Ancient to Modern

David N. Lorenzen

Ancient to Modern

Religion, Power, and Community in India

edited by
Ishita Banerjee-Dube
and
Saurabh Dube

OXFORD
UNIVERSITY PRESS

OXFORD
UNIVERSITY PRESS

Oxford University Press is a department of the University of Oxford.
It furthers the University's objective of excellence in research, scholarship,
and education by publishing worldwide. Oxford is a registered trademark of
Oxford University Press in the UK and in certain other countries

Published in India by
Oxford University Press
YMCA Library Building, 1 Jai Singh Road, New Delhi 110 001, India

First Edition published in 2009
Second impression 2014

ISBN-13: 978-0-19-569662-2
ISBN-10: 0-19-569662-X

Typeset in AGaramond 11/12.7
by Eleven Arts, Keshav Puram, Delhi 110 035

For David N. Lorenzen
In friendship and admiration

CONTENTS

ILLUSTRATIONS

PREFACE

The idea of a volume of essays in honour of David N. Lorenzen was hatched between the two of us—with Ishita providing the lead—around three years ago. The conspiracy was concretized over a splendid dinner with Romila Thapar at her home in New Delhi. With a tentative list of contributors in hand, when we approached David's friends and interlocutors, colleagues and friends, the response was overwhelming. (Indeed, only one scholar found it impossible to meet the admittedly hurried deadline that we set for the authors.) A promise is one thing, while to deliver on it is another. All the contributors sent their papers within the stipulated time frame. Besides, there is a little more to the picture. Together, we have managed to cover not only the different epochs of history but the overlapping arenas of its study—religion and community, ideology and power—that have interested David over a long and distinguished career.

And so, we would like to begin by thanking the contributors to this volume: for writing their essays, responding to endless queries, ironing out minor glitches, and rarely losing their humour through the process. It has been a pleasure for both of us—together and separately—to work once more with the Oxford University Press team. Our students and friends provided pleasant distractions. Finally, along with the other authors of the work, we would like to acknowledge our warm gratitude to David Lorenzen for his intellectual contribution and generous friendship, delivered to some over many years and to others over several decades.

Ishita Banerjee-Dube
Saurabh Dube

INTRODUCTION

Ishita Banerjee-Dube
Saurabh Dube

There are very few scholars of South Asia who have concerned themselves with vastly different eras in the history of the subcontinent, while addressing a clutch of common concerns. David Lorenzen has a prominent place within this limited legion. It is a matter of great pleasure, then, to present a book of essays in honour of this distinguished scholar. The reach and scope as well as the unity and influence of Lorenzen's scholarship should be evident from the presence, in the volume, of a range of questions and subjects, centring nonetheless on religion, power, and community through time. All of this ought to be obvious, as well, from the stature of the contributors to this book, scholars studying the ancient, medieval, and modern worlds of Indian history. Registering such variety as well as unity, the 'Introduction' has three parts. First, we provide a short intellectual portrait of David Lorenzen. Next, we explore the critical categories of religion, power, and community. Finally, we consider how these themes are played out in the chapters themselves.

PORTRAIT OF THE HISTORIAN AS A CRITICAL INTELLECT

David Lorenzen is a remarkable scholar. Our effort here is to highlight aspects of his contributions to worlds of learning, while keeping in view his becoming modesty. It follows, too, that the statement ahead draws on our close intellectual association and warm personal friendship with David, as colleagues at El Colegio de México, over the last decade: but the terms of such closeness appear only between the lines in the brief description.

After taking his first degree at Wesleyan University, Lorenzen conducted his doctoral research under the supervision of A.L. Basham—at the School of Oriental and African Studies, London and later at the Australian National University, Canberra—and then taught at Wisconsin State University during the cultural and political upheavals of the Vietnam years between 1968 and 1970. Over the last three-and-a-half decades, Lorenzen has been a faculty member of the Centre for Asian and African Studies, El Colegio de México in México City. He has also held visiting professorships at the University of Iowa and Harvard University.

During this time, Lorenzen taught a range of courses on the history of the subcontinent (extending from the ancient to the contemporary period) and South Asian society and religions (especially Hinduism and Buddhism). He also conducted a variety of seminars concerning questions of historical and anthropological theory. In several theoretical seminars that we have participated with David at El Colegio de México, the two of us have been struck by his openness toward contending ideas expressed by students and faculty, itself indicative of his truly liberal qualities as a teacher and a person. When combined with his wide-ranging interests and intellectual generosity, these qualities make David an amiable critic and an accessible scholar. Unsurprisingly, over the years there have been many, many colleagues and students who have learned much and gained greatly from his genial and generous persona.

David Lorenzen's contributions to the world of scholarship extend even farther. He has played a significant role in promoting the critical study of Hindu traditions and Indian history—in scholarship on South Asia in the English language across different continents to be sure, but equally in studies of the subcontinent in the Spanish language in Ibero-America. In addition to his research and teaching, Lorenzen has done this in distinct capacities, including as the editor of the journal *Estudios de Asia y Africa* and as director of the PhD programme at the Centre for Asian and African Studies. This Centre is the largest and most prestigious of its kind in Latin America that trains masters' and doctoral degree students from many parts of the Spanish-speaking world.

As is generally acknowledged, David Lorenzen is one of the foremost scholars of cultural history and popular religion in pre-colonial India. Based on his doctoral research, Lorenzen's first book was a path-breaking study of the Kapalikas and the Kalamukhas, two extinct Hindu sects that were also considered as having been lost to history.[1] It is not simply that this is the only major work on the subject. It is also that the book continues to be widely used, discussed, and cited three decades later. This is true also of several of Lorenzen's other writings based upon the Sanskrit tradition, some of them included in his recent collection of essays *Who Invented Hinduism*?, especially those on the life of Sankara and on warrior-ascetics in pre-colonial India.[2]

From the middle of the 1970s, Lorenzen began a large project studying the Kabirpanth, a popular religious formation in north and central India with an extensive constituency among the lower castes within Hindu society. This research is based upon a combination of meticulous textual study of the Hindi language and related vernacular materials and fieldwork among the Kabirpanthi ascetics. The project has resulted in several books and scholarly essays in the English and the Spanish languages, constituting a truly impressive corpus in scholarship on devotional and popular Hinduism.[3] It warrants emphasis, too, that Lorenzen's interests in classical and popular Hinduism have led to other valuable publications, from edited volumes and a co-authored book through to several essays, including the remarkable, much cited, and widely taught 'Who Invented Hinduism?'[4]

David Lorenzen's ever active research agenda currently concerns a significant project on the relationship between Franciscan missionaries and Hindu society, particularly in the eighteenth century. This study represents a new direction in Lorenzen's work, while building on his earlier interests and scholarly training. Together, it critically conjoins Lorenzen's extensive work in the Franciscan archives and long years of study of varieties of Hindi and Italian language materials with his strong background in textual interpretation and keen interest in broader theological and philosophical issues.

The project makes salient contributions to historical scholarship. While the past three decades have seen important research on eighteenth-century India, much of this work has been concerned with issues of political economy and state formation, often tending to treat questions of religion and culture as derivative upon politics and economy.[5] Lorenzen's project not only redresses this imbalance, but brings to light previously unused sources for important regions in north India that have themselves been little studied in writings on eighteenth-century South Asia. Equally, in the South Asian context, research on evangelical entanglements, understood broadly, has so far been rather limited, and rarely conducted in a dialogue with the newer pathways that have been initiated elsewhere.[6] Lorenzen's project addresses several of the important questions in the field, particularly through its focus on the relationship of Franciscan friars with beliefs and practices in the subcontinent in the eighteenth and nineteenth centuries. Much of this is evident in Lorenzen's recent and forthcoming publications as well as in his ongoing writing, including an intellectual biography of Marco della Tomba.[7] Significant strands of this research and writing are crucially present, too, in his magisterial *Who Invented Hinduism?*

From the beginning, David Lorenzen has shown an abiding interest in theoretical issues, but expressed such concerns in distinctive ways. He has always read widely, very widely, mercifully ever escaping the strictures and limitations of mere scholarly specialization. In doing this, he has been guided as much by his formative interests in biology, psychology, and philosophy as he has by his long engagements with Marxism, anthropology, and history. David is a modernist who wants to find patterns in the past and the present, but without excising the constitutive details of social arenas through the means of analytical abstractions. If he is sensitive to the particularities of historical worlds and contemporary ones, mere platitudes of cultural difference do not suffice for him. David is a humanist who finds similarities between African-American Blues and the compositions of *nirgun bhakti* (devotion to a formless Lord/Absolute), yet he also always probes—in the critical tradition (as distinct from lazy assertions) of the Enlightenment spirit—the received wisdom and ready assumptions of modern knowledge. All of this suggests an intellect that cannot be easily pigeon-holed, simply compartmentalized, into a neat slot.

Unsurprisingly, in temporal terms, as has been discussed, Lorenzen's scholarship has straddled the ancient, the medieval, and the modern periods of Indian history, his research interests extending forward in time from the first era to the last one. It follows that the contributions to this volume cover all three. Conceptually and empirically, Lorenzen's writings have focused on religion, power, and community, their meanings and expressions and textures and transformations across history. This fact, too, is registered by the chapters of the present work. And so it is to these key categories that we now turn.

KEY CATEGORIES

The concepts and entities of religion, power, and community are contentious issues and fraught terrains both in academic and everyday arenas. Registering this fact, the discussion ahead presents our own understandings of these categories-entities. It is an indicative, rather than an exhaustive, account. Moreover, far from eliciting a wider consensus, we are acutely aware that the delineations would be contended by the contributors to the volume and the person it honours. But we are also confident that the different authors and Lorenzen himself would be in broad sympathy with our efforts. Together, the deliberations in front not only reflect recent scholarly developments but crucially open up spaces for dialogue and debate. The latter is also the point and purpose of this book, which is entirely in tune with the spirit and substance of David Lorenzen's extraordinary scholarship.

In writing of religion, our reference is to much more than a hermetically sealed off domain of the sacred, a static repository of timeless traditions, an issue to which we shall return. Instead, we understand religion as involving inherently experiential, intriguingly historical, sets of signifying beliefs and practices. At the core of religion, then, there exist meaningful constructions and actions, shifting perceptions and practices that simultaneously shape and are in turn shaped by social worlds. Here are to be found perceptions and practices that are variously tied to processes of power, entailing articulations of authority and domination and their negotiation and subversion. Together, the processual character and the symbolic-substantive nature of religion are intimately bound to social transformations.[8]

What we have just said might be differently expressed, expanded on, in the following way. To us, ensembles of religion reach far beyond mere inventories of particular customs and traditions and specific rituals and beliefs. Rather, they refer to simultaneously symbolic and substantive, structured and fluid meanings and imaginings, norms and practices, and rituals and dispositions. These provide means through which social relationships within and between groups/classes/communities/castes are perceived, experienced, and articulated precisely as part of hierarchical linkages between variously ordered worlds of the human and the divine. Here, religion appears as formatively implicated in the production and reproduction of social life, turning upon the ways in which belief systems, ritual practices, and everyday actions are insinuated and lived within determinate relationships, predicated on processes of power. Since these relationships and processes change, transformations are central to religion.

None of this is to present a totalized (and totalizing), even tendentious (and oddly seamless), definition of religion. Far from this, our emphases seek precisely to open up the category by querying certain durable, usually overlaying, dispositions toward religions. The first of these concerns frequent portrayals of religion as a principally coherent domain, which is virtually autonomous from modalities of power. Such portraits underplay formations of dominance, contentions of authority, and terms of dissonance within religions, patterns of power that entail relationships of gender, caste, and community as well as those of class, race, and office. The second set of dispositions involve representations of religion as mainly discrete and chiefly bounded, as ever looking inwards and turning on itself. Here, religion appears as uncertainly in tune and unsteadily out of tenor with wider expressions of societal transformations, from elaborations of state formation and political economy across history through to articulations of empire and nation in modern times. The last of the enduring orientations toward religion under discussion entail authoritative understandings that only ambivalently explore the temporal dimensions of the values, beliefs, symbols, and rituals that they examine. Instead of approaching these elements of religion as being formed and transformed by historical subjects, they are rendered rather, along with religions themselves, as uneasily encompassing or/and uncomfortably encompassed by continuities, shifts, and ruptures shaping the past and the present.

Our emphases emerge from both scholarly discussions as well as contemporary expressions of religion, and we briefly provide a few instances here. Turning to academic understandings, consider the orthodox Marxist conception of religion as an ideational superstructure that derives from a material base, which has also influenced David Lorenzen's thinking. On the one hand, in pointing to the salience of wider societal and political processes in formations of religions, Marxist understandings broke with readings of religion as exclusively marked by an innate and exclusive, inner logic. On the other hand, by predicating the superstructure on the base the orthodox Marxist schema rendered religion as epiphenomenal, while imbuing abstractions such as modes of production with a life of their own.[9] Overlooked thereby were the indissoluble attributes of social, historical, and ritual processes, including the presence of religion here.

The critical rethinking of orthodox Marxist conceptions—and of earlier disciplinary understandings—of religion have exactly emphasized that such processes consist of specific practices of historical subjects within relationships of power: practices and relationships entailing tacit stocks of knowledge and action and changing contours of meaning and agency that define religion. Clearly, we have learned from these and related discussions as we have from the manner in which such critical engagements have been carried forward in recent years. Especially important for us have been the increasing recognitions not only of the intensely differentiated nature of religions but of their insistent interplay with wider formations of region, state, nation, and globalization, including transnational processes of empire, diaspora, and modernity.[10]

The recognitions should not be surprising. Far from being efficaciously erased by historical designs of capital and consumption, secularism and democracy, nation and globalization, as was once imagined, religion finds today increasingly assertive expressions and ever more salience in schemes of modernity. From the fourth world to the first world—from impoverished indigenous peoples to privileged ethnic constituencies, and from violent religious militants to their equally zealous opponents—at large in the present are subjects of modernity who variously, vigorously lay claims on 'religion' to enunciate its terms and textures in intriguing, powerful ways. Such urgent assertions of religion—and of 'culture' and 'custom', 'civilization' and 'tradition'—feature at once in projects of unity and division, involving strategies of survival and designs of destruction. At stake, indeed, are ironies and challenges for rethinking religion as concept and entity, especially by exploring its enmeshments with power.

For us, power extends far beyond the exercise of authority grounded solely in control over political and economic resources. Instead, power is expressed through manifest and diffuse processes—turning on cultural schemes, disciplinary routines, representational regimes, and discursive practices—of domination, hegemony, control, and subject-formation. If these processes inform everyday social relationships structured by the interlocking of different procedures of social division and governmental command, there is even more to the picture. On the one hand, we are doubtful of inherited assertions regarding power as being exclusively repressive—of what Foucault once described as the privileging of only its 'no-saying' attributes. We register rather that the dark, durable, and dangerous dimensions of power reside exactly in its productivity, its proclivity toward and fecundity in the formation of regimes and subjects. On the other hand, precisely this recognition does not lead us to endorse ominous visions projecting the all-encompassing sway of disembodied power, relentlessly ruling through already worked-over subjects and principally subjectless histories. Instead, we submit that the very productivity of power in the shaping of subjects is ever accompanied by the same subjects reworking the pervasive terms of power.

To argue in this manner, to make such claims, is to underscore that analytically fatal mistakes surround understandings of power or hegemony as a closed system or ever efficacious mechanism of cultural and ideological dominance, just as theoretically grave errors attend the reification of subaltern autonomy and agency. These are issues that we have explored elsewhere, explicitly and implicitly.[11] The point now is that if our inclusive working definitions set the stage for a discussion of the complex dynamic between religion and power, the dynamic itself reveals the negotiated and interrogated, reworked and contested attributes not only of these categories-entities but also of those of community and history.

Recent years have witnessed critical rethinking of pervasive projections of community as an ineluctably anachronistic, tightly bounded entity, as tending toward consensus in its expression, as entailing allegiance to primordial tradition, and as broadly opposed to modernity. This has had compelling consequences. Communities have come to be understood as active participants in wider processes of colonialism and empire, state-formation and modernity, and nation and nationalism, which imbue such processes—themselves made up of diverse relationships of meaning and power—with their own terms and textures.[12] Unsurprisingly, there have been explorations of the many meanings of community as construed by historical subjects as well as governmental regimes, especially the symbolization and elaboration of boundaries of communities as providing substance to differences and identities of their members.[13]

To start off, this has involved examinations of the constitutive location of community within wide-ranging processes of power as well as of its internal divisions as expressed in terms of property, gender, law, and office.[14] Moreover, such efforts have been fortified by incisive accounts of communities as questioning and contesting dominant projects of meaning and power, including those turning on Hinduism and caste and empire and nation, unravelling their challenge to authority in a historically and ethnographically layered manner.[15] Finally, there have been diverse endeavours to write greater heterogeneity into the concept of community. Indeed, recent reconfigurations of the category have derived further support from the thinking through of the antinomy between community and state, moves that have queried the analytical binaries of modern disciplines, which are closely tied to totalizing templates of a universal history and exclusive blueprints of a Western modernity.[16] The effects of such procedures have been felt in the critical and contending rethinking not only of community but also of history.

Three overlaying emphases have played a salient part in recent reconsiderations of history.[17] To begin with, it has been diversely admitted that forms of historical consciousness vary in their degree of symbolic elaboration, their ability to pervade multiple contexts, and their capacity to capture people's imaginations. Second, it has been increasingly noted that history does not just refer to events and processes out there, but that it exists as a negotiated resource at the core of shifting configurations of social worlds. Finally, there has been an opening up of critical questions considering both: the coupling of history-writing with the modern nation, and the haunting presence of a reified West in widespread beliefs in historical progress. Together, in approaching the past and the present, such efforts toward critical history-writing have often bound the impulse to cautiously probe and affirm social worlds with the desire to carefully narrate and describe them. The endeavours have taken truly seriously requirements of evidence and fidelity to facts. Yet they have also sieved historical evidence through critical filters and construed facts unexpected, facts that speak in the uneasy echoes of limiting doubt rather than deal in dead certainties.[18]

The emphases outlined above have not resorted to oppositions involving cyclical notions of the past as characteristic of the East and linear conceptions of history as constitutive of the West. Nor have they approached the assertive appropriations and enunciations of the past in historical and contemporary worlds by submitting to views that each of these visions is equally true. Rather, they have precisely probed such overwrought blueprints and solipsistic schemes by tracking expressions of history as made up of interleaving, conflict-ridden processes of meaning and authority.[19] In this terrain, the explorations have extended from tracing the variability and mutability that can inhere in the perceptions and practices of the past of historical communities through to tracking the persistence of oppositions between myth and history in authoritative projections;[20] and from unravelling the uses of the past and their contending validities in the making of worlds, especially the play of power in the production of history, through to the placing of question marks on pervasive projections of the West and nation as history, modernity, and destiny.[21] Unsurprisingly, the understandings and emphases concerning religion, power, community, and history are played out in distinct ways in the chapters in this volume, and it is the task of describing these endeavours that we now undertake.

CRUCIAL CONCERNS

True to the spirit of David Lorenzen, who has 'never ceased to tease and test and question many modernist assumptions embedded in colonial and postcolonial reconstructions of the religious history of South Asia',[22] each chapter of this volume probes and unsettles established understandings and accepted verities pertaining to religion and texts, sects, and communities. They also engage and extend the myriad aspects of Lorenzen's work in different directions. Together, through their diverse approaches, the chapters effectively articulate plural perspectives that underpin understandings of religion, community, power, and their mutual imbrications.

Opening our considerations, Romila Thapar and R. Champakalakshmi examine the Puranas and Puranic Hinduism with different concerns and emphases. Thapar analyses the Puranas as a distinctive genre of texts in order to underscore their purpose and 'intention'. She points out their inherent nature as sectarian texts associated with a particular deity. This meant that a careful process of selection—of inclusion and exclusion—underlay their composition. Such texts underwent frequent reformulation to incorporate new religious forms, beliefs, and groups into Puranic Hinduism. This process entailed the induction of an additional mythology around the deity that conferred legitimacy on these new forms and practices, effectively 'extending the reach of both sect and text'. At the same time, hostility to sects considered 'heretic' was markedly present in such scenarios.

Thapar substantiates her argument through a critical analysis of the treatment of Buddhism in the Puranas. In his journey from the early to the later Puranas, roughly corresponding to a period when Buddhism was at the height of its glory through to its decline, the figure and form of the Buddha evinced key transformations. Initially perceived as a threat, as a socially and culturally challenging entity, and being conflated with Mahavira, the Buddha eventually got incorporated as an avatar of Vishnu, albeit with a distinct twist. The Buddha is created by Vishnu himself as *Mayamoha*—delusion and illusion personified as a teacher—who leads the *asuras*, *daityas*, and *danavas* (demons) astray by preaching a fake doctrine opposed to the Vaishnava doctrine and Vedic ritual. This diverted the asuras from the correct path and weakened them thereby making it easy first for the gods and—in the later Puranas—for Kalki (the last incarnation of Vishnu) to defeat them. As such, although Buddhism came to be integrated into the Puranas, those teachings that questioned the *varna* (class/caste) organization and what this entailed in terms of sacred and social obligations, were stridently decried. Conversely, the intense contention over belief and ritual as well as the incessant strife over doctrines and social-order(ing) in the religious section of the Puranas, came to be considerably tempered in the more 'mundane' section of the 'vamsanucarita', which listed genealogies and dynastic succession. Here projections of political power conspicuously lacked any commentary on the rulers listed. This separation of political rule from sectarian identity was pragmatic: it indicated at once the Brahman endorsement of kingship, and enabled rulers to be patrons of more than one sect. All of this serves to underscore the acute entanglements of religion, power, and (sectarian) community.

Putting a distinct spin on these matters, Champalakshmi's rich examination of regional religious traditions in southern India between the sixth and the seventeenth centuries CE raises important questions concerning the assimilative nature of Puranic Hinduism. Through a detailed exploration of the evolution of the Kaumara (Subrahmanya), Ganapatya, and Sakti cults in the Tamil region from the early historical period onwards and of the clear ties of these cults with the non-Sanskritic literary and cultural tradition of Sangam and bhakti literature, she argues that the Puranic process was distinctly plural in its regional manifestations, especially in areas peripheral to the Ganges valley. Indeed, it was not until the establishment of the Vijayanagara kingdom in the fourteenth century that the independent regional cults of southern India were brought within the fold of Puranic Hinduism. This involved investing these cults with new mythologies and, more interestingly, linking them with Sankara of the Vedantic tradition, 'a strict and stark absolutist'. Here, Vijayanagara's efforts to establish a supra-regional state through the accommodation of new military chiefs who brought distant regions under control—and the inclusion of newer agricultural and non-agricultural groups into temple ritual and administration—required a legitimating ideology that superseded regional and local forms. The turn to the normative Sanskritic tradition was the means to create this pan-Indian cultural universe.

It was precisely in this context that the Advaita of Sankara, which had 'no visible importance in his own period', that is, the eighth and ninth centuries, was reinforced through two simultaneous measures: the equation of the Brahman of Advaita with the godhead of the Puranic deities; and the conferring on Sankara of the epithet of *Sanmata Sthapanacarya*, or the one who reorganized through the Vedantic tradition the pre-existent six forms of worship along orthodox lines. The fourteenth to the seventeenth centuries also saw the production of biographies of Sankara. These credited him with the establishment of *mathas* (monastery) on the cardinal points of India. They also endowed Sankara with a mythical origin as an incarnation of Shiva who took human form in order to revive the Vedic faith and to save orthodoxy. It is equally the case, however, that such labours of religious leaders and political rulers could not root out the tension between the 'mainstream' (Sanskritic) and the 'local/popular' (vernacular) traditions, a tension that persists until today. By allowing these explorations to dispel notions of a monolithic Hinduism, Champakalakshmi questions Lorenzen's statement that the religion of the Puranas 'displays many continuities with the earlier Vedic religion', even as she agrees with his argument that the greatly expanding mythology of Puranic religion lay at the heart of the development of what we now understand as Hinduism.

In the next chapter, 'Never Have I Seen Such Yogīs Brother'—a title inspired by a song attributed to Kabir that has been used by Lorenzen in one of his important essays—David Gordon White takes us on a roller-coaster ride through intriguing worlds of yogis, warriors, and sorcerers in ancient and medieval India, a journey that is a *tour de force*. By means of an incisive reading of varieties of early South Asian texts and images pertaining to yoga and then by mutually 'confronting' text and image, White critically queries the inextricable association of the yogi and the lotus posture, formulated and popularized by the Bhagavad Gita, and uncritically accepted since by most scholars. White argues that the lotus posture symbolized royal sovereignty in ancient India; it was far from being the distinctive feature of a yogi. What is more, Hindu, Buddhist, and Jain texts do not uphold blithe, pervasive identifications between heat-producing austerities, breath control, self-mortification, and meditation on the one hand, and yoga on the other.

White shows that the terms yoga and *yogin* appear several times in the Mahabharata and the Bhagvad Gita, as they do in the coeval *Yoga Sutra*. While the terms express a variety of meanings, the narrative descriptions of the practice of yoga in the Mahabharata reveal a remarkable uniformity. They consistently depict 'dying as a yogic event' by means of which 'a hero wills his luminous soul or lifebody to rise up out of his recumbent if not comatose physical body.' Yoga here means 'yoking'—as in the Vedas. For the warrior, it is a departure for the heavens, the sun and the world of Brahman beyond. For the non-warriors, who are 'yoked to yoga', it symbolizes exit from one's body by means of entry into another body. In Tantra, too, yoga means '"yoking" the mind-body complex of another being to one's own, often by overpowering them and entering them.' Such practices of yogic possession fit in very well with narrative accounts of yogins—notorious since late medieval times—that depict their capacity as warriors to turn battlegrounds into charnel grounds and of assaulting and vanquishing enemy citadels. Indeed, the most enduring image of the yogin in popular South Asian traditions is that of a terrifying outsider that penetrates sleeping villages at night to carry off naughty children or unprotected women. This is proof that the association of the yogin is more with a powerful, dangerous Bhairava-like figure and less with 'a meditating sage absorbed in quietistic introspection'. White concludes with a double entendre: the image of Mohenjodaro seal 420—identified by Sir John Marshall in 1931 as a male god seated in the typical lotus posture of the yoga, a proto-yogin—and unchallenged by scholars till today, provides the best illustration of a flawed classification, namely that of 'a proto-char sau bis [420, fake in Hindi] yogi'. All of this holds up a mirror to the prevailing power of persuasions and predilections from the past and in the present in representations of religions.

Also in the pursuit of the text and the image but traversing a differing trajectory, Benjamín Preciado-Solís explores portrayals of the horrific in Buddhist Tantric worlds. His chapter follows a captivating path, treading through texts full of minute, gory details of death and destruction, while matching textual traces with powerful images, paintings that meticulously reproduced such intricacies in vivid, repulsive-yet-enticing illustrations. Here, Preciado argues that in this particular path of meditation the texts were to serve as guides for the initiate, further enjoining the painter to create its material representation. Intrigued that the peaceful doctrine of Buddhism could yet produce 'depictions of ferocious cruelty and violence', Preciado launches a search for the sources of the disparity.

Through an exhaustive, careful scrutiny of texts and iconography preserved in the contemporary Buddhist world, he tracks the beginnings of horrific (*ghora*) depictions in the Pali canon and Buddhist Sanskrit texts that pre-date Tantric Buddhism by many centuries. Preciado-Solís points out further that a concept of the ghora 'was included as one of the categories in Indian theories of art' with the horrific being one of the eight original *rasa*s (moods) associated with artistic production. Instances of the use of this rasa abide in the Ramayana and the Mahabharata, in the drama *Malatimadhava* of Bhavabhuti, and in the well-known collection *Vetalapanchavimsati* (Twenty-five Tales of a Phantom). In fact, contrary to common contention, the fount of the horrific imagery of Tantric Buddhism was not witchcraft and black-magic but the orthodox Buddhist tradition—although cults turning on magic got incorporated into Tantric practices.

Here, the Buddhist tradition effectively expressed the aesthetics of the horrific—an important trend within Indian literary and visual arts—to produce artistic masterpieces that span the entire Buddhist world.

Next, the contributions by Purushottam Agrawal and Linda Hess cogently cover the medieval period and the modern one in order to trace, respectively, the fortunes of the Ramanandi and Kabirpanthi ascetic orders. In the process, both forcefully foreground the contingent and contentious nature of religious community. Agrawal's intensively researched discussion of Ramanand—the guru of prominent *sants* such as Kabir, Raidas, and Pipa—breaks new ground in solving the 'puzzle' that surrounds the chronological times and contrasting configurations of Ramanand. It also offers valuable insights into the construction of traditions by members of a religious order. Ramanand, a 'unique figure in the religious and literary history of northern India', has been credited with questioning and challenging Brahman supremacy as well as upbraided for upholding Brahman orthodoxy and orthopraxy. Thinking through these contentious claims and the paradox they imply, Agrawal argues that in determining Ramanand's world view, modern scholarship accords privilege to two Sanskrit works believed to have been written by him. At the same time, it is not only that the little that is known of Ramanand comes from medieval vernacular sources, since Sanskrit writings of the time took no notice of him at all. It is also that, according to Agrawal, concerning Ramanand's world view there is absolute divergence between the Sanskrit works and the Hindi compositions attributed to him. Herein lie the roots of the divergent projections of Ramanand.

By means of exhaustively combing vernacular and Sanskrit texts in the manner of a historian detective, Agrawal distinguishes between a 'Hindi Ramanand' and a 'Sanskrit Ramanand'. He argues that 'the privileged position of Sanskrit Ramanand is not rooted in any serious research but in [an] uncritical acceptance of [a] very recently constructed image of Ramanand as an orthodox Acharya of the Ramawat Sampraday.' Here it is ironic that Bhagawadacharya, the most active participant in the creation of the Brahman image of Ramanand in the twentieth century, was himself a critic of Brahman supremacy, a member of the 'radical' section of the Ramanandi ascetic order. Bhagawadacharya created the 'Sanskrit Ramanand' in order to sever all links with the orthodox, upper-caste followers of Ramanuja—to whom the Ramanandis also traced their lineage till the beginning of the twentieth century—as well as to grant respectability to the constituency of middle- and lower-caste Ramanandi followers, who were looked down upon by the Ramanuji order. This involved Bhagawadacharya in pushing back Ramanand's chronological span by a century, turning him into a native of north India, and producing Sanskrit writings in the guru's name. The success of this 'radical' attempt was signalled by the widespread acceptance of the 'Sanskrit Ramanand' in scholarship. The 'Hindi Ramanand' and a 'bhakti sensibility' were marginalized as a heterodox guru was transformed into a conservative one. Yet, the puzzle regarding Ramanand's chronological span and split ideology lingered, a mystery that now stands solved.

Linda Hess shifts attention to contestations over Kabir, Ramanand's disciple, in the twentieth and twenty-first centuries. Her richly textured account unravels tensions intrinsic to the construction and conservation of a community formed around a militant figure, one who opposed institutional authority and ritual paraphernalia. Hess begins her account with the well-known story of Kabir's death and the ensuing fight among his Hindu and Muslim followers over whether his body was to be buried or cremated—a conflict that was resolved with the miraculous disappearance of the body and its substitution by flowers. This worn tale allows Hess to make a telling comment. The fight over the dead body of a formidable figure who deliberately occupied an 'ambiguous space' between Hindu and Muslim communities, she suggests, has 'a special bite: the fighting devotees have to forget Kabir's central teachings in order to engage in conflict.' From this point of entry and departure, Hess spins a fascinating tale out of discrete yet overlaying elements and fragments: from an enthusiastic filmmaker's unexpected clash with Kabir devotees in Gujarat over his cinematic portrayal of Kabir as an ordinary but inspiring human being and not as a divine incarnation; to a gifted singer-actor's failure to persuade Kabirpanthis of Uttar Pradesh (UP) that his one-act play depicting Kabir as a married man with children—and not as a celibate ascetic—was 'true' to the facts; to the intricate tensions and tussles among leaders and followers of the two main branches of the Kabirpanthi sect, at Varanasi in UP and Damakheda in Chhattisgarh, over interpretations of Kabir's teachings and the significance of sectarian rituals.

All of this sets the stage for Hess to recount the debates and dissensions that followed the negotiations of sectarian hierarchy by a poor, low-caste, popular singer of rural origins from the Malwa region. This lay follower of the sect, who was opposed to ritual, nonetheless accepted an offer from the guru at Damakheda to become a *mahant* (head of a temple or sectarian religious branch) of the order. The decision evoked a wide variety of responses from among the members of Kabirpanth as well as its educated middle-class sympathizers. In the midst of an order that privileges the exalted position of its guru and his functionaries as well as the significance of sectarian ritual, the singer continued to claim that he possessed no special status simply on account of being a mahant and held on to his belief that rituals were important only for the preservation of the community. This aroused the ire of the guru who revoked the singer's right of being a mahant. The 'top-down-bottom-up tale' not only suggests new ways of studying the history of religion but reveals the ways in which the intense emotions and energies invested in the construal and continuance of communities spur their members toward making strident claims on legendary heroes, origin myths, and ritual practices. At stake is the permeation by power of communities, passions, and struggles, which takes us back to Hess' opening irony. If inspiration from Kabir once created the Panth, the Panth now continues to create Kabir.

The following three chapters—by Ines G. Županov, Thomas R. Trautmann, and Saurabh Dube—all diversely deal with Lorenzen's recent research interest in missionaries and converts in modern Indian history. The first two of these contributions complement each other in valuable ways. Here, both Županov and Trautmann discuss the 'titanic shift of authority' that followed the entry of British scholar-administrators into the portals of Orientalist knowledge in the late eighteenth century.

Županov focuses on the life and work of Paulinus a S. Bartholomaeo, an Italian Carmelite missionary who lived in south India between 1776 and 1789 and published a series of books and articles concerning the subcontinent upon his return to Rome. She lucidly unpacks the painstaking research that went into Paulinus a S. Bartholomaeo's scholarly works, redolent with Orientalist ideas, while divulging at the same time his predicament of being a missionary Orientalist. It was on account of the fact that Paulinus remained a professional missionary even as he worked as a professor of Indian languages in Rome that his expertise was not taken seriously enough by his peers, the British and French students of Indian languages and culture and members of rising 'scientific societies' such as the Asiatic Society of Bengal. In Rome itself, his 'incredible erudition and expertise in Indian languages' sat awkwardly with his career as a missionary. Paulinus a S. Bartholomaeo was, however, offered the unique opportunity of organizing an 'Indian collection' at a museum in Veletri by Stefano Borgia. There, he invested a lot of time and energy in trying to 'preserve, describe, classify and publish'—but without the help of 'learned Brahmans'—manuscripts and objects that he and his predecessors had brought back from India.

Županov's in-depth, sensitive account shows how Paulinus a S. Bartholomaeo's passion for a comprehensive knowledge of India was connected to the Jesuits preceding him as well as to later Orientalists. He not only collected natural objects and manuscripts but took a keen interest in plants, seeds, and remedies, enquiring into the causes and cures of common illnesses that afflicted people in south India. At the same time, he learnt Sanskrit in order to get first-hand information of what the classical texts contained. If Paulinus a S. Bartholomaeo's interest in botany brought him close to William Jones, he closely followed his Jesuit predecessors in gaining knowledge of 'pagan' truth with the purpose of replacing it with the true truth of Christianity. And it was exactly this transitory and ambiguous location between two distinct worlds that caused his fall into oblivion—once professional, 'scientific' Orientalists came to dominate the scene.

Trautmann picks up the tale from where Županov leaves it. Critically motivated by Lorenzen's statement regarding the 'imbalance of knowledge-production' among the missionaries and Orientalists—with the balance clearly tilted in favour of the scholar-administrator Orientalists of British India—he puts a distinct spin on the subject. Trautmann places the 'missionary' and the 'Orientalist' in different comparative framings in order to draw out the extensive, critical implications of their relationship. He examines the period after 1770 and argues that while the difference between the missionary and the Orientalist was 'strongly marked discursively and in policy', many missionaries were Orientalist scholars and many Orientalist scholars had strong Christian beliefs, thus making for 'all possible gradations of intermediate cases'. And yet, at a deep level, in the British mind, the two remained entirely distinct from each other. At stake were Orientalist and missionary engagements with Indian culture, particularly religion.

The sharp opposition lay in the great debates of the early nineteenth century that accompanied the 'age of reform' in Britain and in British India. The growing force of Evangelism and its 'unsympathetic gaze upon Hinduism and the Indian past' played a key role here. The Evangelical thrust of joining Christianity with social reform and education worked alongside the Utilitarian push for parliamentary reform at home and a reformist policy in British India. Together, they questioned the Orientalist ideology of 'sympathetic engagement with Hindusim'. Orientalist scholarship continued but lost most of its major political battles—and its specific significance—as the basis of government policy. Trautmann ends with a tale within the tale, turning on the widely campaigned and intensely fought for chair of Sanskrit at Oxford. This was a battle between the renowned Orientalist H.H. Wilson and the missionary W.H. Mill. Throughout the skirmishes, Wilson's lack of morality and degraded Christian character were used to jeopardize his position so that Wilson finally won with a very narrow margin. Pointing to the subsequent collaboration between Mill and Wilson on scholarly projects, Trautmann urges us to reflect on whether, even in the midst of aggressive assertions of the typological opposition, the Orientalist and missionary completely separated themselves in the manner of watertight compartments. In these ways he suggests newer possibilities for finding 'fruitful paths of inquiry'.

Shifting the focus of enquiry from European scholars to Indian Christians, Saurabh Dube's essay discusses the interplay of conversion and life history, embedded within processes of evangelical entanglements between Euro-American missionaries and central Indian peoples. It explores distinct autobiographies and biographies of converts to Christianity in the Chhattisgarh region of central India, especially accounts written between the 1920s and the 1940s. At first, these slender manuscripts and slim typescripts, writings pertaining to native evangelical workers, seem to be wholly formulaic in nature. Yet, careful attention to the very ordinariness and precise details of the texts reveals how they constitute key registers of evangelical entanglements. Indeed, by sieving such writings through the critical filters of an ethnographic sensibility—including reading them alongside materials collected during fieldwork in Chhattisgarh among Indian Christians—makes it possible to unravel how materials of life history imbue notions and narratives of conversion to Christianity with their own salience.

By focusing on the details and dynamics of accounts of Indian Christians, their drama and divergence, their exact surplus of faith in the Book and particular renderings of the Word, the essay explores the distinction and difference at the heart of these narratives—accounts and narrative that were at once vernacular and colonial, simultaneously contrary and common. As a word, conversion carried exclusive connotations only in one of the accounts explored in the chapter: but even this most singular rendering of the category-entity came with its own twist, forcefully split and shaped by the wide-ranging making of myth and narrative, history and legend at the core of evangelical entanglements. As an event, conversion was described in inherently different ways in the life history narratives. As a resource, conversion—to be born into or to become the member of a new faith—allowed life stories of Indian Christians to be plotted in distinct ways, quite as these accounts usually remained rooted in the common and the quotidian. On the one hand, the precise diversity, difference, and distinction at the heart of these tales exceed the singularity of lives entailed by dominant designs of conversion. On the other hand, the very commonness of these life stories, including efforts to dramatize their constitutive terms, militate against the melodrama implied by inherited imaginings of conversion.

In the two chapters that follow, Frank Conlon and Jack Hawley take as their point of departure—albeit unto different purposes—Lorenzen's powerful essay 'Who Invented Hinduism?' Drawing inspiration from Lorenzen's unwillingness to accept uncritically arguments regarding the 'invention' of Hinduism under colonialism, Conlon revisits the Bombay region between the seventeenth and nineteenth centuries. Probing the different meanings and usages of caste and community by Indians and the British, he presents an intricate picture that queries the simplifications often inherent in assertions regarding the 'invention of tradition'. Conlon's explorations of category and community tell us that in the seventeenth century, caste in the Bombay region had salience for the Europeans 'insofar it might be used to recruit population to the new port to promote its economic development'. During the eighteenth century, caste was 'employed as a category to which the East India Company's Indian subjects belonged, and through which some measure of governance and maintenance of order might be obtained.' The arrival of the missionaries in the nineteenth century changed the situation since they 'appropriated' caste as the fundamental symbol of the backwardness of Indian culture, ascribing to it a 'changeless' nature.

Yet, Conlon reminds us, it would simply not do to stop here. For the very moment of the Western appropriation of caste also witnessed a simultaneous counter-development, which was no less a part of a period of extensive social and political change. Now different Indian peoples experimented with caste institutions and ideas in tune with the changed circumstances, while Brahman 'pundits' insisted on the static nature of caste. Indeed, Conlon's survey of the myriad understandings and articulations of caste by both the Europeans and the Indians over two hundred years has wide implications. It illustrates that even prior to British rule caste was 'real enough' to merit broad-based attention and that pre-colonial powers tried to use it as much as colonial regimes. Afterwards, too, the genealogies of caste were shaped as much by the colonizer as by the colonized. Taken together, Conlon aptly argues for the requirements of our own times to move beyond ready assertions of the endless 'invention' through imperial intervention of traditions, institutions, and pasts, in order instead to accord to Indians—their actions and intentions—a place in history.

Hawley adopts a somewhat different tack on questions of cultural construction in colonial contexts. He takes the bait offered by Lorenzen's separation between 'constructionist' scholars, who believe that Hinduism was imagined or invented by the British in the nineteenth century, and others that reject such a view. (In 'Who Invented Hinduism?', Lorenzen places Hawley in the first group and himself among the second set.) Seeking to further take forward the terms of 'constructivism', Hawley tracks the multiple ways in which the 'eternality' of Hinduism came to be posed, albeit only at the end of the nineteenth century. At this juncture, the need to make the claim that Hinduism was *sanātana* (eternal) arose from the 'pressure of the modern spirit and Christian criticism' as well as from the indigenous challenge posed by Hindu reformist groups such as the Arya Samaj. What was crucial to the claim was not 'so much the ancient origins of Sanātana Dharma' but 'its uninterrupted persistence through time.' Hawley asserts that such claims were made on the basis of the 'livedness' of dharma, a livedness that was sustained through teachings in the classrooms, whose walls were ever expanded by public oratory and print culture.

Hawley closely examines the content and structure of two text books, one written in Hindi in 1878 by Pundit Gurusahay of Shajahanpur (UP) who ran a *pathshala* (school) and the other in English in 1903 by Annie Besant for the students of the Central Hindu College and Collegiate School in Banaras (Varanasi). The texts are markedly different in terms of language, purpose, perspective, readership, and circulation: but they nonetheless share 'an explicit devotion to the cause of Sanātana Dharma'. Gurusahay proclaimed the universality and eternality of the Vedic religion by defending its *varnashramadharma*, while inveighing severely against the 'perverts' who started sects and lineages by scooping out some segments of the religion of the Vedas and circulating it under their own names. At the turn of the century, Annie Besant superseded this narrow universal whose frame of reference was the motherland and the interior landscape of Hinduism by a fully articulated universal that embraced the entire world and all its religions. Significantly, operating in tandem, the texts by Gurusahay and Besant marked out a terrain that continues to be recursively invoked in contemporary definitions of Sanātana Dharma—endlessly on offer today.

Ishita Banerjee-Dube and Daniel Gold both focus on the multiple meanings, perceptions, and articulations of community. Banerjee-Dube draws inspiration from Lorenzen's wide-ranging work on religious texts to focus on the work of Bhima Bhoi, the poet-philosopher of Mahima Dharma, a radical religious order of nineteenth-century Orissa. She explores two distinct yet overlapping processes: the creation of a contingent community of Mahima Dharmis around Bhima Bhoi; and the 'appropriation' of the poet in twentieth-century endeavours to express a regional identity centred on the Oriya language. The chapter makes its way through the history of the Oriya language and the early attempts to forge a community around the vernacular and the cult of Jagannath in order to highlight the salient features that gradually came to epitomize Oriya pride and identity. Next, it critically analyses the key elements of Mahima Dharma, particularly its intricate relationship with the cult of Jagannath as portrayed in the compositions of Bhima Bhoi. If these compositions were amenable to diverse deployments, Bhima Bhoi himself has been contendingly assessed by the Oriya literati in the nineteenth and twentieth centuries.

Focusing on the processes that made Oriya and Jagannath vital elements of Oriya nationalism in the late nineteenth and early twentieth centuries—as well as the gradual shifts in these patterns after Independence—Banerjee-Dube argues that the distinct assessments of Bhima Bhoi were directly linked to the former developments. Initial reservations about an 'unlettered' poet of 'low' origin and heterodox ideas, one who had also transgressed the unwritten rule of celibacy adhered to by religious preachers, changed dramatically as the 'rustic', the religious, and the radical figure increasingly came to signify the 'soul' of Oriya language after Independence. Bhima Bhoi's low birth, lack of formal education, distance from western ideas and proximity to the early 'Sudra' poets of the language resulted in his elevation to the status of a 'national' poet of Orissa along with the early poets. Indeed like these poets, who set the Oriya language on its independent career by a clear rupture with Sanskrit meter and style and also broke the stranglehold of Brahmans on religious ideas by providing vernacular renderings of important religious texts, Bhima Bhoi made high ideals of an indescribable Absolute accessible to all in his vernacular compositions, returning to the tradition of religious piety in Oriya literature and causing a break with the recent experiments with English style.

Daniel Gold's essay, based on his fieldwork in a marginal neighbourhood of Gwalior in 2005, is an evocative account of the many meanings and dimensions of community criss-crossed by identities of religion, caste, community, friendship, and affect as well as by the space of the neighbourhood. Part of an extended study of urban religion in Gwalior city, Gold's situated analysis brings alive the dynamics of socio-religious and political community in the everyday lives of the residents. Indeed, the site of the neighbourhood—on a hill named after a Satyanarayan temple that it houses—is crucial for the analysis.

Identities are informed by where the household is located on the hill. Apart from the fact that the houses lower down claim closer ties to the city, the steps that go up through the middle of the hill to the

Satyanarayan temple, also divide the hill into western middle-class (and middle-upper caste) and poor (lower-caste) eastern sections. Residents of the two sections share the steps but hardly intermingle; within each section members of different castes and religions interact with different degrees of intimacy. Again, the two main castes of dalits who populate the eastern section present significant contrast in economic condition and cultural priorities. In addition to intra- and inter-caste and class tensions that give different twists to communitarian identity, Gold's description vividly portrays how religion often plays second fiddle in notions of identity. Muslim artists make a clear separation between religion and art in lovingly polishing images of Hindu deities or enthusiastically acting out the roles of Sita or Lakshman, along with *qawwali* performances and visits to Sufi shrines, while women of the family receive Hindu neighbours on Holi even though they are ambivalent about Hindu festivals. At the end, Gold discusses how a 'circumstantial' hilltop community came into being when the local Congress government carried out raids to evict the 'squatters', the poorest and the least rooted people who live near the top of the hill. Coherence here came through 'accidental political sparks' and not through 'cultural and personal identities' as in the case of the residents lower down on the hill.

Contingency and contradiction have ever been part of formations and articulations of religion and community, critically shot through by power.

NOTES AND REFERENCES

1. David N. Lorenzen, *The Kapalikas and the Kalamukhas: Two Lost Saivite Sects*, 2nd rev. edn (Delhi: Motilal Banarsidass, 1991). First published in 1972 by the University of California Press.

2. David N. Lorenzen, *Who Invented Hinduism? Essays on Religion in History* (New Delhi: Yoda Press, 2006).

3. See, for example, David N. Lorenzen, *Kabir Legends and Ananta-das's Kabir Parichai* (Albany: State University of New York Press, 1991); David N. Lorenzen, *Praises to a Formless God: Nirguni Texts from North India* (Albany: State University of New York Press, 1996); David N. Lorenzen (ed.), *Bhakti Religion in North India: Community, Identity, and Political Action* (Albany: State University of New York Press, 1995); David N. Lorenzen, 'The Kabir Panth and Social Protest', in W. H. McLeod and K. Schomer (eds), *The Sants: Studies in a Devotional Tradition of India* (Delhi: Motilal Banarsidass, 1987), pp. 281–303; and David N. Lorenzen, 'Traditions

of Non-caste Hinduism: The Kabirpanth', *Contributions to Indian Sociology*, vol. 21, no. 2, 1987, pp. 263–83. We provide only the barest minimum of Lorenzen's writings in the Spanish language here.

4. For instance, David N. Lorenzen (ed.), *Religious Movements in South Asia: 600–1800* (New Delhi: Oxford University Press, 2004); David N. Lorenzen and Benjamín Preciado-Solís, *Atadura y liberación: Las religiones de la India* ['Bondage and Liberation: The Religions of India'] (Mexico City: El Colegio de México, 1996); David N. Lorenzen, 'Who Invented Hinduism?', *Comparative Studies in Society and History*, vol. 41, no. 4, 1999, pp. 630–59.

5. See, for example C.A. Bayly, *Indian Society and the Making of the British Empire* (Cambridge: Cambridge University Press, 1988); C.A. Bayly, *Rulers, Townsmen and Bazaars: North Indian Society in the Age of British Expansion, 1770–1870* (Cambridge: Cambridge University Press, 1983); and David Washbrook, 'Progress and Problems: South Asian Economic and Social History', *Modern Asian Studies*, vol. 22, 1988, pp. 57–96. See also, Seema Alavi, *The Sepoys and the Company: Tradition and Transition in Northern India 1770–1830* (New Delhi: Oxford University Press, 1995); C.A. Bayly, *Empire and Information: Intelligence Gathering and Social Communication in India, 1780–1870* (Cambridge: Cambridge University Press, 1997).

6. Such issues are discussed in Saurabh Dube, *Stitches on Time: Colonial Textures and Postcolonial Tangles* (Durham: Duke University Press, 2004). Consider also the discussion in Dube, this volume.

7. For instance, David N. Lorenzen, 'Marco della Tomba', in M. Hortsmann (ed.), *Images of Kabir* (New Delhi: Manohar, 2002), pp. 33–43; David N. Lorenzen, 'Europeans in Late Mughal South Asia: The Perceptions of Italian Missionaries', *The Indian Economic and Social History Review*, vol. 40, no. 1, 2003, pp. 1–31; David N. Lorenzen, 'Marco della Tomba and the Brahmin from Banaras: Missionaries, Orientalists, and Indian Scholars', *Journal of Asian Studies*, vol. 65, no. 1, 2006, pp. 113–41; David N. Lorenzen, *The Scourge of the Mission: Marco della Tomba in Hindustan* (New Delhi: Yoda Press, forthcoming).

8. For us, writings that initiated these and related critical considerations of religion include works such as Talal Asad, 'Anthropological Conceptions of Religion: Reflections on Geertz', *Man*, (n.s.) vol. 18, 1983, pp. 237–59; and Jean Comaroff, *Body of Power, Spirit of Resistance: The Culture and History of a South African People* (Chicago: University of Chicago Press, 1985). See also, Pierre Bourdieu, *Outline of a Theory of Practice* (Cambridge: Cambridge University Press, 1977); Gerald M. Sider, 'The Ties that Bind: Culture and Agriculture, Property and Propriety in the New Foundland Village fishery', *Social History*, vol. 5, 1980, pp. 1–39; and Herman Rebel, 'Cultural Hegemony and Class Experience: A Critical Reading of Recent Ethnological-historical Approaches (parts one and two)', *American Ethnologist*, vol. 16, 1989, pp. 117–36, 350–65.

9. None of this is to deny the emergence of sophisticated versions of the base-superstructure model, especially the one offered by the French philosopher, Louis Althusser. However, the basic problem with the base-superstructure metaphor is that it displaces or, at any rate, cannot adequately account for meaningful practice. This also holds true for Althusser's model. Louis Althusser and Etienne Balibar,

Reading Capital (London: New Left Books, 1970); Raymond Williams, *Marxism and Literature* (Oxford: Oxford University Press,1977), pp. 81–2; Raymond Williams, 'Base and Superstructure in Marxist Cultural Analysis', *New Left Review*, vol. 82, 1973, pp. 3–16.

10. A broader elaboration of these twin issues is contained in Dube, *Stitches on Time.* See also Robert W. Hefner, 'Multiple Modernities: Christianity, Islam, and Hinduism in a Globalizing Age', *Annual Review of Anthropology*, vol. 27, 1998, pp. 83–104; Brian K. Axel, *The Nation's Tortured Body: Violence, Representation, and the Formation of the Sikh 'Diaspora'* (Durham: Duke University Press, 2001); Ana Maria Alonso, 'The Politics of Space, Time, and Substance: State Formation, Nationalism, and Ethnicity', *Annual Review of Anthropology*, vol. 23, 1994, pp. 379–400; and Robert Foster, 'Making National Cultures in the Global Ecumene', *Annual Review of Anthropology*, vol. 20, 1991, pp. 235–60.

11. For instance, Dube, *Stitches on Time*; Ishita Banerjee-Dube, *Religion, Law and Power: Tales of Time in Eastern India, 1860–2000* (London: Anthem Press, 2007); Saurabh Dube, *Untouchable Pasts: Religion, Identity, and Power among a Central Indian Community, 1780–1950* (Albany: State University of New York Press, 1998).

12. Wider explorations of these issues are contained in Saurabh Dube, 'Anthropology, History, Historical Anthropology', in Saurabh Dube (ed.), *Historical Anthropology* (New Delhi: Oxford University Press, 2007). The essay also discusses the place of the collective subaltern studies' endeavour in putting questions of community on historical and ethnographic agendas as well as the earlier limitations and recent transformations within the project of renderings of communities.

13. The examples ahead are illustrative, and they are mostly drawn from the period of history we are most familiar with. This is not meant to diminish the critical significance of scholarly developments for other eras regarding the issues being discussed here.

14. Harjot Oberoi, *The Construction of Religious Boundaries: Culture, Identity, and Diversity in the Sikh Tradition* (Chicago: University of Chicago Press, 1994); Rowena Robinson, *Conversion, Continuity, and Change: Lived Christianity in Southern Goa* (New Delhi: Sage, 1998); Veena Das, *Critical Events: An Anthropological Perspective on Contemporary India* (New Delhi: Oxford University Press, 1995); Prem Chowdhry, *The Veiled Woman: Shifting Gender Equations in Rural Haryana 1880–1980* (New Delhi: Oxford University Press, 1994); Malavika Kasturi, *Embattled Identities: Rajput Lineages and the Colonial State in Nineteenth-century North India* (New Delhi: Oxford University Press, 2002); Dube, *Untouchable Pasts*; Charu Gupta, *Sexuality, Obscenity, and Community: Women, Muslims, and the Hindu Public in Colonial India* (Delhi: Permanent Black, 2002). See also, Sandra Freitag, *Collective Action and Community: Public Arenas and the Emergence of Communalism in North India* (Berkeley: University of California Press, 1990); Gyanendra Pandey, *The Construction of Communalism in Colonial North India* (New Delhi: Oxford University Press, 1990).

15. Shail Mayaram, *Resisting Regimes: Myth, Memory and the Shaping of a Muslim Identity* (New Delhi: Oxford University Press, 1997); David Hardiman, *The Coming of the Devi*: *Adivasi Assertion in Western India* (New Delhi: Oxford

University Press, 1987); Ranajit Guha, *Elementary Aspects of Peasant Insurgency in Colonial India* (New Delhi: Oxford University Press, 1983); Dube, *Untouchable Pasts*; Banerjee-Dube, *Religion, Law and Power*. See also, Anand Pandian, 'Securing the Rural Citizen: The Anti-Kallar Movement of 1896', *The Indian Economic and Social History Review*, vol. 42, 2005, pp. 1–39.

16. For instance, Ajay Skaria, *Hybrid Histories: Forest, Frontiers and Wildness in Western India* (New Delhi: Oxford University Press, 1999); Dipesh Chakrabarty, *Provincializing Europe: Postcolonial Thought and Historical Difference* (Princeton: Princeton University Press, 2000); Banerjee-Dube, *Religion, Law and Power*; Dube, *Stitches on Time*.

17. A broader discussion of these issues is contained in Dube, 'Anthropology, History, Historical Anthropology'.

18. See especially, Peter Redfield, *Space in the Tropics: From Convicts to Rockets in French Guiana* (Berkeley: University of California Press, 2000); Dube, *Stitches on Time*.

19. Shail Mayaram, *Against History, Against State: Counterperspectives from the Margins* (Delhi: Permanent Black, 2004); Yasmin Saikia, *Fragmented Memories: Struggling to Be Tai-Ahom in India* (Durham: Duke University Press, 2004); Dube, *Stitches on Time*. See also, Velcheru Narayana Rao, David Shulman, and Sanjay Subrahmanyam, *Textures of Time: Writing History in South India* (Delhi: Permanent Black, 2001); Wendy Singer, *Creating Histories: Oral Narratives and the Politics of History-Making* (New Delhi: Oxford University Press, 1997).

20. Shahid Amin, *Event, Metaphor, Memory: Chauri Chaura 1922–1992* (Berkeley: University of California Press, 1996); Ann Gold and Bhoju Ram Gujar, *In the Time of Trees and Sorrows: Nature, Power, and Memory in Rajasthan* (Durham: Duke University Press, 2002); Skaria, *Hybrid Historie;* Dube, *Untouchable Pasts*; Banerjee-Dube, *Religion, Law and Power*.

21. Michel-Rolph Trouillot, *Silencing the Past: Power and the Production of History* (Boston: Beacon Press, 1995); Gyanendra Pandey, *Routine Violence: Nations, Fragments, Histories* (Stanford: Stanford University Press, 2005); Chakrabarty, *Provincializing Europe*; Dipesh Chakrabarty, *Habitations of Modernity: Essays in the Wake of Subaltern Studies* (Chicago: University of Chicago Press, 2002); Dube, *Stitches on Time*. See also, Ashis Nandy, 'History's Forgotten Doubles', *History and Theory*, vol. 34, no. 1 (1995), pp. 44–66; Vinay Lal, *The History of History: Politics and Scholarship in Modern India* (New Delhi: Oxford University Press, 2003).

22. David Gordon White, this volume, p. 86.

1. THE PURĀṆAS
HERESY AND THE 'VAṂŚĀNUCARITA'

Romila Thapar

The Purāṇa as a genre is referred to in the Vedas both individually as were the *gāthās*, *nāraśamsis*, *akhyānas*, and others; and as a compound as in *itihāsa-purāṇa*.[1] The distinctions among the former are not invariable. The category of *purāṇa* refers to that which is believed to be of the ancient past. In this sense it includes mythology as well as what might have been projected as a historical tradition. When purāṇa becomes the label for a distinctive genre of texts by the mid-first millennium AD it is better-defined, is associated with an author however mythical he may have been, and is included as part of a tradition. This was said to have been originally associated primarily with the bards—the *sūta* and the *māgadha*—who together with the *vandin,* eulogist, and *cāranas*, professional singers and reciters, and others were to record what was said by the king.[2] It gradually came to be the preserve of the Bhṛgu brāhmaṇas frequently linked to the historical tradition. This transference coincided with a low status for bards in the *dharma-śāstras*.[3] Many Purāṇas claim that they were recited by the sūtas to the *ṛṣis* in the Naimiṣa forest at the time of the twelve-year *sattra* sacrifice, a claim that is also made for one of the recitations of the Mahābhārata.[4] The Naimiṣa forest seems to become a generalized locale for sacrificial rituals.

The Purāṇas as texts record the religious beliefs and practices associated with a particular deity. They also reflect the assimilation of other religious forms and beliefs that went into extending the reach of both text and sect.[5] The concept of the *pañcalakṣana* was a departure from the format of the Vedas as also was the cosmology of past time periods and the future to come. The Purāṇas were serving a different function. They endorsed, at least in theory, the normative behaviour and values conforming to the dharma-śāstras, such as in the discussion of the *acāravyavahāra*, relating to the organization and functioning of society. Claims were made to the usual forms of legitimizing a religious text, such as divine revelation, but such claims were hardly necessary for the more mundane sections such as the vaṃśānucarita in the *Viṣṇu Purāṇa.* This pertains to the succession and descent of ancient heroes and heads of clans coming down to dynastic succession in the kingdoms. Not every Purāṇa, however, included these lists and in the very few that did they were not as systematically arranged as in the *Viṣṇu Purāṇa.* The *Viṣṇu Purāṇa* was virtually the only Purāṇa that to a large extent conformed to the *pañcalakṣana* format.

Such texts were subject to reformulation as and when necessary.[6] A likely occasion would be when the deity was being given an additional mythology often to introduce new forms of worship frequently in an effort to incorporate new groups into Puranic Hinduism. Inductions such as these could result from the conquest of groups outside the existing caste society where such groups were being incorporated into the social and economic system of the conquerors. They could also result from a process of osmosis, as for example, from the cutting of forests and the settling of land so cleared where erstwhile forest dwellers had to be assimilated. This was a process that could take a few generations as is evident from inscriptional evidence.[7] The propagation of existing religious beliefs and the integration of new ones would require patronage, social sanction, and the interweaving of myths and rituals.

Parallel to what has been called acculturation, and implicit in the perspective of religious sects was the necessity of choosing what was to be included and what excluded. In the formulation of sectarian texts, dedicated to the worship of Viṣṇu, Śiva, and other deities, it is understood that some ideologies would have been excluded and that sometimes the exclusion may have arisen from confrontations. The nature of the Purāṇa can perhaps be better understood if there is awareness of its ignoring certain beliefs and practices, although this may be difficult to assess, and to recognizing its hostility to others.

Among the heterodox sects, referred to sometimes as the *pāṣaṇḍas*, the Jainas in particular had their own corpus of Purāṇas which served much the same function in focussing on the belief and worship particularly of the *tīrthānkaras*. The Buddhist schools had no specific texts called Purāṇas, but some did approximate to the Puranic genre in their projection of the Buddha such as the Mahāvastu. Both the Jainas and the Buddhists are seen as hostile to Puranic Hinduism and perhaps the hostility is greater towards Buddhism, possibly because the competition was more widespread. The absence of a deity in Buddhism may have been problematic although it could have been overcome by treating the Buddha as a virtual deity, similar to the treatment of Mahāvīra in the Jaina Purāṇas.

The Jaina tradition intentionally encouraged the writing of texts parallel to some of the existing texts of popular religion from the brahmanical tradition.[8] The Jaina epic, the *Pauamacariyam,* questions by implication the Vālmīki *Rāmāyaṇa*, and the narratives of the Jaina *Ādi Purāṇa* counter existing views. The Jaina *Harivaṃśa* is another such example where even the title was retained. Such texts may have to some extent acted as a check on the denigration of the Jainas in the Hindu Purāṇas. The Buddhists did not have a recognizably parallel tradition and were in any case stronger contenders for a popular religious support than the Jainas. They were doubtless viewed as greater rivals by the Pauranic authors. The currency of these distinctive Purāṇas would have encouraged sectarian loyalties.

The authorship of these various Purāṇas differed. The Vaiṣṇava and Śaiva Purāṇas are attributed to Vyāsa and his disciples and recur in every age; there have been twenty-eight so far.[9] Some of the Jaina Purāṇas are given individual authors. The audience for these texts were largely those who heard them recited, mainly an upper caste, *dvija* audience. Eventually, the more important locations for the recitations of the Purāṇas were temples. Given this, patronage—especially royal patronage—for the construction of temples became a matter of intense competition. Royal patronage also took the form of making grants of land, either to the Buddhist *vihāra*s or more frequently to learned brāhmaṇas. Such grants were used to embellish the vihāras. In the case of brāhmaṇas if the grant was large enough it could become the base from which a few generations later claims were made to kingship. The mention of the *brahma-kṣatra* as a caste of origin increases in the first millennium AD, and more often applies to brāhmaṇas who have taken on kṣatriya functions.

I would like to consider the treatment of Buddhism in the Purāṇas from a few salient perspectives pertinent perhaps to the intention of the Purāṇas: the Buddha as a member of a lineage, the references to his teaching, and statements about those Mauryan rulers listed in the vaṃśānucarita section whom the heterodox sects claimed as their patrons. The third of these themes is in the context of the first two as evident from the Purāṇas.

In the descent list of the Ikṣvākus after the start of the Kali age, Śākya occurs as the name of a person and not of a clan.[10] Prior to the Kali age Daśaratha and Rāma were listed in the Ikṣvāku lineage. Since this segment begins with the Kaliyuga, the list takes the form of a prediction of those to come and is as follows:

...sañjayasya sutoḥ śākyah śākyac śuddhodhano 'bhavat śuddhodanasya bhavitā siddhārtho rāhulah sutaḥ prasenajit tato bhāvyaḥ kṣudrako bhavitā....[11]

This translates in a genealogical pattern as:

...Sañjaya
Śuddhodana
Siddhārtha—only in a few *Purāṇas*
Rāhula/Rātula
Prasenajit
Kṣudraka...

The Ikṣvākus are associated with *kula-vardhanāḥ* (increasing the status of the family) or in alternate readings *śuddha-vaṃśa-jāḥ* (born of a lineage of status). In a couple of Purāṇas they are also described as *śūrāś ca kṛta vidyāśca satya-sandhā jitendriyāḥ* (heroes, men of learning, truthful and self-controlled). It is further predicted that three generations down from the last name will see the end of the lineage. As members of the Ikṣvāku lineage they would have been kṣatriyas.

Not all the Purāṇas include Siddhārtha, and some give alternate names such as Suddhārdha or Śākyārthe.[12] They knew them as Śākyas but do not distinguish between a clan name and a member of the clan. Buddhist texts explain the name Śākya and it is not the name of a person.[13] The Purāṇas are not meticulous about any descent list. The contemporary Buddhist sources were consistent about the Buddha's descent but obviously were not consulted. Presumably these narratives of origin from Buddhist sources were regarded as unimportant by the authors of the Purāṇas despite the centrality of Buddhism in the period when the earliest Purāṇas were being composed. This can perhaps be seen as a comment on how the heterodox sects were viewed by brāhmaṇa authors.

The Śākyas were a chiefdom and had no king, as was also the case with some other clans of the time of the Buddha.[14] Given that the Purāṇas generally ignored clans that were chiefdoms and therefore ignored many clans contemporary with the Śākyas, such as the Mallas, Koliyas, Vṛjjis, or the Jñātrikas to which Mahāvīra belonged, the latter need not have been included. The reason for this may have been that the Śākyas were said to be descended from Ikṣvāku, the much respected founder of the Śuryavaṃśa. Or, to reverse the argument, was the Buddhist tradition trying to link the Śākyas to Ikṣvāku in order to give them a Śuryvaṃśa lineage? This would also have tied in with their connections to Kosala. Some Purāṇas refer to Siddhārtha as the son of Śuddhodana.[15] It is surprising that nothing further is said about him in the genealogical segments since he features in the mythology of evil elsewhere in the Purāṇas.

Yet there are some echoes of similarities with Buddhist narratives. The story of the ancestral figure of Okkāka goes through many permutations of legends involving the patriarch banishing his older sons in favour of the son from his younger favourite wife.[16] Like Ikṣvāku, Okkāka is also an ancestor of the Śākyas. It has been suggested that Ikṣvāku could be a Sanskritized form of the Pāli name Okkāka. Ikṣvāku has also been linked to *ikṣa* (sugarcane), in a later Buddhist tradition narrating an origin myth of the Śākyas.[17] He was called Okkāka because when he spoke a light emanated from his mouth.[18] A similar statement is made in the *Śatapatha Brāhmaṇa* about Videgha Māthava who is said to have carried Agni in his mouth.[19]

Prasenajit echoes the Pasenadi of the Pāli texts. He was a contemporary of the Buddha, was politically important, and ruled Kosala.[20] He was anxious to have close kinship links with the Śākyas and asked to marry into the Buddha's family. The Śākyans held themselves as being of superior status and therefore sent him a young woman born of a Śākyan and a *dāsī* (female slave). The son from this marriage discovered the fraud and therefore wrecked vengeance on the Śākyas.[21] That the Ikṣvāku dynasty came to a close just a few generations later would be borne out by Buddhist sources which do not mention a long subsequent history.

The section on genealogies and succession lists seems to have no cross-links with those on mythology and religious sects and vice versa. It is almost as if the Siddhārtha of the Ikṣvāku lineage was in no way connected to the Buddha. Were these sections written by different authors whose agendas did not overlap? It is likely that a separation was maintained between succession lists that recorded presumed genealogies of ruling families and statements of religious sectarian opinions. Even if this section of the Ikṣvāku descent list was originally prior to the spread of Buddhism as a religion, it still could have been commented upon from the religious sectarian perspective had there been an integration of various sections of the text. The religious sectarian sections of the Purāṇas where the Buddha has an ambiguous role ignore the Śākyas. This is quite apart from genealogies not intended to be taken literally but rather as pawns in a game of status and politics.

It has been suggested that the absence of other kṣatriya tribes in the descent lists was because they had been absorbed into caste society or because they were opposed to Puranic Hinduism.[22] Some are given the status of *vrātya* kṣatriyas in Manu.[23] The Licchavis have a high status in Buddhist and Jaina texts being described as kṣatriyas of the Vasiṣṭha *gotra*.[24]

As has been pointed out the root *budh* has given rise to various forms.[25] As a noun in the name of the Buddha it occurs in the Purāṇas such as, Buddhadeva, Buddharūpa, and so on; and generally in association with an *avatara* of Viṣṇu. In the religious context the Buddha is referred to as the Buddha and generally not as Siddhārtha as in some of the genealogical sections. He is said to have been born in the land of the Kīkaṭas, another name for Magadha in the early sources.[26] Yāska states that the name derives from the inhabitants who reject Vedic sacrifices and this has been glossed as *anārya nivāsa*.[27] He was perceived therefore as socially and culturally different. There is also in one case a conflation of the Buddha and Mahāvīra when it is said that the Buddha was the son of the Jina, came from Kīkaṭadeśa and was an avatara of Viṣṇu, born to destroy the heretics.[28]

Some later Purāṇas made the Buddha into an incarnation of Viṣṇu and left it at that, the assumption being presumably that he and his teaching were thereby incorporated into Vaiṣṇava worship. Hence the occasional description of his being *śānta*, calm, and associated with yoga.[29] But clearly this was not acceptable to sectarian Vaiṣṇavas who then constructed a myth to explain why the Buddha had been made into an avatara of Viṣṇu despite preaching a doctrine not in conformity with Vaiṣṇava belief. It was maintained that what he taught was opposed to Vedic ritual and therefore the power of those to whom he preached—the asuras, daityas, and dānavas—was weakened and they were defeated in their struggle against the *devas*, those conforming to Vedic dharma. In a strongly sectarian manner it is said that the former were diverted from the correct path. Incorporation and exclusion therefore, become parallel processes.

The references to the Buddha as an avatara of Viṣṇu were late, dating from the mid-first millennium AD onwards.[30] This was a critical period for the future of both Buddhism and Puranic Hinduism. Judging by Hsüan Tsang's account, Buddhism was declining in parts of *madhya-deśa* and many parts of the peninsula, although not in eastern India. The earlier popularity of Buddhism in the subcontinent had obviously not been forgotten. It was therefore necessary to come to terms with this popularity. In the contestation between the two, the putting down of Buddhism as a popular religion would have been less effective if it had been only a philosophical critique. It was more easily done through associating its teachings with what was regarded as 'the Other' of Indian culture from the perspective of the brahmanical tradition and by insisting on the incorrectness of its teachings. For this purpose a mythology had to be constructed. The confrontations were with what were regarded as the heresies, the argument being that the presence of *nāstika* doctrines—those opposed to conformity with the Vedic dharma—would destroy society.[31]

The Kaliyuga was projected as the age of decline when heresies flourish. The *varṇāśramadharma* was not observed so the essential rules of caste were broken. The Śūdras were dominant, became kings and performed the *áśvamedha* sacrifice normally only permitted to the twice-born castes. Various evil-minded persons wandered about as mendicants and were maintained through alms.[32] Characteristic of the heretics was their opposition to the dharma of the Vedas.

The initial incorporation of the Buddha was the story of the Buddha as Māyāmoha. Subsequently he was projected as an avatara of Viṣṇu. The context is the deceptive teachings of both Buddhist and Jaina monks. Māyāmoha, with a double emphasis on delusion and illusion is personified as a teacher. The basic story is simple and echoes the primeval myth of the deva-asura confrontation. The *Viṣṇu Purāṇa* narrates the story of devas, gods, and asuras and daityas, demons, at war resulting in the defeat of the devas, who appeal to Viṣṇu for help. The appeal is yet another occasion for glorifying Viṣṇu. Neither devas nor asuras are specifically defined. They seem to be terms used in a broad sense to differentiate between 'us' and 'them'. The asuras observe the varṇa and recognize religious rites which make them somewhat invulnerable. Yet they are enemies. Therefore, some intervention from a deity is required.[33] Viṣṇu, conceding the appeal of the devas produced an illusory form from his body and gave him to the devas, saying that this would lead the asuras astray; or for that matter even those devas who did not observe the Vedic dharma.[34] This was Māyāmoha. He went among the asuras assembled at the Narmada and was naked, shaven-headed and holding a peacock feather. He was obviously meant to represent a Digambara monk. His teaching of *anekāntavāda* and questioning the Vedic formulae was to divert them from the asceticism required of Vedic practioners and to attaining *mokṣa*. Nakedness also referred to not being clothed in the Vedas.[35] His doctrine spread among the daityas and they discarded the Vedas.

Māyāmoha then put on some red robes and preached *ahiṃsā* to them, asking them to desist from sacrificing animals. He was thus converted into a Buddhist *bhikkhu*. Under the influence of this teaching the asuras gave up their adherence to the Vedic dharma. Māyāmoha ensured that a variety of *pāṣaṇḍa* sects, were able to follow his teaching. Many became contemptuous of the Vedas, their deities, sacrificial rituals, and the brāhmaṇas. They began to pose rational questions that contradicted brahmanical belief.[36] This has been read as an attempted refutation of the Yogācāra and Śūnyavāda doctrines.[37] The insistence of the heretics on believing only that which can be rationally explained has also been viewed as linked to the question of the divine revelation of the Vedas. Ultimately the asuras were weakened, which finally led to their defeat by the devas.[38]

The concluding section is a diatribe against all pāṣaṇḍas where the word has by now changed its meaning from all sects—as used in the Aśokan edicts—to specific sects opposed to brahmanical doctrines and to Puranic religion. The shift in meaning suggests that the latter may have been large in number. Described as sinners because they contest the Vedas, it is said to be a sin to even speak with or be sociable to, such heretics.[39] Frauds, those who have strayed from the path of religious observances and rites, self-serving, wicked, and those given to questioning authority by arguments involving causal reasoning, should be avoided altogether. The attack on causal argument—*hetukaḥ*—was doubtless also directed at philosophical schools such as Sāmkhya and Nyāya. This is a strongly sectarian position on tenets, quite apart from the hostility towards those who are mendicants of the heterodox persuasion, who do not observe the prescribed brahmanical rituals and who are excluded from the *śrāddha*s.

There are other versions of the story with some changes. The *Matsya Purāṇa* states that Bṛhaspati preached the Jinadharma to the powerful sons of Rāji. When Indra discovered that they were upholding a dharma contrary to the Vedas, he destroyed them.[40] The moral of the story is that those who deviate from the Vedic dharma are pāṣaṇḍas and should be avoided. The gods should destroy them. Elsewhere Bṛhaspati in the guise of Śukra preaches to the asuras and diverts them from the correct path. The real Śukra curses them but adds that it was their destiny to be diverted.[41] In another variant Bṛhaspati in a sense authors the heretical religion through creating Māyāmoha.[42] Disguised as Śukra he preaches heresy to the asuras: that rituals were invented by greedy priests, that deities and brāhmaṇas both consume intoxicants and meat, that Śiva and Viṣṇu as deities cannot impart religious doctrines, and so on. The heretics then opposed animal slaughter in rituals and the irrationality of the Vedas. Embedded in the mythology is a question raised in a later Purāṇa, namely, how could the gods have created a fraudulent teacher? It receives an ambiguous answer: that the gods are prone to human weaknesses.[43]

In the later Purāṇas of post-Gupta times the Buddha is projected as an avatara of Viṣṇu. Although the background story remains the same, his status as an avatara is somewhat different from his being Māyāmoha. As an avatara of Viṣṇu the Buddha can be one of ten or more avataras.[44] Viṣṇu took birth as the Buddha or in one text as Siddhārtha, the son of Śuddhodana, and taught the asuras to doubt and oppose the dharma of the Vedas. The daityas and asuras did so and because of this were weakened and were not only defeated by the devas but also ended up in hell.[45] The story comes with eulogies of the various incarnations and the Buddha figures among them, generally the penultimate and prior to Kalki. The story as narrated is an attempt at assimilating Buddhists. However, when the teachings are referred to, and even more the description of those who teach and accept the teaching, then the acrimony against and the vilification of, the heretical sects is stridently stated.

To read these stories as merely negating the separate identity and continued existence of the heterodox Sramanic sects[46] is to simplify the intention of the Purāṇas. They were in essence sectarian texts and aware of the need to confront those regarded as heretical. Sramanic views were recognized as being antithetical to the Vedic. More often than not the litmus test of heresy has to do with acceptance of the Vedic dharma. This may have been symbolic not so much of the texts as of the social and ritual mores of Vedic Brahmanism.[47] The definition of the Vedic dharma was less focused on the performance of Vedic ritual and more on the observance of varṇāśramadharma. The definition of heresy was at one level an objection to the belief and ritual propagated by certain sects. But at another and more emphatic level it was an objection to such sects denying the varṇa organization of society and all that this entailed in terms of sacred and social obligations as encoded in the dharma-śāstras and *gṛhya-sūtras*.

The use of *māyā* as a prefix is also a comment on Sramanic teaching being ultimately illusory. Even though the Purāṇas themselves depart from Vedic views on belief and ritual, they nevertheless continue to endorse the Vedas. There were conflicting views even among the authors of the various Purāṇas. It could also be possible that the Sramanic sects were being treated as a front for questioning the Vedic dharma by some of its own adherents. The reference to hetukaḥ touched on philosophical thought other than that of the heresies.

Inter-sectarian confrontations between Vaiṣṇavas and Śaivas are also reflected in some Purāṇas but infrequently compared to the opposition to the *śramaṇa*s and they tend to be later in date. A general statement is that the presence of nāstikas, often identified with śramaṇas, destroys a society. The term is used in various senses, from atheists to those who supported other sectarian views. More specifically, the image of *māyāpuruṣa* in the form of a Jaina *muni* is conjured up by Viṣṇu to disturb the rituals of those worshipping Śiva.[48] The māyāpuruṣa is told to compose a śāstra in *apabrahṃśa*, a language used by some Jaina authors, and the śāstra was to counter the *śruti*s, *smṛti*s, and varṇāśramadharma. Viṣṇu urges Nārada to persuade Śiva to follow the new doctrine which is clearly a caricature of Buddhism. Such rivalry reflects a competition over patronage and support rather than a refutation of doctrine. In the instances quoted above the intervention of and association with, heretics, symbolizes the rivalry. This is dissimilar to the confrontation between Puranic Hinduism and the Sramaṇic sects.

Where hostility is expressed against sects such as the Pāśupatas, Vāmacaras, Kapālikas, and Kālamukhas within the Śaiva tradition and the Pañcarātras within Vaiṣṇavas,[49] the hostility seems due less to religious sectarianism and more to their not observing the social norms. This would have been the case with the Pāśupatas and the Kapālikas.[50] Even more curious are the appeals to the Buddha and to Kalki as incarnations of Viṣṇu for protection against the pāṣaṇḍas and the sins of the Kaliyuga.[51] This could be an indicator of the assimilation of Buddhism or else that the character of Buddhism itself had so changed, as in Vajrayāna Buddhism, that it could barely be distinguished from other Puranic sects.

Admittedly, the papering over of differences was more at the level of their popular perception. The brāhmaṇa authors of the Purāṇas were well aware of diverse sectarian positions that theoretically at least affected belief, ritual, and social practice. These may have started to become interchangeable, requiring adjustments on the part of both brāhmaṇa authors and Sramanic teaching.[52] Nevertheless the key issue remained that of who controlled the social norms. Presumably the decline of Buddhism by the early second millennium AD (apart from eastern India) created a confidence among the authors of the Purāṇas to induct the Buddha more directly without depicting him as Māyāmoha. As has been pointed out, the *Padma Purāṇa* provides evidence of interpolations. Among the more interesting is when an *ācārya* of the Madhva sect identifies *pāṣaṇḍins* as those who worship Śiva and denounces the *māyāvada* of Ṣankarācārya as *pracchanna bauddha*, crypto-Buddhism, as indeed did some others as well.[53]

This was also the period of philosophical debates across a large spectrum ranging from the Cārvākas to Vedanta. Critiques of the philosophy of Vedic Brahmanism were common and are summarized together with the views of other schools in texts such as Mādhava's *Sarvadarśana-saṃgraha*. Some argued that the material world was all that existed and others insisted on *ātman* being central.[54] These are important in the context of sectarian competition. Philosophical schools were in a sense implicitly challenging sectarian texts in as much as there was some accommodation of variant views in the former whereas the latter appear to be more rigid. Some overlapping views, however marginal, are present in the Mīmāmsā, Sānkhya, Buddhist, and Cārvāka theories. These philosophical debates are not reflected in Puranic sectarianism. The Purāṇas were intended to propagate the worship of a deity and were not texts concerned with philosophical discourse. Can we argue that there is a suggestion of Viṣṇu also being a crypto-Buddhist, given the manner in which the Buddha as an avatara is projected in the Purāṇas?

The confrontation between sectarian positions is not a direct one in which arguments may have been raised to denigrate the other sect point by point. The intention here is to declare its teachings incorrect and conducive to evil behaviour. The criterion of correctness is based on observing the Vedic dharma, although the Puranic rituals themselves do not observe the dharma except in theory. Sometimes this endorsement is weak as in the preference for *tapas* over *yajña* or in statements such as *ahiṃśa paramadharmaḥ*.[55] The central deities—Viṣṇu and Śiva—were marginal in the Vedic system and the central deities of the latter—Indra and Agni—are marginal to Puranic Hinduism. The form of worship changed with yajñas often being replaced by *pūjā* so that offerings avoided the killing of animals. Icons, unknown to the Vedic system, were now worshipped in temples which became permanent sacred spaces. By the end of the first millennium AD temples had become complex institutions funded by grants of land and requiring a hierarchy of administrators and servitors. Cosmologies and mythologies were different as were the ritual requirements of *vratas* and *tīrthas*. Was the insistence on conforming to the Vedic dharma largely a front for sectarian conflicts involving issues of social positioning rather than merely belief and ritual ?

The belief and practice of Puranic Hinduism was in itself different from the religion of the Vedas. It was influenced in many ways by the śramaṇa sects although the stance was always one of hostility towards them. The inherent hostility was compared by Patañjali to that of the mongoose and the snake.[56] The projection of the Buddha in the Purāṇas is therefore ambiguous. He is not inherently evil but preaches a doctrine that was opposed to the Vedic religion. He is not a *rākṣasa* but is an incarnation of Viṣṇu although this avatara has a different function, almost inverting the concept. He does not come into a direct confrontation with the personification of evil who he then annihilates, restoring the world to goodness, as do the other human incarnations of Viṣṇu. There is no one-to-one action as in the case of Narasiṃha, Rāma, and Paraśurāma. The Buddha comes to preach a false doctrine, which because it is false, initially weakens those who are prone to evil and this enables them to be finally defeated. It is a long-term investment requiring a fresh mythology to introduce this change in the concept of an avatara.

The Buddha as Māyāmoha was created from a deity even if he was illusory. This was a reversal of Buddhist belief although it was by now acceptable to many practising Buddhists despite the Buddha as also much of Buddhist philosophy having denied it. In a sense the story of Māyāmoha, possibly a later interpolation,[57] may be a reflection of a historical condition. What had earlier been regarded as heresies were being gradually eroded and being replaced by new heresies in the early second millennium AD. Brahmanical thinking was becoming dominant but not entirely so. The defeat of the asuras and daityas and the victory of the devas could have been an analogy referring to this change in relation to the Sramanic sects.

The Vedic system had to be invoked by the Purāṇas largely to endorse the social model of varṇāśramadharma, which had its roots in the Vedic system but which was formulated in post-Vedic times. The greatest fear among the authors of the Purāṇas concerns the changes in social organization in the Kaliyuga. This is in part a reflection of what was actually happening and in greater part a projection of what could happen once the stringency of the normative rules of caste were questioned. The Kaliyuga was viewed as the time when the caste hierarchy was turned upside down and the śūdras were effectively the dominant caste with the brāhmaṇas paying respect to them. The Sramanic sects were opposed to the varṇāśramadharma and their teaching was not supportive of this system. The matter gets aggravated when kings become patrons of the pāṣaṇḍas.[58] This perhaps irked the Puranic authors even more than the differences in belief and ritual.

Given all, this one wonders why the comparatively bland vaṃśānucarita section was included, especially in the *Viṣṇu Purāṇa.*

It lists the descent of those of high status from earliest times and ends with the kings of various dynasties bringing the information up to the Gupta period. Recorded as a genealogical pattern it is present in only a few Purāṇas. Where it is included it seems extraneous. The inclusion of a separate and distinct vaṃśānucarita section in the Purāṇa was more likely to ensure its preservation as a record embedded in an important religious text as well as to give status to at least the heroes of legend who were accorded the status of kṣatriyas.

There appears to be a difference in objectives between those that maintained the vaṃśānucarita section and those that composed and edited the other parts of the Purāṇa. This is suggested by the absence of negative attributes associated with these rulers who were known to have been, or claimed to have been, followers of the heterodox sects. The reference to the politically powerful early Mauryan emperors is an example.

The dynastic lists subsequent to the lineages of the heroes include the statement that future rulers will be from a variety of castes, including Śūdras and *mlecchas*.[59] The Mauryas will follow the Nandas. The Nanda dynasty will be founded by Mahapadma, a son of the Śiśunāga king Mahānandin by a śūdra woman.[60] Subsequent kings will be śūdras. It is not clear whether this applies only to the Nandas or to their successors as well. Mahāpadma will exterminate all the kṣatriyas. This in itself would have made it necessary for other varṇas to become rulers but the choice of śūdras is significant. The uprooting of kṣatriyas suggests his having conquered the chiefdoms of the middle Ganga valley in order to establish his *eka-cchattram*, sole sovereignty. The Nandas will be uprooted by the brāhmaṇa Kauṭilya who will establish Candragupta of the Mauryas as king. A brāhmaṇa would have thought it his duty to uproot śūdra kings, but curiously the person he instals is described in other sources as a *vṛṣala,* low caste. Only the Buddhist and Jaina sources give the Mauryas the status of kṣatriyas. No comment is made on these deviations from the rules of varṇa and presumably, it is expected in the Kaliyuga.

The low status of the Mauryas is asserted in sources other than the Buddhist. In Viśākhadatta's play, *Mudrārākṣasa*, dating to the mid-first millennium AD, Candragupta is referred to variously.[61] He is described as Maurya*putra*, the suffix putra suggesting a clan affiliation. It is also said that he was brought up by a shepherd and that Cānakya recognized his potential and adopted him. Cānakya calls him vṛṣala more than once although others refer to him as *āryadeva* and deva. Underlying the status of minister and king, it also sets out the superiority of the brāhmaṇa over the śūdra. The Maurya succession was regarded as important to the Indian past as is evident even in later commentaries in the AD second millennium on texts that refer to the Mauryas, such as the *Mudrārākṣasa*.

Post-canonical Buddhist sources insist on the *kṣatriya* status of the Mauryas and go further and provide them with kinship links to the Śākyas. The region from which they came was full of peacocks (*mayura: mora*), hence the name Moriya/Maurya.[62] This attempted link with the Śākyas gave the Mauryas the appropriate kṣatriya status. It also effectively connected the coming of Buddhism to Sri Lanka through Mahinda, the son of Aśoka, with the clan of the Buddha.

A late Jaina tradition held that Candragupta became a Jaina in his last years, abdicated the throne, and travelled together with the Jaina seer Bhadrabāhu to south India.[63] The same text mentions that Candragupta came from a village of peacock-breeders, hence the name Maurya from mora and was gifted by his father to Cānakya. Peacock-breeders would have been ranked low in the caste hierarchy.

Candragupta's son, Bindusāra is said to have been close to the Ājīvikas. This was not an insignificant sect at this time as is evident from votive inscriptions issued by two Mauryan rulers, Aśoka and Daśaratha, inscribed at the Barabar and Nagarjuni Hill Caves.[64] Contemporary with the writing of the Purāṇas there is evidence of what appears to be a Vaiṣṇava attempt to chisel away the name of Ājīvika in three of the inscriptions. The sect is said to have had access to the court of Bindusāra,[65] who had an interest in philosophical ideas since he requested that a sophist be sent to him from Greece.[66] Aśoka's adherence to Buddhism is clear from his edicts.

If the claims of the heterodox sects were correct then the first three and most influential of the Mauryan rulers were all heretics in the eyes of the brāhmaṇas. The Purāṇas suggest their low varṇa status but are silent about their heterodoxy. The one who comes in for flak on both counts in other texts is Aśoka whose patronage gave visibility to the heterodox sects in the Mauryan Empire. It has been thought that the garbling of the name Aśokavardhana in the various Purāṇas was meant as disrespect. But names in the Purāṇas are known to be garbled merely out of scribal error. Little is said about him in the Purāṇas but there are many snide remarks on his name, *devānampiya* (the beloved of the gods), in other texts.[67] The discussion among grammarians about the use of this word is a sharp attack, even if indirect, on Aśoka.

It is interesting that the word was initially used as an honorific. It is used thus later by the grandson of Aśoka, Daśaratha in one of his inscriptions.[68] Patañjali treats it as such.[69] The *Mahāvaṃsa* composed in the AD sixth century, claims that the Sri Lankan ruler Tissa, also used it as a title, associating it with Aśoka.[70] By the AD eleventh century the term had come to acquire the derogatory and sarcastic meaning of one who is foolish or ignorant—*mūrkha*, as is stated by Kaiyaṭa.[71] Aśoka had not been erased from people's memory since he is known to Kalhaṇa and written about in the *Rājataraṅginī*.[72] He is described as a supporter of the *Jina-śāsana* who built many vihāras and *caityas* and was reckoned as a praiseworthy king. This contradicts the Puranic presentation of the Sramaṇic religions or even the definition of devānampiya by contemporary grammarians. As a royal title, devānampiya had been replaced by the more high-sounding *mahārājādhirāja* and other similar titles in the early first millennium AD. The change in the meaning of devānampiya in brahmanical sources doubtless had to do with their sectarian confrontation with Buddhism and their view of Aśoka's connection to Buddhism. The silence of the Purāṇas about Aśoka is all the more striking since Buddhist sources of the time were highlighting Aśoka as a sectarian hero. He is said to have killed eighteen thousand Ājīvikas and burnt alive Nirgrantha *upāsakas* and offered a gold coin for the head of each Jaina monk.[73] An assertion of difference with if not hostility towards, brāhmaṇas, is evident in the terms used by Buddhist authors such as, *brahmanjātiyapāsaṇḍa* (brāhmaṇas who taught false doctrine) and *brahmane brahmapakkhike*.[74]

Whereas heretics in general are vilified, kings known to be personally committed to heretical sects are not condemned where they are mentioned by name in the Puranic dynastic lists. The politics of royal patronage where kings were patrons of brahmanical and Sramaṇic sects is evident from the time of Aśoka who calls for both brāhmaṇas and śramaṇas being respected. There appears to be a deliberate intention to keep the dynastic lists free from comment as far as religious patronage was concerned, although caste status is clearly referred to. The 'vaṃśānucarita' is punctuated by narratives of early heroes. Such narratives are absent in the dynastic section. Yet so much could have been made out of the Buddhist projection of the wicked Aśoka, Caṇḍasoka, prior to his 'conversion' and his becoming Dhammasoka.

Measured by archaeological remains Aśoka's patronage to Buddhism was extensive. It has been suggested that some aspects of the Māhābhārata in particular were a response to or an attempt to whittle down the influence of this patronage.[75] It is even described as a brahmanical manifesto provoked by the imperium of Aśoka.[76] Aśoka was not only having *stūpas* and *caityas* constructed but was cutting at the roots of the Vedic dharma. His edicts do not mention varṇa or jāti, his insistence on ahiṃsā was inimical to animal sacrifice, he was averse to various rituals and ceremonies and made a rather skeptical use of the gods to propagate his notion of *dhamma*. He was doing what was expected of a Māyāmoha. It would have been normal for brahmanical sectarian texts to target him.

The Buddha avatara of Viṣṇu presents something of a paradox in Puranic sources. This is apparent in the nature of how he is depicted.[77] Viṣṇu creates the Buddha to harm 'the Other' through conversion to heresy, but then is incarnated as Kalki in order to destroy the heretics. The way in which Māyāmoha functions contradicts the *bodhisattva* and the *arhat* ideal, which presumably it was intended to do. The Buddha avatara was perhaps an attempt to appropriate heresy even though overtly decrying it. It is interesting that the Buddhists did not object to such an appropriation. The Vaiṣṇavas tended not to directly confront what was regarded as heresy as did the Śaivas. Episodes of Śaiva–Buddhist and Śaiva–Jaina conflict are referred to from the mid-first millennium onwards.[78] There are fewer instances of such conflicts between the Vaiṣṇavas and the heterodox sects. Was heresy in some ways sublimated in the story of the Buddha avatara of Viṣṇu? Vaiṣṇava–Śaiva confrontations might have taken precedence over the confrontation between brahmanical thinking and heresy. The same argument of false doctrine is used by Madhvā against Śaivism and against Śankarācārya.[79]

The Buddha avatara possibly introduces a change in the concept of incarnation and of evil. The Buddha as Māyāmoha is not Viṣṇu reborn as a man but is created by Viṣṇu from himself. Evil is not that which is associated with individual behaviour and actions but with sectarian beliefs and the ordering of society. Much importance is given to the centrality of argument and logic among those opposed to the Vedas detracting the virtuous—*hetuvādavimohitaḥ*. The Buddha avatara as a protector together with Kalki reflects a decrease in the prevalence of Sramaṇic heresy. To that extent it records a change in the relationship between the Sramaṇic sects and Puranic Hinduism. The experience of this heresy prepares the scene for heresies within the Śaiva and Vaiṣṇava tradition. It could be argued that the Buddha avatara, although it precedes Kalki is to some degree, a consequence of the need for Kalki, since heretics have to be created in order that they may be destroyed. This is also not unconnected with the increasing significance of Maitreya in the Buddhism of the early first millennium AD, parallel to the saviour-figure cults of the eastern Mediterranean.[80] There is a problem however, in co-relating the dimension of time as given in the theory of the *yugas* with these sentiments. If the Buddha precedes Kalki fairly closely, then he has to be dated in the last phase of the Kaliyuga, far further into the future than is permitted by the dating of the Kaliyuga in human years. Even if it is assumed that at the time of the composition of the *Viṣṇu Purāṇa* this stage of the Kaliyuga had arrived, it would be contradicted by the linear dating of the Kaliyuga as given for instance in the Aihole inscription of Pulakesin II. This dates the start of the Kaliyuga to 3102 BC but the total length of the Kaliyuga was calculated as 432,000 years.[81] Chronology was of little consequence in narrating these sectarian hostilities.

The richness of the contentions over belief, ritual, and social ordering in other sections of the Purāṇa is a contrast to the pared-down statements of projections of political power in the 'vaṃśānucarita'. That lists of dynastic succession lack a commentary on those listed is perhaps a statement that rulership was perceived as distinct from the sectarian identity of the ruler. The prestige of kingship over other forms of polities was established by the mid-first millennium AD as is also evident from the focus on dynasties as part of the 'vaṃśānucarita'. The brāhmaṇa endorsement of kingship is also evident from a variety of other texts. The śūdra status of the Mauryan emperors meant that they were not conforming to the varṇāśramadharma central to Vedic dharma. Even if not adhered to in many other texts, this distinction would also have made it possible for rulers to be patrons of more than one sect, as most had to be.

ACKNOWLEDGEMENTS

I would like to thank Kunal Chakrabarti for his helpful comments on an earlier draft.

NOTES AND REFERENCES

1. These were hymns, hero-lauds, and narratives about heros. *Itihasa* literally means 'thus indeed it was' and *purāṇa* refers to legends and traditions.

2. *Padma Purāṇa*, 2.28.88.

3. In the Vedas, the sūta is described as *ahantiya* (*Atharvaveda* 3.5.7; *Taittirīya Saṃhita* 4.5.2) whereas in Manu (10. 11, 26) he is of a low caste. Māhābhārata, Ādiparvan, 122.4 ff.; 126. 15; *Bhagavata Purāṇa*, 10. 23–32.

4. For instance, *Matsya Purāṇa*, 1.5 ff.

5. For a recent study of this aspect see Vijay Nath, *Puranas and Acculturation* (Delhi: 2001); W. Doniger (ed.), *Purana Perennis, Reciprocity and Transformation in Hindu and Jaina Texts* (Albany: 1993); K. Chakrabarti, *Religious Process, The Puranas and the Making of a Regional Tradition*, Delhi, 2001.

6. R.C. Hazra, *Studies in the Puranic Records on Hindu Rites and Customs* (Delhi: 1975), second edition, pp. 6–7.

7. R. Thapar, 'Perceiving the Forest: Early India', *Studies in History*, n.s., vol. 17, no. 1, 2001, pp. 1–16.

8. P.S. Jaini, 'Jaina Purāṇas: A Puranic Counter Tradition', in Doniger (ed.), *Purana Perennis*, pp. 207–49.

9. *Viṣṇu Purāṇa*, 3.3.11 ff.; cf. 6.15 ff.

10. *Viṣṇu Purāṇa*, IV. 22. 1. ff.

11. F.E. Pargiter, *The Purana Text of the Dynasties of the Kali Age* (Delhi: 1975) (reprint), pp. 9–12.

12. Ibid., 11, fn. 53.

13. *Sumaṅgala-vilāsinī*, 1.258.

14. *Majjhima Nikāya*, I. 457; I. 228; *Dīgha Nikāya*, I.91; II.164.

15. *Agni Purāṇa*, 16.2.; *Matsya Purāṇa* 271.12.

16. *Dīgha Nikāya*, 1.92; *Mahāvastu*, 1.348; *Mahāvaṃsa*, 2.12–16; *Dīpavaṃsa*, 3. 41–45.

17. S. Beal, *Romantic History of Buddha* (London: 1907), 18 ff.

18. *Sumaṅgala-vilāsinī*, 1.258.

19. *Śatapatha Brāhmaṇa*, 1.4.1.14–19.

20. *Dhammapada-aṭṭhakatha*, 1.338.

21. *Dhammapada-aṭṭhakatha*, 1.339 ff.; *Jātaka* 4.144 no. 465.

22. Vijay Nath, *Puranas and Acculturation* (Delhi: 2001), pp. 38–42.

23. Manu 10.22.

24. B.C. Law, *Tribes in Ancient India* (Poona: 1973), second edition, p. 302.

25. R.S. Bhattacharya, 'Buddha as Depicted in the Purāṇas', *Purāṇa*, vol. 24, no. 3, 1982, pp. 384–404.

26. *Garuḍa Purāṇa,* 1.1.32; *Bhāgavata Purāṇa,* 1.3.24.

27. *Nirukta* 6.32.

28. *Garuḍa Purāṇa,* 1.1.32; 86.11; 196.11.

29. *Agni Purāṇa,* 49.8; *Śiva Purāṇa,* II. 15.16.11. quoted in Bhattacharya, 1982.

30. Hazra, *Puranic Records of Hindu Rites and Customs,* pp. 1–8.

31. R.N. Dandekar, 'Heretical Doctrines in the Purāṇas', *Purāṇa,* vol. 37, no. 1, 1995, pp. 3–20.

32. *Viṣṇu Purāṇa,* VI.1. 10–60; *Matsya Purāṇa,* 144. 1–47; *Bhāgavata Purāṇa,* 12.2. 1–15; *Kurma Purāṇa,* 1.29.

33. *Viṣṇu Purāṇa,* 3.17.37–39.

34. *Viṣṇu Purāṇa,* 3.17.41–44.

35. *Viṣṇu Purāṇa,* 3.18.35 ff.

36. *Viṣṇu Purāṇa,* 3.18.24.

37. Dandekar, 'Heretical Doctrines'.

38. *Viṣṇu Purāṇa,* III, 17–18; *Devibhāgavata Purāṇa,* 4.13.

39. *Viṣṇu Purāṇa,* 3.18.99 ff.

40. *Matsya Purāṇa,* 24. 37–49.

41. *Matsya Purāṇa,* 47. 182–228.

42. *Padma Purāṇa,* Srstikhanda 13, quoted in Dandekar.

43. *Devibhāgavata Purāṇa,* 4.12–14. quoted in Dandekar.

44. *Matsya Purāṇa,* 47.247; *Bhāgavata Purāṇa,* 1.3.24, 6.8.19, 10.40.22.

45. *Agni Purāṇa,* 16.2.

46. Nath, *Puranas and Acculturation,* p. 21.

47. *Viṣṇu Purāṇa,* 3.18.35 ff.

48. *Liṅga Purāṇa,* 71, quoted in Dandekar.

49. V. Raghavan, 'The Viṣṇu Purāṇa and Advaita', *Purāṇa,* vol. 23, no. 2, 1981, pp. 149–52; 'The Sūta-Saṃhita', *Annals of the Bhandarkar Oriental Research Institute,* vol. 22, nos 3–4, 1947, pp. 236–53.

50. Hazra, *Puranic Records on Hindu Rites and Customs,* p. 202; David N. Lorenzen, *The Kapalikas and the Kalamukhas: Two Lost Saivite Sects* (Delhi: Motilal Banarsidass, 1972).

51. *Garuḍa Purāṇa,* 1.202.

52. Chakrabarti, *Religious Process,* pp. 132–54.

53. *Padma Purāṇa,* Uttarakhāṇḍa, 263, quoted in Hazra, *Puranic Records on Hindu Rites and Customs,* p. 126; S. Mayeda, *A Thousand Teachings* (Tokyo: 1979), pp. 3–10; G.C. Pande, *Life and Thought of Śankarācārya* (Delhi: 1994), pp. 268–70; David N. Lorenzen, 'The Life of Ṣankarācārya', in F. Reynolds and D. Capps (eds), *The Biographical Process* (The Hague: 1975).

54. R. King, *Indian Philosophy,* Edinburgh 1999, 16 ff.; D.P. Chattopadhya, *Lokayata* (Calcutta: 1959), pp. 28–30.

55. *Matsya Purāṇa,* 143.13; 143.40–41; 148.32.

56. S.D. Joshi (ed.), *Patañjali Vyākaraṇa Mahābhāṣya* (Poona: 1968), 2.4.9; 1.476.

57. Hazra, *Puranic Records on Hindu Rites and Customs,* pp. 24–5.

58. *Bhāgavata Purāṇa*, 5.6.9–11.

59. Pargiter, *Dynasties of the Kali Age* (Delhi: 1975) (rpt), pp. 27–9; *Viṣṇu Purāṇa* 4.24.20–21; *Bhāgavata Purāṇa*, 12.1.8–10.

60. Pargiter, *Dynasties of the Kali Age*, 25.

61. Act II.6; Act VII.12.

62. *Vaṃsatthapakāsinī*, I, 5, 179–80.

63. Harisena, *Bṛhatkathākośa*, A.N. Upadhyaya (ed.) Bombay, ch. 143; *Parisiṣṭaparvan*, H. Jacobi (ed.) (Calcutta: 1891), VIII, 415 ff.

64. J. Bloch, *Les Inscriptions d'Asoka* (Paris: 1955), 156; D.C. Sircar, *Select Inscriptions Bearing on Indian History and Civilisation* (Calcutta: 1965), p. 79.

65. P.L. Vaidya (ed.), *Divyāvadāna*, Darbhanga, 1959, C-370, 233; *Divyāvadāna*, Cowell and Neil (eds) (Cambridge: 1886), XXVI, 370 ff.

66. Athenaeus, III, 444.

67. For a comprehensive coverage, see M.M. Deshpande, 'Interpreting the Āsokan Epithet *devānampiya*', to be published in a volume edited by P. Olivelle, *Asoka in History and Historical Memory*, forthcoming.

68. Sircar, *Select Inscriptions Bearing on Indian History and Civilisation*, vol. I, Calcutta, 1965, pp. 79–80.

69. *Mahābhāṣya* on Panini, 2, 4. 56 and 6.3.21.

70. R. Thapar, *Asoka and the Decline of the Mauryas* (Delhi: 1997), pp. 135–6.

71. *Pradīpa*, on 2.4.56; quoted in Deshpande.

72. I. 101–7.

73. S. Mukhopadhyaya (ed.), *Aśokāvadāna* (New Delhi: 1963), pp. 67–8; also in Vaidya, *Divyāvadāna*, C 427, 277.

74. *Samantapasādika*, I. 38; *Mahāvaṃsa*, 5.34.

75. A. Hiltebeitel, *Rethinking the Mahābhārata*, (Chicago: 2001); N. Sutton, 'Aśoka and Yudhisthira', *Religion*, vol. 27, 1997, pp. 331–41; J.L. Fitzgerald, *The Mahābhārata*, vol. 7 (Chicago: 2004), pp. 114 ff. M. Biardeau, *Le Mahābhārata* (Paris: 2002).

76. M. Biardeau quoted by A. Hiltebeitel in 'Buddhism and the Mahābhārata', in F. Squarcini (ed.), *Boundaries, Dynamics and Construction of Traditions in South Asia* (Firenze: 2005), pp. 107–32.

77. W. Doniger O'Flaherty, *The Origins of Evil in Hindu Mythology* (Berkeley: 1976), pp. 199–211; 'The Image of the Heretic in the Gupta *Purāṇas*', in B.L. Smith (ed.), *Essays on Gupta Culture* (New Delhi: Oxford University Press, 1983), pp. 107–27.

78. R. Thapar, 'Cultural Transaction and Early India: Tradition and Patronage', in Romila Thapar, *History and Beyond* (New Delhi: Oxford University Press, 2001), pp. 17–20.

79. O'Flaherty, *The Origins of Evil in Hindu Mythology*, p. 209.

80. R. Thapar, 'Millenarianism and Religion in Early India', in Thapar, *Cultural Pasts*, pp. 946–62.

81. *Epigraphia Indica*, Aihole Inscription of Pulakeśin II, VI, 7; R. Thapar, *Time as a Metaphor of History* (New Delhi: Oxford University Press, 2000).

2. ŚAṄKARA AND PURANIC RELIGION

R. Champakalakshmi

In hagiographical tradition and biographies Śaṅkara is hailed as *Ṣaṇmata Sthāpanācārya*, the one who established the six forms of Puranic religion, namely, the Śaiva, Vaiṣṇava, Śākta, Saura, Gāṇapatya, and Kaumāra. The Puranic process is central to the development of religion in India, within the amorphous framework of what came to be called Hinduism. In the post-Vedic Period (post-600 BC), confronted by the challenge posed by the Sramanic Buddhism and Jainism to the Vedic religion and their socio-religious dominance, the brāhmaṇas realized the need for reworking their tradition through the incorporation and assimilation of regional and folk forms, rituals, beliefs, and practices[1] in order to evolve a new syncretic religion, that is, the Puranic religion. The Puranic process thus represents 'an instrument for the propagation of brāhmanical ideals of social reconstruction and sectarian interests, a medium for the absorption of local cults and associated practices and a vehicle for popular instructions on norms governing everyday existence'.[2]

The Puranic process which started in the Gupta period (between the fourth and sixth centuries CE) became a universal phenomenon throughout the subcontinent. However, it showed a distinct multiformity in the rich pattern of its regional manifestations, particularly in the regions peripheral to the Ganga valley. Along with the epic, the *Dharmaśāstras*/*Smṛti* literature, the Purāṇas marked a major change from the Vedic religion and in effect organized religion and its social base in the early historical (300 BC–300 CE) and early medieval (400–1300 CE) periods. The Purāṇas even claimed continuity with and authenticity from the Vedas/*Śruti* and the Smṛti in achieving this change. However, they underwent extensive revisions as Puranic structures were adopted in new texts to bring in purely local, vernacular forms in different regions. The Purāṇas grew into a vast corpus with some regionally identifiable texts, rich and variegated in their myths and forms of worship and even social norms suitable to the changing conditions. Later Purāṇas followed new modes of legitimation of the brahmanical order (*varṇa*) whenever and wherever this order was threatened. In the process the *Āgamas*/*Tantras* came to be recognized as an important source of authority on religious matters, particularly temple worship, rituals, and sectarian practices. The chronology of the Purāṇas is thus closely linked to the historical and regional contexts in which they arose. The *Pañcāyatana* form of worship and the *Ṣaṭāyatana* or Ṣaṇmata worship are undoubtedly different ways of grouping the various cults centring on Puranic deities as and when they became significant in the process.

It is, however, important to recognize that the major Puranic developments date to the early medieval period (sixth and twelfth centuries), when a changing socio-political organization based on a land grant system of agrarian expansion deriving legitimacy from the temple, facilitated the emergence of territorial kingship and a brahmanical social order (*varṇāśrama*).[3] Vedic yajña or sacrifice as a legitimating device for royal power became a mere ritual or symbol and was replaced by *dāna* or gift and temple worship both for purposes of legitimation and for the expansion of the agrarian economy. This change is not attributable to any one religious or spiritual leader of the times; it was a widespread phenomenon that involved brāhmaṇas well versed in the Vedas as the donees of land grants, brāhmaṇas who composed the Purāṇas providing a rich mythology around the major gods like Viṣṇu and Śiva, and brāhmaṇa temple priests who followed Āgamic canons for temple rituals and worship.

This was the historical context in which Śaṅkara (788–820 CE) and his philosophy of Advaita based on commentaries on the Upaniṣads, the *Brahmasūtras*, and the *Bhagvadgīta* together known as the *Prasthāna Trayī*—are situated. Although inscriptions or vernacular bhakti hymns datable to the early medieval period hardly grant Śaṅkara any role in the evolution of Puranic religion, conventional belief among the Hindus of the Smārta tradition attribute credit to his Advaita for providing a philosophical base that gave the Puranic deities a universal and transcendental character. This was, however, an indirect result of the transformation of the Advaitic Brahman of Śaṅkara into a godhead at the hands of Vaiṣṇava and Śaiva protagonists of the early medieval period who equated Puranic deities with Brahman, a process indicated first by the *Bhāgavata Purāṇa* of the ninth and tenth centuries believed to have been composed in the Pāṇḍya country and later, by the conscious adoption of this universalization to 'lesser' and/or folk deities like the Goddess, Gaṇapati, Skanda-Kārttikeya, and the revival of the Vedic Sūrya with the same attributes in the Vijayanagara period (fourteenth to the seventeenth centuries).

There is yet another interpretation of the epithet Ṣaṇmata Sthāpanācārya as one who reorganized the six forms of worship along more orthodox lines through the Vedāntic tradition. It is hard to attribute this reorganization to Ādi Śaṅkara, as Śaṅkara is unknown to any of the contemporary sources. It seems to be a major contribution of the spiritual leaders of the Vijayanagara period who responded to the organizational and institutional needs of the brahmanical tradition, particularly of the Śṛngeri *maṭha* (monastery), which is claimed to have been established by Śaṅkara himself. The reorganization of the Puranic Ṣaṇmata is thus authenticated by the medieval spiritual leaders from the fourteenth to the seventeenth centuries, by ascribing it to Śaṅkara himself, although it occurred during the Vijayanagara period which sought to restore temple worship and brahmanical (Hindu) orthodoxy threatened by the intrusion of alien religions like Islam which affected the existing socio-political organization. Why a stark absolutist like Śaṅkara was invoked by the followers of the Advaitic/Śaṅkara tradition for the Ṣaṇmata Sthāpanā can be understood not merely as a response to the threat posed by Islam but needs to be situated within larger processes that marked a changing socio-political situation. A series of developments in south India's socio-religious organization from the twelfth century onwards leads to the evolution of canonical traditions and religious communities and culminated in the sectarian reorganization and consolidation under Vijayanagara.

In pre-twelfth-century peninsular India, the spread of the Puranic–Āgamic religion can be traced to about the fourth century of the Christian Era in the Deccan and Andhra, where the Vedic, Puranic, and Āgamic forms came to be accepted (almost as a package) as brahmanical tradition, the Puranic ideology assisting in the evolution of monarchical forms of polity or lineage polities, the brāhmaṇa-kṣatriya nexus dominating society and polity. The more important Deccan kingdoms from the fourth to the fourteenth centuries for instance, the Cāḷukyas of Bādāmi, the Rāṣṭrakuṭas of Malkhed, the Cāḷukyas of Kalyāni, and the Vengi Cāḷukyas of Andhra, the Hoysaḷas of south Karnataka, and the Kākatīyas of Warangal promoted the Puranic religions of Śaivism and Vaiṣṇavism while invoking other deities like Skanda-Mahāsena in the *praśasti* portion of their inscriptions. Vaiṣṇavism and Śaivism were also adopted in the Tamil region by the Pallavas of Kāñci and the Pāṇḍyas of Madurai (from the sixth to the ninth centuries CE), who introduced the *Brahmadeya* and the temple as the institutional forces for their propagation and claimed descent from the Sūrya or Candra Vamśa of the Puranic tradition. Through this patronage of the ruling families, Śaivism and Vaiṣṇavism developed huge pantheons which incorporated non-Vedic and non-brahmanical elements such as the mother goddess and the tribal or folk deities. Each region contributed, synchronically or diachronically, and in different degrees to the development of the Puranic tradition.

This process can be clearly traced in Tamil literature. The change from the rich corpus of early Tamil classics (third century BC to third century CE) to the bhakti hymns of the Āḻvār and Nāyanār (from the sixth to the ninth centuries) signalled the spread of the Puranic-brahmanical tradition. The Sangam *tiṇai* (eco-zonal) deities such as Māl, Murukan (Vēlan and Cēyōn), and Koṟṟavai were incorporated into the Puranic Vaiṣṇava and Śaiva pantheons and transformed into regional or universal deities, with the natural landscape of the Sangam classics giving place to the temple landscape of the early medieval period. The Tamil region therefore, assumes greater importance as representing a major cultural variant of the Puranic religion evolving through the 'bhakti movement' of the Āḻvār and Nāyanār, propagated through the vernacular language and idiom in their emotionally powerful hymns expressing devotion to a personal god housed in the temple. The Tamil hymnal literature expresses a protest against caste (varṇa) hierarchy, status, and privileges, particularly against orthodox Vedic Brahmaṇism, the Caturvedis, who were recipients of impressive land grants as Brahmadeyas from the ruling families. The temple, therefore, became the focal point of social organization and ritual ranking among various castes, occupational groups, and ethnic/tribal populations, all of which were being brought into temple society through bhakti as the legitimating ideology for socio-political organization. The temple as an institutional means of integration proliferated and marked the growth of an agrarian society through land grants and in effect superseded the Brahmadeyas as the integrative force.[4] Yet, both Brahmadeyas and temples were interlinked through the managerial functions of the brāhmaṇa landholders. They were also controlled by non-brāhmaṇa or vēḷāḷa landholders of the *Ūr* and *Nāḍu* (agrarian settlement and peasant region respectively). The Cōḷas (from the ninth to the thirteenth centuries) consciously promoted the vernacular bhakti and under Cōḷa royal patronage Śaivism consolidated itself, providing substantial ideological support to Cōḷa power. The most significant temples of the Drāviḍa style with a rich repertoire of sculptures and paintings were erected during their period. The Tamil Śaiva textual/canonical tradition starting from the Tamil hymns (*Tēvāram*) to the hagiographic and philosphical treatises, evolved between the eleventh and the fourteenth centuries with spiritual leaders from the vēḷāḷa community assuming control over the organization of the canon and the Śaiva maṭhas headed by vēḷāḷa cult leaders.[5]

The Vaiṣṇava and Śaiva bhakti saints also tried to invest the Tamil hymns with authority and establish them as scriptures—*maṟai*—by ascribing to them a status equal to the Vedas.[6] In this respect the Śrīvaiṣṇavas were more successful in relating the Sanskrit Vedic tradition to Tamil Vaiṣṇava doctrine and practice than the Tamil Śaivas, due to a conscious rendering of the Tamil bhakti in Puranic structures that is, the *Bhāgavata Purāṇa*, which represents not only the culmination of the Āḻvār bhakti, but also offers the first evidence of the influence the Advaitic idea of Brahman, probably as propounded by Śaṅkara, considerably modifying it by making that Brahman *saguṇa* and equating it with Viṣṇu. Though the author or authors of this Purāṇa are not known, it is indisputable that it was composed in south India (Pāṇḍya country) in the late ninth or early tenth century, and stands at the beginning of a millennium of intensive debate on the Vedānta.[7] Śaṅkara is not mentioned in any of the Vaiṣṇava works on the Vedānta and yet in the intellectual discourse of the post-Śaṅkara period his

Advaita seems to have had a clear impact, not in its pristine and absolutist form but in a modified form, which would enable the Puranic religion to consolidate itself.

Among the pre-Śaṅkara Vedāntins mention is made of a Drāviḍācārya who is identified with Nammāḻvar or Śaṭakopa (Śaṭhakopa?), a Śūdra saint, whose *Tiruvāymoḻi* is called the *Drāviḍa Veda* in the Vaiṣṇava exegesis and commentarial literature from the fourteenth century onwards, the Vaiṣṇava teachers making incongruous analogies, while drawing parallels with the Vedas. The highly stimulating debate on the Vedānta, which Rāmānuja's *Viśiṣṭādvaita* (qualified non-dualism) evoked from the twelfth century to provide a philosophical thrust to Śrīvaiṣṇavism led to the evolution of the Ubhaya Vedānta, more appropriate for the devotional cult, which the stark absolutism of the Advaita or non-dualism of Śaṅkara could not provide. Thus it may be argued that it is Rāmānuja's *Viśiṣṭādvaita*—which drew upon the Vedāntic and Advaitic non-dualistic position, but introduced a different philosophical/metaphysical base of qualified non-dualism by acknowledging the individual self and its capability of becoming one with the universal Brahman—that was more suitable for the temple-based bhakti and was a major instrument in the construction of the Puranic tradition as a pan-Indian religion. While all the developments relating to bhakti and temples as the most influential instruments of socio-religious integration are corroborated by inscriptional records and temples of this period, hardly any epigraphic reference to Śaṅkara or his Advaita is known. An inscription from Cambodia dated in the seventh or ninth century[8] is, however, believed to refer to Śaṅkara and his doctrine, but the identification and reading of the inscription are beset with a number of problems. It is not till the fourteenth century AD, that is, the Vijayanagara period, that any authentic record is available on Śaṅkara. Hence, if Śaṅkara is believed to be the *sthāpaka* (founder/reviver) of the six Puranic cults, it is hard to establish a direct connection of his scheme of spiritual experience with any of the Puranic cults, except perhaps the indirect adoption of the Vedāntic Brahman as the Saguṇa Brahman by the Vaiṣṇavas in the *Bhāgavata Purāṇa* and by the Śaiva Siddhāntins, particularly Umāpati Śivācārya in the fourteenth century.

To show how the Puranic religions evolved over the early medieval centuries, it would be more useful to study the development of the

Vaiṣṇava, Śaiva, Śākta, and Subrahmaṇya (Kaumāra), and Gāṇapatya cults in the Tamil region. Of these the first two are too well known to be repeated here. The other three are significant from the point of view of their early incorporation into the Śaiva religion and their later revival as major deities in their own right by the fourteenth century AD.

KAUMĀRA

The Kaumāra, derived from Kumara or Subrahmaṇya,[9] developed through a complex process of the merging of deities called Skanda, Kārttikeya, Mahāsena, Subrahmaṇya, Ṣaṇmukha and above all, Murukan (Cēyōn and Vēlan) of the Sangam Tamil texts. Murukan, a Tamil deity associated with hilly tracts (the *Kuṟiñci* eco-zone) in the early historical period, became universalized through a process of acculturation by the formal Sanskritic-Puranic religious system, first as a regional deity of Tamiḻakam as attested by the *Tirumurukāṟṟuppatai* and *Paripāṭal*, classified as Sangam works but datable to the fifth and sixth centuries CE, with six sacred centres forming a sacred geography for Subrahmaṇya. The tribal deity Murukan was transformed into a transcendental god, synthesizing an essentially local, folk, or popular cult with the cult of (Subrahmaṇya) (or Skanda-Kārttikeya) of the Sanskritic-brahmanical forms of worship within the larger Puranic pantheon.

Research on the cult of Murukan has tended to either seek the Dravidian or more specifically the Tamil roots of the cult or to derive its origin from Sanskritic tradition and localize the Sanskrit myths associated with Skanda-Mahasena, the warrior god. In the early Tamil context, Murukan as the child-god and the god of love belongs to the *Kuṟiñci tiṇai* and is given the pride of place as the Tamil deity par excellence. In conventional belief his identity with the Sanskritic Skanda–Kārttikeya was achieved even before the time of the composition of the post-Sangam text *Tirumurukāṟṟuppatai* (hereafter *TMP*). Such a view ignores the changing contexts of his worship as a regional deity in the early historical and early medieval periods representing important socio-economic transformations.

The evolution of the cult has to be situated within the broader cultural processes in Tamiḻakam wherein bhakti became the key instrument of the propagation and establishment of the Śaiva and

Vaiṣṇava religions as the major religious systems. Murukan's sacred geography first emerges in the *TMP*. In the Sangam works his worship is not space specific. The sacred space was 'flexible' in the sense that a temporarily sanctified space was created for the performance of rituals such as *veṟiyāṭal, vēlanāṭal*, and *kuravai* dance.[10] By the time of the *TMP*, Murukan ceases to be only a Kuṟiñci god. He is believed to have performed the vēlanāṭal and veṟiyāṭal in other eco-zones like the *Marutam* and *Neital*, a claim that takes him out of a local context and places him in a regional one, as centres in other eco-zones get sanctified and marked as 'permanently' sacred for his worship. This goes hand in hand with the rise of an agrarian economy centred on the temple with land as the major item of gift, which slowly replaced an uneven pattern of subsistence economic activities of the different eco-zones. The six sacred shrines cover the traditional Toṇḍai Nāḍu, Cōḷa Nāḍu, and Pāṇḍi Nāḍu (later *maṇḍalams*) and are located within the rice-producing areas and their edges in close proximity to the hill and forest resource areas, that is, at points of convergence of different eco-zones whose resources could be mobilized through the temple. Temples were symbols of royal power and superordinate integrating forces and along with royalty were the largest consumers of such resources as agricultural products, pastoral products, and forest and hill products. It may also be noted that the Kongu Nāḍu does not figure in this distribution of sacred centres of Murukan in the *TMP*. Thus at a relatively early stage Murukan is transformed into a 'universal god'.[11]

The six sacred centres are distributed in the traditional eco-zones, described as *paṭaivīṭu*, military camp, highlighting the warrior aspect of the god. The *TMP* seems to be a compilation of the images of Murukan which emerged over a period of time, the variations marking the intra-regional diversity. While retaining the imagery peculiar to the *akam* (love) poems of the Sangam, Puranic mythology is brought in through the verses associating Murukan with gods such as Viṣṇu, Śiva, and Indra, pointing to a merging of his identity with the Puranic Skanda-Kārttikeya. The name Subrahmaṇya does not occur in the *TMP*, a name by which he comes to be known only from the late Pallava and Pāṇḍya inscriptions of the ninth century. The *TMP* and the *Paripāṭal*, which also has verses on Murukan, are placed in a period of transition from heroic poetry to the age of bhakti literature,[12] though bhakti as an ideal is implicit in these works.

Over a period of time the mythology of Subrahmaṇya integrates the six centres. At one level the *Sthala-purāṇas* of a much later period, that is, from the sixteenth to the eighteenth centuries link the centres through the stories of his birth, his destruction of Cūra, Tāraka, and his marriage to Deivayānai and Vaḷḷi (a Tamil tribal/hunter girl), his association with Brahmā, and above all with Śiva as the latter's son. At another level the integration of the temples of other deities within the geographical region, such as Tirupparankuṉṟam, Aḻagarmalai, and Svāmimalai, is achieved through localized myths such as the ritual journey of Subrahmaṇya to Madurai to attend the wedding of Mīnākṣi-Sundareśvara and Murukan's marriage with Vaḷḷi of the Kuṟavar tribe. Common mythology links more distant geographical zones signifying the importance of the sacred geography created in the *TMP*. The gradual change in the mode of worship from one of Shamanistic practices like the possession of women by Murukan and Vēlan with the spear, the Shaman priest with red robes, his cock banner and peacock mount, as also the offering of goat, millet, rice mixed with blood and so on, which is pronounced in the descriptions of Paḻamutircōlai and Kuṉṟutorāṭal sections, is underplayed later and brāhmaṇas as officiating priests become prominent. The only reference to Murukan as the son of Koṟṟavai is in the Paḻamutircōlai section of the *TMP*, whereas as the son of Śiva his incorporation in the larger Śaiva pantheon is of greater importance.

The crystallization of the Murukan cult as that of Skanda-Kārttikeya was one of the most significant aspects of the Tamil Śaiva tradition in the early medieval period (between the sixth and thirteenth centuries). However, it did not result in the evolution of a separate or independent sectarian tradition, for he was incorporated in the Śaiva pantheon and found a special position in the Pallava shrines (*garbha gṛha*) as a part of the composite Somāskanda icon in the Pallava and some Pāṇḍya shrines. The composite icon of Somāskanda is the cult object in all Pallava shrines.[13] Also significant is the Subrahmaṇya aspect with the attributes of Brahmā predominant in the early Pallava and Pāṇḍya cave (rock-cut) temples. In a few separate shrines he is represented as Subrahmaṇya, the warrior aspect of the god, shown with the ornament called the *cannavīra*. The iconography of Murukan, on which the most authentic work so far is that of Mme. L'Hernault,[14] develops as a highly complex one and while Brahmā,

Agni, and Indra associations dominate in images from the seventh to the ninth, it is only in the post-thirteenth-century representations that the spear, the six heads and twelve arms, and the two consorts become conspicuous, with no evidence of a standardization of his iconography.

It is significant that wherever the Skanda or Subrahmaṇya icon is found in cave temples of the seventh to ninth centuries, he is represented more often as one of the five deities, Śiva, Durgā, Skanda, Vināyaka, and Viṣṇu. In south India, the representation of the Pañcadevata (in *Pañcāyatana* worship) never included Sūrya. Sūrya was introduced in Śaiva temples as a subsidiary deity and this Vedic deity got incorporated into the Puranic sectarian worship only after the late medieval religious changes ascribed to Śaṅkara's establishment of Ṣaṇmata. For Subrahmaṇya or Skanda, on the contrary, no sectarian affiliations developed till late medieval times, when the six sacred centres of the Tamil Murukan came to be converted into a sacred geography of Subrahmaṇya worship in the form of paṭaivīṭus. Significantly, it was only by the fourteenth century that the *TMP* was included in the Śaiva textual or canonical tradition.

The fourteenth century also saw a conscious attempt to return to orthodoxy. A Vedic origin was sought for the Puranic religions and sects, and Skanda-Kārttikeya-Subrahmaṇya was made the central deity of the Kaumāra cult, believed to have been reorganized on orthodox lines by Śaṅkara. This was a development of the Vijayanagara period under the aegis of the Smārta tradition evolved by the followers of Śaṅkara, the Śṛngeri, and Kāñcī Śaṅkara maṭhas being pre-eminent. A complex mythology combined the Sangam Tamil myths or stories and the Puranic myths culminating in the *Sthala Purāṇas* of the fifteenth to the eighteenth centuries, and in the *Kandapurāṇam* of uncertain date, containing layers of myths of different periods and different historical contexts.

Clearly, there are significant gaps in the history of the evolution of the Subrahmaṇya cult. In the early medieval period Skanda was only a deity, albeit an important one, in the Śaiva pantheon. In the Vijayanagara period, an independent sectarian development takes place aroud the cult of Kumara, and the six paṭaivīṭus attain importance for Subrahmaṇya worship only after the Kaumāra sect emerges as one of the six or Ṣaṇmata attributed to Śaṅkara by the spiritual leaders of the Śaṅkara tradition nearly six centuries after Śaṅkara. I turn now to a brief survey of the changes in the six centres of Murukan worship, which mark the three distinct phases of the Puranic process.

Tirupparankuṉṟam

In Tirupparankuṉṟam, the early historical Jain cave shelters with Tamil Brāhmī inscriptions, located at the hill top in Tirupparankuṉṟam,[15] were abandoned around the third and fourth centuries. Cave shrines were excavated with cells for Śiva, Viṣṇu, and Durgā (with Somāskanda relief in the Śaiva cell) in 773 CE. Here Murukan is not the main deity for he is represented only in one of the lateral spaces as a subsidiary deity along with Vināyaka on either side of the Durgā cell. The inscriptional reference is not to Subrahmaṇya but to the shrine of Śiva and its consecration in the reign of Pāṇḍya Varaguṇa I (ninth century). After a long gap of about four centuries the records reappear from the thirteenth to the eighteenth centuries.[16] These later Pāṇḍya inscriptions invariably record grants of land as *devadāna* and so on, probably to the temple of Tirupparankuṉṟamuḍaiyār, the lord of the place, who is assumed to be Subrahmaṇya. Grants were also made to other deities, particularly to the goddess (Bhagavatī Āḻvār and Tirukkāmakkōṭṭam-Durgā). The incorporation of Subrahmaṇya in this polytheistic temple, where the main cells are dedicated to Śiva, Viṣṇu, and Durgā is significant as he becomes part of a larger tradition (Pañcadevata/Pañcāyatana?) in the early medieval period, although his association with this place is older as indicated by the *TMP*. Interestingly it also coincided with the remarkable increase in the brahmadeyas and devadānas in this region.

Popular local myths like that of the divine marriage of Deivayānai with Murukan, and myths of the Puranic genre explain Murukan's association with Vedic and other divinities, such as Brahmā and Indra, and Murukan coming to Tirupparankuṉṟam as a brāhmaṇa to accept the gift of land by the legendary king Śibi, who needed one more brāhmaṇa to complete the traditional number 108. Thus the early associations of Murukan with this centre are increasingly established through myths and legends in a continuing context.

Tiruccendūr

In Tiruccendūr (Tiruccīralaivāy) on the east coast (35 miles from Tirunelveli) the main icon, a standing figure, is not of Ṣaṇmukha, although the *TMP* refers to the Ṣaṇmukha aspect while describing this centre. Referred to as Centil and Neṭuvēḷ in early Sangam poems, the main deity gets the name Subrahmaṇya only in the ninth-century inscription of the Pāṇḍya Varaguṇa II (874 CE).[17] Other inscriptions refer to grants such as gold coins for various requirements of the deity, including camphor, an import from Sumatra. Again after a long gap, inscriptions of the thirteenth century record land grants. Local traditions speak of Subrahmaṇya worshipping Śiva at a shrine built by Ṃaya, the divine architect, to cleanse himself of the impurity incurred on killing Cūrapadma, probably based on a story in the *Kandapurāṇam*. The fire ritual is central to the Skanda Saṣṭi festival here, as it is related to the myth of the birth of Subrahmaṇya on new moon day and the story of Agni's intercourse with Svāhā.

Paḻani

In Tiruvāvinankuṭi (Paḻani and Āykkuṭi) Murukan is represented in the form of a mendicant and the temple received a land grant in the early ninth century from a member of the *brahmadeya sabhā* of Virakerāḷacaturvedimangalam.[18] Later in the thirteenth century a Pāṇḍya inscription[19] records a land grant to the *paṇḍarāttār-śudra* priests of the temple in Āykkuṭi, which included wet and dry lands, all forest lands, groves, houses and their tenants—all the resources available in the region. Devadāna grants proliferated, pointing to an expansion of agricultural activities. Āykkuṭi was also a centre of the Vēḷir, pastoral chiefs and descendants of the Yādavas and the *Sthala Purāṇa* link it to the sage Agastya. In the *TMP*, however, the Puranic influences are limited to the allusion of the Puranic gods and their visit to the hill abode of Murukan.

Svāmimalai (Tiruvērakam)

Situated in the rich delta of the Kaveri amidst agrarian settlements (brahmadeya and *ūr*) the temple of Svāminātha on an artificial hill is dedicated to the deity as a bachelor, represented in the shrine with a *daṇḍa* (sceptre) in the right hand and with a sacred thread, which had by now replaced the warrior *cannavīra* in the Subrahmaṇya icons. The inscriptions of this temple date only from the sixteenth century and refer to the Vijayanagara period grants,[20] although tradition tries to push back the antiquity of Subrahmaṇya worship by stating that the early Pāṇḍya king who built a temple for Mīnākṣi Sundareśvara near this temple also made endowments to the Subrahmaṇya temple. The *TMP* describes brāhmaṇas performing Vedic sacrifices and rituals, acting as officiating priests of the temple (of Subrahmaṇya). The temple is closely associated with the story of Śiva being taught the *brahma jñāna* by Svāminātha. A variant of this myth exalts Śiva and not Subrahmaṇya by giving reasons for the event, according to which, Śiva willingly forgot the sacred *mantra* in order to please the devas and learnt it from his son, thereby retaining the importance of both the deities.

Tiruttaṇi

Tiruttaṇi, known as Taṇikai and Taṇiyal, is situated in the traditional region of the Pallavas, that is, Toṇḍaimaṇḍalam and is the fifth Murukan centre. It can be clearly dated to the late Pallava period on the basis of the Tiruttaṇi-Vēlañjēri bilingual copper plates of the reign of Aparājita (late ninth century),[21] recording a gift of the village Pudur in Taṇiyal Nāḍu in the Kuṉṟavartanakkōṭṭam. This centre was combined with the great *agrahāra* of Mēliruñjēru, the residents of which are said to be the foremost among the learned people and eminent in the Vedas and *Vedāngas*. The devadāna and the brahmadeya were made as a joint gift to Ṣaṇmukha, the son of Maheśvara, who is pleased to stand on the hill of the agrahāra, Śrīmat Taṇiyal. Land was also granted in the time of the Cōḷa Rājendra I to Subrahmaṇya Piḷḷaiyār.[22] The gift included all lands in the manner of the Aykkuṭi grant mentioned above. It is significant that the *Kōṭṭams* of this region were pastoral-cum-agricultural units within which the *nāḍus* (peasant units) were located. The hill, the forest, and the agricultural land were brought under a systemic agrarian organization with the brahmadeya and the temple as the integrating forces.

The myths of Taṇikai are all concerned with the gods seeking the favour of Murukan. Murukan killed Tārakāsura to help Tirumāl recover his attributes—the Cakra and Śankha. The other deities, Brahmā and Viṣṇu as Rama, also sought his favour. These are late myths of the *Sthala Purāṇa* variety found in the *Taṇikācalapurāna* and *Taṇikaipurāṇa*. Murukan himself is said to have come to Taṇikai, meaning a calm serene spot, after killing Cūrapadma and the battle with the hunter gatherer tribes to win Vaḷḷi's hand in marriage. These myths are in strong contrast with the imagery of the old tribal deity Murukan in the *TMP*, which describes the Shaman priest, the jungle tribes, 'the strong mountain folk who drink wine with their kin, sweet liquor, honey-brew in long bamboos'.[23] Murukan himself dances the kuravai on the hills with the women to the beat of the battle drums (*TMP*, 5).

A̤lakarmalai (Pa̤lamutircōlai)

A̤lakarmalai, sacred both for Māl and Murukan, has the smallest of Murukan temples—a modern structure which dates only from the seventeenth century. The deity enshrined here is Murukan with his two consorts. The *TMP* offers an interesting picture of his worship here, where 'goats are slaughtered, grains of rice offered in several pots with flowers, his cock banner is raised in the festival of festivals'. Murukan is here referred to as the 'son of six women'. Two traditions seem to blend here, one the *Vēlanēṭal* and sacrifice and the mention of Ko̤r̤r̤avai and at the same time the allusion to Krittikas as such, though not by their name.

Thus the emergence of the sacred geography of the Murukan cult as delineated in the *TMP* is not without contradictions in terms of cult practices, the degree of brahmanical dominance or vice versa on the deity's individual status and the myths associated with these centres. The Kongu region is conspicuously out of this regional pilgrimage circuit for almost all the Murukan temples of that region are post-thirteenth century and are greatly outnumbered by the goddess or Amman temples. Puranic Śiva and Viṣṇu dominate the entire Tamil religious tradition from the sixth century to the Nāyak period, a time span in which three distinct developments occur. The first was the Purāṇization of all cults, rituals, beliefs, and myths and the emergence of bhakti and the temple as the major instruments of this transformation from the seventh to the ninth centuries. The second was the ideological significance of bhakti in the evolution of a regional state and culture between the ninth and the thirteenth centuries, when the Puranic Śaiva and Vaiṣṇava religious systems subsumed other cults and their deities. A resurgence of the popular and folk traditions through the revival of deities like Murukan and the mother goddess as independent deities with their own individual temples took place in the post-thirteenth-century period when

Murukan is not only reinstated as the chief deity in his earlier abodes like the *aṟupaṭaivīṭu,* but also enshrined in new temples sanctified by their brahmanical associations while retaining their tradtional ritual practices and modes of worship, serving as the tutelary deities of the lower strata of society and being drawn into a pilgrimage network expanding the sacred geography of their respective cults.

GĀṆAPATYA

A similar development can be seen in the worship of Gaṇapati, who is incorporated into the Śaiva Puranic pantheon as a son of Śiva and represented in temple niches (on the north wall of the shrine) as one of the *parivāra devata*s in the early medieval period. However, he is often also represented in cave temples from the seventh to the ninth centuries as a part of the *Pañcadevata*/Pañcāyatana worship in south India especially in the Tamil region. Gaṇapati was a deity with independent traits and has been worshipped as the leader of the *gaṇa*s and as Vighneśvara, the remover of obstacles. From the fourteenth century, he gets the status of a Puranic deity, and separate shrines are built for him not only within the temple precincts of Śiva shrines but independently with brahmanical ritual and worship. Interestingly, it is only in the Vijayanagara inscriptions that invocatory verses are addressed to him as a deity. He also becomes the focus of a separate sectarian organization, which the late medieval Śaṅkara/Smārta tradition assigns to Ādi Śaṅkara himself, although not as important as the Śaiva and Vaiṣṇava organizations.

Gaṇeśa is said to function on multiple levels, from the level of the subsidiary gods to that of the supreme deities. His worship crosses sectarian boundaries.[24] Like the mother goddesses, Gaṇeśa also passed through a process of change from a predominantly malevolent to a benevolent deity when both were being incorporated into Puranic Hinduism, respectively, as the consort and son of Śiva. In the Purāṇas he becomes well defined as the leader of Śiva's army of gaṇas (hence Gaṇapati). He is seen as a deity controlling transitions and new states (that is, marriage). Gaṇeśa's liminal role as guardian and as lord of beginnings, as mediator between the material and divine worlds are well known in many regions. Yet important regional differences exist even within India in the perception of Gaṇeśa.

Vināyaka, as another name of Gaṇeśa, seems to have no direct connection with the Vināyakas, who in the Mahābhārata (MBH) are malignant demons, *bhūtas*, *rākṣasas*, and *paiśācas*. The single reference to Gaṇeśa in the *itihāsa* is in sharp contrast with the important role Gaṇeśa plays in the Purāṇas. The terms Gaṇeśa and Gaṇapati in the MBH invariably refer to Śiva. Gaṇeśa appears rather late in the Puranic tradition. Yet attempts have been made to trace him back to the Vedas and to pre-Vedic times, although, according to A.K. Narain's study of Gaṇeśa in early art and literature, his image and iconic attributes can hardly be related to a Vedic or Puranic Brāhmaṇic context.[25] Two texts belonging to the Black *Yajur Veda*, the *Maitrāyaṇīya Samhita*, and *Taittirīya Āraṇyaka* have Gāyatris and refer to Dantin, Vakratuṇḍa, and Hastimukha, suggestive of Gaṇeśa and interestingly it is Sāyana (fourteenth century) who explicitly establishes the identification in his commentary on the Āraṇyaka.[26]

The Gaṇeśa stories are a perfect illustration of the 'variants and multiforms', that are characteristic of Puranic literature generally marked by a plurality of traditions.[27] The numerous stories surrounding Gaṇeśa concentrate mainly on three incidents—his birth and parenthood, his elephant head, and his single tusk. In the birth stories it is Pārvati not Śiva, who is anxious to have a son. Śiva accepted him as her son and hence he is Vināyaka, born *nāyakena vinā*, without the intervention of a husband. His mount, a field rat, is said to be a totem of at least one Dravidian tribe, the Oraons pointing to a Dravidian origin. It is not clear whether he is married or not although Siddhi and Buddhi, success and wisdom, which are associated with him, are often treated as his consorts.

The Puranic myths provide a wide variety of explanations for his form—as violently losing his human head after birth, the elephant head being placed on his body as a substitute. As doorkeeper to Pārvati's inner chamber, he denies entry to Śiva and in the battle that followed, his human head was cut off by Śiva's *triśūla* and then as a boon to Pārvati the elephant head was attached. He is also called Gāngeya, for Ganga also called him her son.

The earliest known representation of Gaṇeśa in south India is at Piḷḷaiyārpaṭṭi in a cave shrine, an image six feet tall, with two arms and trunk turned to the right with no *ankuśa* or *pāśa*, but in *ardha padmāsana*, *motaka* in the right hand in *kaṭi hasta* and left hand on the hip, right tusk longer and left shorter. Known variously as Erukkāṭṭūr, or Ekkāṭṭur, Marutankuṭi, Tiruvīnkaikkuṭi, and Rājanārāyaṇapuram in inscriptions, this centre has cave shrines for Gaṇapati, Śiva as Linga, as Tiruvīnkaikkuṭi Mahādeva, Lingodbhava, and Sankaranarayana. After the early fifth-century inscription, Pāṇḍya inscriptions reappear only between the twelfth and the fourteenth centuries, recording grants to the early Śiva (cave) temple and the later structural one or Tirumarutankuti nāyanār. When Piḷḷaiyār became the main deity (named Desi Vināyaka Piḷḷaiyār) in the fourteenth century, a *gopura* was added in the north and grants to Piḷḷaiyār were made in 1305. The Nagaram or assembly of traders of Rājanārāyaṇapuram has been in charge of most of the temple's functions and continue to do so to this day.[28]

ŚĀKTA

The same process can be discerned in the case of the worship of the goddess, a tribal, popular/folk deity in the early historical period, with benevolent and malevolent traits, later subordinated to the Puranic sectarian forms of worship as the consort or divine mother. The revival of her worship with independent shrines and temples with Āgamic canons and rituals in the thirteenth and fourteenth centuries is again a development of the medieval times in south India. Even in existing Śiva temples dating from the seventh century the goddess acquired a separate shrine after the twelfth and thirteenth centuries, replacing Śiva (Tiruvālavāyuḍaiyār) as the main deity in some like the Mīnākṣi shrine in the second *prākāra* of the Madurai Sundareśvara temple. It may also be emphasized that the Kāñci Kāmākṣi temple is of later origin and the inscriptions of the temple date from the fifteenth century, just as the Śṛngeri Śāradā *pīṭha* (lit. pedestal, but here denotes seat/cult centre) appears around the same period. Their importance is due to the reorganization under Vijayanagara royal patronage (but ascribed to Śaṅkara's Ṣaṇmata) which brings Śakti worship to the fore. Both the Śāradā pīṭhas of Śṛngeri and Kāñci Kāmakōṭi are assigned to Śaṅkara.

Several studies have shown that the Śakti cult, in its Puranic articulation, combined Aryan and non-Aryan forms of worship.[29] In most studies on the goddess, primacy is given to the Sanskritic tradition mainly based on the ritual and/or Sanskrit mythic content[30] often ignoring local/vernacular traditions. In Tamil bardic poetry, tribal forms of worship (sacrifice of blood and flesh to the devils etc.) are predominant while 'the presence of Vedic religion, of brahmanism... may be traced as a very feeble, unimportant superstratum'.[31] A distinct cultural tradition was developing 'in which common 'folk' elements were intrinsically amalgamated with typical Tamil features', while the impact of Upaniṣadic ideology was more restricted.[32]

Tamil local legends are replete with instances of the ferocious and malevolent goddess wreaking destruction on all that stood in her path, including her husband Śiva. Shulman uses the *Talapuraṇās* to relate their mythic corpus to the changes, locating these myths within the context of the increasing brahmanical presence in the Tamil region and the nature of incorporation and contestation at work.[33] By the time the *Tēvāram* (Śaiva bhakti hymns) and other texts were composed, the goddess had been brought into the fold of Puranic Brāhmaṇism. Yet there is enough evidence from inscriptions, temple art and architecture, and later myths to suggest that the goddess retained a certain independent identity/space, despite changing sacred spheres from 600 to1300 CE.

In the Sangam classics and post-Sangam works the goddess is variously known and eulogized as Aṇanku (*Naṟṟiṇai,* poem 165; *Akanāṉūṟu*, ll, 14, 16, 366), the beautiful and dangerous goddess. Aṇanku is interpreted as directly related to the sexuality of women, an aspect to which greater attention needs to be paid.[34] She is the mountain goddess to whom the hunters (Maṟavar) offer sacrifice propitiating her for rain. She is Koṟṟavai, Cūli, or Durgā, the bestower of victory in war or (*Kuṟuntokai*, poem 218) and who is skilled in the *tuṇankai* dance (*TMP,* ll.457–61). She is Mudiyōḷ the goddess of the *pālai tiṇai*, the original mother, the goddess who bore in her great womb (Mōṭṭu), the progenitor of the powerful god of the hilly regions that is, the red god Murukan, (*TMP*—6, ll.256–9). The *Patiṟṟuppattu* is replete with the horrific forms of the worship of the goddess reputed to live on the Ayirai mountain, demanding blood sacrifices in return for victory and rich booty (poems 65, 66, 79, and 88). She is also the *Kāṭuṟai kaṭvuḷ* or the forest deity (*Porunarāṟṟuppaṭai*, ll. 51–2). She is Kali, residing in inaccessible terrains like the desert, forests, and hills with her large retinue of ghosts, spirits, and demons (*Maturaikkāñci*—l.20, and 631–3, *Akanāṉūṟu,* poems 198 and 366.)

Thus images of power and aggression dominate. It is this variety of features, as a goddess of war and victory, beauty, and power and as the mother that led her to her subsequent associations with the goddesses in the Puranic pantheon. The integration of many local elements with the goddess of victory began during the Sangam period itself but nowhere is her affiliation with Śiva mentioned in the Sangam works.

The *Cilappatikāram* (Vēṭṭuva Vari-canto-12), a post-Sangam epic, provides the most graphic example of the amalgamation of tribal/folk and brahmanical forms of worship of the goddess. It refers to her as the slayer of the buffalo demon Mahiṣa, as Durgā and Śālini and as the sister of Viṣṇu. Most striking is a detailed description, where the goddess is likened to Śiva with the moon in her coiffure, an unwinking eye on her forehead, a throat darkened by poison, the serpent Vāsuki as her girdle, mount Meru as her shoulder bangles, the elephant hide as her upper garment, and a lion's skin as her skirt, with a trident in her bangled hands. According to Dikshitar, the goddess appropriated these aspects from Śiva.[35]

In the invocation to the *Kalittokai,* a post-Sangam work, lord Śiva is described as having the goddess Umā always by his side, Murukan as being born of the union of Śiva and Umā, the daughter of the king of mountains, that is, the Himalayas (*Paripatal,* Poem 5), through the machinations of the god of love, Kāma. In most studies of 'divine hierogamies' (sacred marriage) 'marriage' is stressed as the factor that mediates the transformation of the malevolent female deity into a benevolent one, the subrodination of woman to man.[36]

The language of bhakti saints reveals that the incorporation of the goddess within the brahmanical tradition, though significant in the Tamil context, was not a smooth incorporation of a 'little' tradition within the 'great' one. In literary traditions, there was a constant oscillation between the two sets of belief—violent and benign—with regard to the goddess demonstrating the absence of a homogenoeus conceptualization with continuity running parallel to change in the tradition of goddess worship.

The continuity in the goddess traditions could be obscured by the many new and diverse associations that were made through their incorporation into the Śaiva divine household. Yet at some levels the goddess (especially in sculptural representations) continued to be perceived in her own right. The Mahiṣasuramardini episode probably based on the the *Devi Mahātmya* story has quite a few representations on the cave panels at Māmallapuram, while the Pēy kalaippāvai (mounted on a darting stag or deer as described in the the *Cilappatikāram*, canto 12, l.70) continues to be depicted, although the lion mount of Caṇḍikā/Ambikā, the slayer of the demon Maḥisa, are all collapsed in this figure. The Varāha and Ādivarāha cave temples have panels depicting both the stag and the lion as her mount. In Māmallapuram, the Draupadi *ratha* and other shrines represent the human sacrifice. The identification of various goddesses as consorts of Śiva does not indicate that all these female deities are one and the same. Folk goddesses of a similar nature continue to be worshipped for various reasons, especially for prevention and cure of diseases/epidemics.

The small Piṭāri (Bhaṭāri) temples mentioned in the Pallava, Pāṇḍya, and early Cōḷa inscriptions points to the existence of independent shrines for the goddess in this period.[37] From the ninth to the twelfth centuries, when they are identified spouses of Śiva, separate gifts in the form of ornaments and services to the goddess are made in Śiva temples. From the twelfth century, Kāmakkōṭṭam or goddess shrines are accorded space within the enlarged Śiva temples marking an important change in the status of the goddesses. The marginalization of the female goddess suited the imperial ambitions of the Cōḷas.

The importance of the motif of dance in assigning a subordinate position to the goddess cannot be overestimated. While most of the dances like the *marakkāl*, the *tunaṇkai*, Śiva's *koṭukoṭṭi* and *pāṇṭarankam* were associated with Koṟṟavai-Durgā in the early period (*Perumpāṇāṟṟuppatai.*, ll. 457–61; *Cilappatikāram*, canto 6, l.39), the early medieval Cāḷukya sculptures in Paṭṭadakal, in the Pallava Kailāsanātha temple at Kāñci, and paintings in Panamalai establish Śiva as the great dancer. In the Naṭarāja temple at Cidambaram, the goddess (Kāli?) is shown outside the *sabhā* (hall) dancing in the courtyard, with the king Rājarāja witnessing the dance. The Ūrdhva tāṇḍava of Śiva, a posture that the goddesss is unable to emulate, symbolizes the liberation of humanity (souls) from materiality, that is, the rampage of Kāli who would have swallowed all that came in her path.[38] Yet in Cidambaram, Dārāsuram, and Gangaikoṇḍacōḷapuram female dancers perform all such *karaṇa*s or movements.

The goddesses which coalesced in the great goddess of the *Devi Mahātmya* had their origin in non-brahmanical cultures, although several scholars insist that the worship of the great goddess was known to Brāhmaṇism from the earliest times.[39] The Devi is mostly associated with Śiva as wife in her passive form and as his Śakti in his war-like aspect. It is she who finally restores order in the world and it is through her grace that success is gained in worldly endeavours. However, in the early medieval and later periods this power gets attributed to Śiva, not to the goddess.

The goddess was never completely subdued, which is evident from the fact that a number of grants were made in her favour from the seventh century and innumerable devi shrines were constructed in the fourteenth century in the Tamil country. On the basis of Census Reports of 1961, Burton Stein points to the proliferation of goddess shrines (along with that of Gaṇesa and Murukan), particularly Amman temples[40] in Kongumaṇḍalam and Pāṇḍimaṇḍalam of the Tamil region from 1300 to 1750. According to him, this illustrates a significant shift in the sectarian affiliation of most Tamils, a turning away from Śiva to other deities, most notably to goddesses. Ethnographic evidence suggests that most non-brāhmaṇa Tamilians maintained multiplex sectarian affiliations, seldom shifting from one to another, but more often adding to their affiliational connections through time. The vēḷāḷas of Kongu are all worshippers of Śiva, but the family gods are various Śaktis, or female destructive spirits who have Śūdra Pūjāris. Stein tries to show that the relationship between the declining rate of construction of Śiva temples and the rising rate of Amman temples was complementary in Kongu and in the Pāṇḍya country.

The sacred credentials of non-Vedic, tutelary deities were raised to a higher order when their worship was taken over by the dominant cultivating groups, specially the peasant subcastes, of a locality without divesting them of their local significance. Simultaneously, vertical and horizontal or spatial integration of the agrarian region was strengthened by the linkage of all such tutelaries to local Śiva shrines and through these to the great regional Śiva centres, thus homogenizing temples known across the subcontinent with very local shrines in order to establish the numerical increase in these temples. This makes Stein's findings quite tentative. The explanation should be sought in the changing socio-economic context from the twelfth century, when artisans and craftsmen, apart from traders, were increasingly reviving their earlier affiliations with folk/popular deities and their worship. In a period of increasing crafts production, groups of artisans and craft specialists, generally assigned a lower caste status in the brahmanical tradition, became socially and economically ascendant, and asserted their presence by reviving links with popular deities of regional traditions. This accounted for the elevation of Murukan, Amman, and Gaṇeśa cults to the higher tradition. This point needs to be kept in mind in the context of the reorganizational activities of the Smārta successors of Śaṅkara, who sought to establish not only a Puranic basis but even a Vedic origin to all such cults.

ŚAṄKARA AND ṢAṆMATA

At this point it would be useful to put forth the generally accepted views on Śaṅkara's date and the important events of his life as narrated in the traditional biographies.[41] Conventional dates assigned to Śaṅkara go back to a period as early as the sixth and fifth centuries BC. Early medieval dates ranging between 650 and 775 are assigned by G.C. Pandey on the basis of the dates of other authors and philosophers such as Kumarila and Maṇḍanamiśra, which according to him would agree with the date in the Śṛngeri tradition. While historians generally subscribe to the date 788–820 CE (the dates followed in this essay) the tradition about succeession lists (of the monastic establishments) are not earlier than the fourteenth and fifteenth centuries.

The legendary biographies of Śaṅkara which 'combine features of age-old hagiography and royal panegyrics' presume a lost ancient basis for the medieval legend of Śaṅkara. The extant biographies of Śaṅkara date from the fourteenth to the eighteenth centuries, the earliest being at least five or six centuries later than the historically accepted dates of Śaṅkara. Of these biographies the most popular is Mādhava's *Śaṅkara Digvijaya (SDV)*, dated from the fourteenth to the seventeenth centuries.[42] The seventeenth and eighteenth centuries witnessed a growing search for the biographical traditions of Śaṅkara, and the Mādhavīya, according to Pandey seems to have met this need most successfully.

The identification of Mādhava with Vidyāraṇya is complicated by the fact that there were many Mādhavas—Mādhava, the brother of Sāyana, Mādhava, the son of Sāyana, and Mādhava, the minister and general of Vijayanagara. There is also the possibility of a fourth Mādhava who became Vidyāraṇya. Biographies of divergent dates from the thirteenth to the sixteenth centuries are claimed by the Śṛngeri and Kāñcī pithas as written by their *ācāryas*. Among them feature the one by Vyasācālīa/Vidyāśankara, of the Śṛngeri monastery, who is said to be the teacher of Mādhava Vidyāraṇya. Another work is that of Ānantagiri, who claims to be a disciple of Śaṅkara and is identified with Anandajñāna (eleventh century) in the Śaṅkara lineage of the Kāmakōṭipīṭha.

Later biographies of the seventeenth century follow a 'patterned imagination' providing a mythical origin to Śaṅkara. 'Puranic' and Āgamic texts give a highly mythologized account of Śaṅkara, which is recurrent in later literature, namely, the idea that Śaṅkara was an incarnation of Śiva, born to rescue Vedic faith and social ethos from the hostile attacks of diverse heterodox faiths, through an exposition of Advaita. To help the revival of the Vedic faith and to save orthodoxy, he is believed to have undertaken disputation with rival sects and schools, established new temples and monastic centres of worship, and synthesized Smārta-Puranic cults under the aegis of the Advaita. Biographies before the *Saṅkara Vijaya,* if they existed, apparently relied on a continuing debate on Advaita as well as the new Puranic mythological perspective, emphasizing the 'religious' and 'synthetic' aspects of the life and works of Śaṅkara. They claim that Śaṅkara established the six modes of worship, the Ṣaṇmata. It appears that Śaṅkara's biography is expounded by different works from the standpoints of the different monastic traditions, that is, the *Guru-Vamśa-Kāvyà*, of the Śṛngeri tradition.

The accounts of his early life, meeting with Kumarila, Maṇḍanamiśra, and philosophical debates and the like, are common to most biographies including the fact that he lived only for 32 years and died at Kāñcī or in Kerala or in the Himalayas. Beyond these, there are widely varying accounts of diverse journeys and pilgrimages, debates, and the founding of the monastic centres and the installation of images, *yantras*, and *lingas* with little consistency about the number, nature, or order of these events, apart from many obscurities and contradictions.

Śaṅkara's peregrinations and organizational activities led to the establishment of maṭhas at Vārāṇasi, Kashmir, Badari, Jagannātha (Pūri), Dvāraka, Śṛngeri (Ṛṣyaśrngāśrama) on the Tungabhadra where goddess Śāradā was permanently located in the maṭha, and at Kāñcī where the goddess Kāmākṣi (Kamakōṭi pīṭha) was consecrated and where he founded both Śiva and Viṣṇu Kāñcī or in other words renovated the temples of these two sects. Each of these maṭhas has its own monastic lists of pontiffs which vary considerably due to the multiplication of Śaṅkaras (Ādi and Abhinava) with artifical gaps created by an ante-dated chronology. Different versions of his visits to various places in India form a pan-Indian pilgrimage network, through a mention of all important sacred places. They include: Paśupatinātha (Nepal), Ujjayaini, Śrīśaila, Śeṣācala, Narasimhagiri (Ahobila?), Venkaṭagiri (Tirupati?), Gokarṇa (the shrine of Mūkāmbika), Setu (Rāmeśvaram), where he debated with the Śāktas, Jambukeśvaram, where he decorated the Akhilāṇḍeśvarai image with the *tāṭankas*, and Kālaṭi in Kerala, his birth place, Vyāghrapura (Chidambaram), Tirupati and Anantanārāyaṇa in Travancore, and finally Kāñcī, where he is said to have reformed the worship of the goddess Kāmākṣi. The exact order of his visits is, however, not possible to follow.

Several questions arise at this juncture: Did Śaṅkara himself institute Vedāntic maṭhas as organized institutions for the *sannyāsins* of his school? Or were they established in the late medieval period, that is from the fourteenth century, and then ascribed to Śaṅkara? The uncertainty arises from the fact that there is no authentic record or traditions, either of Śaṅkara or his maṭhas till the fourteenth century. Medieval monastic institutions claiming to derive their traditions from Śaṅkaracarya assigned to him a mythical origin and/or a divine incarnation in order to legitimize and popularize their influence.

Apart from records of properties gifted to the monastery from time to time, no epigraphic material is available that allows for a reconstruction of the early history of the Śṛngeri maṭha prior to Vidyāraṇya. Its history can be traced only on the basis of the epigraphic materials available from Vidyāraṇya's time but mainly relies on the *GVK* and also *SDV* in order to trace the changes in Śṛngeri maṭha, which is claimed to be non-sectarian.[43] A case in point is the legend of goddess Śāradā. She is Sarasvati (who had taken the form of Maṇḍanamiśra's wife Ubhayabhārati, with whom Śaṅkara had a debate), who bestowed a boon on Śaṅkara by accompanying him to Ṛṣyaśṛnga Āśrama (in Śṛngeri) on the bank of the Tungabhadra. The establishment of the Śrīcakra below the image of Śāradā, the *sphaṭika liṅga* of Candramaulīśvara and a *mūrti* of Gaṇapati carved out of a block of crystal with a ruby in the middle are assigned to Śaṅkara. Vidyāraṇya, the eleventh Jagadguru of Śṛngeri maṭha after Śaṅkara, is believed to have installed the present golden image in place of the sandal wood image of Sri Śāradā consecrated by Śaṅkara. Vidyāraṇya got rich land-endowments and insignia of authority from the founders, the Sangamas of Vijayanagara, which are mentioned in the *GVK*. An inscription at Śṛngeri, of the period of Harihara II, gives a complete list of the gifts.[44] The Śṛngeri maṭha grew to be a centre of organized temple worship and of feeding pilgrims, with priests and a huge body of servants, and came to have several branches, of which the Bangalore and Kālaṭi ones are important.[45]

According to Pandey, the monastic list of pontiffs at Śṛngeri from Vidyātīrtha in the thirteenth century has a fair degree of historical corroboration. The Kāñcī Kāmakōṭi pīṭha received gifts from AD twelfth century,[46] the earliest being that of the Telugu Cōḷa ruler Vijaya Gaṇḍa Gopāla in AD 1111. Other grants of lands and villages made by the Vijayanagara rulers Vira Narasimha Deva dated Ś. 1436 (1514 CE) and by Nāyaka rulers like Vijaya Cokkanātha of Madurai (1708 CE) for the maṭha's centre at Tiruvānaikkōyil (Jambukeśvaram) in the island of Śrīrangam and the last grant by the Qutub Shahi, Tana Shah, in 1677 CE, are attested by contemporary archives like the Sarasvati Mahal Library, Tanjavur, and the Madras Central Record Office. On account of disturbed conditions, the maṭha was transferred from Kāñcīpuram to Tanjavur and then from Tanjavur to Kumbha kōṇam (or Kumbakonam). Yet continuous patronage by the Tanjavur rulers and special honours bestowed on the Śaṅkaracārya of Kāñcīpuram by the Nawabs of Arcot and Travancore sovereigns and by British officers show that it was Kāñcī, which was the main piṭha while those in other holy places such as Jambukeśvaram and Vārānasi were branches.

Śaṅkara, the most original thinker after the Buddha and an extraordinary philosopher, became the source of a new and distinct tradition within the Vedānta. He gave up ritualistic religion when he took up *sannyāsa* and the wandering life of a mendicant. Traditional accounts attribute to him 400 literary works of diverse character, most of which are apocryphal. The *Brahmasūtra Bhāṣya*, the commentaries on the the ten classical Upaniṣads and the Bhagavad Gīta, that is, the *Prasthāna Trayī*, are universally and justly accepted as authentic works of Śaṅkara. However, benedictory verses and those which are Tāntric and quote the Purānas and even Śrutis ascribed to him by the tradtional biographies are uncharacteristic of Śaṅkara.

G.C. Pandey holds that it would be unfair to limit Śaṅkara's authorship only to versified logical philosophy. He also stresses the importance of doctrinal rather than stylistic criteria in determining the authenticity of Śaṅkara's works. As Śaṅkara is remembered as a great religious and spiritual leader, not merely as a philosophical commentator, some of the hymns and *stotras* (such as *Ānandalahari, Soundarya Lahari,* and *Dakṣiṇamūrti* stotra among others) attributed to him are accepted as his by some scholars. Moreover, although Śaṅkara laid stress on *jñāna* as a means of liberation, it is believed that he also acccepted bhakti as a requisite for the prior purification of mind, with God or Saguṇa Brahman figuring quite prominently in his thought. This accounts for his recognition of the need for preparatory *sādhanā* and Advaitic Āgamas which culminate in pure jñāna *mārga*. It is significant that Robert E. Gussner states that the stotras were the result of a medieval tendency to popularize the Vedānta by bringing it near to the bhakti movements,[47] a view which is more in keeping with the historical context and processes which led to the establishment of a Smārta tradition in the fourteenth and fifteenth centuries during the Vijayanagara period.

Buddhism, the great rival of the Vedānta, which was more rational and universal as a philosophical religion than the Vedānta, is believed to have influenced Śaṅkara and the pre-Śaṅkara Vedāntin Gauḍapāda, his teacher's teacher. However, Vedānta replaced Buddhism in India and became the principal expression of its spiritual culture and philosophy. Both Gauḍapāda and Śaṅkara were familiar with the Upaniṣadic and Mahāyānic thought, especially Vijñānavāda of the Sūnyavādins of the Madhyamika school, who first made systematic use of the distinction of two standpoints, absolute and empirical. Śaṅkara presented a new interpretation of the Vedānta as his principal concern seems to have been the restoration of Vedānta to its original meaning from which it had been distracted by misinterpretations and obscured by an overgrowth of the ritualistic Smārta-Puranic religion. His interpretation of the Vedānta not only led to its philosophical renovation but also became the basis of connecting it with the new ethos of the Smārta-Puranic religion.

Śaṅkara seems to have upheld the validity of the traditional Vedic social order as defined by the *Dharmasūtras* and *Smṛtis*, restricting the option of mendicancy to the brāhmaṇas, while its relative importance in the traditional scheme of social life elevated in practice the role of the sannyāsin as compared to that of the priest in the early medieval period. As David Lorenzen points out

> in his major works, those agreed to be genuinely his, Śaṅkara has little to say about matters which directly pertain to social relations. He does, however, largely accept the orthodox Brāhmaṇical theodicy of *karma* and *samsara* which in fact embodies a conservative social ideology heavily skewed in favour of the higher varṇas.[48]

Śaṅkara seems to accept without question the traditional account of the creation of the four varṇas. Further, Śaṅkara 'admits the right of the Shudras to acquire knowledge of the *Itihāsa* and *Puranas*, but not the *Veda*', 'virtually limiting the possibility of salvation to Brahmins, alone, when he insists only Brahmins have a right to become ascetics (sannyasis), since sannyasa is, in practical terms, a prerequisite for Brahma knowledge. His debate with Ubhayabhārati, a woman, not permitted by orthdoxy is justified by the claim that she is none other than the goddess of learning, the story thus vitiating the liberal social ethic implied by Śaṅkara's willingness to debate with a woman.'

G.C. Pandey believes that the essential kinship of Śaṅkara's Advaita to Śākta Advaita cannot be denied and that it requires no effort to reconcile Śākta worship with Advaitism for Śāktism was non-dualistic. Hence the authenticity of the exquisite work *Saundaryalahari,* which, according to Pandey, breathes the spirit of non-dualism and of the *Prapañcasāra* in which Śaṅkara's approval of Tāntricism emerges more clearly. The Smārta tradition adds Sūrya and Gaṇeśa to Viṣṇu, Śiva, and Śakti to create the tradition of Pañcadevopāsana, in which even minor cults got included. The sun has an honoured place in Vedic religion and is the accepted symbol of Brahman in the Vedānta.

Śaṅkara's support, essentially in the form of a *saguṇopāsana*, is evoked to establish the Puranic cult of the sun for ensuring health and freedom from diseases. In south India, the sun is a mere attendant deity till the cult is said to have been made part of the Ṣaṇmata.

The Smārta–Puranic religion of the age was, it is suggested, working towards a vast religious synthesis. This is ascribed to the bhakti saints of the south, and Śaṅkara is also believed to have contributed to it. However, there is hardly any evidence in the bhakti hymns of Śaṅkara's contribution and, more importantly, historical processes do not attest to the emergence of the Ṣaṇmata during the early medieval centuries when the two major Puranic religions evolved around Śiva and Viṣṇu. While the chronolgy of the Śaṅkara lineage or succession till the fourteenth century is a matter of great doubt, there must have been some teachers who followed Śaṅkara's Advaita and indulged in intellectual debates, which did not directly influence the Puranic process. The original contribution of Śaṅkara apparently was to organize mendicants into orders and connect them with definite monastic centres in terms of residence, schooling, and guidance. If Śankarite monasteries existed even before the fourteenth century, the nature of such monasteries underwent a great change with the emergence of the Vijayanagara kingdom in the fourteenth century and the patronage it extended to these monasteries, especially at Śṛngeri. These monasteries now acquired a new affluence and authority in addition to their traditional religious influence and prestige.

Bhakti and the temple developed a religion of ritual. Of considerable significance was their ideological potential for the regional state under the Cōḷas, a major dynasty. The complexity of the historical processes in the period from the fourteenth century outlined above does not support Pandey's simplistic explanation, that

...only when the religion appeared inadequate in public life before the onslaughts of Islam that a more personal religion of spirituality received emphasis in the 13th–14th centuries, and it was then that the voice of Śaṅkara came to be heard effectively in the religious domain as distinct form a mere philosophical debate or contemplation.

Śaṅkara's Advaita was not relevant for the regional state in the early medieval period. In the larger pan-Indian politics of power that developed from the fourteenth century, legitimacy was sought in Vedic and Vedāntic roots in greater antiquity, which must have become a pressing need under Vijayanagara and hence Śaṅkara was invoked.

CONCLUDING REMARKS

Let me bring together the different threads in the above survey to understand the nature of the religious synthesis brought about in the Vijayanagara period. How does this period differ from that of pre-Vijayanagara south India? In the pre-Vijayanagara period, the historical processes which determined the development of religion were predominantly regional. Although the early medieval period witnessed an amazing spread of brahmanical/Puranic religion, the regional, vernacular forms were conspicuously different in the Deccan, Andhra, and Tamil regions due to the nature of folk/popular traditions which confronted the brahmanical forms. Hence the nature of acculturation, assimilation, and even acceptance of local forms were different. The Tamil region, with a strong non-Sanskritic literary and cultural tradition, illustrates this experience more clearly than other regions. The visible presence of local folk deities and their undiminished importance is clear from a study of the Murukan and Koṟṟavai cults. It is also seen that with their folk attributes these deities get almost totally absorbed into the Puranic forms in the early medieval period, and there is a revival of their independent worship with separate temples and/or shrines within the larger Puranic Śaiva and Vaiṣṇava temples in the thirteenth and fourteenth centuries, in which they seem to be taking over the Puranic structures in their own right. The expansion of the temple precincts to accommodate a number of shrines for the goddess, Subrahamṇya and Gaṇeśa in the Śaiva temples and of the goddesses and other minor deities in the Vaiṣṇava temples is a conspicuous feature of this period. Simultaneously, separate temples for Amman and Murukan cults, came into existence in all the regions, particularly in the Kongu region, where brahmadeyas and bhakti centres were hardly present.

Politically, there was a lack of clear configurations, with the regional powers like the Cōḷas and Cāḷukyas having declined and their place taken by ruling families and minor chiefs of lesser territorial significance. Turkish invasions introduced new militant powers in the search for richer avenues of resources. On the economic front, traders and craftsmen gained greater influence from the twelfth century and sought enhanced social status vis-à-vis the brahmanas and *vāḷāḷas*. The temple was the only means of providing space to the newly emerging economic groups and to the mixed rural and urban economy.

Vijayanagara inherited this mixed economy and a society in a constant state of flux. In addition, there was a major shift in the centre of power to the Deccan and rivalry from the Bahmani sultanate. Vijayanagara therefore, aimed at a larger territorial integration and delegated power to military chiefs (Nayakas) for more effective control of distant and different cultural regions. The migration of such warrior chiefs to the peripheries and their participation in temple building and endowments is a conspicuous feature of this period. This led to significant changes in patterns of ownership of land, causing disintegration of some older Brahmadeyas and peasant organizations like the nāḍu as well as an increase in craft production, intensive urbanization, and a fair degree of monetization and commercialization. Temple society expanded since new entrants into all these spheres of activity had to be accommodated within the same legitimating framework. The maṭha emerged as the community's leading instrument of integration. Incidentally, the vertical right-(*Valankai*) and left-(*Iṭankai*) hand divisions served as the paradigm for the incorporation of all lower agricultural and non-agricultural groups into temple ritual and administration, albeit below the brāhmaṇa elite and non-brāhmaṇa landowning and warrior groups. Most of the lower strata of society revived the worship of their folk deities, not in their original form but in imitation of the great tradition.

Vijayanagara was trying to establish a supra-regional state covering at least four culture regions of south India—Tamil, Telugu, Kannada, and, to a lesser extent, Kerala. This required a legitimating ideology which could supersede regional and local forms of authority. A reordering of the regional forms in relation to the normative Sanskritic tradition would have been the only way in which a pan-Indian cultural universe could be created as an ideological base for the Vijayanagara state. Vijayanagara promoted a rigorous Sanskritization, in fact a Vedicization, which included a harking back to the Vedic tradition, and adoption of the Vedāntic position as propounded by philosopher-thinkers like Śaṅkara and Rāmānuja, and, most significantly, an authentication of local cults under the rubric of the Purāṇas by equating their central deities with the Brahman/universal soul of the Vedāntic Advaita and Viśiṣṭādvaita philosophy.

Two phenomena became dominant in the process. Śaṅkara's Advaita, which had no visible influence in his own period—the eighth and ninth centuries—was now reinforced by the Vedāntic ideas of Brahman. The second was the fact that for the first time serious commentaries on the Vedas were written by Sāyaṇācārya, and Mādhava-Vidyāraṇya. Authentic biographies of Vedāntins like Śaṅkara and Rāmānuja were also composed, supposedly based on earlier ones now not extant. Vedic authenticity, which was reversed in Tamil hymnal literature, was sought again in the Vedānta for re-establishing the Smārta tradition through the establishment of Śaṅkara maṭhas in the cardinal directions of the subcontinent. The maṭha henceforth became a major force in south India to uphold and preserve the Śaiva, Vaiṣṇava, and Smārta traditions. It is significant that Mādhava-Vidyāraṇya, who is closely linked to the foundation of the Vijayanagara state, is claimed to be an incarnation of Śaṅkara and is believed to have moved to Śṛngeri from Kāñcīpuram. Various philosophies also came to be debated upon vigorously as is evident in the early works of Mādhava in Śṛngeri such as the *Sarva Darśana Sangraha.*[49]

However, mere Sanskritization and a search for Vedic sources for all community traditions were inadequate, especially for the courtly style of Vijayanagara. As the Mahanavami festival indicates, elaborate ceremonies around folk forms of culture and religion were also organized at the annual courtly festival along with Vedic ceremonies. While commentaries on the Vedas and the philosophical systems conferred on Vijayanagara rulers a pan-Indian legitimacy, regional forms of ceremonial practice proclaimed them as lords of the southern regions.

Among other significant developments, there were attempts at synthesizing northern Sanskritic and popular southern traditions in the canons of the respective sects, particularly the Śaiva Siddhānta system, claimed to be based on the Tamil *Tēvāram* hymns. This system now began quoting both Āgamic and Vedic scriptural authority and included regular Vedic chants and rites of worship in the temples although the Āgamas and Vedas are antithetical canons. Umāpati Śivācārya, a philosopher of the early fourteenth century, made a significant contribution to the evolution of the Śaiva Siddhānta canon by bringing together the Vedānta and Śaiva Siddhānta. While drawing heavily upon the hymnal tradition, basic to the theology and philosophy of the Śaiva Siddhānta, he simultaneously tried to establish the 'continuous and pre-dominant' influence of the Vedic tradition. Umāpati's unique contribution lies in his making the whole hagiographical history available to us in his *Cēkkiḻār Purāṇam* and *Tirumuṛai kaṇḍa purāṇam.* Umāpati, it is said, made a bold departure in tapping all the older sources of tradition, but at the same time carving a new path for the transformation of Tamil bhakti tradition into the Śaiva Siddhāntic tradition in an aesthetically more pleasing atmosphere of rapprochement through the dance of Śiva.[50]

Śaiva Siddhānta teachers like Umāpati Śivācārya (and his predecessor Meikkaṇṭār) resolved tensions between two conflicting traditions and rival groups of scriptures. Umāpati, like Rāmānuja, took a position different from Śaṅkara, qualifying the latter's non-dualism by making Śiva the Saguṇa Brahman just as Rāmānuja had equated Viṣṇu with Brahman. This created a sense of 'communitas' among the Śaiva and Vaiṣṇava lay followers, who now had gurus (spritual leaders) and canonical/textual traditions. Thus a powerful rival school was subsumed in these schools of philosophy. It may be pointed out, however, that the Śaiva Siddhānta maṭhas were invariably headed by non-brāhmaṇa (vēḷāḷa) gurus and the Śrīvaiṣṇava maṭhas (whether of the northern Vaṭakalai or southern Tenkalai schools) were headed by brāhmaṇas. Subsequently, the Smārta, Śaiva, and Vaiṣṇava sects claimed that Śaṅkara had given them an unassailable base for their central concepts of godhead, that is, of the the Śaiva, Vaiṣṇava, Śākta, Saura, Gāṇapatya, and Kaumāra cults. The non-Vedic Śākta, Kaumāra, and Gāṇapatya cults now acquired huge temples and brahmanical modes of worship. Moreover, a new sacred geography emerged which placed local temples in a wider pilgrimage network, with *Sthala Purāṇa*s and *Mahātmya*s glorifying the temple centres by claiming legendary origins in order to attract pilgrims. It was from the sixteenth century that this genre became prominent in south India. Through all this evolved a major tradition—the Smārta—which invoked Śaṅkara as the founder or reviver of Ṣaṇmata, six forms of Puranic religion. It represented an attempt to Vedicize major non-Vedic and lesser but popular/folk cults and synthesize Vedic and non-Vedic, and contestatory vernacular/regional practices into a monolithic tradition, by Purāṇizing lesser divinities and emphasizing that only a

Vedic-brahmanical origin could provide a pan-Indian character to all the regional and local cults. The Smārta tradition, with its entirely brahmanical organization, was an attempt to counter the influence of the Śaiva Siddhānta tradition.

The question that needs to be posed is: Did Vijayanagara rulers and preceptors (cult leaders) try to homogenize all forms of worship under Sanskrit norms through a revival of Vedic orthodoxy and by granting Vedic authority to the non-Vedic traditions? Under Bukka I, was there an attempt even to include the Jain community in his *rājaśāsana*, (Rāmānuja śāsana) which was issued to resolve a conflict between the Vaiṣṇavas and Jains? Jina Darśana was declared to be no different from Vaiṣṇava Darśana and Vaiṣṇava cult leaders were ordered to help in the reconstruction of many Jain temples. Would these developments under Vijayanagara have provided the basis for all future attempts, including those during the nineteenth and twentieth centuries to establish a consciously constructed common source for all religious systems and communities?

Visions of a monolithic Hindu tradition are believed to have been first projected by colonial reconstructions of the past. More importantly, these reconstructions were influenced by imperialist concerns with imposing imperial legal structures and British rule of law in dealing with the conflicting claims of different communities to socio-religious privileges and status hierarchy. Such reconstructions may well have been based on the ways native interpreters coming from specific social and religious backgrounds projected their understandings of a 'Hindu' past to the colonial administrators. Attempts from above, at consolidation and 'Vedicization' of diverse religious systems and resolution of tensions between Sanskritic and vernacular traditions, such as that under Vijayanagara, probably had a role to play in colonial constructions of a homogenous Hindu community, although such attempts at synthesis brought into existence a rich cultural mosaic now known as Hinduism.

David Lorenzen argues in a recent work[51] that evidence of a Hindu self-identity may be found in vernacular Hindi literature prior to 1800 in the texts composed by popular religious poet-singers of north India, most of them members of the non-brāhmaṇa castes. This literature, he adds, 'establishes a Hindu religious identity through a process of mutual self-definition with a contrasting Muslim order' and during the centuries of rule led by Muslim sultans and Emperor... Hindus developed a consciousness of a shared religious identity based on the loose family resemblance of the variegated beliefs and practices of Hindus, whatever their sect, caste, chosen deity or theological school.

Such an understanding of the pre-1800 developments might well aid the cause of the present communal forces who try to present a monolithic Hindu tradition and a false cultural nationalism.

Lorenzen's statement that the religion of the Puranas, which took shape between 300–600 CE, displays continuities with the earlier Vedic religion is highly problematic because it takes the continuity for granted. But his claim that the principal features and emphases, particularly the greatly expanding mythology of the gods Viṣṇu, Śiva, and Devi of the Puranic religion make it something new that marks the beginnings of a medieval and modern Hinduism is valid since this Puranic process lies at the core of the development of what we now understand as Hinduism.

NOTES AND REFERENCES

1. R.C. Hazra, *Studies in the Puranic Records on Hindu Rites and Customs,* (Dacca: University Press, 1940), p. 243.

2. Kunal Chakrabarti, 'Anthropological Models of Cultural Interaction and the Study of Religious Process', *Studies in History,* vol. 8, no. 1, 1992, pp. 123–4. See also Kunal Chakrabarti, *Religious Process. The Puranas and the Making of a Regional Tradition* (New Delhi: Oxford University Press, 2001), for the Puranic process in Bengal.

3. B.D. Chattopadhyaya, *The Making of Early Medieval India* (New Delhi: Oxford University Press, 1997), Introduction.

4. See R. Champakalakshmi, 'From Devotion and Dissent to Dominance. The Bhakti of the Tamil Āḻvārs and Nāyanārs', in R. Champakalakshmi and S. Gopal, eds, *Tradition, Dissent and Ideology, Essays in Honour of Romila Thapar* (New Delhi: Oxford University Press, 1996), pp. 135–63.

5. R. Champakalakshmi, 'Puranic Religion: The Evolution of the Tamil Saiva Tradition', in Satish Saberwal and Supriya Varma (eds), *Traditions in Motion: Religion and Society in History* (New Delhi: Oxford University Press, 2005), pp. 173–204.

6. Champakalakshmi in Champakalakshmi and Gopal (ed.), *Tradition, Dissent and Ideology,* pp. 135–63.

7. Friedhelm Hardy, *Viraha Bhakti, The Early History of Kṛṣṇa Devotion in South India* (New Delhi: Oxford University Press, 1983), Part Five.

8. G.C. Pandey (ed.), *Life and Thought of Sankaracarya* (Delhi: MLBD, 1994), pp. 41–54, The Date of Śaṅkara.

9. See R. Nagaswamy, 'The Origin and Development of Kaumaram', in R. Nagaswamy (ed.), *Sankara and Shanmata,* Souvenir of the Conference on Sankara and Shanmata (Madras: 1969), pp. 126–30. The essays in this volume generally argue that the six *maṭhas* were established by Śaṅkara and trace their origin in the Vedic tradition.

10. Fred Clothey, *The Many Faces of Murukan: History and Meaning of a South Indian God* (The Hague: Mouton, 1978), p. 27.

11. Ibid, p. 34.

12. Kamil Zvelebil, *Tamil Traditions on Subrahmanya-Murukan* (Madras: Institute of Asian Studies, 1991).

13. R. Champakalakshmi, 'Iconographic Programme and Political Imagery in Early Medieval Tamiḻakam: The Rajasimhesvara and The Rajarajesvara', in B.N. Goswamy (ed.), *Indian Art: Forms, Concerns and Development in Historical Perspective, History of Science, Philosophy and Culture in Indian Civilization*, vol. VI, part 3, ed. (New Delhi: Oxford University Press, 2000), pp. 217–64.

14. L'Hernault, *L'Iconographie De Subrahmanya Au Tamil Nad,* Publications de Francais D'Indologie, no. 59, 1978.

15. Iravatham Mahadevan, *Early Tamil Epigraphy. From the Earliest Times to the Sixth Century* AD, Cre-A and Harvard, Harvard Oriental Series, 62, Chennai, 2003, Part 3, Corpus of Tamil Brahmi Inscriptions.

16. 339 of *Annual Report on Indian Epigraphy* (*ARE*), 1918 and 240–5 of *ARE* 1941–2.

17. 26 of *ARE* 1912; *South Indian Inscriptions* (*SII*), vol. XIV, pp. 12–17.

18. 609 of *ARE* 1893; 300 of *ARE* 1955–6.

19. 611 of *ARE* 1893; Other records—*SII*, XVII, 401–3.

20. 496 and 497 of *ARE* 1907.

21. R. Nagaswamy, *Tiruttani and Velanjeri Copper Plates* (Madras: Tamil Nadu State Department of Archaeology, 1979), pp. 3–22.

22. Ibid, p. 31; 438 of *ARE* 1904.

23. A.K. Ramanujan, *Poems of Love and War* (New Delhi: Oxford University Press, 1985), p. 226.

24. Robert Brown (ed.), *Ganesh: Studies of an Asian God* (New York: State University Press, 1992).

25. A.K. Narain, 'Gaṇeśa: A Proto-History of the Idea and the Icon', in Brown (ed.), *Ganesh*, 1992, pp. 19–48.

26. Ludo Rocher, 'Gaṇeśa's Rise to Prominence in Sanskrit Literature', in Brown (ed.), *Ganesh*, 1992, pp. 69–83. The name Vighnesa is said to occur in the *Bhagavad Gita*, X-23.

27. Wendy O' Flaherty, *Asceticism and Eroticism of Siva* (London: Oxford University Press,1973), pp. 16–21.

28. Sa. Ganesan, *Pillaiyarpatti Talavaralaru,* fifth edition, 1992.

29. Pushpendra Kumar, *Sakti Cult in Ancient India* (Varanasi: Bharatiya Publishing House,1974), pp. 90–1 and 277–8.

30. Wendy O'Flaherty argues, on the basis of Samkhya philosophy, that the goddess is seen affecting the god in Puranic mythology like Prakrti affects Purusa,

by animating him and causing the blossoming of his latent powers. 'The Shifting Balance of Power in the Marriage of Siva and Parvati' in Hawley and Wulff (eds), *The Divine Consort Radha and the Goddesses of India* (Delhi: MLBD, 1984), p. 132. Also Tracy Pitchman, *The Rise of the Goddess in Hindu Tradition* (Delhi: Sai Satguru Publishers, 1997), p. 5.

31. Kamil Zvelebil, *The Smile Of Murukan* (Leiden: E.J. Brill, 1973), p. 21.

32. F. Hardy, *Viraha Bhakti,* The Early History of Krishna Devotions in South India (New Delhi: Oxford University Press, 1983), p. 141.

33. David Shulman, *Tamil Temple Myths* (Princeton: Princeton University Press, 1980), pp. 8–10.

34. See Lawrence Babb, *The Divine Hierarchy Popular in Central India* (New York, London: Columbia University, 1975), pp. 205–6.

35. V.R.R. Dikshitar, tr. *Silappatikaram* (Madras: Kazhakam, 1978).

36. George L. Hart, *The Poems of the Ancient Tamils* (Berkeley: University of California, 1975), pp. 23–4.

37. Pitari temples in Sendalai (eighth century CE), rock-cut temples in Mamallapuram for Durga (seventh century), Makalam referred to in a Śiva temple at Niyamam (eighth century), in a Brahmadeya called Arincikai Caturvedimangalam and other places.

38. *Tiruvacakam, Tirucalal, l.14.* The Urdhva Tandava in his vision is the 'going up rather than getting entangled in the mire' and in the ultimate analysis 'matter is spiritualised', Dorai Rangaswamy, *The Religion and Philosophy of Tevaram* (University of Madras, 1958), p. 497.

39. V.S. Agarwala, 'The Glorification of the Great Goddess', *Purana*, 1963, pp. 64–89; Dasarath Sharma, 'Verbal Similarities between the *Durga Sapatasati* and the *Devi Bhagvata Purana* and Other Considerations', *Purana*, pp. 90–113.

40. Burton Stein, 'South Indian Temples', *Indian Economic and Social History Review*, vol. 14, no. 1,1977, pp. 11–42 (Table 1).

41. This whole discussion on the life and thought of Śankara is based on the authoritative work of G.C. Pandey, *Life and Thought of Sankaracarya,* 1994 and David Lorenzen's article 'The Life of Sankaracarya', in F.W. Clothey and J.B. Long (eds), *Experiencing Siva: Encounters with a Hindu Deity* (New Delhi: Manohar Publishers, 1983), pp. 155–75.

42. Herman Kulke, 'Maharajas, Mahants and Historians. Reflections on the Historiography of Early Vijayanagara and Sringeri', in Anna Libera Dallapiccola and Stephanie Zingel-Ave Lallemant (eds), *Vijayanagar: City and Empire* (Stuttgart: Frantz Steiner Verlag, 1985), pp. 120–43.

43. Yoshitsusgu, Sawai, 'The Smarta Tradition of Srngeri. The Faith of the Ascetics and Lay Smartas: A Study of the Sankaran of Srngeri', PhD Thesis, Wienna University, USA, pp. 22–33.

44. *Annual Report of the Mysore Archaeological Report, 1928*, p. 17.

45. Sawai, p. 34 and no. 47. Controversy exists between the Śṛngeri and Kāñcī maṭhas. They provide different succesion lists with dates for each guru. The Puri maṭha's list lacks dates. They differ from Śṛngeri in dating Śaṅkara to 509–477 BCE.

46. N. Ramesan, 'Sri Kamakoti Pitha of Sri Sankaracarya', in Nagaswamy (ed.), *Sankara and Shanmata,* pp. 372–86.

47. Robert E. Gussner, quoted by G.C. Pandey with an incomplete reference to the *Journal of American Oriental Society* (*JAOS*), 1978, pp. 259–67.

48. David Lorenzen, *Who Invented Hinduism? Essays on Religion in History* (New Delhi: Yoda Press, 2006), Chap. 6, p. 121.

49. Sheldon Pollock, 'Sanskrit Literary Culture from the Inside Out', in Sheldon Pollock, ed., *Literary Cultures of South Asia* (New Delhi: Oxford University Press, 2002), pp. 94–5. Pollock says that Sayana, the celebrated minister and general, was more attracted to religious and philosophical texts and his editing and commentarial labours on the Vedas reached industrial magnitude during the reigns of Harihara I and Bukka (AD 1336–77).

50. David Smith, *The Dance of Siva, Art and Poetry in South Asia* (Cambridge University Press, 1996), pp. 104–7.

51. Lorenzen, *Who Invented Hinduism,* Chap. 6, pp. 120–43.

3. 'NEVER HAVE I SEEN SUCH YOGĪS, BROTHER'

YOGĪS, WARRIORS, AND SORCERERS IN ANCIENT AND MEDIEVAL INDIA

David Gordon White

Since the publication of his ground-breaking *Kāpālikas and Kālāmukhas* in 1972,[1] David Lorenzen has never ceased to test and tease and question the validity of the many modernist assumptions embedded in colonial and post-colonial reconstructions of the religious history of South Asia. A case in point is his 'Warrior Ascetics in Indian History', an early and important revisioning of the pivotal role of religious orders in the economic, political, and military landscapes of medieval, Mughal, and colonial India.[2] Lorenzen's article—which situates the so-called Sannyasi Rebellion of the late eighteenth-century within a broader history of ascetic militancy—opens with a song attributed to the north Indian poet-saint Kabīr,[3] the first line of which is 'Never have I seen such yogīs, Brother.' In the present study, which examines the person (or persona) of the yogī (or yogin) in a variety of early South Asian sources, I will argue against the implicit model of the yogin in this poetic verse, and demonstrate that there existed a conceptual link between yoga, combat, killing, and dying that was very likely more ancient than the 'classical' formulations of yoga found in the Bhagavad Gītā (BhG) and the *Yoga Sūtras* of Patañjali (YS).

ASSUMING THE LOTUS POSITION

In his authoritative archaeological survey of the Mohenjo-Daro site written in 1931, Sir John Marshall confidently identifies the now-famous figure represented on seal 420 (Fig. 3.1) as:

Fig. 3.1: Mohenjo-Daro seal 420 *ca.* 2500–2000 BCE. Based on Parpola, M-340. Restoration by John C. Huntington. Courtesy: John and Susan Huntington Archive

a male god, who is recognizable at once as a prototype of the historical Śiva....The God, who is three-faced, is seated on a low Indian throne in a typical attitude of *Yoga*, with legs bent double beneath him, heel to heel, and toes turned downwards. His arms are outstretched, his hands, with thumbs to front, resting on his knees....The lower limbs are bare and the phallus (*ūrdhvameḍhra*) seemingly exposed, but it is possible that what appears to be the phallus is in reality the end of the waistband....[T]he attributes of the deity are peculiarly distinctive. In the first place, he is three-faced (*trimukha*)....The second feature of this pre-Aryan god that links him with the historical Śiva is his peculiar Yogī-like posture...Śiva is pre-eminently the prince of Yogīs—the typical ascetic and self-mortifier, whence his names *Mahātapaḥ*, *Mahāyogī*. Primarily, the purpose of yoga was the attainment of union (*yoga*) with the god by mental discipline and concentration; but it was also the means of acquiring miraculous powers, and hence in the course of time the yogī came to be regarded as a magician, miracle-monger, and charlatan. Like Śaivism itself, *yoga* had its origin among the pre-Āryan population, and this explains why it was not until the Epic Period that it came to play an important part in Indo-Āryan religion...Śiva is not only prince of Yogīs; he is also lord of the beasts (*paśupati*), and it is seemingly in reference to this aspect of his nature that the four animals—the elephant, tiger, rhinoceros and buffalo—are grouped around him.[4]

While many scholars have taken issue with Marshall's identification of the image on this seal with the five-headed male Hindu god Śiva, few, if any, have ever challenged his assumption that the humanoid figure is seated in a yogic pose, and is, by extension, a *yogī* or *yogin*.[5] It is this assumption that I wish to question. First of all, is the cross-legged pose of this enthroned figure necessarily a yogic posture? If such were the case, a number of figures from many other parts of the ancient world would also have to be qualified as yogīs (or their female counterparts). These would include a number of other figures from the Indus Valley Civilization of equal antiquity to the figure on seal 420. Some of these images, from the Indus Valley site of Harappa, show figures in identical postures, often enthroned, and sometimes in stylized buildings, which some scholars have identified as shrines.[6]

Following the watershed of the Indus Valley seals, no South Asian images of figures in 'yogic' posture appear for the next two thousand years, until a circa first century BCE bas relief medallion of the goddess Śrī (Fig. 3.2), from the Bharhut *stūpa* in central India. Here, Śrī is seated on a lotus and flanked by elephants in a configuration later associated with the iconography of the goddess of prosperity, Gaja-Lakṣmī.[7] Identified with royal sovereignty, Śrī is closely associated with the lotus flower in an account from the Mahābhārata (MBh), an epic dating from the same period as this medallion. In it, Śrī weeps tears that become golden lotuses, and is identified with Draupadī, the queen of the five Pāṇḍava brothers.[8] From the same century, two bronze coins, issued by the Scythian kings Maues (*ca.* 90–80 BCE) and Azes (*ca.* 57–10 BCE), each represents the respective kings seated in a cross-legged posture upon a cushion. These coins, which bear both Greek and Kharoshti inscriptions,[9] date from the period in which

Fig. 3.2: Śri seated on lotus, Bharhut, *ca.* first century BCE. Courtesy: John and Susan Huntington Archive

the Śakas, the Indo-Scythians, were extending their realms from their Central Asian homeland into north-western South Asia.

Well to the west (but linked with both South and Central Asia by the Silk Road), in Anatolia, the first two centuries of the common era saw a profusion of sculptural and numismatic representations of the famous Artemis of Ephesus type, images which—in addition to the goddess's famous bodices comprised offerings of bull testicles (often mistaken to be multiple breasts)—also featured vestments (called 'ependytes' [from the Greek *epénduma*][10]) upon which were figured bulls, bees, flowers, and human figures in cross-legged postures uncannily similar to that of the figure on Mohenjo-Daro seal 420.[11]

These figures are not found on all representations of Artemis: in many cases, they are replaced by 'winged Nike' figures, whose lower limbs simply disappear, as in the case of the famous sculpture housed in the National Museum in Naples, Italy.[12] Scholars have identified the animal imagery in this goddess's iconography as a vestige of earlier cults of a great western Asian 'Mistress of Animals.' Hiltebeitel, in his 1973 analysis of Mohenjo-Daro seal 420, argues for an identification of that figure as a priest of an ancient 'Buffalo Mother Goddess,' who would have been the forerunner of the later Hindu goddess Durgā, the 'Slayer of the Buffalo Demon'.[13]

Further to the west but from the same period as the Bharhut image of Śrī, one finds another cross-legged figure represented as a 'Lord of Animals', that has been identified as the Celtic horned god, Cernunnos (Fig. 3.3). The most famous of these is figured on an inner panel of the first-century BCE Gundestrup Cauldron, an artefact which, although it was unearthed in far north-western Denmark in the late nineteenth century, is thought by some scholars to have been manufactured in the south-eastern portion of the Balkan peninsula near the Black Sea. All other images of Cernunnos hail from France or Italy, the earliest extant image being from Val Camonica, in the Italian Alps.[14] Cernunnos is generally represented in a cross-legged posture; however, this posture is not unique to the god. Other male deities, from the second century BCE Provence and Narbonne in France, are also represented in a cross-legged pose.[15] Scholars also agree that much of Cernunnos's iconography is inspired by ancient Near Eastern prototypes, and it should be recalled that in New Testament times, an eastern extension of the Celts was Anatolia, where they were called the Galatians by the apostle Paul.[16]

Returning to South Asia, where nearly all early stone sculpture that has survived down to the present day is Buddhist, a number of seated Buddhist and Jain figures are shown in what today would be called a 'full lotus' posture. These include the earliest anthropomorphic representation of Buddha Śākyamuni from the Mathura school, dated to the first to second centuries CE, in which the Buddha is seated upon a dais with eyes wide open and his right arm upraised;[17] and a first-century CE Jain *āyāgapaṭṭa* depicting a Jīna, probably Mahāvīra, seated in a cross-legged posture upon a dais with an open flower behind him, also from Mathura.[18] The reverse of a bronze tetradrachm coin of the Kushan emperor Kaniṣka (*ca.* 100–132 CE) depicts a cross-

Fig. 3.3: Celtic horned god Cernunnos, Gundestrup Cauldron, *ca.* first century BCE. Courtesy: Kit Weiss, National Museum of Denmark

legged figure seated on a low bench-like throne, which is identified by a Bactrian inscription as 'Buddha Maitreya'.[19] From the third century CE onward, one finds a proliferation of sculpted Buddha figures, ranging from central India to the Swat Valley, in which the Buddha is shown seated in 'full lotus posture' with eyes half closed and hands held slightly clasped on his lap.[20]

Here, I will leave aside these intriguing iconographic parallels—between figures who are sometimes horned, sometimes enthroned, and sometimes surrounded by or clothed in representations of animals—to concentrate on the wide-ranging iconographic detail of their cross-legged posture. Is it a yogic posture?[21] If so, then what is one to make of the fact that, following the Indus Valley images, it does not 'resurface' for nearly two thousand years, and that when it does so, it appears at nearly the same time in four geographically distant regions, that is, at Bharhut in central India, in Scythian Central Asia, in Anatolia and Thrace, and in France and Italy? If it is it correct to assume that the posture of the figure represented on seal 420 is a yogic posture, then is this figure a yogin? What is a yogin? If we are to hope to make some sense of these images in their South Asian contexts, then we must attempt to confront image with text. Let us begin with the Buddhist and Jain images, which, apart from that of the goddess Śrī, are the earliest South Asian representations of figures in what may be interpreted as the 'yogic' lotus posture.

There is, in fact a textual record from the Buddhist canon that discusses what may have been the yoga of the period of these sculptures. This record, which has been documented and studied in detail by Johannes Bronkhorst, is enlightening on a number of points. The *Majjhima Nikaya* ('Middle-Length Sayings') figure among the earliest Buddhist scriptures and are considered to have been a part of the Buddha's original teachings to the monks of his fledgling community. A set of teachings in that corpus, dating to no later than the third century BCE, refer disparagingly to a non-Buddhist, probably Jain, method of cultivating the mind, called 'meditation' (*jhāna*/*dhyāna*).[22]

This technique involved, among other things, extreme fasting and complete stoppage of breath, and clenching the teeth while pressing the tongue upward against the palate. According to the text, this practice only gave the Buddha headaches, copious sweating, a sensation of roaring in the ears, great pain, and mental distraction.[23] Against this entirely unsatisfactory set of techniques, the Buddha proposes his own method, which he calls the Four Dhyānas,[24] precisely the non-ascetic, non-self-mortifying path he took to realize enlightenment: this, I would argue, is the practice pictured in the many sculptural representations of the Buddha seated in 'lotus posture' with half-closed eyes. Note, however, that at no point is the term yoga mentioned in the Buddha's teachings, neither with reference to the Jain techniques that the Buddha disparages, nor the one that draws him effortlessly toward enlightenment. The operative terms are, in both cases, jhāna/dhyāna.

One of the practices criticized by the Buddha closely resembles a description found in a Hindu source from a slightly later period. In the context of a discussion of the 'sixfold yoga', the *Maitri Upaniṣad* (MU), datable to the first centuries CE, states that through the fixing of the mind (*dhāraṇā*), effected by 'pressing the tip of the tongue against the palate and suppressing speech, mind, and breath, one sees brahman through insight.'[25] This description also appears to anticipate that of a technique known as the *khecarī mudrā*, which is found about a thousand years later in *haṭha yoga* texts.[26] In addition to containing the earliest mention of the term 'yogin' in the Hindu scriptural record,[27] this MU passage also comprises the earliest Indian mention of a sixfold yoga, whose components it lists as: *prāṇāyāma* (which may or may not have meant breath control here[28]), *pratyāhāra* (withdrawing the senses), *dhyānam* (meditation), dhāraṇā (fixing the mind), *tarka* (insight), and *samādhi* (concentration). Five of these components are found in the eight-limbed yoga formulated in the YS. Markedly absent from the MU list is *āsana*, 'seated posture'. What does this do for tentative identifications of figures seated in a cross-legged pose as yogins?

I would argue that in the centuries around the beginning of the common era, the lotus posture was a mark of royal sovereignty: royal gods or goddesses, their priests, and kings, sat enthroned in this posture, upon a dais, lotus, or cushion. When Buddhas and Jīnas began to be represented anthropomorphically, their cross-legged posture was originally an indication of their royal sovereignty, rather than of any meditative or yogic practice. This hypothesis is supported by a sculpted image from Swat, dated to the first century CE or later, which has been identified as *either a prince or a bodhisattva*. As Cribb has noted,

> While crossed legs and folded hands, postures associated with the practice of meditation, are characteristic of Buddha and Bodhisattva images, and thus suggest that the figure with its bejeweled body is a Bodhisattva, a notable precedent for these postures within a secular context exists in the image of the seated king on the Maues coin.[29]

Elsewhere, a copper coin minted in Taxila under the reign of the first Kushan monarch Kujula Kadphises (middle of the first century CE), depicts a cross-legged figure in an identical pose to that of the Buddha Maitreya on the bronze tetradrachm of the later Kaniṣka, mentioned above, with one important difference: on the reverse of the earlier coin, it is the king himself that is seated in lotus posture.[30] Here, I would suggest that the term 'lotus posture' (*padmāsana*) derives not from the pose itself, which in no way resembles a lotus, but rather from a lotus (*padma*) throne or seat (*āsana*). Such a throne, which is altogether appropriate for the royal goddess Śrī, would also be so for the Buddha, whose royal origins are so emphasized in early iconographic and textual traditions.

YOGA IN THE EARLY HINDU TEXTUAL RECORD

Recall here that in his identification of the cross-legged figure of Mohenjo-Daro seal 420 as a proto-Śiva, Marshall noted that 'Śiva is pre-eminently the prince of Yogīs—the typical ascetic and self-mortifier, whence his names *Mahātapaḥ*, *Mahāyogī*.' It should be noted from the outset that the textual record, from Hindu, Buddhist, and Jain sources, does not authorize an identification—which most historians have blithely assumed—between heat-producing austerities (*tapas[ya]*),[31] breath control (prāṇāyāma), self-mortification, and meditation (dhyāna) on the one hand, and yoga on the other. The terms denote different procedures with overlapping goals; the meanings of the terms vary from source to source; and we have no conclusive evidence for knowing whether they were practised in combination with one another. Of equal significance is the fact that the epithet *mahāyogin* is nowhere applied to the god Śiva prior to the second century BCE to fourth century CE MBh.[32] Of course, one sees very little of Śiva at all prior to the great epic; and nowhere is his so-called 'forerunner' Rudra characterized as a yogin in earlier scriptural sources.

If we are to understand what connection there was, if any, between seal 420 and the earliest Indian narrative accounts of yogins, then we would do well to look at the various uses of the terms yoga and yogin in the MBh. As Peter Schreiner has noted,[33] the term 'yog' appears nearly 800 times in the MBh, of which well over 300 in the didactic teachings of the 'Mokṣadharma' section of the epic's twelfth book, the Śānti Parvan, and nearly 150 in the BhG alone. Generally speaking, didactic or doctrinal discussions of yoga, such as they are found in these two sources, are ambiguous on the meaning of yoga. Both present a multiplicity of meanings for the term, an indication that there were likely many 'yogas' in the air in this period: the same situation is reflected in the coeval YS, whose compiler attempted to reconcile a variety of doctrines and discussion originating from Buddhist, Samkhyan, and 'Yoga' philosophies. When, however, one looks at *narrative* descriptions of the practice of yoga in the great epic, one finds a remarkable uniformity.

In fact, one of the two most common epic uses of the term yoga, when narrativized as a practice undertaken by human practitioners, depicts 'dying as a yogic event'[34] by means of which a hero wills his luminous soul or lifebody to rise up out of his recumbent if not comatose physical body. Humans who are 'yoked to yoga' (*yoga-yukta*) transcend their human condition and rise up to the heavens, as in the case of the awesome Bhīṣma,[35] the heroic Balarāma[36] and Kṛṣṇa,[37] as well as the five Pāṇḍavas, who, together with Draupadī, ascend the snowy fastnesses of the Himalaya to meet their death.[38] Very often, the apotheosis of epic heroes is linked to the sun, as for, example, the warrior Bhūriśravas, who, knowing his end is at hand,

entered into [the state of] going forth [from life] (*prāya*) on the battlefield....Desiring to go to the World of Brahman, he thereupon offered his vital breaths into [his] breaths. He fixed his eye on the sun with his mind placid, in internal acquiescence. Meditating on the great Upaniṣad, that sage became yoked to yoga.'[39]

Similarly, Droṇa, upon hearing the announcement of the death of his son, 'yokes himself to yoga.'[40] Here as well, the sun is evoked in a number of ways. As Droṇa rises toward heaven, it appears that two suns have seemingly merged into a single point, following which he enters into the moon,[41] 'which was shining like the sun'[42] Although not a warrior, the epic Śuka, upon deciding to attain *mokṣa*, 'undertakes yoga' as he gazes upon the rising sun, and is as if drawn across the heavens by his eyes, which are fixed upon the solar orb.[43]

These epic accounts of yogic apotheosis appear to draw upon the same tradition as a passage from the circa sixth-century BCE *Chāndogya Upaniṣad* (ChU),[44] which postulates that the solar rays that creep into the channels of the individual subtle body also constitute the path taken by the dead:

Like a road between two villages goes from one to the other, so too the solar rays go to two worlds, this world below and the world above....But when he is departing from this body, then he progresses aloft (*utkrāmati*) along these very rays (*raśmibhiḥ*)....No sooner does he cast his mind to it, than does he go to the sun. That, verily, indeed is the door of the world (*lokadvāram*), an entrance for those who know....[45] On that subject, this verse: 'There are a hundred and one channels of the heart. One of these passes up to the crown of the head. Progressing aloft (*utkramaṇe*), one goes to immortality....'[46]

The third- to first-century BCE *Kaṭha Upaniṣad* (KU) reproduces the same passage, and links it directly to the practice of yoga, in one of the very rare uses of the term in the entire corpus of the classical Upaniṣads.[47] The MU calls the channel that leads to immortality the *suṣumnā*, along which—through the junction (*yukti*) of breath, the syllable *oṃ*, and the mind—one may progress aloft (*utkramet*).[48] This same channel, 'transpiercing the solar orb, progresses beyond (*atikramya*) [the sun] to the World of Brahman. They [the dead] go by it to the highest station (*parāṃ gatim*).'[49] Elsewhere, the *Praśna Upaniṣad* (PU) explains that the sun gathers all living beings (or life-breaths, *prāṇān*) into its rays (*raśmiṣu*) as it moves across the sky.[50] The first- to second-century CE *Praśna* and the MU are coeval with the MBh, which like the MU evokes the piercing of the solar orb, and links said piercing to the practice of yoga in the following aphorism: 'Two penetrate the orb of the sun: the recluse (parivrad), and the hero who, yoked to yoga (*yogayukta*), has lain down his life on the battlefield.'[51]

These Upaniṣadic and epic accounts also resonate with the earliest of all Indian discussions of yoga—that is, those found in the Vedas. As Boris Oguibénine has noted, the *Ṛg Veda* (RV) first uses the term yoga to refer to 'yoking' a horse to a war-chariot.[52] Later, however, the term is applied to the Vedic poet, who yokes his mind to poetic inspiration, to conjugate his words to both the world of the sacrifice and the world of heaven. In this usage, the 'yogas' of the fire god Agni are what permit him to move between the sacrificial ground on earth and the realm of the gods in heaven.[53] Oguibénine summarizes:

Here one finds incontestable traces of a single unique conception of the [poetic] word as stretching across a gap, and serving to cross over it to connect its two endpoints and create a link between them. One recognizes the same characteristics in the role of the officiating poet in the ancient Vedic sacrificial rite: to construct explanatory correlations and identifications by establishing correlative links between phenomena of different orders, notably between microcosm and macrocosm, between the ritual world and the mythic world, between the human and the divine....To give voice to a correlative link of this sort is to create a means for reducing the distance that separates these phenomena, and to move across this gap, which brings us....to the idea of 'expedition' and 'departure' and 'journey' that [the French Indologist Louis] Renou recognized in the [Vedic] concept of yoga[54]....When [the Vedic poets] underscore [the idea of] yoga, it is its extension that is at play....The warrior aspect of yoga is also linked to departures, journeys, and [military] expeditions.[55]

I have already outlined the epic use of the term 'yoga' in the sense of a warrior's departure for the heavens, the sun and the World of Brahman beyond. What of the yoga of the 'recluse who practices yoga,' the second member of the epic aphorism quoted above? In the MBh, the yoga of non-warrior figures who are 'yoked to yoga' is a different one. The best-known narrativization of yoga of this type involves the Pāṇḍava king Yudhiṣṭhira and his Kaurava uncle Vidura, both of whom are incarnations of the god Dharma. After the final battle has been won, Yudhiṣṭhira withdraws to a hermitage, in the vicinity of which he comes upon Vidura alone in the forest. Yudhiṣṭhira announces himself, at which point Vidura,

fully fixed his gaze upon the king, having conjoined with his faculty of sight the faculty of sight in him. And the wise Vidura, who was fixing his breaths in his breaths and his senses in his senses, also verily entered [Yudhiṣṭhira's] limbs with [his own] limbs. Using his power of yoga (*yogabalam*), he did enter into the king's body. Vidura was seemingly set ablaze with the fiery splendor of the righteous king. Then the king likewise saw that [that] body of Vidura, whose eyes were dull and glassy, and which was propped up against a tree, was devoid of consciousness. He then felt himself to be several times stronger [than before], and the righteous king of great splendor, the son of Pāṇḍu, recalled his entire past; and...the practice of yoga (*yogadharma*) as it had been recounted [to him] by Vyāsa.[56]

In this case, the yogic transfer is final: Vidura has left his now dead body behind to permanently cohabit the body of Yudhiṣṭhira. Other epic accounts of more temporary yogic transfers explicitly designate solar rays—already seen in the ChU and PU passages quoted above—as transfer media. So, for example, a story from the Mokṣadharma-parvan describes a female mendicant (*bhikṣukī*) named Sulabhā who, giving up her former body through yoga (*yogatas*), has taken on the appearance of a beautiful woman to appear before King Janaka of Mithila.[57] Thereafter, she instructs him on the nature of mokṣa after first entering his body:

That connoisseur of yoga entered (*praviveśa*) into the king, having conjoined (*saṃyojya*) his consciousness with [her] consciousness, [his] eyes with [her] eyes, and [his] rays (*raśmīn*) with [her] rays (*raśmibhiḥ*). With the bonds of yoga did she bind him....[58]

Then, at the conclusion of a 160–verse 'inner dialogue' that takes place inside the king's body, Sulabhā states: 'Just as a solitary mendicant would dwell for one night in a an empty citadel, so indeed do I dwell tonight in this body of yours.'[59] A similar scenario is found in the epic account of Vipula, a hermit who protects his guru's wife from the god Indra's advances by yogically (*yogena*)[60] entering into her body.

With [his] two eyes [locked] into her two eyes, having conjoined (*saṃyojya*) his rays in her rays, Vipula was entered into [her] body like the wind into the sky.[61]

Other epic figures who undertake this sort of yogic entry into a foreign body include Kāvya Uśanas[62] and Bharadvāja.[63] Many such non-warrior yogins are identified in the MBh as Bhargavas, descendents of the Vedic sage Bhṛgu. As Robert Goldman has argued,[64] the Bhargavas are a problematic lineage, specialists of Atharvavedic charms and spells who are generally portrayed negatively in the epics as 'military brahmins'[65] whose supernatural powers are often linked to violence, sorcery, confusion, and hostility to gods. With the Bhargavas, we perhaps find ourselves in the presence of an epic bridge between the 'warrior aspect of yoga' that Renou identified in the Vedic literature,[66] and Tantric yogins, to whom we will turn shortly. A passage from the Mokṣadharma section of the didactic epic typologizes the 'Bhargava type' of epic yogin:

practitioners of yoga who are without restraints and endowed with the power of yoga (*yogabalānvitāḥ*) are supreme beings (*īśvarāḥ*) who enter into [the bodies of] the Prajāpatis, the sages, the gods, and the great beings. Neither Yama nor angry Antaka nor death of terrible prowess has dominion over the yogin who is possessed of immeasurable splendor. The practitioner of yoga may act upon many thousands of bodies (*ātmanām*) [at a time], and having obtained [their] power, walk the earth with all of them. And having moreover obtained the objects of his senses, he may again undertake terrible austerities [and] further condense [them, i.e. those other bodies], like the sun does [its] rays of light.[67]

Both of these types of yogic departures from one's body, either into or through the sun or into the body of another creature via the conduits of solar rays, are described aphoristically in the much neglected third section (*pada*) of the YS, which is devoted to supernatural powers:

YS 3.26: 'From perfect discipline (*saṃyama*) on the sun, knowledge of the worlds.'

YS 3.38: 'From loosening the fetters of bondage to the body and from awareness of the bodily processes, the mind's [power of] entering into another [being's] body (*cittasya paraśarīrāveśaḥ*).'

YS 3.39: 'From mastery of the upward breath (*udāna*)... progressing aloft [out of the body] (*utkrānti*).'

It should be noted here that, while a single verse of the YS mentions āsana ('sitting'; 'posture') as one of the eight limbs of yoga, this source does not describe any of the postures of yoga per se. It is only in Vyāsa's circa fifth-century commentary on this verse that any of the sorts of postures later associated with yogic practice are named. The same is the case in the MBh, as E. Washburn Hopkins observed in a groundbreaking article written over a hundred years ago:

'Posture' is a chief concern of the Yogin, but to the Muni this technicality is unknown. Through the whole of the earlier epic I believe there is but one case even suggesting the Yogin [sic] 'posture,' whereas the tales are many which show that the Munis either stood, or hung themselves upside down....[68]

YOGA AND YOGINS IN TANTRIC AND NON-SCRIPTURAL SOURCES

In the fourth century CE, the earliest extant sculptural representations appear of Lakulīśa, the legendary founder of the Pāśupata order who, according to myth, arose when Śiva himself entered into the body of a burning corpse on a cremation ground in western India. In his earliest sculptures, Lakuliśa is represented as a standing figure, iconographically similar to representations of *gaṇas* in the Kushan period.[69] Lakuliśa is termed a yogin in many textual descriptions,[70] and following the fifth- to sixth century he is often portrayed seated upon a lotus in what might be identified as a yogic posture or with a yoga-band (*yoga-paṭṭa*) wrapped around his knees.[71] The earliest textual references to this cloth band date from the same period (Fig 3.4).[72]

I am convinced, however, that Lakulīśa's 'yoga' was not the yoga of postures and mind and breath control, but rather a yoga of the same sort as that described in the MBh. Doctrinally, the Pāśupatas took the yogic god Śiva to be their model, and accordingly, yoga was considered by them to be the union or contact of the individual soul with God, by virtue of which the human practitioner partook of the attributes—that is, the eight supernatural powers (*siddhis*)—of the god Maheśvara.[73] Pāśupata yoga is illustrated in a story from the eleventh-century Kashmiri *Kathāsaritsāgara* (KSS), concerning a certain Vāmaśiva, a Pāśupata 'Lord of Yoga', who, in imitation of Śiva, enters into the body of a corpse on a cremation ground:[74]

In the...cremation ground there lived an old yogin of the Pāśupata sect...[who] was like a second Maheśvara[75]....A young Brahmin had been brought to the cremation ground for burning. When the yogin saw the being that the crowd was mourning, that barely adolescent body, he resolved to enter into it, weary as he was of his own great age. He quickly went to an isolated spot and, shouting with all his might, began to dance with the appropriate gestures and postures. At that moment, the ascetic

Fig. 3.4: Lakuliśa, Mathura, *ca.* fifth–sixth century CE. Courtesy: State Museum, Lucknow, India

(*tapasvin*), abandoning his own body out of a desire for youthfulness, thereupon entered into the corpse of the Brahmin boy by means of yoga (*yogāt*). At that moment, the young Brahmin, revived, arose from the heaped up pyre and began to yawn....[76]

The principle behind this practice is stated aphoristically in the same collection, in ways reminiscent of the MBh account of Yudhiṣṭhira and Vidura:

He who, through yogic yoking (*yogayuktitas*), freely enters into the body of another and penetrates his internal senses and his external senses, with inviolate mind and intellect, as if going from one house to another, such a knower is a Lord of Yoga (*yogeśvara*), [who] immediately recalls everything [about the body he has left behind].[77]

This yoga, of entering into the body of a corpse (often on a cremation ground), is of course a case of *paraśarīrāveśa*, the supernatural power mentioned in the MBh and YS 3.38. Haunting cremation grounds in imitation of Bhairava—a horrific form of Śiva often referred to in the Tantras as the god of tantric yogins—is an important part of the lifestyle of the tantric yogin, and descriptions of figures of this type are common in medieval Indian literature. The identification with Bhairava is stated explicitly in the *Svacchanda[bhairava] Tantra* (SvT), a seminal Kashmiri Tantra dating from about the tenth century:

in this way the yogin lives on (*vartate*). He is able to remain the same by means of another [person's body] (*pareṇa*), and Death cannot carry him off, not even for a billion eons....The yogin, by means of his spontaneous (*svacchanda*) yoga, by living in a world of the spontaneous, joins the ranks of the spontaneous, and becomes identical with Svacchanda [Bhairava].[78]

The most complete description of techniques for a yogin's forced entry into the *living* body of another person is found in the early ninth-century *Netra Tantra* (NT)—a Kashmiri Tantra closely linked to the SvT—which, in its twentieth chapter describes three types of yoga: the supreme (*para*), the subtle (*sūkṣma*) and the gross (*sthūla*). The female yoginīs—who are ambiguously portrayed as both superhuman minions of Śiva and human sorceresses possessed by the superhuman yoginīs—are said in this text to yoke (*yojayante*) *paśu*s (creatures, victims) with Śiva through these three types of yoga, yogas that an experienced yogin may, moreover, employ to ward off the same predatory yoginīs.

Supreme yoga simply consists of the yoginīs' liberation of paśus by internalizing them, that is, eating them, and thereby digesting and destroying the three impurities that separate them from Śiva, in the same way that initiation (*dīkṣā*) by a guru liberates a disciple. Subtle yoga, the text continues, is practised by Mothers and Guhyakas to draw into themselves, by means of their yogic virility (*yogavīryataḥ*), the life force of their victims.[79] The text then goes on to explain how this type of yoga may also be practised by a human connoisseur of yoga (*yogavit*). What the text describes is in fact a succession of forays into a foreign body by different constituents of one's own yogically empowered mind-body complex, without the yogin ever entirely 'leaving himself' or 'losing himself' in that foreign body.

Having entered it via the path of yoga, one envelops that other lifebody (*jīva*) with one's own, and merges with it. One then detaches oneself from that body, taking over its action capacities. Now operating at a distance, from inside one's own body, the yogin next smashes and cuts away the *śakti* of that other body, appropriating it for himself.[80] The connoisseur of yoga (yogavit) heats up and melts down, with the 'solar quality of his consciousness' (*citsūryatvena*), the other body's life essence, which is contained in its *śakti*, 'in the same way that [the] rays [of the moon, according to Kṣemarāja's commentary on this verse] are heated and melted by the rays of the sun (*raśmibhirarkavat*).'[81] He then should yoke (*yojayet*) all of those liquefied and condensed faculties and bodily constituents together in that other body's heart.[82] Then,

> having laid hold of that with his own mind, he should enter [that body again]. Then, advancing into that body-citadel (*puram*) from every side, the yogin should take all that he has melted down and seized and bring it immediately into his own self. In that moment, he brings that other lifebody [into himself], through the use of seals and spells (*mudrāmantraprayogataḥ*). This is the way a yogin should practice subtle yoga.[83]

The yogin described in this NT passage is not simply appropriating the empty shell of a body that has been vacated by its rightful owner—that is, its soul—upon death. By the twelfth century CE, that type of paraśarīrāveśa had become so banal as to figure in a Jain treatise on yoga.[84] His is rather a hostile takeover, an attack on another body-citadel, which involves controlling, subduing, driving away, and even killing another self or soul. Here, then, yoga merges with the types of sorcery or zombification recounted in the Twenty-five Vampire Tales, which form a portion of the late eleventh-century KSS, the 'Ocean of Rivers of Story'. In fact, the KSS material is but a ripple on an ocean of literature on 'sinister yogins', literature found in every South Asian language, ancient and modern, Sanskritic and vernacular, from Nepal to Sri Lanka.

By emulating the divine model Bhairava, the tantric yogins of South Asia have carried forward a body of theory and practice whose origins may be traced back to at least the first millennium BCE. Here, yoga means 'yoking' the mind-body complex of another being to one's own, often by overpowering them, and entering them—that is, possessing them—via the conduits of the solar rays that radiate outward from every human body, and most especially from the eyes. As we have seen, these acts of yogic possession are of three principal types. They may be symbiotic, as in the case of initiation, in which a guru enters into the body-citadel of the disciple (like Sulabhā does for King Janaka), following the Tantric model of the penetration (*āveśa*) or co-penetration (*samāveśa*) of human consciousness with the Bhairava-consciousness of the Tantric godhead; or commensalist, as in the cases of the appropriation of dead bodies by living yogins like the Pāśupata yogin from the KSS; and predatory or parasitic, as in the case of the 'subtle yoga' described in the NT.

These practices dovetail with many historical accounts of yogins, who have been notorious, since the late medieval period at least, in their roles as warriors capable of transforming battlegrounds into charnel grounds, and of assaulting and vanquishing enemy citadels (*puram*). As David Lorenzen demonstrated nearly thirty years ago, historical accounts of regiments (*ākhāḍa*s) of warrior yogins are multitudinous, and it should be noted that the original name of what is commonly known today as the militarized 'Ancient Regiment' (Jūnā Ākhāḍa') of the Dasnāmi order was 'Bhairava Regiment'.[85] Regiments of yogins imply a multiplicity of bodies, in the context of which the advertised power of a yogin to inhabit multiple bodies at the same time obviates the need for enlisting new recruits.

It is the same type of yoga that has also permitted a single individual—Gorakhnāth, the legendary founder of the Nāth Yogīs, for example—to leave a myriad of burial tumuli (samādhis) scattered across South Asia, tumuli said to house the bodies he left behind when he chose to inhabit other, younger, fresher bodies. In this respect as well, the tantric yogin imitates the divine model of Bhairava, which multiplies himself into the eight or sixty-four Bhairavas who are engaged in constant battle with the demonic forces that would otherwise invade the citadel of a worshipper's body, or a temple, a home or any other inhabited space.

Finally, the yogin is, in popular South Asian traditions, none other than the bogey-man or the stock figure of the villain, the terrifying outsider who penetrates sleeping villages under the cover of night to carry off naughty children or unprotected village women. This, I would argue is the most perennial and pervasive understanding of the person/a of the yogin in South Asia: not a meditating sage absorbed in quietistic introspection, but rather, a powerful, terrifying Bhairava-like figure who penetrates the cosms of other peoples bodies, villages, citadels, and armies to conquer his own death by taking the lives of others.

There are other yoga traditions, whose South Asian roots may be traced back to the BhG, the YS, the *Yogaśataka* of Gorakṣanātha and other scriptural sources. To varying degrees, these traditions involve the meditation, breath control, and postures that are the principal descriptors of the colonial category of 'classical yoga'. None, however, appear to be as ancient, perennial, and pervasive as the yoga traditions that have been treated in the present study, in which case the referent of the normative term 'classical yoga' is in need of revision. Better still, the term should simply be abandoned. It is something of a historical irony that in current parlance, the emic term employed by wandering ascetics (who in north India most often call themselves *bābas* or *sādhus*) for a false ascetic or charlatan is '420 Yogi' (in Hindi, *cār sau bīs jogī*). Many times in my interactions with Nāths, Nāgas, and other members of the itinerant (and formerly military) religious orders, I have heard this term used, derisively, for persons who wore the garb of the yogin in order to enjoy the food and shelter offered to holy men by charitable organizations at various pilgrimage sites. In this contemporary usage, the figure 420 is said to refer to the paragraph in the colonial Indian penal code that defines 'cheating and dishonesty inducing delivery of property' as a punishable offence. In the light of the preceding, the same modifier may be applied to the image, on Mohenjo-Daro seal 420, identified by Marshall as a 'proto-Śiva': rather than representing a proto-Śiva or a proto-yogin, it stands as a monument to a flawed classification system: a proto-*cār sau bīs yogī*.

ABBREVIATIONS

BhG	Bhagavad Gītā
ChU	*Chāndogya Upaniṣad*
KSS	*Kathāsaritsāgara* of Somadeva
KU	*Kaṭha Upaniṣad*
MBh	Mahābhārata
MU	*Maitri Upaniṣad*
NT	*Netra Tantra*
PU	*Praśna Upaniṣad*
RV	*Ṛg Veda*
SvT	*Svacchanda Tantra*
YS	*Yoga Sūtras* of Patañjali

NOTES

1. David N. Lorenzen, *The Kāpālikas and Kālāmukhas: Two Lost Śaivite Sects* (New Delhi: Thomson Press, 1972).

2. David N. Lorenzen., 'Warrior Ascetics in Indian History', *Journal of the American Oriental Society*, vol. 98,1978, pp. 61–75. Lorenzen acknowledges earlier contributors to this history in the footnotes to his article: these include J.N. Farquhar, 'The Fighting Ascetics of India', *Bulletin of the John Rylands Library*, vol. 9,1925, pp. 431–52; W.G. Orr, 'Armed Religious Ascetics in Northern India', *Bulletin of the John Rylands Library* 24 (1940), pp. 81–100; J.M. Ghosh, *The Sannyāsis in Mymensingh* (Dacca: Pran Ballav Chakrabarty, 1923); J.M. Ghosh, *Sannyāsi and Fakir Raiders in Bengal* (Calcutta: Bengal Secretariat Book Depot, 1930); Bernard S. Cohn, 'The Role of the Gosains in the Economy of Eighteenth and Nineteenth Century Upper India', *Indian Economic and Social History Review*, vol. 1, 1964, pp. 175–82; and Dirk H.A. Kolff, 'Sannyasi Trader-Soldiers', *Indian Economic and Social History Review*, vol. 8, 1971, pp. 213–20. Since 1978, two important histories of military asceticism in India have appeared: Dirk H.A. Kolff, *Naukar, Rajput and Sepoy: The Ethnohistory of the Military Labour Market in Hindustan, 1450–1850* (Cambridge: Cambridge University Press, 1990); and William Pinch, *Warrior Ascetics and Indian Empires* (Cambridge: Cambridge University Press, 2006).

3. Shukdev Simha (ed.), *Kabīra-bījaka*, (Allahabad: Nilabha Prakashan, 1972), p. 102.

4. John Marshall, *Mohenjo-daro and the Indus Civilization, being an official account of archaeological excavations at Mohenjo-daro carried out by the Government of India between the years 1922 and 1927*, 2 vols (London: Arthur Probsthain, 1931), vol. 1, pp. 52–4.

5. Mircea Eliade, *Yoga: Immortality and Freedom*, second edition (Princeton: Princeton University Press, 1970), p. 355; Alf Hiltebeitel, 'The Indus Valley 'Proto-

Śiva', Reexamined Through Reflections on the Goddess, the Buffalo, and the Symbolism of *vāhanas*', *Anthropos,* vol. 73, nos 5–6, 1978, pp. 768–9; Stella Kramrisch, *The Presence of Śiva* (Princeton: Princeton University Press, 1981), pp. 10–11; Wendy Doniger O'Flaherty, *Śiva, the Erotic Ascetic* (New York: Oxford University Press, 1981), p. 9.

6. Jonathan Mark Kenoyer, *Ancient Cities of the Indus Valley Civilization* (Karachi: Oxford University Press, 1998), pp. 113–15 (Figs 6.20 [H95–2487]; 6.24 [Harappa cat. no. 27]; and 6.25 [H94–2263]).

7. Coomaraswamy, *La sculpture de Bharhut,* translated by Jean Buhot (Paris: Editions d'Art et d'Histoire, 1956), plate 40, fig. 124. The medallion is discussed on p. 83.

8. MBh 1.189.9–48, especially vv. 9, 11, and 39.

9. Elizabeth Errington and Joe Cribb, *The Crossroads of Asia: Transformation in Image and Symbol in the Art of Ancient Afghanistan and Pakistan, An exhibition at the Fitzwilliam Museum, Cambridge, 6 October–13 December 1992* (Cambridge: Ancient India and Iran Trust, 1992), p. 63, figs 27 and 28. The seated royal figure is on the reverse of the Maues coin and the obverse of the Azes coin. Both coins are held in the British Museum, London (1859–3–1–68 and 1894–5–6–604).

10. Robert Fleischer, *Artemis von Ephesos und Verwandte Kultstatuen aus Anatolien und Syrien* (Leiden: Brill, 1973), p. 91.

11. Ibid., plate 8 (Artemis Ephesia in Jerusalem, E 13); plate 34 (Artemis Ephesia in Tripoli, E 60); and plate 35 (Artemis Ephesia, formerly in Bonn, now lost, E 66).

12. Ibid., plate 11: discussion and bibliography, pp. 8–9. This sculpture is item no. 665 in the Naples collection.

13. Hiltebeitel, 'Indus Valley "Proto-Śiva"', pp. 773–92.

14. Jørgen Jensen, *Danmarks Oldtid, Aeldre Jernalder 500 f.Kr.–400 e.Kr.* (Copenhagen: Gyldendal, 2003), pp. 206–21; Paul-Marie Duval, 'Cernunnos, le dieu aux bois de cerf', in *Dictionnaire des Mythologies et des religions des sociétés traditionnelles et du monde antique,* ed. Yves Bonnefoy, 2 vols (Paris: Flammarion, 1981), vol. 1, p. 152.

15. Ibid., vol. 1, p. 152; Ole Klindt-Jensen, *Gundestrupkedelen* (Copenhagen: Nationalmuseet, 1961), p. 11.

16. Ibid., p. 50; Geoffrey Barraclough, *The Times Concise Atlas of World History* (London: Times Books Limited, 1982; Maplewood, Hammond, 1986), p. 15, map 6.

17. Stanislaw J. Czuma, *Kushan Sculpture: Images from Early India* (Cleveland: Indiana University Press, 1985), fig. 12 (text p. 64). This sculpture is housed in the Museum of Fine Arts, Boston, David Pulsifer Kimball Fund 25.437.

18. Ibid., fig. 3 (text p. 53). This sculpture is housed in the State Museum, Lucknow J. 250.

19. Errington and Cribb, *Crossroads of Asia,* fig. 199, p. 200.

20. A stunning example is a seated Buddha from Gandhara, dating to the first half of the third century CE: Czuma, *Kushan Sculpture,* fig. 108 (text, p. 197: Cleveland

Museum of Art, Bequest 61.418). I am grateful to Phil Wagoner for kindly referring me to the sources indicated in notes 17–20.

21. A study that simply juxtaposes seal 420 with photographs of contemporary yoga guru T.K.V. Desikachar practising the *mūlabandha* posture, and concludes that the image on the seal is therefore that of a yogin, is Yan Y. Dhyansky, 'The Indus Valley Origin of a Yoga Practice', *Artibus Asiae*, vol. 48, nos. 1–2, 1987, pp. 89–108.

22. Johannes Bronkhorst, *The Two Traditions of Meditation in Ancient India* (Delhi: Motilal Banarsidass, 1993), pp. 19, 23.

23. Ibid., pp. 1–5.

24. Ibid., pp. 22–4.

25. MU 6.20, quoted ibid., p. 48.

26. David Gordon White, *The Alchemical Body: Siddha Traditions in Medieval India* (Chicago: University of Chicago Press, 1996), pp. 158–9.

27. MU 6.10, noted in E. Washburn Hopkins, 'Yoga-technique in the Great Epic', *Journal of the American Oriental Society*, vol. 22,1901, p. 334.

28. In the Dharma Sūtra literature, that is, several centuries before the common era, *prāṇāyāma* denoted a type of penance and religious rite for removing the taint attaching to acts and omissions that were condemned by the society of the time. At this stage, *prāṇāyāma* had not been identified as a component of yogic practice: P.V. Kane, *History of Dharmaśāstra*, 5 vols, second edition (Poona: Bhandarkar Oriental Research Institute, 1968–77), vol. 5, part 2, p. 1436. Buddhist references to six-limbed (*ṣaḍaṅga*) yoga are substantially later, appearing in the *Guhyasamāja Tantra* and its *Sekoddeśa* and other commentaries.

29. Errington and Cribb, *Crossroads of Asia*, p. 169, fig. 167. See above, no. 9.

30. John M. Rosenfield, *The Dynastic Art of the Kushans* (Berkeley: University of California Press, 1967), pp. 14–15 and plate I, fig. 6. Rosenfield notes the resemblance in composition between this and the Scythian coins described above (note 9). Like those coins, that of Kujala Kadphises also bears Greek and Kharosthi inscriptions. A coin of Vima Kadphises, Kujala's successor and Kaniṣka's predecessor, portrays that king in the same cross-legged pose on its obverse, seated upon a cloud or 'rocky prominence'. On its reverse is a representation of Śiva: ibid., pp. 23–4 and plate II, no. 20. I am grateful to Daniel Michon for this reference.

31. The sole early counter-example of which I am aware is a statement from the *Śvetāśvatara Upaniṣad* (2.12) that a body 'cooked in the fire of yoga' will no longer experience old age or suffering. Kāvya Uśanas's yoga is identified with his tapas in MBh 12.278.12,16, 26.

32. Śiva is termed a *mahāyogin* in MBh 5.66.14 and 12.278.28. The term is applied far more frequently to the epic god Viṣṇu/Kṛṣṇa. Śuka, Vyāsa, and other sages bear the same epithet.

33. Peter Schreiner, 'What Comes First (in the *Mahābhārata*): Sāṃkhya or Yoga?' *Asiatische Studien/Etudes Asiatiques*, vol. 53, 1999, p. 756.

34. Peter Schreiner, 'Fire—its literary perception in the *Mahābhārata*', in Maya Burger and Peter Schreiner (eds), *Studia Religiosa Helvetica Jahrbuch*, vol. 4/5, (Bern: Peter Lang, 1999), p. 141; and Peter Schreiner, 'Yoga—Lebenshilfe oder Sterbetechnik?', *Umwelt und Gesundheit* (Köln), vol. 3, no. 4 (1988), pp. 12–18.

35. MBh 13.154.3–6.

36. MBh 16.5.11–15.

37. MBh 16.5.18–25.

38. MBh 17.1.28, 44; 17.2.1.

39. MBh 7.118.16b, 17a–18b.

40. MBh 7.165.35b.

41. This passage reflects the notion that a component of the transmigrating human body is basically fluid and *lunar* in nature. In his commentary on *Chāndogya Upaniṣad* 5.10.6, found in his *Brahmasūtra Bhāṣya*, Śaṅkara coherently delineates the relationship between the soul, the subtle body, the body of enjoyment—and the moon.

42. MBh 7.165.39a–41a, 41c–42b

43. MBh 12.319.5b–24b, discussed in Hiltebeitel, *Rethinking the Mahābhārata*, pp. 302–3.

44. On the dates of the principal Upaniṣads, see Patrick Olivelle, *Upaniṣads* (Oxford and New York: Oxford University Press, 1996), pp. xxxvi–vii.

45. ChU 8.6.2,5.

46. ChU 8.6.6.

47. KU 6.16, which is framed by 6.11, which 'defines' yoga, and 6.18, the final verse of the Upaniṣad, which alludes to the 'entire set of yogic rules taught by Death'.

48. MU 6.21.

49. MU 6.30.

50. PU 1.6.

51. MBh 5.33.52 (*178 in the critical edition, following 5.33.52 in the K2.4.5; D8.10; K1; and D2.7 manuscripts): *dvāv imau puruṣau loke sūryamaṇḍalabhedinau/ parivrāḍyogayuktaśca raṇe cābhimukho hataḥ//*.

52. Boris Oguibénine, 'Sur le terme *yóga*, le verbe *yuj*-et quelques-uns de leurs dérivés dans les hymnes védiques', *Indo-Iranian Journal*, vol. 27 (1984), p. 85.

53. RV 2.8.1, cited ibid. p. 85.

54. Ibid., p. 87.

55. Ibid., p. 89, citing Louis Renou, 'Quelques termes du Ṛgveda, d. *yoga*', *Journal Asiatique* (1953), p. 178.

56. MBh 15.33.24–29.

57. MBh 12.308.7b, 10a, 12ab. For a discussion, see James L. Fitzgerald, 'Nun Befuddles King, Shows *Karmayoga* Does Not Work: Sulabhā's Refutation of King Janaka at MBh 12.308', *Journal of Indian Philosophy*, vol. 30 (2002).

58. MBh 12.308.16b-17b.

59. MBh 12.308.190ab.

60. MBh 13.40.50a.

61. MBh 13.40.56.

62. MBh 12.278.9–20.

63. MBh 13.31.29–30, noted in Brockington, 'Yoga in the *Mahābhārata*', p. 18.

64. Robert Goldman, *Gods, Priests and Warriors: The Bhṛgus of the Mahābhārata*

(New York: Columbia University Press, 1977), pp. 81–128, summarized in Hiltebeitel, *Rethinking the Mahābhārata*, pp. 110–13.

65. Goldman, *Gods, Priests, and Warriors*, p. 99.

66. See above, note 54.

67. MBh 12.289.24–25.

68. Hopkins, 'Yoga-technique in the Great Epic', p. 369.

69. U.P. Shah, 'Lakulīśa: Śaivite Saint', in Michael Meister, ed. *Discourses on Śiva: Proceedings of a Symposium on the Nature of Religious Imagery* (Philadelphia: University of Pennsylvania Press, 1984), pp. 96–7 and plates 79, 80.

70. Ibid., pp. 96, 100

71. Ibid., plates 81–3 and 86–93.

72. Sir Monier Monier-Williams, *A Sanskrit-English Dictionary etymologically and philologically arranged with special reference to cognate Indo-European languages* (London: Oxford University Press, 1899; Delhi: Motilal Banarsidass, 1984), s.v. 'yoga-paṭṭa,' cites the 5th–7th c. CE *Padma Purāṇa*, the *ca.* 625 CE *Harṣacārita*, and Hemādri's (1260–1309*) Caturvargacintāmaṇi.*

73. *Pāśupata Sūtra* 1.21–26 and the 'Pañcārthabhāṣya' commentary (attributed to Kauṇḍinya), pp. 6, vv. 8–9; p. 41, vv. 17–18; and p. 148, v. 18, cited in Minoru Hara, *Pāśupata Studies*, ed. by Jun Takashima (Vienna: Institut für Südasien-, Tibet-, und Buddhismuskunde, 2002), pp. 34–35.

74. KSS 12.30.23a, 37a.

75. KSS 12.30.21b, 22b.

76. KSS 12.30.31–35.

77. KSS 8.2.60–1.

78. SvT 7.258, 260.

79. NT 20.27ab.

80. NT 20.28a–31b.

81. NT 20.32a–33a.

82. NT 20.33b–34a.

83. NT 20.34b–36b.

84. Hemacandra, the author of an important Jain treatise on yoga entitled the *Yogaśāstra*, discusses entering into the bodies of dead creatures, including humans (Olle Quarnström, *The Yogaśāstra of Hemacandra, A Twelfth Century Handbook on Śvetāmbara Jainism* (Cambridge, MA and London: Harvard University Press, 2002), p. 142).

85. Lorenzen, *Kāpālikas and Kālāmukhas*, p. 46.

REFERENCES

Aranya, Swami Hariharananda (ed. and tr.), *Yoga Philosophy of Patañjali Containing his Yoga aphorisms with the commentary of Vyāsa in the original Sanskrit, and annotations thereon with copious hints on the practice of Yoga* (Calcutta: University of Calcutta, 1981).

Barraclough, Geoffrey ed., *The Times Concise Atlas of World History* (London: Times Books Limited, 1982; Maplewood, NJ: Hammond, 1986).

Brahmasūtra Śāṅkara Bhāṣya with the Commentaries of Bhāmatī, Kalpataru and Parimala, 2 vols, ed. by K.L. Joshi (Ahmedabad and Delhi: Parimal, 1981).

Brockington, John, 'Yoga in the *Mahābhārata*', in Ian Whicher and David Carpenter (eds), *Yoga: The Indian Tradition* (London: RoutledgeCurzon, 2003), pp. 13–24.

Bronkhorst, Johannes, *The Two Traditions of Meditation in Ancient India* (Delhi: Motilal Banarsidass, 1993).

Chāndogya Upaniṣad, ed. with French tr. by Emile Sénart (Paris: Belles Lettres, 1971).

Cohn, Bernard S., 'The Role of the Gosains in the Economy of Eighteenth and Nineteenth Century Upper India', *Indian Economic and Social History Review*, vol. 1 (1964), pp. 175–82

Coomaraswamy, Ananda K., *La sculpture de Bharhut*, tr. by Jean Buhot (Paris: Editions d'Art et d'Histoire, 1956).

Czuma, Stanislaw J., *Kushan Sculpture: Images from Early India* (Cleveland: Indiana University Press, 1985).

Dhyansky, Yan Y., 'The Indus Valley Origin of a Yoga Practice', *Artibus Asiae*, vol. 48, nos 1–2, (1987), pp. 89–108.

Duval, Paul-Marie, 'Cernunnos, le dieu aux bois de cerf', in Yves Bonnefoy (ed.), *Dictionnaire des Mythologies et des religions des sociétés traditionnelles et du monde antique*, 2 vols (Paris: Flammarion, 1981).

Eliade, Mircea, *Yoga: Immortality and Freedom*, second edition (Princeton: Princeton University Press, 1970).

Errington, Elizabeth and Joe Cribb, *The Crossroads of Asia: Transformation in Image and Symbol in the Art of Ancient Afghanistan and Pakistan, An exhibition at the Fitzwilliam Museum, Cambridge, 6 October–13 December 1992* (Cambridge: Ancient India and Iran Trust, 1992).

Farquhar, J.N., 'The Fighting Ascetics of India', *Bulletin of the John Rylands Library* 9 (1925), pp. 431–52.

Fitzgerald, James L., 'Nun Befuddles King, Shows *Karmayoga* Does Not Work: Sulabhā's Refutation of King Janaka at Mbh 12.308', *Journal of Indian Philosophy*, vol. 30 (2002), pp. 641–77.

Fleischer, Robert, *Artemis von Ephesos und Verwandte Kultstatuen aus Anatolien und Syrien* (Leiden: Brill, 1973).

Ghosh, J.M. *The Sannyāsis in Mymensingh* (Dacca: Pran Ballav Chakrabarty, 1923).

———, *Sannyāsi and Fakir Raiders in Bengal* (Calcutta: Bengal Secretariat Book Depot, 1930).

Goldman, Robert, *Gods, Priests and Warriors: The Bhṛgus of the Mahābhārata* (New York: Columbia University Press, 1977).

Guhyasamāja Tantra, ed. by Benoytosh Bhattacharyya (Baroda: Oriental Institute, 1931).

Hara, Minoru, *Pāśupata Studies*, ed. by Jun Takashima (Vienna: Institut für Südasien-, Tibet-, und Buddhismuskunde, 2002).

Hiltebeitel, Alf, 'The Indus Valley "Proto-Śiva", Reexamined through Reflections on the Goddess, the Buffalo, and the Symbolism of *vāhanas*', *Anthropos*, vol. 73, nos 5–6, (1978), pp. 767–97.

——, *Rethinking the Mahābhārata: A Reader's Guide to the Education of the Dharma King* (Chicago: University of Chicago Press, 2001).

Hopkins, E. Washburn, 'Yoga-technique in the Great Epic', *Journal of the American Oriental Society*, vol. 22 (1901), pp. 333–79.

Jensen, Jørgen, *Danmarks Oldtid, Aeldre Jernalder 500 f.Kr.–400 e.Kr.* (Copenhagen: Gyldendal, 2003).

Kabīra-bījaka of Kabīradāsa, ed. by Shukdev Simha, (Allahabad: Nilabha Prakashan, 1972).

Kane, P.V., *History of Dharmaśāstra*, 5 vols, second edition (Poona: Bhandarkar Oriental Research Institute, 1968–77).

Kaṭha Upaniṣad, in Sivananda (1983).

Kathāsaritsāgaraḥ kaśmīrapradeśavāsinā Śrīrāmabhaṭṭsanūdbhavena mahākavi Śrī Somadevabhaṭṭena viracitaḥ, ed. by Jagadish Lal Sastri (Delhi: Motilal Banarsidass, 1970).

Kenoyer, Jonathan Mark, *Ancient Cities of the Indus Valley Civilization* (Karachi: Oxford University Press, 1998).

Klindt-Jensen, Ole, *Gundestrupkedelen* (Copenhagen: Nationalmuseet, 1961).

Kolff, Dirk H.A., *Naukar, Rajput & Sepoy: The ethnohistory of the military labour market in Hindustan, 1450–1850* (Cambridge: Cambridge University Press, 1990).

——, 'Sannyasi Trader-Soldiers', *Indian Economic and Social History Review*, vol. 8 (1971), pp. 213–20.

Kramrisch, Stella, *The Presence of Śiva* (Princeton: Princeton University Press, 1981).

Lorenzen, David, *The Kāpālikas and Kālamukhas: Two Lost Śaivite Sects* (New Delhi: Thomson Press, 1972).

——, 'Warrior Ascetics in Indian History', *Journal of the American Oriental Society*, vol. 98 (1978), pp. 61–75.

Mahābhārata, 21 vols, ed. by Visnu S. Sukthankar, *et al.* (Poona: Bhandarkar Oriental Research Institute, 1933–60).

Maitri Upaniṣad, ed. with a French tr. by Marie-Louise Esnoul (Paris: Adrien Maisonneuve, 1952).

Marshall, John, *Mohenjo-daro and the Indus Civilization, Being an official account of Archaeological Excavations at Mohenjo-daro carried out by the Government of India between the years 1922 and 1927*, 2 vols (London: Arthur Probsthain, 1931).

Monier-Williams, Monier [Sir], *A Sanskrit-English Dictionary etymologically and philologically arranged with special reference to cognate Indo-European languages* (London: Oxford University Press, 1899; Delhi: Motilal Banarsidass, 1984).

Netratantram [Mṛtyuñjaya Bhaṭṭāraka] with the Commentary Udyota of Kṣemarājācārya, ed. by Vajravallabh Dwivedi (Delhi: Parimal Publications, 1985).

O'Flaherty, Wendy Doniger, *Śiva, the Erotic Ascetic* (New York: Oxford University Press, 1981).

Oguibénine, Boris, 'Sur le terme *yóga*, le verbe *yuj*-et quelques-uns de leurs dérivés dans les hymnes védiques', *Indo-Iranian Journal*, vol. 27 (1984), pp. 85–101.

Olivelle, Patrick, tr., *Upaniṣads* (Oxford and New York: Oxford University Press, 1996).

Orr, W.G., 'Armed Religious Ascetics in Northern India', *Bulletin of the John Rylands Library* 24 (1940), pp. 81–100.

Pāśupata Sūtra with Pañcārthabhāṣya of Kauṇḍinya, ed. by R. Ananthakrishna Sastri (Travancore: Tranvancore Sanskrit Series, 1940).

Pinch, William, *Warrior Ascetics and Indian Empires* (Cambridge: Cambridge University Press, 2006).

Praśna Upaniṣad, in Sivananda (1983).

Quarnström, Olle, *The Yogaśāstra of Hemacandra, A Twelfth Century Handbook on Śvetāmbara Jainism* (Cambridge, MA and London: Harvard University Press, 2002).

Renou, Louis, 'Quelques termes du Ṛgveda, d. *yoga*', *Journal Asiatique* (1953), pp. 177–80.

Rosenfield, John M., *The Dynastic Art of the Kushans* (Berkeley: University of California Press, 1967).

Schreiner, Peter (1999a), 'Fire—Its Literary Perception in the *Mahābhārata*', in Maya Burger and Peter Schreiner (eds), *Studia Religiosa Helvetica Jahrbuch*, vols 4 and 5 (Bern: Peter Lang, 1999), pp. 113–44.

——, (1999b), 'What Comes First (in the *Mahābhārata*): Sāṃkhya or Yoga?', *Asiatische Studien/Etudes Asiatiques*, vol. 53 (1999), pp. 755–77.

——, 'Yoga—Lebenshilfe oder Sterbetechnik?', *Umwelt und Gesundheit* (Köln), vols 3/4 (1988), pp. 12–18.

Shah, U.P., 'Lakulīśa: Śaivite Saint', in *Discourses on Śiva: Proceedings of a Symposium on the Nature of Religious Imagery*, Michael Meister (ed.) (Philadelphia: University of Pennsylvania Press, 1984).

Sivananda, Sri Swami, *The Principal Upanishads: Isa, Kena, Katha, Prasna, Mundaka, Taittiriya, Aitareya and Svetasvatara Upanishads with Text, Meaning, Notes and Commentary* (Sivanandnagar: Divine Life Society, 1983).

Svacchandatantram, with the commentary of Kṣemarājā, 2 vols, ed. by Vrajavallabha Dvivedi (Delhi: Parimal Publications, 1985).

Śvetāśvatara Upaniṣad, in Sivananda (1983).

White, David Gordon, *The Alchemical Body: Siddha Traditions in Medieval India* (Chicago: University of Chicago Press, 1996).

Yogaśāstra of Hemacandra. In Quarnström (2002).

Yoga Sūtras of Patañjali. In Aranya (1981).

4. VISUALIZATIONS OF THE HORRIFIC IN BUDDHIST TANTRIC LITERATURE

Benjamín Preciado-Solís

The first time that I ever saw a Tibetan painting, thirty years ago, I was surprised by the horrific figure of Mahākāla, exquisitely painted as a fat black demon dancing wildly, drunk with blood in the midst of an ocean of blood where further demons of horripilant countenances dance too in an orgy of death. In the painting fiendish figures were surrounded by pieces of corpses. Heads, hands, arms, and legs freshly severed from the dead bodies were strung together to form horrifying adornments to the bodies of the drunken demons. The vision of that black landscape with hellish scenes made me wonder about its meaning and what it represented. It was obvious that the artist was an accomplished master and that he dedicated his best efforts to representing those horrible scenes in minutest detail to produce that shocking effect that had moved me. Everything was so perfectly depicted it seemed that the painter knew exactly where to paint each figure with what gory detail.

These terrible depictions full of blood and death often produce the same effect in people that see them for the first time. How is it, one wonders, that such a peaceful doctrine as Buddhism has produced such depictions of ferocious cruelty and violence, of sadistic torture and horrendous crime? What aesthetic canons have produced those masterpieces of exquisite art, of horrific perfection? It is generally said that tantric Buddhism took such imagery from the witchcraft and black magic cults that existed in India from time immemorial and that it used the imagery to awake internal psychic forces in the individual who meditates on them. The visual images are supported by textual descriptions intended to show the particular details of every image and scene to be represented either physically or mentally. There are extensive catalogues of descriptions of images called *Sādhanās* intended to teach the correct method of visualization and meditation for each deity as well as the results to be obtained from such practice. One of such treatises is the *Sādhanā Mālā*, a collection said to be written in the twelfth century in eastern India. In it we find numerous descriptions full of minute details about horrific images. The *Sādhanās* are special texts written for this purpose, but we also find in the Tantras such descriptions of terrible deities and their entourage of corpse-devouring fiends:

The worshipper should conceive himself as the god (Heruka) who stands on a corpse in the Ardhaparyanka attitude. He is well clad in human skin and his body is besmeared with ashes (Fig. 4.1). He wields the Vajra in the right hand and from his left shoulder hangs the Khatvânga with a flowing banner, like a sacred thread. He carries in his left hand the Kapâla full of blood. His necklace is beautified by a chain of half-a-hundred severed heads. His face is slightly distorted with bare fangs and blood-shot eyes. His brown hair rises upwards and forms into a crown which bears the effigy of Aksobhya. He wears a Kundala and is decked in ornaments of bones. His head is beautified by five skulls. He bestows Buddhahood and protects the world from the Mâras (wicked beings).

> Śavasthaṁ ardhaparyaṅkaṁ naracarmasuvāsasaṁ I
> Bhasmoddhūlitagātrañca sphuradvajrañca dakṣiṇaṁ II
> Calatpatākākhatvāṅgaṁ vāme raktakaroṭakaṁ I
> Śatārdhamuṇḍamālābhiḥ kṛatahāramanoramaṁ II
> Iṣaddaṁṣṭrākarālāsyaṁ rakatanetraṁ vilāsinaṁ I
> Piṅgorddhvakeśaṁ Akṣobhyamukuṭaṁ karṇakuṇḍalaṁ II
> Aśthyābharaṇaśobhaṁ tu śiraḥ-pañcakapālakaṁ I
> Buddhatvadāyinaṁ dhyāyāt jaganmāranivāraṇaṁ II[1]

The worshipper should think himself as Yamântaka, one-faced and two-armed, who stands in the Pratyalīdha attitude, carries the a skull full of blood in the left hand and a white staff surmounted by a yellow head still wet with blood, in the right. He is decked in ornaments of snakes and his brown hair rises upwards. He wears garments of tiger-skin, bears the image of Aksobhya on the crown, and is embraced by his Svâbhâ Prajñâ. He stands on the orb of the sun over the double lotus on the back of a buffalo. He (the worshipper) should also meditate upon the

Fig. 4.1: ‘He is well clad in human skin…’, Tibetan woodprint, eighteenth century. Photograph: Benjamín Preciado-Solís

Bhagavatî (Prajñâ) who is one-faced, two-armed, and has variegated ornaments. She stands in the Pratyâlîdha attitude, is intoxicated with wine, wears garments of tiger-skin which slips down her waist and remains in yâb-yum with the god, both standing in the Pratyâlîdha attitude. Thus meditating....

‘Ātmānaṁ Yamāntakaṁ ekamukhaṁ dvibhujaṁ pratyālīḍhapadaṁ raktaparipūrṇakapālavāmakaraṁ sārdrapītamuṇḍāṅkitasitadaṇḍadakṣiṇakaraṁ nāgābharaṇavibhūṣaṇaṁ piṅgalordhvakeṣaṁ vyāghracarmāmbaradharaṁ Akṣobhyamukuṭinaṁ svābha-Prajñāliṅgitaṁ mahiṣopari viśvadalakamalasūryasthaṁ dhyāyāt. Bhagavatīñca dvibhujaikamukhīṁ, vicitrābharaṇaṁ ālīḍhapadasthitāṁ madavihvalāṁ skhaladvyāghracarmāṁśukām Bhagavatā saha sampuṭayogena pratyālīḍhenāvasthitām evaṁ vicintya...'[2]

These iconographic descriptions are meant both to guide the meditator in his visualizations and the painter in the creation of the material representation. Even the production of the painting must be done with materials taken from the cemeteries according to the Hevajra Tantra, 'By a painter who belongs to our tradition, by a yogin of our tradition, this fearful painting should be done and it should be painted with five colours reposing in a human skull and with a brush made from the hair of a corpse.'[3] By these methods and with these materials were painted the masterpieces that we admire today in the great museums of the world. The eighteenth-century thangka representing Mahākāla kept in the Museum Volkenkunde, Leiden, is a fine example of this art. All devouring Time is represented as a ferocious menacing black giant with three staring reddish eyes that protrude from its sockets and a dangerous open mouth showing sharp white fangs ready to cut throats. He has four arms, with a sword and a spear held by the upper hands and a skull cup brimming with mixed brains in the lower ones. From his neck hangs a long garland of human heads and he sits upon a contorted corpse. The demonic figure is surrounded by a halo of flames and is in the midst of a group of dancing demons and demonesses who have the heads of wild beasts.

There was a Tantric practice in use in the twentieth century witnessed in the 1930s by the French traveller and writer, Alexandra David-Neel. She remembers in her book *Mystiques et magiciens du Tibet* how the practitioner of the rite of *chöd* imagines a female deity that comes out of his own head and with a sharp sword beheads him, then cuts his members, tears his skin and opens his belly, while a host of hungry demons waits for the feast. His entrails fall down, the blood runs freely and the repulsive fiends bite, tear, and chew with ugly noises. The practitioner of the rite then repeats liturgical words offering his body. He claims that he pays his debts in this way, offering the body that he loves and cares so much for. He offers his flesh for the hungry ones, his blood for the thirsty, his skin for the naked, and his bones to warm up the cold suffering ones.

The National Museum of History, Taiwan, keeps a thangka depicting Vajravārahi a female deity of terrible character dancing upon a corpse, the dead body of the god Bhairava. Her Sādhanā describes her image in detail:

The worshipper should think himself as the goddess Vajravārahi whose colour is red like the pomegranate flower and who is two-armed. She exhibits in her right hand the vajra along with the raised index finger, and shows in the left the skull and the khatvanga. She is one-faced and three-eyed, has dishevelled hair, is marked with the six auspicious symbols, and is nude. She is the essence of the five kinds of knowledge, and is the embodiment of the sahaja pleasure. She stands in the Pratyalidha attitude, tramples upon the gods Bhairava and Kālaratrī, wears a garland of heads still wet with blood which she drinks.

Ātmānaṁ Bhagavatīṁ Bajravārāhīṁ dāḍimakusumaprakhyāṁ dvibhujāṁ dakṣiṇakareṇa vajratarjanīkākarāṁ vāmena karoṭakhaṭvāṅgadharāṁ ekānanāṁ trinetrāṁ muktakeśāṁ ṣaṇmudrāmudritāṁ digambarāṁ pañcajñānātmikāṁ sahajānandasvabhāvāṁ, pratyālīḍhapadākrānta-Bhairava-Kālarātrikāṁ sārdramuṇḍamālālaṅkṛtagātrāṁ sravadrudhiraṁ pibantīṁ bhāvayet.[4]

The example in the National Museum of History differs only in small details from this description of the Sādhanā. Instead of the *vajra,* (thunderbolt, symbol of the highest illumination) in her right hand she brandishes a butcher's knife to cut the bodies of those brave enough to invoke her.[5] In the Hermitage Museum of Saint Petersburg, Russia, there is another example of a painting of the same goddess.[6] What is important to point out is the horrific character of the deity, who drinks blood from the heads she has just cut from the bodies. She is surrounded by six companions all of the same murderous character, drinking blood and adorned by garlands of heads. These scenes are repeated constantly in the Tantric Buddhist iconography and leave us wondering about the meaning of this sort of imagery.

Here we see again the imagery of death and destruction represented through these deities. They generally wear garlands of heads or skulls and drink blood or brains from a skull-cup. They stand or dance upon a corpse and generally give the impression of ferocious violence intended to provoke intense fear in the spectator. All this imagery is part of the scenery of the cemetery or cremation ground (*smashāna*), a place in ancient India where dead bodies were burnt and sometimes just abandoned. The smashāna acquired in Tantric Buddhism the status of most appropriate place for meditation; it was the natural setting for Tantric yogīs. This is quite evident from the role the smashāna came to play in the design of the *mandala* (graphic device or painting for meditational purposes) of these deities. A scheme of eight smashānas was developed around the central part of the mandala and the main deity. This meant that the meditator had to pass through these cemeteries to attain the vision of the divinity. Each one of the eight smashānas had a particular imagery:

Homage to the blessed Lokeśvara. Having to declare the eight cemeteries, it is said:

To the East there is the cemetery called Gtum-drag. In it there is the tree aura on which is its lord (the yaksa) Gtum-drag white in colour, he has the head of an elephant. Near the tree: Dban-po, lord of the corresponding region. He is yellow in colour, his right hand holds the vajra and his left one is in the attitude of threatening; his vehicle is Sa-srun the white elephant. Near him is Vâsuki the serpent of yellow colour; above is the cloud sgra-sgrogs of blue colour.

To the north is the cemetery Tshan-tshin-can. In it is the Tree of 'Illumination' on which is its lord Gahvara. He has a human head and is of yellow colour. Near the tree is Lusnan lord of the corresponding region, yellow in colour; his right hand is in the attitude of protection and the left one has a club. His vehicle is a corpse. The serpent is Hjog-po of red colour. Above is the cloud smugs-pa of white colour.

To the west is the cemetery Hbar-bas-hkhrigs-pahi-ken-rus. In it stands the tree Mya-nan-med/Aśoka on which is its lord Hbar-bas-hkhrigs-ken-rus who has the head of a sea-monster and is yellow in colour. Near the tree is the lord of the corresponding region Varuṇa, white in colour. His vehicle is the sea-monster (*chu-srin, makara*); his right hand is in the attitude of the mudrâ of menacing and in the left he holds a noose. The serpent is Stobs-kyi-rgyu/Karkotaka, green in colour. Above is the cloud drag-po/ghora of white colour.

To the south is the cemetery Hjigs-sde/Bhisana. In it is the tree barura/bibhîtaka (a variety of myrobolan) on which is its lord Hjigs-sde/ Bhîsana, who has a human head and of black colour. Near the tree is the lord of the corresponding region, namely Gsin-rje/Yama, of black colour. In the right hand he holds a club and in the left a noose; his vehicle is the buffalo. The serpent is Padma, of white colour. Above is the cloud hkhrigs-pa/âvarttaka of yellow colour.

In the region of the god of the fire (south-east) is the cemetery Dpal-gyi-nags/Lakṣmīvaṇa, in which stands the tree karañja; above it is its lord Dpal-gyi-nags/Laksmîvana, who has the head of a goat and is of white colour. Near the tree is the lord of the corresponding region Byin-za/Hutâsana (namely fire), of red colour. In the right hand is the rosary and in the left the vessel of consecrated water; his vehicle is the goat. The serpent is Pad-machen/Mahâpadma, of white colour. Above is the cloud hkhyil/ghûrnita of red colour.

In the region of the south-west (*Bden-bral, Nirrti*) is the cemetery Hjigs-pahi-mun-pa/Ghorândhakâra. In it stands the tree udumbara on which is its lord Hjigs-pa/Bhîsana, who has the head of a buffalo and is of black colour. Near the tree is the lord of the corresponding region Srin-po Bden-bral/Nirrti of black colour. His right hand is in the mudrâ of menacing and his left holds a human head. The serpent is Mthah-yas/ Ananta, of blue colour. Above is the cloud sgra-sgrogs/garjita of white-yellow colour.

In the region of the wind (north-west) is the cemetery Kîli-kîlar-sgrogs-pa/Kilikilârava in which stands the tree srid-sgrub/arjuna; above it is its lord Kîli-kilar-sgrogs who has the head of a buffalo and is grey in colour. Near the tree is the lord of the corresponding region, the god of the wind, of white colour. He holds two standards in both hands. His vehicle is the antelope. The serpent is Rigs-Idan/Kulika, of variegated colour. Above is the cloud hbebs-pa/varsana of green colour.

In the region north-east is the cemetery Ha-har-rgod-pa/Attahâsa; in it stands the tree nyagrodha on which is its lord Ha-har-rgod-pa, who has the head of a bull and is white in colour. Near the tree is the lord of the corresponding region Dban-Idan/Isâna, of the light blue colour. In the right he holds a trident and in the left a skull; his vehicle is the bull. The serpent is Dun-syon/Sankhapâla of yellow colour. Above is the cloud gtum-mo/canda, multicoloured. All the lords of the regions have human heads and two hands.[7]

Fig. 4.2: 'Two horrible skeletons swirl and move in a mockery of dancing...', Tibetan fresco, western Tibet. Photograph: Benjamín Preciado-Solís

As we can see the smashāna or cremation ground was an essential place for Tantric practice, either in actual or in an imaginary form. The landscape is filled with funeral pyres, dead bodies in different stages of decay, and scattered human bones as well as wild beasts and birds that prey upon the corpses. The yogī dwells in these horrible surroundings and meditates upon death, decay, and destruction as the essence of reality. One other image related to the smashāna, particularly in Tantric Buddhism, is that of the dancing skeletons, a bizarre scene in which we are witnesses to a macabre performance. Two horrible skeletons swirl and move in a mockery of dance pretending to be gay and elegant men and women, gentlemen and, ladies forgetting their dismal fleshless condition (Fig. 4.2). The grotesque scene induces a sense of revulsion and fosters serious thought about the human condition.

It has been generally accepted that this horrific imagery is characteristic of Tantric Buddhist cults. This is true but we can also trace the origin of the horrific imagery as well as the meditation practices to much earlier times in the history of Buddhism. Both, the terrible (*ghora*) images and the smashana practices can be found in the Pali canon and in Buddhist Sanskrit texts pre-dating Tantric Buddhism by many centuries. We have also to point out that a concept of the horrific (ghora) was included as one of the aesthetic categories in Indian theories of art. The horrific ghora is one of the eight original *rasas* or aesthetic categories associated with artistic works. We find examples of the use of this aesthetic resource in numerous Sanskrit works such as the Rāmāyaṇa and Mahabhārāta and, even closer to the theme that we are dealing with, in the drama *Malatimadhava* of Bhavabhuti and in the collection of stories *Vetalāpanchavimsati* (Twenty-five Tales of a Vampire). The Buddhists took this aesthetic theory and incorporated it into their artistic productions both plastic and literary. Take, for instance, the description of the emaciated body of Śākyamuni after his ascetic practices:

And my body which took for food only a single berry became extremely thin and weak. O monks, like the knots of the âsîtakiî plant or the knots of the kâlika plant were my limbs and their joints. Like the sides of the crab, so also were my sides. My rib cage was like an old stable with its sides caved in, so that light shines through—so likewise, you could see light shine through my body. The vertebrae of my spine were like the uneven contours of a braid of hair—high and low, uneven. So were the vertebrae of my spine. Like a gourd cut too young which has withered and finally dried up completely, my head withered until it looked old and wrinkled and dry. Like the reflections of the stars in a well during the last month of summer when the water is so low the reflections are difficult to see, so also my eyeballs sank in, becoming difficult to see. Like the foot of the goat or the hoof of the camel were my shoulders, my stomach, my chest, and the rest.[8]

This minute description shows the deep interest shown by the poet in the scene, and his artistic mastery in portraying the state of emaciation reached by the Buddha through his austerities. But we not only find such exquisite stylistic relish on the horrible in the texts, we have visual representations of the famished Śākyamuni in the art of the Gandhara region in the so called Indo-Greek style. There is, of course, the famous meditating Buddha of the Lahore Museum in Pakistan, a masterpiece that carefully depicts the appearance of the body of Śākyamuni. Bones, tendons, sinews, and veins are seen under the parched skin of the ascetic.

We find also this meticulous care put in the representation of the human body in the images not of emaciated anchorites, but in those of muscular guardians of the doors of palaces and temples (*dvārāpālas*). The tradition of representing ferocious door guards was taken from India into China and we find many examples in Chinese art of these terrible giants threatening to tear into pieces the fool who tries to cross the threshold of the sacred precinct. In the Lung Men caves we can see various gigantic carvings of dvārāpālas showing their carefully delineated muscular bodies and their beastly grimaces, ready to pounce and break bones, eat flesh, and drink blood. In the collection of the National Museum of History in Taiwan, we can see a pair of ceramic guardians that very well exemplify the type of ferocious Chinese dvārāpālas.[9]

The demonic visions are also present in the pre-Tantric Buddhist texts. The well-known scene of the temptation of Śākyamuni is

Fig. 4.3: 'Some were eating human flesh and blood…', Tibetan woodprint, eighteenth century. Photograph: Benjamín Preciado-Solís

an excellent example of representations of terrible demons in the Buddhist tradition:

The demons' heads and their hands and feet were twisted and distorted; their bellies were distended; their heads and faces and eyes were flaming, shining with a terrible fierceness; their eyes shone red and flashing like those of the venomous black serpent; their canine teeth stuck out, enormous and frightful; their tongues hung from their mouths, thick and rough like matting.

Some of the demons spewed forth venom; others, like garudas, grasped sea-snakes in their hands. Some were eating human flesh and blood, gnawing on hands and feet, heads, livers, entrails, and bones (Fig. 4.3). Their bodies were of different colors: greenish, dark blue, reddish brown, blue, red, and yellow. Some had crooked eyes or eyes hollow like wells, eyes inflamed or torn out and hanging; eyes slyly squinting or twisted; eyes flashing and deformed.

Some of the demons approached proudly, carrying fiery mountains and riding atop other fiery mountains. Others made their way toward the Bodhisattva grasping uprooted trees. Some had ears like goats, hogs, or demons; like the hanging ears of an elephant, or the ears of a boar. Some had no ears at all. Some looked like skeletons with emaciated bodies but stomachs distended. Others had stomachs like pitchers and feet like skulls. Their skin and flesh were shriveled, their ears, noses, hands, and feet, or eyes and heads were missing. Some in their desire to drink blood were cutting of each others' heads...Some of the demons were wearing garlands of severed human fingers and garlands made of human bones and skulls.[10]

This description from the *Lalitavistārā* is a clear example of the aesthetic interest in the representation of horrific and terrible scenes. Here again, the poet seems to enjoy the occasion to show his mastery of style in the depiction of a tremendous orgy of violence and aggression. Such scenes, so common in Tantric Buddhism as we have just seen, were prevalent in Buddhism many centuries earlier. This particular image has been represented thousands of times, both in painting and sculpture, throughout the Buddhist world. There is a very famous piece from the Amarāvati stūpa kept at the Guimet Museum in Paris that shows a similar scene. In these sculptures one sees the dependence of the Buddhist writers on the aesthetical canons of ancient India, as it is also evident the dependence of visual iconographic art on the literary texts. The artists are clearly guided in their representations by the texts produced from literary and religious motives. The close association between the texts of the Sādhanās and the Tantric images is also not original to Tantric Buddhism.

An interest in the decaying body can also be found in the Pāli canon. In a passage from the *Satipatthana Sutta* we find an instruction for the monks to meditate on the parts of the body:

Furthermore...just as if a sack with openings at both ends were full of various kinds of grain—wheat, rice, mung beans, kidney beans, sesame seeds, husked rice—and a man with good eyesight, pouring it out, were to reflect, 'This is wheat. This is rice. These are mung beans. These are kidney beans. These are sesame seeds. This is husked rice.' In the same way, monks, a monk reflects on this very body from the soles of the feet on up, from the crown of the head on down, surrounded by skin and full of various kinds of unclean things: 'In this body there are head hairs, body hairs, nails, teeth, skin, flesh, tendons, bones, bone marrow, kidneys, heart, liver, pleura, spleen, lungs, large intestines, small intestines, gorge, feces, bile, phlegm, pus, blood, sweat, fat, tears, skin-oil, saliva, mucus, fluid in the joints, urine.' 'In this way he remains focused internally on the body in & of itself, or focused externally...unsustained by anything in the world. This is how a monk remains focused on the body in & of itself....It is as if a monk would see a body left in the *smashana,* one, two or three days alrady dead, swollen, whitish, starting to rot. Then he gathers his thoughts on that body: This body of mine will also pass through the same process, it will be like this, still it has not come to that.[11]

This description of the parts of the human body is the immediate antecedent to the meditation on a corpse. This practice is not exclusive to Tantric Buddhism and was developed from the earliest times by the Buddhist monks. Shantideva wrote his famous treatise, the *Bodhicaryavātara,* in the seventh century and there he prescribes a meditation on a dead body. It is the body of a woman who was the cause of carnal temptation to the meditator:

Here is the body for which you honoured the procuress, for which you accepted sin and shame, for which you risked your own life and destroyed your fortune. That body by whose embraces you enjoyed supreme delight is but these bones; here they are, free now, you can hold them in your arms as you desired, why don't you rejoice? Here is the face of your beloved...that face is now devoured by vultures as if they could feel your own despair. Look at it, why do you now go away? That same face that you jealously guarded from other's glances, why don't you protect it now? Seeing this lump of flesh devoured by vultures and jackals you realize that she whom you adorned with garlands and sandal-oil is now the food of others. If you shiver looking at this motionless skeleton, why did you not fear it when it was alive? When it was covered with flesh it caused your passion, why is it repugnant to you without its flesh?[12]

The terrible experience of contemplating the corpse of a loved person may cause such a shock as to take one to abandon the world and retire into a religious life. That is exactly what happened to the Duke of Gandia when he saw the rotten corpse of Queen Isabel of Portugal, wife of Emperor Charles the V. That vision would lead the Duke to renounce the world and join the Jesuit order to become, after his death, Saint Francis of Borja.

There is a practice of meditation on the 'Ten Perceptions of Putrescence' found in several Pāli texts such as the famous *Visuddhi Māggā*. One version of this meditation appears in the *Vimuttimāggā*, a Pāli text of around the ninth century, no longer extant in its original language but found only in a Chinese translation. In it, we find a long practice of meditation on the decaying signs of a corpse. Bloatedness, festering, worminess, and other nauseating states of putrescence are described in detail in a horrific scene worthy of the most extreme Tantric texts:

Q. What is the perception of bloatedness? What is the practising of it? What are its salient characteristics function and near cause? What are its benefits? How is the sign grasped?

A. 'The perception of bloatedness': The state of being swollen throughout like a cast off smelly corpse which distends its bag of skin—this is called 'bloatedness.' The viewing of bloatedness with right knowledge—this is called 'perception'. The training and the undisturbed dwelling of the mind on that perception—this is called the practicing of it. The sending forth of the mind into the perception of bloatedness is its salient characteristic. The disgust connected with the perception of bloatedness is its function. Reflection on malodour and impurity are its proximate cause.

'What are its benefits?': Nine are the benefits of the perception of bloatedness. Thus: A man is able to gain mindfulness with respect to the interior of his body, he is able to gain the perception of impermanence and the perception of death. He increases disgust and overcomes sense-desires. He removes the clinging-to-form and well-being. He fares well and approaches the ambrosial.

'How is the sign grasped?': The new yogi who grasps the sign of the putrescence of bloatedness goes alone, without a companion, established in mindfulness, undeluded, with his faculties drawn inwards and his mind not directed at external things, reflecting on the path of going and coming. Thus he goes to the place of putrescent corpses. Avoiding contrary winds, he remains there, standing or sitting, with the putrescent sign before him, and not too far from nor too near it. And that yogin makes a rock, an ant-hill, tree, bush, or a creeper, near the place where the putrescent thing lies, one with the sign, one with the object, and considers thus: 'This rock is impure, this is the impure sign, this is the rock'. And so also with the ant-hill and the others…

Why does he go without a companion? It is for the sake of acquiring calmness of body. 'Established in mindfulness' means: 'Owing to nondelusion the faculties are drawn inwards and the mind does not go to external things'.

Why does he reflect on the path of going and coming? It is for the sake of acquiring calmness of body. Why does he avoid contrary winds? It is for the sake of avoiding malodour. Why does he sit neither far nor near the sign? If he sits far, he cannot grasp the sign. If he sits near, he cannot get a dislike for it, or see its nature. If he does not know its nature, he is not able to grasp that sign. Therefore, he sits neither too far from nor too near it. Why does he consider the sign on all sides? It is for the sake of non-delusion. Non-delusion is thus: When a yogin goes to a still place and sees the putrescent sign, fear arises in him; at such a time if the corpse appears to stand up before him, he does not stand up, but reflects. In this way he knows, recollects, rightly understands, regards well and fully investigates the sign. In the same way he considers all signs. This is (the indication of) non-delusion.

Q. Why does he grasp the sign in ten ways? A. It is for the sake of binding the mind...

One, two or three nights after death, the body becomes discoloured, and appears as if it were stained blue. This is the discolouration sign. This discolouration is called the blue sign. The understanding of this through right knowledge is called the perception of discolouration….

'Festering': Two or three nights after death, the body festers and matter exudes from it like ghee that is poured out. This is the festering of the body. The understanding of this through right knowledge is called the perception of festering...

'The fissured' means: 'What resembles the scattered parts of a body that has been hacked with a sword'. Again, a corpse that is thrown away is also called the fissured, The understanding of this through right knowledge is called the perception of the fissured...

'The gnawed': (leavings of a) corpse on which crows, magpies, brown kites, owls, eagles, vultures, wild pigs, dogs, jackals, wolves, tigers, or leopards have fared—this is called 'the gnawed...'

'The cut and the dismembered': Corpses, lying in various places, of those done to death with stick, sword or arrow—these are called, 'the cut and the dismembered...'

The blood-besmeared state of the body and the severed limbs is known as 'the blood-stained...'

'Worminess': The state of a body covered with worms as with a heap of white pearls is called 'worminess'. The understanding of this through right knowledge is called 'the perception of worminess...'

What is 'the bony'? The state of bones linked chain-like by means of flesh, blood and sinews or by sinews without flesh and blood, or without flesh and blood is called 'the bony...'

This is in accordance with the teaching of the *Abidhamma:* 'One dwells without passion and the rest practises the first meditation, *jhâna*, rightly, dwells on the perception of bloatedness and causes the arising of the boundless object.' The great Elder Singâlapitâ uttered this stanza:

The heir of the Buddha, he,
the almsman, in the fearful wood,
has with 'bony-precept' filled
this earth, entirely.
I think this almsman will,
in no long time, abandon lust.[13]

In this text translated from the Pāli into Chinese by Tipitaka Sanghapala of Funan and now into English, we can see the high degree of importance given to this kind of meditation. We have edited the passage to make it shorter but the methodical care put into the explanation of every detail of the practice is still evident. The signs of putrescence are described and explained in detail one by one. The monk is led step by step through all the stages of the meditation and taught the meaning of it and its results. With this we close our review of the sources of the horrific (ghora) imagery of Tantric Buddhism and confirm that its origin comes from the orthodox Buddhist tradition and not from black magic cults, even if these cults are also incorporated within the Tantric practices. We have also shown that the aesthetics of the horrific was an accepted trait within Indian literary and visual theories of art and that Buddhist Tantric art taps that tradition in order to produce the superb works of art found all over the Buddhist world.

Horror and fear as human sentiments or emotions are always present in religious systems and values. In fact, there are assumptions that the origin of religion can be found in the fear and horror of death. Both Buddhism and Hinduism can be considered as religious systems built on the theme of salvation or liberation. But salvation or liberation from what? From the grip of death, both in this world and in the after life. Ultimately, all religions try to give an answer to the mysteries of life and death, which form the core of religious and philosophical enquiries. In this context, the sentiment of horror and the horrific beings and situations have been utilized to communicate several notions that fulfill specific mechanisms within each religious tradition or school.

In the three examples that we have presented from Buddhism, we find three different uses of the horrific in different contexts. First, as part of the temptation of the Buddha to be. The texts and later iconography emphasize the horrific character of a part of the visions confronted by Siddhārtha Gautama during the final process of his enlightenment. Devils, demons, ghouls, witches, and other horrific creatures prey over the solitary yogī in search of liberation, virtually at the doorstep of salvation, trying to prevent him from his goal. In this example we have the image of the hero-saint overcoming all perils and fears through his unshakable determination and valour. The horrific image in this case is used to underline the greatness of the act of liberation and that of the obstacles encountered.

The second example of the use of horrific images in the Buddhist tradition is similar in certain respects to the first one but is different in quality and context. In both the enlightenment seeker is striving

Fig. 4.4: 'The yogi...must overcome his fears and remain calm and firm...', Rāvaṇa-kā khāi cave, Ellora, Maharashtra. Drawing by James Burgess. Photograph: Benjamín Preciado-Solís

to reach the goal of liberation, but in the former one we have the hero-saint directly facing the jaws of hell while in the latter one the protagonist is an ordinary monk following the process of training his senses and mind. In this case the practitioner must contemplate the horrifying process of rotting and decay of a corpse, all the time meditating on the impermanence of all phenomena, and especially of the human body. At the same time he must maintain calmness and steadiness in the disturbing surroundings of the charnel ground, the smashāna, favourite haunting place of *rākṣasas*, *piśācas*, and *preta*, (demons, ghouls, and hungry ghosts).

Is this place, the smashāna, and these beings, the horrific inhabitants of the charnel ground, we find the central attributes of the third example. Here we have a different ideology at play, no longer involving the liberation ideal but entailing the obtaining of magical power which now moves the seeker into these dangerous and terrible surroundings. The yogī, as in the second example, must overcome his fears and remain calm and firm, but he has also to defeat the dangerous creatures that roam around him in order to dominate them and obtain their powers for his own benefit (Fig. 4.4). Here we are in the Tantric milieu, where the hero- saint is turned into a hero-magician and warrior, an intrepid and fearless man that dares to enter the realm of the demons and challenge them and subdue them by the force of his unshakable will. We may have doubts about the reality of the magical powers to be obtained but the strength of character and sheer will power are clearly evident in the secret rituals in the horrific charnel ground.

Is it the case that Indian society had a morbid taste for tales of haunted places, charnel grounds infested with ghouls, and animated corpses? Or do these stories and pictures of fearless men, brave heroes that dominated their own fears and vanquished the forces of hell, carry other lessons?

NOTES

1. *Sâdhanamâlâ*, B. Bhattacharya, *The Indian Buddhist Iconography.* (Calcutta: Firma K.L. Mukhopadhyay (Calcutta, 1958), p. 155.
2. Ibid., p. 513. Bhattacharya, *The Indian Buddhist Iconography*, p. 167.
3. Hevajra Tantra I.10.19–27
4. B. Bhattacharya, p. 218.
5. Cat. 6883. no. 127, *Catalogue of Exquisite Collection*
6. M. Rhie, and R. Thurman, *Wisdom and Compasión. The Sacred Art of Tibet.* p. 258, (New York: Harry N. Abrams, 1991).
7. Rnal-hbyor-pa. Small treatise on the eight cemeteries. Tucci, 1935, vol. III–2, pp. 175–9.
8. *Lalitavistāra Sūtra, the Voice of the Buddha.* 1983, p. 506.
9. Cat. 75 and 91, nos. 40 and 41 *Catalogue of Exquisite Collection.*
10. *Lalitavistāra Sūtra,* (1983).
11. *Satipatthana Sutta, the Foundations of Mindfulness,* 1993.

12. *Bhodhicaryavātara* 8.2.
13. Arahant Upatissa, 1995.

REFERENCES

Bhattacharya, B., *The Indian Buddhist Iconography* (Calcutta: Firma K.L. Mukhopadhyay, 1958).

Casey Singer, Jane, *Selection 1994. Rossi Gallery* (London: Rossi Publications,1994).

Chandra, Lokesh, *Buddhist Iconography* (Delhi: International Academy of Indian Culture, 1991).

Clark, W.E., *Two Lamaistic Pantheons* (New York: Paragon, 1965).

David-Neel, Alexandra, *Mystiques et Magiciens du Tibet* (Paris, Plon, 1929).

Finot, Louis, 'Manuscrits Sanskrits de Sadhanas retrouves en Chine', *Journal Asiatique* (Jul–Sept. 1934), pp. 1–86, Paris.

Huntington, Susan, *The Pala-Sena Schools of Sculpture* (Leiden: E.J. Brill, 1984).

Lalita-vistara, P.L. Vaidya (ed.), Buddhist Sanskrit Texts, No. 1, Darbhanga, The Mithula Institute, 1958.

Lhundup, Geshe y Hopkins, J., *Teoría y Práctica del Budismo Tibetano* (Barcelona: Ediciones Aura, 1977).

____ *Lalitavistara Sutra, the Voice of the Buddha* (Berkeley: Dharma Publishing, 1983).

Li Jicheng, *The Realm of Tibetan Buddhism* (Pekin: Foreign Languages Press, 1991).

Lohia, Sushama, *Lalitavajra's Manual of Buddhist Iconography* (New Delhi: Aditya Prakashan, 1991).

Mallman, M.T. *Introduction a l'iconographie du tantrisme bouddhique* (Paris: Bibliotheque du Centre de Recherches sur l'Asie Centrale, 1975).

Meisezahl, R.O., 'L'Etude iconographique des huit Cimetieres d'apres le traite Smasanavidhi de Luyi' in *Geist und Ikonographie des Vajrayana-Buddhismus* (VGH Wissenschaftsverlag, St Augustin).

Rhie, M. and Thurman, R., *Wisdom and Compassion: The Sacred Art of Tibet* (New York: Harry N. Abrams, 1991).

Samten, Ngawang, *Mañjusri: An Exhibition of Rare Thankas* (Varanasi: Central Institute of Higher Tibetan Studies, 1986).

____ *Satipatthana Sutta: The Foundations of Mindfulness*, tr. Nyanasatta Thera (Kandy: Buddhist Publication Society, 1993).

Snellgrove, David L., *Indo-Tibetan Buddhism* (London: Serindia Publications, 1990).

Trungpa, Chögyam, *Visual Dharma: The Buddhist Art of Tibet* (Berkeley: Shambhala, 1975).

Tucci, Giuseppe, *Teoría y práctica del mandala* (Barcelona: Barral Editores).

____ *Tibet. Land of Snows* (New York: Stein and Day, 1967).

____ *Tibetan Painted Scrolls* (Rome: Librería dello Stato, 1949).

____ *The Temples of Western Tibet and Their Artistic Symbolism*, (New Delhi (reprint 1989): Aditya Prakashan, 1935).

Upatissa, Arahant, *The Path of Freedom (Vimuttimagga)*. Tr. from the Chinese (Kandy: Buddhist Publication Society, 1995).

Von Glassenapp, H., *Misterios Budistas* (Buenos Aires: Editorial Schapire, 1965).

Waddell, L. Austine, *Tibetan Buddhism* (New York: Dover Publications, 1972).

Wayman, Alex, *The Buddhist Tantras: Light on Indo-Tibetan Esotericism* (Delhi: Motilal Banarsidass, 1990).

Farrow, G.W. and Menon I., *The Concealed Essence of The Hevajra Tantra*. With the commentary Yogaratnamala (Delhi: Motilal Banarsidass, 1992).

5. IN SEARCH OF RAMANAND
THE GURU OF KABIR AND OTHERS

Purushottam Agrawal

Ramanand is a unique figure in the religious and literary history of northern India.[1] He is widely celebrated as the guru of famous saint-poets Kabir, Raidas, and Pipa. Yet, Ramanand remains obscure so far as his own life is concerned. On the one hand, he has been a source of inspiration for many intellectuals who have questioned and criticized Brahmin supremacy until as late as the early twentieth century. On the other, more recent academic scholars often describe him as the epitome of Brahmin orthodoxy and orthopraxy. The irony lies in the fact that it was one such interrogator of Brahmin supremacy within the Ramawat *sampraday* (sect)—an early twentieth-century scholar named Bhagwadacharya—who contributed most directly to the construction of the Brahmin image of Ramanand.

It is interesting to note that whatever little we know of Ramanand is gathered from medieval vernacular sources—the hagiographies found in the Sant and Vaishnava traditions and the poetic compositions attributed to him in the Adi Granth and *Sarvangis* (collections of compositions of various bhakta poets)of Rajjab and Gopaldas. By contrast, Sanskrit writings from medieval north India take no notice of Ramanand at all.

Yet modern scholarship clearly privileges two Sanskrit works attributed to him, the *Ramarchan Paddhati* and the *Vaishnava Matabaj Bhaskar* in determining his world view. We will also discuss a third, the *Ananda-Bhashya*. For the sake of convenience let us call Ramanand as reflected in the *Sarvangis* and Adi Granth, the 'Hindi Ramanand' and Ramanand reflected in Sanskrit works attributed to him, the 'Sanskrit Ramanand'. I hope to demonstrate that the privileged position of Sanskrit Ramanand is not rooted in any serious research but in uncritical acceptance of a recently constructed image of Ramanand as an orthodox acharya (preceptor and teacher) of the Ramawat sampraday. Because of this acceptance the Hindi Ramanand has been effectively marginalized in academic discourse on the bhakti sensibility.

Similarly interesting is the fact that all pre-modern references to Kabir make the following two points: Kabir was born a Muslim weaver, and he was a disciple of Ramanand. But modern scholarship, particularly in the Western academy, has convinced itself that Ramanand could not have been even a contemporary of Kabir, not to talk of any connection between the two. David Lorenzen and Pinuccia Caracchi however, remain exceptions to this scholarly consensus.

As far back as 1978, Richard Burghart noted the 'poverty of information' regarding the life and views of Ramanand.[2] Over the last three decades, this poverty has not decreased in any way. William Pinch observes in this context:

> Indeed it can be argued that the increasing interest in Sant studies has pushed Ramanand and Ramanandis into the background. Guru Nanak is included among the Sants, as are several figures claimed by Ramanandis as members of Ramanand's original circle of disciples, most notably Ravidas and Kabir. Sants are bound to each other in the clarity of scholarly hindsight by a disdain for Brahminical knowledge and ritual, an outspoken disregard for idols and images, and a dedication to egalitarian poetic verse—all of which lends to the study of Sant literature a distinctly counter-elitist, folk-culture appeal.[3]

If one were to go by the Hindi compositions attributed to Ramanand which have been preserved in Adi Granth and *Sarvangis*, Ramanand himself would come out as someone who, having a 'disdain for Brahminical knowledge and ritual, an outspoken disregard for idols and images and a dedication to egalitarian poetic verse' would be a figure quite suitable for 'a distinctly counter elitist, folk culture appeal'. But the Sanskrit Ramanand gets in the way. Charlotte Vaudeville, having cited a pada (a poem) by 'Hindi' Ramanand (found both in the Adi Granth and the *Sarvangi* of Rajjab) has this to say: 'If this pad was really composed by Ramanand, the latter should indeed be considered a true follower of the Sant-Mat: idol worship is clearly rejected, the supreme lord is conceived of as invisible and all-pervading, solely revealed through the *sabda* uttered by Satguru.'[4] But since 'modern Ramanandis...claim their orthodoxy in matter of worship and caste...'—that is, since they take 'Sanskrit' Ramanand as their authority—'that liberal saint (which comes out in the Hindi compositions) may have been another Ramanand but of that other Ramanand, we know nothing: he may have been influenced by Nath-panthi beliefs and, at the same time, cultivated a preference for the Vaishnav name of Ram.'[5]

Vaudeville's idea that the 'liberal saint Ramanand' was someone else is not unprecedented. Ramchandra Shukla, the eminent literary historian and critic writing his '*Hindi Sahitya ka Itihas*' ('a history of Hindi literature') way back in the 1930s, cites the same pada and comes to the same conclusion (the nature of his sympathy was different though.) 'It is clear from this citation that such *padas* could not have been composed by Vaishnava Bhakta Ramanand. Maybe some other Ramanand penned them.'[6]

Ignoring the circumstances and the context that led to the construction of Ramanand as 'Acharya' by the modern Ramanandis, Vaudeville and many others have also failed to take note of the interesting fact that even the Sanskrit Ramanand is quite liberal, so far as caste is concerned. It was bound to be so, because the Sanskrit Ramanand was being constructed precisely in order to bestow 'orthodox' approval on the lack of strict observance of Brahminical rules of conduct by modern Ramanandis. The crux of the matter for the 'radical' Ramanandis in the early twentieth century was to counter the arrogance of the Ramanujis—that is, adherents of the Ramanuja or Sri Vaishnava sampraday—who prided themselves on their accurate observance of caste rules and 'superiority' accruing from the same.[7] The Ramanujis made no effort to hide their contempt for the Ramanandis, many of whom came from the middle and lower castes.

Any observer who has looked into the social base of the Ramanandi sampraday and its lay followers—the author of *Dabistan-e-Mazahib* in the seventeenth century, Buchanan and Wilson in the nineteenth century, and Peter Van der Veer and William Pinch in the late twentieth century, for instance—have noted that most of the members came from the middle and low castes. Hence, the Ramanandis could hardly observe caste rules as 'accurately' as the upper-caste Ramanujis.

Consequently, they were treated as 'country cousins' by the Sanskrit-speaking, caste-rules-observing Ramanujis. This 'inferior' status of Ramanandis was reinforced through symbolic gestures in everyday life and on symbolically significant occasions like the Kumbh gatherings, where they were supposed to come after the Ramanujis in the ritual baths and processions. Indeed, they were made to carry the palanquins of Ramanuji Mahants and Acharyas on such occasions.

In this essay, we will hear the voices and closely examine the attempts of 'radical' Ramanandis like Bhagwadacharya, who, angry at this humiliation, sought to sever all connection with the Ramanujis. As indicated before, this was done by pushing back Ramanand to the fourteenth century and by making him a native of north India. This claim was established on the basis of Sanskrit writings attributed to Ramanand. The 'traditionalists' among the Ramanandis, those who upheld the late floruit and southern origin of Ramanand, fiercely resisted the attempts of such 'radical' Ramanandis, but accepted several of the Sanskrit texts as genuine. The point I wish to elaborate in this essay is that in taking the 'evidence' advanced in favour of Ramanand's early floruit at face value, which was to privilege the Sanskrit Ramanand over the Hindi one, academic scholars have completely missed the context of such 'evidence' and consequently the irony of the situation. In fact, this early and Sanskrit Ramanand is not supported by historical evidence, and is the creation of modern Ramanandis. Little did the 'radical' Ramanandis realize that their modern construction of a Sanskrit Ramanand belonging to the fourteenth century would distance the historical Hindi Ramanand of the fifteenth century from his traditionally accepted circle of disciples, causing what is nowadays seen as chronological and biographical improbability. This was the unintended consequence of putting the past into the service of the present without any regard for plausible evidence—the cost of creating 'traditions' at will.

By the time Ram Chandra Shukla was writing his canonical volume—*Hindi Sahitya ka Itihaas* ('A History of Hindi literature') in the course of the 1920s, the 'radical' faction of modern Ramanandis led by Bhagwadacharya and Raghuvaracharya had succeeded in creating the fourteenth-century figure of 'Acharya' Ramanand as the founder of an independent sampraday, a person who did *not* belong to the spiritual lineage of Ramanuja, and who did not come from the south, but from Prayag. In addition, he had a *bhashya* on the Vedanta Sutras to his credit. After all, in the Brahminical tradition one is not recognized as an acārya unless one has authored a bhashya. The 'authentic' Sanskrit text *Ramarchan Paddhati* was attributed to Ramanand in the early twentieth century and the 'authenticity' of various manuscripts vigorously debated—the purpose being either the approval or the rejection of traditional '*guru-paramparas*' that indicated the connection between Ramanuja and Ramanand. 'Ancient' manuscripts were produced as and when required to aid the ongoing struggle of 'independence' from Ramanuji hegemony. The 'poverty of information' noted by Burghart has aided the radical Ramanandi construction of the floruit and world view of Ramanand. The presumption of an eternal Brahminical 'conspiracy of appropriation' has itself become an important datum: if so much was suppressed, is its value not automatically certified as soon as it is once again 'brought to light'?

It is on the basis of such 'evidence' that modern scholarship has completely rejected the unanimity of medieval traditions regarding Ramanand's relationship with Kabir and others. Winand Callewaert, for example, has the following to say about Anantdas, the sixteenth-century hagiographer of leading sants:

> He sang about Namdev, Kabir, Raidas, Dhana, Angad, Trilochan and Pipa. More famous Bhakta-s he could not have chosen and four of them (Kabir, Dhana, Pipa and Raidas), he says were initiated by Ramanand. Namdev, Angad and Trilochan were too far away in the past, even for his sense of history to call them disciples of Ramanand.[8]

Unlike Callewaert, Anantdas, of course was not gifted with a proper sense of history, but his sense of chronology seems to be quite precise. He was careful enough to note that 'the first Bhakta who lived in this Kali age was Namdev; he had God in his hands.'[9] According to Callewaert himself, 'The saint Namdev lived around 1300 AD;'[10] hence Anantdas seems to be right in describing him as the pioneer of bhakti proper in 'this kali age.' If indeed he was obsessed with 'Brahminizing' Kabir and others by making them disciples of Ramanand, why not Namdev and others? Why not make Ramanand the pioneer? After all, Anantdas was a Ramanandi himself and Ramanand lived between 1299 and 1410 CE, as Callewaert and others with a rich sense of history would want Anantdas to believe. But obviously, Anantdas knew better.

As noted above, hardly any 'facts' are available about Ramanand's life. But the 'fact' remains that all medieval mentions of Kabir concur unanimously on two points: that he was born a Muslim weaver, and that Ramanand initiated him. Starting with Hariram Vyas, the native of Orchha who first mentioned Kabir in the mid-sixteenth century, through Anantdas writing his *Parchais* at the turn of the sixteenth century to the author of *Dabistan-e-Mazahib* in the mid-seventeenth century, everyone 'knew' that Kabir was 'initiated by Ramanand'. This consensus cannot be dismissed simply as 'attempts to Hinduise Kabir'. Tradition—Hindu, Indian, or any other for that matter—is something more than institutionalized conspiracy!

And yet, such is the power of the Sanskrit Ramanand and the Brahmanical, Sanskrit evidence, that even in the most fiercely 'anti-Brahmanical' factions of modern scholarship, the medieval consensus of the non-Sanskrit (and non-Brahmin) sources regarding the relationship of Ramanand and Kabir has been just dismissed as absolutely inconsequential.

THE PROBLEM OF THE *AGASTYA SAMHITA*

The *Agastya Samhita* is supposedly the most important and irrefutable evidence in favour of Ramanand's early floruit. As a matter of scholarly caution, however, the very fact that the relevant 'chapters from *Agastya Samhita*' (as described by Bhandarkar) give very precise dates of the birth and death of Ramanand and of his twelve disciples—should have warned scholars. We are told in these chapters that Ramanand was born in Prayag (Allahabad) on the seventh day of the *Krishna Paksha* of *Magha* month of *Vikrami Samvat* [VS] 1356, corresponding to 1299 CE; and passed away on the third day of *Vaishakh Shukla* of 1467 *VS*, corresponding to 1410 CE. Such precision is as improbable as the remarkable lifespan; moreover—another sign warranting caution—these are the dates recognized by the Ramawat sampraday.

R.G. Bhandarkar was the first to introduce the 'chapters from *Agastya Samhita*' into the scholarly discussion. Writing about Ramanand in his 'Vaisnavism, Saivism and Minor Religious Systems' (1913), he mentions the floruit of Ramanand as given by Macauliffe, which was in tandem with what all nineteenth-century British Indologists got from the then available sources and their informants, before going on to repudiate it on the basis of the *Agastya Samhita*:

Mr Macauliffe mentions Mailkot as the place of his birth and says he must have flourished in the end of the fourteenth century and the first half the fifteenth century, which, he states, corresponds with a reckoning, which gives 1398 AD as the date of the birth of Kabir. The authority I have consulted states that that he was born at Prayaga as the son of a kanyakubja Brahmina named Punyasadana and his wife Susila. The date of his birth is given as 4400 of the Kali age, equivalent to 1356 of Vikrama Samvat. This corresponds to 1299 or 1300 AD and is more consistent with traditional statement the there were three generations between him and Ramanuja. The date of Ramanuja's death is usually given as 1137 AD, though it makes him out as having lived for 120 years. The lapse of three generations between 1137–1300 AD is a more reasonable [*sic*] supposition than between 1137 and the end of the fourteenth century. This last date, therefore, given for Ramanand is manifestly wrong and that occurring in the book I have consulted appears to be correct in all probability.[11]

Bhandarkar cites his source in a footnote—'chapters from the *Agastya Samhita* with a Hindi translation by Rama Narayana Das completed in Samvat 1960, corresponding to 1904 AD' Indeed, Rama Narayana Das's *Agastya Samhita* also gives the exact dates of the twelve famous disciples of Ramanand. The question, however, is: are these 'chapters' really from '*Agastya Samhita*'? Or did the same person—Rama Narayana Das—compose both the Sanskrit 'original' and its Hindi translation? And why was the authority of the *Agastya Samhita* invoked to authenticate these chapters?

The book cited by Bhandarkar describes itself as the '*Shri Ramanand Janmotsva Katha* ('the narrative celebrating the birth of Shri Ramanand') taken from the 'Bhavishya Khand' ('canto of the future') of the *Agastya Samhita*, commented upon by the 'resident of Ayodhya, Pandit Rama Narayana Das,' and finished in Vikrama Samvat 1960'.[12] This book was published by 'Vaishnava Rama Dasji' of Dakore from Mumbai in VS 1963, that is, 1906 CE. Sitaramsharan 'Rupkala' in his commentary on the *Bhaktamal* of Nabhadas (first published in 1903) also refers to the 'life of Ramanand' as stated in *Shri Agastya Samhita Bhavishyottar Khand*, but explains that the edition consulted by him was 'available from 'Hazarilal Ganeshprasad' of

Kunjgali, Kashi.'[13] The text, however, is undoubtedly the same, as borne out by a couple of *slokas* (a two-line Sanskrit meter, couplet) cited by 'Rupkala'.

Thus the earliest reference to the 'Bhavishya' or 'Bhavishyottar Khand' of the *Agastya Samhita* is in 1903. The *Agastya Samhita* proper contains nothing like a 'Bhavishya Khand'—or an 'Atit Khand' ('canto of the past') for that matter. The tenuousness of this source doesn't seem to have bothered any scholar dealing with the floruit of Ramanand. In fact, the only scholar who has analysed the *Agastya Samhita* in some detail is Hans Bakker, but his main concern is the development of the Rama cult in medieval north India, not the time and temperament of Ramanand. Bakker accepts the fourteenth-century floruit of Ramanand, and other scholars following the lead of Bhandarkar, have assumed the 'chapters' to be part and parcel of the *Agastya Samhita*.

I have in my possession three copies of the *Agastya Samhita*. One of these is a digital copy of the manuscript originally preserved in Lalchand Research Library, Lahore, now found as manuscript no. M-826 in the library of DAV College, Chandigarh. It consists of 56 folios, five of which are missing. The manuscript is described as, 'ancient, incomplete and mutilated'. The second one is a photocopy of the edition published from Hitwadi Library, Calcutta in the Bengali year 1315, corresponding to 1909 or 1910. This has the slokas in Bengali characters along with a Bengali translation by Shri Kamal Krishna Smrititirtha, who informs the reader in the preface, 'I have determined the text on the basis of four manuscripts—one from the Asiatic society, one from Sanskrit College and two from my own village.'[14] The third is the *Agastya Samhita*, *Purva Bhag* (the first half), published in VS 2042 (1985) from Haridwar with a Hindi translation by Pandit Mahavir Prasad Mishra, who says in the preface, 'this work was found in "VidyaVaridhi library" in mutilated and lamentable condition, and my paternal uncle Pt. Kanhaiya Lal Mishra had decided to work on it, but nothing took place due to his sudden demise in 1927. I have also consulted the manuscript from the library of Alwar state.'[15] All these copies of the text are exactly the same. Moreover, they tally with the one used and extensively quoted by Bakker.

The *Agastya Samhita* is undoubtedly one of the most important texts of the Rama cult. Hans Bakker rightly places it in the context of 'a tendency to 'Ramatize' older forms of Visnuism' and further explains:

The older Vaishnava theology apparently continued in so far as the idol of Vishnu, now said to be that of Rama was often retained. Neither was there any need to change the essential structure of liturgy (Puja). However, the alterations in the phenomenal aspects of god involved new formulae *(mantras)*, prayers *(stotras)*, mediation *(dhyana)* etc. in order to invoke, visualize and worship the new pantheon. To provide for this need Ramaite cult texts were composed from the 11th–12th centuries, the period from which our first archeological evidence for this new development dated.

The three oldest of these texts appear to be the *Ramapurvatapaniya Upanishad* (RPTUp), the *Ramarakshastotra* of Budhakausika, and the *Agastyasamhita* (AgS). The AgS is by far the most extensive, and not surprisingly it is fully modeled upon the great tradition of Visnuite ritual as laid down in the Pancratra samhitas. The replacement of the vyuha doctrine by the conception of Vishnu's identity with Rama, however explains why it has been labeled as an 'apocryphal' text.[16]

Obviously, the *Agastya Samhita* is an apocryphal text in the sense that its title is supposedly a part of ancient Pancharatra Agamas, but its present text has evolved only after the emergence of the Rama cult. This is the 'most important' text of the Rama cult, since it helps 'Ramatize older forms of Visnuism' on the authority of the ancient, putatively authentic 'Narada' Pancharatra of which it is supposed to be a part. It is also referred to as the 'Agastya Sutikshna Samvada', as it is composed in the form of a dialogue between Agastya and Sutikshna.

Bakker's 'tentative surmise', made on the basis of internal and external evidence, regarding the time and place of the composition of *Agastya Samhita* seems to be correct: 'the *Agastya Samhita* originated in the 12th century in Varanasi, the bulwark of Hindu orthodoxy, in Brahmin circles possibly related in some way or another to Brahmin families attached to the aforementioned sanctuaries.'[17]

Had the scholars who took at face value the 'chapters from *Agastya Samhita*' mentioned by Bhandarkar bothered to compare these with the *Agastya Samhita* proper, the curious fact of a text composed in the twelfth century giving the birth year of Ramanand as 1299 or 1300 would have surely struck them. To be fair, Pinuccia Caracchi has asked 'when were these chapters added to *Agastya Samhita*?' Before going into this, a brief and comparative introduction of the contents of the copies in my possession and the one used by Bakker would be in order.

The manuscript no. M-826 of Chandigarh and the printed copy from Calcutta both contain 32 chapters. The Haridwar edition in its present form consists of 11 chapters, but the commentator Mahavir Prasad Mishra informs in a footnote at the end of the preface, 'The financial assistance received by us could meet the expenses for publishing 11 chapters only, but the work actually has 32 chapters, the publication of the remaining part will depend on the generosity of the donors.'[18]

The chapters in the manuscript and in the Haridwar edition are left untitled, with a colophon at the end of each chapter stating: 'here ends the chapter named 'Param Rahsya Kathanam' (the exposition of the highest mystery) in the Sri *Agastya Samhita*'. The published version from Calcutta also follows the manuscript faithfully, with the commentator adding a 'table of contents' which indicates the theme of each chapter, for the convenience of the reader.

In all these copies, the seventh chapter deals with the 'Rama mantra' followed in the eighth by a genealogy of the gurus who gave this mantra to their disciples. The list starts with Brahma the creator himself and ends with Shaunka, the seer. Chapters 26 and 27 deal with the details of the Ramanavmi vow which has enabled Bakker to decide on the period of this text. Here, it is important to note that the *Agastya Samhita* does not mention any 'historical' person; and only provides names of divine and 'mythological' characters such as Shiva, Rama, Lakshmana, Hanuman, Parvati, Vashishtha, and Vyasa.

Hans Bakker has quoted the *Rama-Mahatmya* (the praise of Rama) in full from the tenth chapter of his copy of the *Agastya Samhita*.[19] It runs into 34 slokas and tallies exactly with all the copies in my possession. Similar is the case with many more slokas cited by Bakker. It is plausible that the edition used by him was based on the manuscripts consulted by Kamal Krishna Smrititirtha in 1909 or 1910 and by Mahavir Prasad Mishra in 1985 and which tally with the manuscript no. M-826 preserved in the DAV College Chandigarh. It bears pointing put that Bakker, aware of 'ten entries under the title '*Agastya Samhita*' in the National Catalogue Catalogorum', only consulted 'the *Agastya Samhita* as edited by Ramnarayanadas'.[20] Why is this important? Let us turn to Caracchi at this point.

Pinuccia Caracchi has translated 'chapters from *Agastya Samhita*' (by Ramnarayanadas, that is, those used by Bhandarkar) into Italian.

In a section of the introduction, entitled: 'Which *Agastya Samhita*?'[21] Caracchi argues, 'It is still to be seen when our text was added to the *Agastya Samhita* and of which *Agastya Samhita* it would be a part?' Believing in the existence of 'three or four *totally different* texts of the *Agastya Samhita*', she refers to the one used by Bakker as '*Agastya Sutikshna Samvada*' and then states:

This, in my assessment is only one of the *Agastya Samhitas* and had numerous editions (Lucknow-1898, Ayodhya-n.d., Calcutta-1910, Mysore-1957), while it appears that all the others are found only in the manuscript form. What are more interesting directly to our study are the five chapters that proclaim to be part of the *Bhavishya Khanda* of the Agastya Sutikshna Samvada. Still, the studies of this *Agastya Samhita* in the manuscript form and its published versions describe it as divided in 32 or 35 chapters, while our text is to be imagined as being part of a work of vast proportions, divided into Khandas which in turn ought to be sub-divided into a considerable number of chapters. (Only the *Bhavishya Khanda* consists at least of 135). On the subject being discussed, it is to be noted that the life of Ramanand does not find place in the editions of Agastya Sutikshna Samvada studied by B. Bhattacharya and Bakker. Even the date of its composition proposed by Bakker testifies in favour of the exclusion of life of Ramanand from it....One then needs to think of another *Agastya Samhita*....Given the considerable number of the manuscripts that are taken under the title of *Agastya Samhita*, a research in the field to trace the manuscript containing the Ramanand Janmotsva would be welcome. This should be in possession of Ramanandi sampraday, as most probably it was a Ramanandi, Pandit Ramnarayanadas who took care of publishing the text translated here.[22]

Caracchi mentions the 1910 Calcutta edition of the *Agastya Samhita* but fails to note that this was based on four manuscripts as explained by the translator, and that there is remarkable consistency between this edition, the Haridwar edition (based on the Alwar manuscript), and the manuscript from Lahore (presently in Chandigarh). She opines that the *Agastya Samhita* containing the relevant chapters 'should be in possession of Ramanandi sampraday'. But is that really so? As indicated at the beginning of this essay, the issue of the floruit of Ramanand is deeply implicated in the controversy over Ramanandis' relationship with Ramanujis. I will discuss it in some detail a little later, but a relevant piece of information will be in order here. By the third decade of the last century, under the leadership of Bhagwadacharya, the 'radical' Ramanandis had almost convinced the majority of Ramanandis that their sampraday was completely independent of Ramanujis and that Ramanand had nothing to do with the spiritual lineage of Ramanuja. But the polemics persisted. It was in the course of such polemics that Balbhadra Das, a firm believer in the Ramanuja–Ramanand lineage, published an edition of the *Vaishnava Matabaj Bhaskar* along with *Ramarchan Paddhati* in 1928. He wrote a lengthy introduction under the title 'Prastuta Prasanga' (literally, 'the matter at hand', although a more appropriate translation would be, 'the present controversy'). Demolishing the arguments and the evidence advanced in favour of 'no connection with Ramanuja' position, he had this to say regarding the 'chapters from *Agastya Samhita*':

> This work claims to be '*Agastya Samhita Bhavishyottar Khanda*'. But *Agastya Samhita* has no such Khanda, in fact it has no Khanda division at all, it is simply divided in the 'Adhyayas' (chapters), 33 in all, running from first to last. This is true of the published version as well as that of the manuscripts. The abovementioned *Bhavishyottar Khanda* starts from the 131st chapter, which proves that the author of this has not even seen the *Agastya Samhita.* Had he seen the Samhita, he would have certainly begun his Khanda from the 34th chapter, not from the 131st.There is still another remarkable feature of this Khanda. It has in the beginning, the *Upakrama* ('invocation'), which makes it an independent work. Had this been a Khanda of the *Agastya Samhita* it would not contain the *Upakrama*....Obviously then, this is nothing but a forgery in the name of *Agastya Samhita.*[23]

This challenge remained unanswered. Even Bhagwadacharya, the prime target of Balbhadra Das, and a person known for his ability to produce 'ancient' manuscripts with remarkable promptness, could not produce any manuscript containing the 'Bhavishyottar' or 'Bhavishya' Khanda. Balbhadra Das, right in catching Ramnarayanadas on the wrong foot, went wrong in stating that, 'the author of this has not even seen the *Agastya Samhita*'. The 'author' actually had edited the 1898 edition of the *Agastya Samhita.*

In the light of the foregoing discussion, it is not difficult to answer the basic question posed by Caracchi: 'when was our text added to the *Agastya Samhita*'? The simple answer is, between 1898 and 1903, and that is why it is not likely to be found in any of the old manuscripts of the *Agastya Samhita* proper. This addition was done by none other than the editor of the 1898 edition of the *Agastya Samhita*—the same Pandit Ramnarayanadas.

Hans Bakker has this to say about the editor of *Agastya Samhita* used by him:

Ramnarayanadas was a Sanskrit scholar who apart from the *Ayodhya Mahatmya* edited several other Rama Bhakti texts, e.g. the *Agastya Samhita* (Lucknow, 1898). He claimed spiritual descent from Bhagavannarayana, a pupil of *Agradas* and lived in the Bara Sthan in Ayodhya under the Mahant ship of Ramamanoharprasda, the 8th Mahant since Ramprasada.[24]

The author of the chapters translated by Caracchi also gives his *guru-parampara* (spiritual genealogy) in four and a half Sanskrit slokas printed just beneath the table of contents. It starts with Anantanada, one of the twelve disciples of Ramanand, who was the guru of Krishandasa, who in turn was the guru of 'Shri Bhagavannarayana'. This author thus clearly claims his 'spiritual descent' from the same person and unambiguously identifies himself as 'Ayodhya Niwasi, Narayana Vanshi' (a resident of Ayodhya, belonging to the house or dynasty of Narayana) at the end of *Shri Ramanandashtakam*, (eight verses in praise of Ramanand) given before the *Ramanand Janmotsva Katha* and also at the end of each chapter of the latter. The 'belonging to the dynasty of Narayana' part of his identity is extremely significant, as will become clear from the following.

Bakker continues:

Until the death of Mahant Ramamanoharprasada, Ramnarayanadas, though himself a Ramanandi, acknowledged the authority of Ramanuja to whom the official Parampara was traced back....After the death of the Mahant of Bara Sthan, however, most Ramanandi branches broke away from the Ramanuji tradition under the influence of Bhagwaddas [or Bhagwadacharya], another chela of Manoharprasada, which resulted in the declaration of 1921. Ramnarayanadas seemed to have been a reluctant follower of this movement, nevertheless he and Ramavallabhasharana are known in Ayodhya as the authors of several forgeries written in the first decades of the present century, such as the Ramarchan Paddhati ascribed to Ramanand and the Shri Janakibhashya, a commentary on the Vedanta sutras ascribed to Ramprasada. The need for such a commentary became felt once the majority of the Ramanandis had ceased to recognize Ramanuja's Shri Bhashya, yet the Shri Janakibhashya was never acknowledged by the Mahants of the Bara Sthan and Ramprasada's authorship is vehemently denied. That, at least, Ramnarayanadas did not shy away from interpolating new ideas into traditional texts is proven by his edition of the Ayodhya Mahatmya.[25]

It was undoubtedly the 'same Pandit Ramnarayanadas'—a 'resident of Ayodhya and belonging to the Narayana dynasty, claiming spiritual descent from Bhagavannarayana'—who did not shy away 'from interpolating new ideas (that is, the five chapters of the Ramanand Janmotsva) into the traditional text'—the *Agastya Samhita*. It is significant that he identified himself as 'belonging to Narayana dynasty' because it symbolically underlines his faith in the traditional view of Ramanand as belonging to the spiritual lineage of Ramanuja. This view was contested vehemently by the radical Ramanandis under the 'influence of Bhagwadacharya'. Ramanuja propagated the Narayana mantra and worshipped the four-armed Narayana (another name of Vishnu), while the radical Ramanandis insisted on the Rama mantra and worshipped the two-armed, bow-carrying Rama.

Ramanarayanadas appended the 'Ramanand Bhavotsaha Ashtakam' (eight slokas celebrating the birth of Ramanand) to his own five chapters. Actually there are ten slokas, the second of which gives the date of the birth of Ramanand as 'Thursday, the 7th of the Krishna Paksha of the Magha Masa of the year 1356 of Vikrami Samvat'. The tenth sloka informs us 'this set of eight was composed by Pandit Shri Ramacharan on Magha Vadi the 8th, 1937 of the Vikrami Samvat'. 1937 VS would correspond to 1880 or 1881 of the Common Era. To the best of my knowledge this is the earliest mention of 1356 VS (that is, 1299 CE) as the year of Ramanand's birth. It seems Ramnarayanadas was only following this lead in his own 'five chapters found in the *Agastya Samhita*'.

The central issue of all the debates and polemics within the Ramanandi sampraday was the guru-parampara, and all paramparas respected traditionally relate Ramanand and Ramanuja in some way. This is why Pandit Ramanarayandas not only referred to himself as 'belonging to the dynasty of Narayana' but also mentioned the years of the birth and death of Ramanuja along with those of Ramanand at the end of the *octave* composed by 'Pandit Shri Ramacharan.' The 'radical' Ramanandis, however, could not countenance even a remote connection between the two and their leader Bhagwadacharya often referred sarcastically to Ramanarayandas' self-description of 'belonging to the dynasty of Narayana'.

Like many a missionary in possession of the only possible version of Truth, Bhagwadacharya had neither patience nor respect for those who dared to disagree even mildly. (This, despite the fact, that he actively participated in the Gandhian National Movement, in fact lived in the Gandhi Ashram in Kocharab, Ahmedabad for quite some time and composed an epic in Sanskrit celebrating the life and achievements of Mahatma Gandhi!) His motto was simple: You are either with us or against us. He wanted nothing less than full loyalty to the cause. Pandit Ramanarayandas, the author of the *Ramanand Janmotsva Katha* (the 'chapters from the *Agastya Samhita*' to which we have often referred), was a Ramanandi who aided the cause of Bhagavadacharya by propagating an early floruit of Ramanand thereby putting in serious doubt the connection between Ramanand and Ramanuja, while not being able to sever the link completely. Apart from claiming to belong 'to the dynasty of Narayana', he also recorded the birth and death of both the acharyas in one place.

Bhagwadacharya came down heavily on such a deviation:

> Well, after all, he belonged to the dynasty of Narayana, so what if he made an irrelevant connection here? And don't you forget, in 1921 he was not able to answer even one of the several questions put to him in a pamphlet published by the general secretary of Shri Ramanandiya Vaishnava Mahamandala. Don't expect to get any relief for your misplaced idea of Ramanand being in the lineage of Ramanuja from such irrelevancies.[26]

After the death of the Mahant (spiritual and temporal head) of Bara Sthan and in the light of Bhagwadacharya's increasing influence, Ramanarayandas was left with no choice than to become 'a reluctant follower', as indicated by Bakker.

The radical faction of Ramanandis succeeded in creating an atmosphere in which it was very difficult to sustain the 'traditional' view of the Ramanuja–Ramanand lineage. And yet, the issue of the floruit of Ramanand was not exactly sacrosanct for this faction. It was apparently all right to uphold any floruit as long as it served the purpose of getting rid of the Ramanuja connection. The radical

Ramanandis referred vaguely to the evidence of the *Agastya Samhita*, with the name 'Agastya' helping them to interpret the word 'Dravid (belonging to the south) Muni' found in the Vaishnava works as a name referring to the sage Agastya rather than to Ramanuja or any other person belonging to the southern Vaishnavas.

Their aim was to construct a 'Sanskrit' Ramanand capable of bestowing orthodox approval on their practical liberalism in the matter of caste rules of purity and pollution. The early or later floruit of Ramanand was only of secondary significance. Bhagwadacharya composed his '*Shri Ramanand Digvijay*' ('The universal victory of Ramanand') in 1927 on the assumption of 1356 VS (1299 CE) being the year of Ramanand's birth, but in the 1967 edition of the same work he quite simply put a footnote to the relevant sloka: 'This Samvat has been proved wrong. Maybe we will need to make it a hundred years earlier.'[27]

But the need did not arise, since the sampraday and the academics had by this time come around to the early floruit and—more importantly, from Bhagwadacharya's point of view—to the image of Ramanand as a 'Sanskrit' Acharya, a 'shastrasiddha' ('well versed in orthodoxy') albeit liberal Acharya, as Hazari Prasad Dwivedi was to describe him in his well-known work on Kabir. [28]

Once Bhagwadacharya succeeded in replacing the Hindi Ramanand with the Sanskrit one, he felt he did not have to bother too much about dates. Ramchandra Shukla, author of the canonical history of Hindi literature, doubted the attribution of 'Vaishnava Bhakta Ramanand's' authority and name to the Hindi compositions that bore his signature in the medieval anthologies. This meant, effectively, that by the end of the third decade of the twentieth century, Ramanand had become an orthodox yet liberal Sanskrit acharya rather than an iconoclastic Hindi poet for many readers of Hindi.

Having accepted the 'consensus' Bhagwadacharya had forged, academic scholars found themselves in a quandary. They now had to discard the traditional consensus that assigned both Ramanand and Kabir to the fifteenth century of the Common Era. In other words, they now had to adjust the dates of Kabir to make them agree with the supposed *Agastya Samhita* dates of Ramanand. And if this adjustment did not somehow work, they had to doubt the Ramanand–Kabir connection. The supposed chapters from the *Agastya Samhita* thus became the benchmark for determining the historicity of the traditional consensus about the Ramanand–Kabir connection. Taking these chapters as *the* evidence, the scholars either tried to prove that Kabir belonged to an earlier date or found the Ramanand–Kabir connection improbable. In the late 1930s, Pitambar Dutt Barthwal insisted on an earlier date for Kabir, on the basis of the 'undoubted' fact that he was a 'disciple of Ramanand'. Parashuram Chaturvedi in the early 1950s analysed the references (to guru) found in the works of Kabir and his contemporaries to argue that it was difficult to uphold the Ramanand–Kabir connection, although he tentatively accepted 1448 CE as Kabir's year of death and maintained that if this date is correct, then Kabir of course could have been a disciple of Ramanand. Hardly any new evidence or argument has been added to the debate since then and most scholars today assign Kabir to the fifteenth century. Chaturvedi's skepticism about Ramanand being the guru of Kabir has been widely upheld.

In his thesis on the Nirguna school of Hindi poetry, first published in 1936, Barthwal, even while noting that Bhavishyottar Khanda is a later addendum to the *Agastya Samhita*, took its dates of Ramanand as traditional and rejected the fifteenth century floruit of Ramanand on the basis of this 'later addendum'. In fact, 'the chronology as accepted' in the work of Barthwal was crucially dependent upon his acceptance of the dates of Ramananda contained in the 'later addendum'—Bhavishyottar Khanda. He adjusted the dates of Kabir accordingly:

> According to prevalent belief, Kabir was born in 1398 AD, which is too late a date for a disciple of Ramananda that he undoubtedly was. He must have at least been 18 years of age to have an intense spiritual craving, which made him seek Ramananda and made the later accept him. Even if we keep a margin of two years for association with Ramananda before his death in 1410 AD, Kabir's birth must be placed before 1390. Namadeva, who died in 1350 AD was surrounded by myth in the time of Kabir. So, we may safely hold Kabir to have been born between 1350 and 1390 AD and accept 1370 as his probable date of birth.[29]

Barthwal, having accepted 1356 VS as birth year of Ramanand, continued to believe confidently and enthusiastically that Ramanand initiated Kabir, Raidas, Pipa, and others, explaining the obvious time-gap with the help of Nabhadas's reference to the exceptionally long life enjoyed by Ramanand. He also used the 'reference to Ramanand' in one of Kabir's own compositions (pada no. 77 of the *Bijak*) and other medieval sources like Hariram Vyas of Orchha and *Dabistan*-e-*Mazahib* to substantiate his argument.

In the introductory essay for *Ramanand ki Hindi Rachnayen* ('the Hindi compositions by Ramanand'), which he compiled from manuscripts found in the Nagari Pracharini Sabha (NPS) as well as from other sources, Barthwal went to great lengths in discussing the metaphysical and ontological questions that arose in reconciling the 'differences in the philosophical position as reflected in the (*Vaishnava Matabaj*) *Bhaskar* and the Hindi compositions of Ramanand.'[30] Yet he used Sanskrit compositions as the main yardstick in this explanation of 'differences' between the Hindi and the Sanskrit Ramanand.

Parashuram Chaturvedi also accepted the 'evidence' provided in the 'chapters from the *Agastya Samhita*' to determine the floruit of Ramanand, but unlike Barthwal, he did not make it the sole criterion for deciding the issue of the Ramanand–Kabir connection. Taking other factors into account, he found it improbable that Ramanand could have initiated Kabir and other Sants. He underscored the absence of any mention of Ramanand on the part of Kabir and others and expressed serious doubt about them even being contemporaries. At the same time, as stated earlier, Chaturvedi tentatively accepted 1448 CE as the year of Kabir's death and naturally found his connection with Ramanand quite probable:

> If this [1448 as the death date of Kabir] is accepted, then Kabir being a contemporary of, in fact, being influenced by Ramanand will also become acceptable....yes in such a situation his birth date will have to be taken to an earlier period than 1455V.S. [i.e. 1398 CE] and may be in that case, this year [1398] will have to be taken as the year of his enlightenment.[31]

Accepting the authenticity of the pada attributed to Ramanand in the *Adi Granth*, Chaturvedi quite enthusiastically wanted Ramanand to be included among the 'early upholders and propagators of the Sant Mat without any doubt.'[32]

It is important to note that, despite being ambivalent regarding the Ramanand-Kabir connection and criticizing Barthwal for reading too much into pada 77 of the *Bijak*, Chaturvedi did not take Sanskrit

Ramanand as a referent and yardstick to explain Hindi Ramanand. Chaturvedi's 'overview' of literature and evidence in this regard is often referred to by those who see in the idea of the Ramanand–Kabir connection, attempts to 'Hinduise Kabir in modern times' (Vaudeville for example) or to bestow 'Brahminical respectability' on the Sants, even in pre-modern times. It is generally ignored that even though Chaturvedi accepted the so-called 'chapters from *Agastya Samhita*' as authentic, and hence found it improbable for Ramanand to be a contemporary of the fifteenth-century Sants, he nevertheless wanted to include the Brahmin Ramanand in his category of the Sants because he accorded priority to the Hindi compositions of Ramanand over the Sanskrit works attributed to him. He wanted to accept an early date for Kabir before accepting the connection between Ramanand and Kabir.

In his detailed study of the Kabirpanth, David Lorenzen took note of the 'the Sant Tradition to which Kabir belonged' as 'the principal expression of non-caste Hinduism'. He rightly emphasized:

> It should be noted that neither the caste Hinduism, nor the non-caste Hinduism is sufficiently homogeneous to be regarded as a single undifferentiated cultural entity. At the same time, however, the varied manifestations of each do have many common characteristics, a certain family resemblance. This is true both at the level of the local, non-standardized little traditions and at the level of more widespread and codified great traditions.[33]

The Hindi Ramanand is crucial for an understanding of the 'varied manifestations' of both caste and non-caste Hinduisms. And so are the attempts to replace him with the Sanskrit Ramanand in the modern times. It is in the context of the 'common characteristics, a certain family resemblance' that both these contradictory images of the same historical person reveal their cultural and historical significance. Hindi Ramanand is critical of 'caste Hinduism' to such an extent that he can be seen as an 'early upholder and propagator' of the Sant world view, even the Sanskrit Ramanand was constructed as being quite liberal within the ideological framework of caste-Hinduism. In both cases, he continues to be a Brahmin by birth and yet transcends the world view traditionally associated with this Brahmin identity.

The problems faced by scholars 'reared on the basic structural oppositions of the caste hierarchy' (to borrow an expression from William Pinch) have only been accentuated by the identity politics that are currently fashionable and the academic discourse that takes these as their base. The assumption that 'Ramanand, being a Brahmin, could only uphold the caste hierarchy'—or that, if at all he opposed it, he must have been someone else, 'of whom we know nothing'—is taken as a basic point of departure in some academic circles today. The simple empirical fact of every individual carrying multiple identities and having the ability to make moral choices is often ignored in this discourse.

Such assumptions, coupled with the 'evidence' of the 'chapters from *Agastya Samhita*' have ruled out the possibility that the 'Brahmin' Ramanand had anything to do with the 'weaver' Kabir. They belonged to two structurally opposed worlds and were not even contemporaries. Even a careful and meticulous scholar like John S. Hawley tends to make sweeping remarks in this particular context, which reflect not only his personal opinion, but also the prevalent consensus and dominant view in a most cogent way:

> Ramanand solves too many problems on too little evidence. He supplies the missing link that would relate Kabir's non-theist 'eastern' Banarasi side to the theist bhakti personality so prevalent in manuscripts that show up farther west. He locates Kabir in a specific monastic lineage—the Ramanandis'—while also providing the means for him to have come from a Muslim family, as his name suggests, and then later be aligned by conversion with a kind of bhakti that at least some Brahmins could call their own. It's all too neat, and too unechoed in the poems [of Kabir] themselves. I have to side with lower-caste critics who think the connection between Ramanand and Kabir was just a pious invention, a way to deny Kabir his roots.[34]

In the first place, if one were to go strictly and exclusively by the manuscripts and their antiquity, 'the oldest dated manuscript' (Fatehpur, 1582 CE) containing the poems of Kabir gives no indication of him being a 'weaver from Banaras'—a fact noted by Hawley himself. Was Kabir then a 'weaver from Banaras'? Second, the 'connection' will not remain 'unechoed in the poems' of Kabir if one listened to the Hindi Ramanand speaking in the medieval sources. Moreover, the Ramanand–Kabir connection was first doubted by Bhandarkar, and then questioned by Parashuram Chaturvedi, and as chance would have it, both of them were 'high caste Brahmins' not 'lower caste critics'. So far as 'roots' are concerned, the bulk of Ramanandis belonged in medieval times and continues to belong in modern times as well to the so-called lower castes and middle level castes. Most of these castes are referred to as 'backward castes' in the legal and political discourse of contemporary India and are distinct from the castes referred to as 'Dalits'. Incidentally, the caste to which Kabir belonged—Julaha amongst Muslims and Koris amongst Hindus—are considered part of the Other Backward Castes (OBCs) and not of Dalits. Hence one can see, even in the work of 'lower caste critics' with whom Hawley wishes to side, an attempt to appropriate Kabir and 'deny him his roots'. If one were to accept the 'authenticity of representation' argument implicit in Hawley's choice of sides, one would have to wait for a Kabir critic belonging to the OBCs to receive an authentic Kabir with authentic roots. In any case, the very idea of the roots of a certain kind is a 'given' rooted more in contemporary politics of identity, and can hardly be considered sufficient to dismiss the fact of the universal medieval consensus so far as this connection is concerned. Moreover, this connection was upheld in medieval India by Brahmins and others. After all, Nabhadas was believed to have been a 'Dom', the lowest of the low in the caste order. And finally, as shown above, the 'irrefutable evidence' of 'the chapters from *Agastya Samhita*'—'just a pious invention', has inadvertently worked against the historicity of the Ramanand–Kabir connection. We could of course find, in future, more solid reasons than these spurious 'chapters' to doubt medieval consensus on the issue, but in the meanwhile let us accept the location of Kabir in the specific 'monastic lineage' of Ramanandis as this lineage itself is of the 'lower castes' and the OBCs. It was on behalf of this social composition of his sampraday that Bhagwadacharya took up the cudgels with the Brahminical Ramanujis.

Unlike many scholars in the field, David Lorenzen goes from 'known to unknown' in order to determine the floruit of Ramanand, and hence argues that there are several independent historical tests that show clearly that Ramanand must belong to the fifteenth century. These include the synchronisms of Kabir with Sikandar Lodi and Virsimha Baghel (and hence Kabir's floruit of about

1480–1520); the 1588 date of Anantdas's *Namdev Parachai*; and the floruit of about 1580–1624 commonly given to Nabhadas. In the traditional genealogy accepted by the Ramanandis and others, Kabir is an immediate disciple of Ramanand, Nabhadas is in the fourth generation of Ramanand's disciples, and Anantdas is in the fifth generation of his disciples. All this fits together nicely and clearly indicates, according to Lorenzen, that Ramanand must belong to the fifteenth century.

Further, he compares the genealogies given by Nabhadas and Anantdas and argues:

What is the main evidence that *supports* the existence of this guru-disciple relation? Quite simply, it is the unanimous claim of tradition that Kabir was a disciple of Ramanand. The exact correspondence of the names in the genealogies of Ramanand's pupils found independently in the works of Ananata-das and Nabha-das is one strong argument in favor of historicity of Ramanand-Kabir connection. Both these works were written within about a hundred years of Kabir's probable death.[35]

Lorenzen has worked with the Kabirpanthis, and all the branches of the Kabirpanth unhesitatingly uphold the Ramanand–Kabir connection till today. Like the Ramanandis, the Kabirpanth also draws its followers mainly from the lower and 'other backward castes'. It is quite interesting that for the Kabirpanthis, the acceptance of this connection in no way diminishes either Kabir's independence of personality and thought or the sharpness of his sarcasm and his attacks on caste hierarchy. Among the contemporary leaders of the Panth, the erudite acharya of the Parakh branch, Abhilashdas, even while underlining the uniqueness of Kabir's world view and spiritual pursuit which makes the idea of a guru redundant, concedes that 'a seeker after all needs a guru, so it is natural that Kabir went to Ramanand.' Most importantly, Abhilashdas mentions 'Sant Nirvan Sahib of Surat (Gujarat), a contemporary of Kabir, as welcoming Kabir into his ashram and singing in a pada that 'Kabir has taken Ramanand as his guru and lives in Banaras.'[36] This reference to 'Sant Nirvan Sahib' obviously deserves to be probed further.

Acharya Vivekdas of the Chaura branch also insists on the initiator–initiated relationship between Ramanand and Kabir. In fact, in his '*Amarpur Desh Apna*' ('I belong to the land of immortals'), an imaginary dialogue between Kabir and his disciple Virsimha Baghel, Vivekdas makes Kabir himself say this of Ramanand by way of explaining the 'difference between the Guru and disciple':

> He never wanted his disciples to be bound with his own tradition. He gave them freedom to choose and take their own ways. That is why the disciples of Swamiji (i.e. Ramanand) branched out in various traditions. This is actually what he wanted. He desired everyone to protect Indian religion and culture in his own way. The times demanded this as well. He was a Saguna Margi only in appearance. Everyone thought that he worshipped Rama and Sita, but it was all only appearance. Deep down, his way was that of the internal reflection.[37]

Obviously the Panth believes more in the 'medieval' Ramanand than in his modern construct, and has a nuanced understanding of the similarity and dissimilarity of his Hindi and Sanskrit versions. This belief and understanding gives the Kabir of its perception an independence of thought and personality as well as a continuity with the 'early upholders and propagators of the Sant Mat' and a location within the 'non-caste Hinduism'.

It will not be presumptuous, one hopes, to claim, in the light of the foregoing analysis that it is positively misleading to rely on the so-called 'chapters from Agastya Samhita' and push the floruit of Ramanand back into the fourteenth century CE. There is no basis whatsoever to dismiss the fifteenth century floruit assigned to Ramanand by a consensus in the pre-modern sources or to privilege the Sanskrit Ramanand over the Hindi Ramanand.

HINDI RAMANAND AND SANSKRIT RAMANAND

This is perhaps the right place to step back from controversies surrounding the Sanskrit Ramanand and describe the Ramanand we meet in Hindi texts—those that could well have been composed in the fifteenth century. Relatively firm dates can be assigned to five padas attributed to Ramanand in the *Sarvangis* of Rajjab and Gopaldas and the *Adi Granth*. Before turning to these, let me mention two works whose date of composition is more difficult to assess. These are the *Gyan Lila*, a work consisting of thirteen couplets, and the *Gyan Tilak*, a dialogue between Ramanand and Kabir.

Apart from these, there are six padas attributed to Ramanand in Hindi. Only one of these padas—glorifying Lord Hanuman—can be put under the category of Saguna Bhakti. Notably, it is not found in any of the manuscripts used by Barthwal to prepare his *Ramanand ki Hindi Rachnayen*. In other words, it is found neither in any of the two *Sarvangis* nor in the *Adi Granth*. Grierson sent it to Shyam Sundar Das who published the same in his article 'Ramawat Sampraday'.[38] In all probability Grierson got it from one of his friends amongst the Ramanandis, perhaps Rupkala. It was this pada of dubious provenance that was used by Ramchandra Shukla and others to imagine the existence of two Ramanands since the 'Vaishnava Bhakta', who authored 'Grierson's pada,' could not have composed the padas that rejected idol worship and celebrated the 'Nirguna' world view. The *Gyan Lila* was found in the library of Jodhpur Durbar and *Gyan Tilak* in the collection of Nagari Pracharini Sabha itself.

If we exclude 'Grierson's pada', we are left with five padas in all. One of these (*kahan jayeie ghar hi lago rang:* 'Where to go? I have found his hue in my very own home') is found in a *Sarvangi* manuscript of 1660 VS (1603 CE) preserved in the collection of the NPS, in the *Adi Grantha*, and also 'in another manuscript of 1771 VS (1714 CE),' according to Barthwal. The same is also found in the *Sarvangi* of Rajjab, quite appropriately given the very first place amongst the padas collected in the chapter dealing with *Tirath Tiraskar*, 'the rejection of pilgrim places.'[39] This pada also appears in Gopaldas's *Sarvangi*, composed in 1627 CE.[40] It was the author of this very pada that Vaudeville wanted 'to be considered a true follower of the Sant mat.' The second of Barthwal's padas (*sahaj suni main chit vasant,* The mind enjoys the eternal spring of Sahaj and Shunya') is also recorded by Gopaldas, with only minor variations in the text.[41] The pada, *taten na kichchu re samsara* ('What I have to do with this world?') presents a similar case.[42] The remaining two padas recorded by Gopaldas, *sahjen sahjen sab gun jaila* ('By and by you get rid of all attributes') and *Hari bin janam britha khoyo re* ('You've wasted your life without God') are also found with slight alterations in the *Sarvangi* of Rajjab.[43]

What kind of a persona emerges form these padas? To put it quite simply, they are so similar to poems attributed to Kabir that one could easily replace the *chhap* or *bhanita* (that is, signature) 'Ramanand' with the signature 'Kabir'. Here are the complete prose translations of the five padas that appear in these early Dadupanthi collections:

Those who ignore the name of Rama and refuse the company of noble souls waste the preciousness of human life. The chanting of His name is the only anchor of life. It enlightens darkened lives and souls; I am here to tell you this by the order of the Lord Himself. Don't waste your life in false pride that comes with wealth and status.

What do I have to do with this world? My only anchor is the name of Rama. I know the illusory nature of worldly pleasures. To go after them is to meet the fate of the ant that gets stuck in molasses. In fact, it is like believing a dream to be true reality. Ego destroys the knowledge of true self. I tell you, meditate on this, for my Guru has taught me the secrets of life and death.

It is only through 'Sahaj' that all attributes of the Self eventually disappear. It is only by the sweet nectar of chanting the true name that you achieve liberation. Ramanand enjoys the eternal company of Rama and partakes in the nectar of His grace.

Where to go? I have found His true hues in my very own home. I am not inclined to go on any pilgrimage. Pilgrim places have only water and stones, while Hari permeates every place in the world. O my Guru, Ramanand is indebted eternally to you, for your Word has freed him of the bondage of Samsara.

My mind enjoys the eternal spring of Sahaj and Shunya, and is not inclined to wander any more. I have reached a 'place' where there is no desire, no OM, no Brahma, no Vishnu and none of his twenty-four avatars. There is no Maya in the place where Ramanand's Swami dwells undisturbed.

Academic scholars are aware of this Hindi Ramanand, of course, but in their world he is expected to prove his credentials on the benchmark provided by the Sanskrit Ramanand constructed by Bhagwadacharya and his followers. Their efforts have borne fruit in that the historical and theoretical primacy of the Hindi Ramanand has been overshadowed.

Bhagwadacharya had a difficult task. In order to construct a Sanskrit Ramanand, independent of Ramanuja, he had to 'find' rare manuscripts of Sanskrit works 'by' Ramanand and fight for their acceptance. He also had to reject similar manuscripts 'found' by others if they did not agree with his own positions on the most crucial issue of guru-parampara. For him the test of the authenticity of any manuscript—Hindi or Sanskrit—was whether it helped to sever the ties between Ramanuja and the Ramanujis or failed to do so.

Let us examine how the Sanskrit Ramanand compares with the Hindi one on all-important issue of caste. The oral tradition attributes a one-liner to Ramanand: *Hari ko bhaje so Hari ka hoi, jat paant poochhe nahin koi* ('One who relates to God belongs to Him. The question of caste does not arise'.) Important as it is in popular memory, this verse is not to be found in any early collections of Ramanand's Hindi works. Richard Burghart argues 'The saying is in Hindi and hence would not be found in the two Sanskrit texts, *Vaishnavamatabjabhaskar* (*Bhaskar* for short) and *Ramarchanpaddhati*, which have also been attributed to Ramanand.'[44] While it is true that it is rare to find a Hindi saying in a Sanskrit work, in this case we need to look a second time. Consider the following slokas from the *Bhaskar,* which I quote from the edition published by Balbhadra Das in 1928 CE:

God in his grace does not care for the caste, purity or the power of anyone seeking refuge in Him.

(Sloka 100, pp. 180–1.)

How would this sloka translate in Hindi? Tolerably close to the famous verse from the oral tradition. And it does not stand alone. Other slokas could also be cited where the text discusses relationships between caste Vaishnavas and others:

The sages and the scriptures enjoin those born in the higher castes to serve Vaishnavas, even those belonging to the lower castes.

(Sloka 107, pp. 184–5.)

Those belonging to the twice-born castes must seek liberation in Hari, who does not care for either rituals or caste.

(Sloka 125, pp. 197–8.)

Those who carry the five Vaishnava marks on their body, whether twice-born, Shudras, or women—are epitomes of piousness. In fact, they are manifestations of Vishnu himself. They are the essence of the holiness of holy places. They purify the place in which they dwell. All sins go away merely by looking at these noble souls. (Slokas 149–150, p. 213.)

Richard Burghart did well in not mentioning the *Ananda Bhashya* amongst the works 'attributed to Ramanand', its authenticity was contested from the beginning and in due course of time even its most enthusiastic upholders discarded it. Similarly the authenticity of the *Ramarchanpaddhati* was always a matter of bitter polemics between the 'traditionalist' and the 'radical' Ramanandis—as it contained a guru-parampara, the real bone of contention between these two factions. Bhagwadacharya and his supporters tried to produce their own version of the *Paddhati*, but ultimately quite bluntly rejected the 'present Ramarchanpaddhati' as nothing but 'forgery'. The case with the *Bhaskar*, however, was different. Contesting factions produced their own versions of the *Bhaskar* as well, but nobody ever questioned the authenticity of the work in its entirety. The 'radical' Ramanandis only eliminated any reference to Ramanuja from the manuscripts 'found' by them. Apart from such contested slokas the '*Bhaskar*' was accepted as authentically representing the philosophical and liturgical views of Ramanand.

The significance of the *Bhaskar* lies in its being the single consensually accepted statement of the views of Ramanandi sampraday as a whole. Whether it really came down from the sixteenth century or was attributed to Ramanand much later, it presents us with the peculiarity of Ramanandi sampraday, which wants to see its 'founder' as an Acharya well versed in Sanskrit, practising and teaching the Saguna mode of worship, yet rejecting the caste hierarchy not only in matters of bhakti but also, by extension, in everyday practice. It calls the Shudra and women Vaishnavas—'epitomes' of piousness, deserving the reverence normally paid to the 'twice-born'. It is extremely suggestive that to clinch this point (whosoever he was and whenever he composed this text), the author of the *Bhaskar* took care to insert into his text a Sanskrit rendering of the Hindi saying 'relates to God, one who belongs to him, the question of caste does not arise'.

The Sanskrit Ramanand of the *Bhaskar* represents continuity with the Hindi Ramanand insofar as the issue of caste is concerned, even though he diverges in conceptualizing the Supreme Being and representing modes of worship. The Sanskrit Ramanand affirms 'non-caste Hinduism'. He had to. After all, those who were constructing the Sanskrit Ramanand in modern times were seeking the seal of orthodox approval on their heteropraxy, which was an inevitable result of the 'diversity' of their sampraday. As Burghart puts it:

One feature of the Ramanandi Sampraday which appears unique in comparison with other ascetic Sampradays is its diversity. During the sixteenth and seventeenth centuries, both devotional and Tantrik disciplines were attributed to Ramanand; both twice-born Hindus as well as members of the servant and untouchable castes, women and perhaps even Muslims were recruited into the Sampraday.[45]

BHAGWADACHARYA IN THE EARLY TWENTIETH CENTURY

In his autobiography, Bhagwadacharya informs us that he was born in 1880 in Punjab into a family of Brahmin immigrants from Uttar Pradesh. He also gives hints of his opponents maligning him as 'some low caste person from Bihar', as he was 'forced to spend his childhood in Bihar and to hide his Brahmin identity'. He reached Ayodhya in 1918 and was almost immediately 'spotted' by those Ramanandis who wanted to take on the haughty Ramanujis, but Bhagwadacharya was a 'novice' of the Bara Sthan, whose mahant favoured the traditionalists. Hence Bhagwaddas (Bhagwadacharya's name in the this phase) had to keep away from the 'controversies' out of respect for the 'command' of his Guru. He sought an outlet in nationalist politics, as he thought the sectarian feud was not going to help anyone:

Vaishnavas (Ramanandis) wanted me to join their ranks in this feud with the Ramanujis. But I avoided all this, for one; my Gurudeva did not want me to join them, secondly I always considered the national service more important. This sectarian feud was not going to serve the nation in any way. I left for Prayaga in order to avoid all this.[46]

In Prayaga, he participated in Congress activities and took the lifelong Khadi vow, but could not keep away from the sectarian feud for long. He came back to Ayodhya and soon found himself in the leadership role of the radical Ramanandis. Along with Balakram Vinayak he decided to 'first of all, form an organization':

The organization was formed immediately and named 'Shri Ramanandiya Shri Vaishnava Mahamandala'. The times were terrible. We had to change the guru-parampara. The difficulty of such a task among the sadhus is beyond imagination for outsiders....We also needed a committee to do research into the Paramparas and find from them that there was no connection between Ramanuja and Ramanand. We formed such a committee as well. It was named Puratatwanusandhayini Samiti (the archeological research committee). I was the general secretary of both.[47]

The times were indeed troubled. There was a spate of pamphlets and notices from both the sides, and all of a sudden, the research committee 'found' a document detailing the requisite parampara. In a debate at the famous Hanuman Garhi temple (in 1920) the radical group presented this parampara as the 'main' evidence of 'no-connection'. The resulting chasm between Bhagwaddas and his guru led to Bhagwaddas being forced to leave Bara Sthan 'voluntarily'. He was immediately welcomed at Maniram ki Chhaoni.

The main evidence in this debate, the parampara just mentioned, was said to have been composed by Agradas of the third generation of Ramanand's disciples. Raghubardas (a friend and comrade of Bhagwadacharya at this point of time, but later on an adversary) had found it 'by chance'; it was being used as wrapping paper. This was only the first in a whole series of research miracles performed by the radical Ramanandis. The parampara was composed by Agradas in the form of a dialogue. In it, Agradas's guru Krishandas requests his guru Anantanand—one of the 12 immediate disciples of Ramanand—to identify the lineage through which the initiatory Rama mantra had passed. The parampara consists of 22 slokas and contradicts all traditional paramparas on the question of Ramanand's belonging to the spiritual lineage of Ramanuja. Bhagwaddas wrote an introduction to this parampara and dismissed all the other paramparas with an argument that had no academic merit but was appealing to his target audience of Ramanandis:

None of the current Paramparas is composed by any of our own Acharyas. We are duty bound to honour a Parampara composed by someone of our own fold. Our committee has found a Parampara that is absolutely different from all others. It is worthy of our special attention and respect as it is composed by Agradasji, who was third in the lineage from Ramanandji himself. We, the Ramanandis, must ponder it. After all, who amongst us dare say that Agradasji was writing any falsehood....This Parampara clearly tells us that Ramanandji did not belong to lineage of

Ramanujaji. This statement is bound to cause a lot of disturbance but is still worthy of very serious attention.[48]

The radical strategy and aim both become clear here. Anybody doubting the authenticity of this parampara would be guilty of sacrilege against Agradas himself. And in order to avoid that one had to accept that Ramanand had nothing to do with Ramanuja. The deliberate confusion between the *Agastya Samhita* proper and its putative chapters composed by Ramanarayandas also came in handy for Bhagwaddas, as he could put the lineage of the Rama Mantra, as given in the eighth chapter of the *Agastya Samhita* proper, into the mouth of Agradas in this parampara which Raghubardas had found 'by chance'. Similarly Bhagwaddas could also refer to 1356 VS, as given in the 'same Samhita', elsewhere in his writings, with the caveat we have heard, namely, that 'the floruit of Ramanand might need to be pushed back by another hundred years.'

The other important aspect of this parampara was its complete erasure of any Acharya of southern origin. This was required to completely cut off the Ramanuji connection and it also implicitly dismissed the popular belief that Ramanand brought Bhakti from the south, a sentiment articulated in another well-known Hindi verse—'*Bhakti dravid upji, laye Ramanand*'—bhakti originated in the south and was brought (to the north) by Ramanand. Here again the *Ramanand Janmotsava Katha*'s idea of Ramanand hailing from Prayaga was helpful to the cause of radical Ramanandis and they upheld it quite vigorously.

The problem, however, was the guru-parampara as given in the *Ramarchan Paddhati* attributed to Ramanand. Here Bhagwaddas and Raghubardas were faced with their own logic of sacrilege: how dare one doubt the parampara given by Ramanand himself? At first the radical group tried to face the awkward situation by rejecting outrightly the *Paddhati* as 'fake' (1923), but they later took a more moderate position, expressing doubts about the 'authenticity' of the text doing the rounds in the name of *Paddhati* (1936) in response to Balbhadra Das's (1928) claim that his edition was based upon a manuscript of the seventeenth century and a litho copy of 1880. It was only in 1958 that Bhagwaddas finally came to an unambiguous declaration on this matter. He said, 'It is beyond doubt that the *Ramarchanpaddhati* and the present *Ananda Bhashya* were never composed by Ramanand'.[49]

The radical faction succeeded, on the occasion of the Ujjain Kumbh in 1921, to bring the bulk of Ramanandis and many leading Mahants to their side. Bhagwadacharya was to call 11 May 1921 'the day of deliverance for the sampraday'. It was on this day, he said, that the Ramanujis failed to respond to the charge that their sectarian texts 'contained insults' to Rama and other Ramawat deities.

The 'deliverance' earned at the Kumbh in 1921 had immediate fallout, as though the Ramanandis were only waiting for this 'intellectual' victory to be translated into some symbolic act. Bhagwadacharya notes with understandable sense of achievement:

The final ritual bath was just a few days away. Up to that point the Ramanujis led the procession, with a prominent Ramanuji entering in a palanquin carried by the Ramanandis....After the victory things changed dramatically. The Ramanujis were excluded from the procession that forms for the final bath. Now they cannot join the Ramanandis in any Kumbh.[50]

Even after this 'deliverance', however, sharp debates and polemics persisted, as is made clear by the dates mentioned above in the context of the controversy over the *Paddhati*. The radical faction was faced with the task of not only 'changing the parampara' but also that of producing a bhashya by Ramanand, as without a bhashya nobody can be considered an Acharya in his own right. The radical faction was aware of this need and had begun the work even before the 'deliverance'. In 1920 Bhagwadacharya made reference to the '*Ananda Bhashya* of 'Swami Ramanandji' which was in the process of being published. The bhashya ultimately appeared in full in 1932 and Bhagwadacharya, along with others of the radical faction, continued to swear by its authenticity in the face of onslaughts on the part of opponents like Balbhadra Das, who pointed out as many as fourteen inaccuracies of grammar and doctrine. The opponents categorically accused Raghubardas of forging it with the sole intent of severing the connection with Ramanujis. Bhagwadacharya vehemently rejected all such charges at this point in time, but after his falling out with Raghubardas, started condemning this bhashya as 'nothing but a forgery perpetuated by Raghubardas'. In his autobiography, he gives the fascinating details of intrigues that went into 'transforming the Janaki Bhashya of Ram Prasad into the Ananda Bhashya and attributing it to Ramanand'. He admits quite candidly, 'being a new and fresh recruit to the cause, I inspired this act of injustice and fraud.'[51]

This confession came in 1958. He also confessed to having 'changed the very body of the *Vaishnavamatabjabhaskar*'. But, just as in case of the early or late floruit of Ramanand, the authenticity of the *Bhashya*, *Paddhati*, or *Bhaskar* hardly mattered now. Bhagwadacharya and his group had successfully metamorphosed 'the wayward disciple of Ramanuji tradition' into the 'founder of an independent tradition, into an Acharya in his own right, an author of Sanskrit works'. As was intended, this metamorphosis took place in the imagination of the Ramanandis, and we now know the dynamics of this metamorphosis. The transformation, however, took place not only in the Ramanandi imagination but also in the imagination of academic scholars.

This change had far-reaching consequences, some of which I have tried to analyse in this essay. Having achieved their 'deliverance', Ramanandis now take the authenticity of all the Sanskrit works attributed to Ramanand for granted, and in the same measure insist on his early floruit. The strategy of Sanskritizing Ramanand in order to subvert the Brahminical hegemony of the Ramanujis has worked well so far as the Ramanandis are concerned, or at least they think so. They have not completely disowned the Hindi Ramanand, but have definitely subordinated him to the Sanskrit one. They also continue to revere his 'low caste disciples' although they are no longer considered to be the authentic transmitters of Ramanand's doctrine. Obviously, then, the Ramanandi 'radicals' have succeeded for the Ramanandi sampraday. But what about Ramanand himself? What has this strategy done to him?

To put it mildly, it has denied Ramanand his roots and has helped undermine the significance of his attempt at transcending the social identity he was assigned at birth. It has weakened the courage of his convictions. Ramanand emerges as an independent thinker both in his Hindi compositions and in whatever little we have in other references made to him in the medieval period. In spite of being born a Brahmin, he was no Brahmin supremacist; in fact, he was quite critical of ritualism and gave fullest space to the individual choice of his disciples. The modern Ramanandis constructed an orthodox, albeit liberal Acharya to replace the historical Ramanand and in so doing reduced the historical facts and evidence to mere instruments at the service of their present project.

This utter instrumentalization of facts and method and complete subordination of the past to the present denying its autonomy is bound to lead to problems of a very serious kind, as we in India have been witnessing in so many contexts. If it is widely accepted that the politics of identity override honest efforts to know the past, both justice and truth stand on perilously weak footing.

The politics of identity has made the idea of 'representation' extremely popular in the academic circles these days. The rejection of the possibility of analysing the relationships between representations and reality has led to the fixation of ascribed identity with the supposedly 'authentic' representation that precludes the possibility of moral choice on part of the individuals who by definition happen to carry multiple identities. In the area of bhakti studies this fixation results in systematic denial of the very core of the bhakti sensibility. This sensibility is seen as an exclusionist representation on the part of various social identities instead of what it really is: a dialogue between various moral actors.

The story of Ramanand is the story of such a dialogue and needs to be probed further. Is it true, as Richard Burghart says, that Ramanand was dwarfed by his disciples in 'Priya Dass' commentary on Nabha Ji's *Sri Bhakta Mala*' [52] or could it be that Ramanand did not care to establish a *panth* or create a cult around him? In that case, would what Burghart reads as 'dwarfing' turn out to be a genuine tribute to Ramanand's personality and temperament?

The story of Ramanand, along with others, helps us see the Indian tradition as something vibrant, not as frozen in time. It also points out some of the processes underlying the emergence and spread of the bhakti sensibility in pre-modern India. This story bears witness to the dynamics that made it possible for some individuals and groups to go beyond the social identities that had been assigned them at birth and seek to construct a parallel moral universe in their imagination—a benchmark in the process of critiquing the existing social order. This story needs to be probed further because Ramanand may have been the most important source of inspiration for the spread of 'non-caste Hinduism' in the whole sweep of Indian—certainly north Indian—religious history.

NOTES AND REFERENCES

1. The story of this essay goes back to the summer of 2000, when I published an article in the Hindi journal *Bahuvachan*, analysing the legends of the Kabir–Ramanand relationship. In this chapter, I tried to look at legends surrounding this key figure in the religious history of north India sympathetically, accepting the common assumption that Ramanand was born in 1299 CE and passed away in 1410. David Lorenzen appreciated my exploration of the legends but disagreed vehemently with the dates of Ramanand. This urged me to work and reflect upon the question of Ramanand's floruit and his role in the bhakti sensibility of north India. The present essay is only a brief report of ongoing research and reflection, made possible by the help and support of many friends and students. I would like to thank the following persons: N.K. Pande, Samir Baran Nandi, Pinuccia Caracchi, Noorin, L.N. Malik, Keshav Mishra, Koslendradas, John S. Hawley and David Lorenzen, Ishita Banerjee-Dube and Saurabh Dube, and my wife, Suman, and children, Ritambhara and Ritwik.

2. Richard Burghart, 'The Founding of the Ramanandi Sampraday' in David Lorenzen (ed.), *Religious Movements in South Asia 600–1800* (New Delhi: Oxford University Press, 2004), p. 231.

3. William Pinch, *Peasants and Monks in British India* (New Delhi: Oxford University Press, 1996), p. 50.

4. Charlotte Vaudeville, *A Weaver Named Kabir* (New Delhi: Oxford University Press, 1993), p. 88.

5. Ibid., pp. 88–9.

6. Ramchandra Shukla, *Hindi Sahitya ka Itihas* (Varanasi, Nagari Pracharani Sabha, Samvat 2035, that is, 1978 CE), p. 86.

7. The Shri Vaishnavas were quite liberal on the issue of caste in their early phase when they had Shudra functionaries in their temples. Ramanuja himself is credited with establishing rather a liberal Pancharatra form of worship in many temples. However, by the fourteenth century, they were divided on the issues of caste and doctrine. The Vijayanagara rulers played a major part in undermining the rights and privileges of the Shudra functionaries in the temples. See Burton Stein, 'Social Mobility and Medieval South Indian Sampradays' in Lorenzen (ed.) *Religious Movements in South Asia*, pp. 80–101. The ruler of Jaipur played a similar role three centuries later to make Ramanandis stick to caste order and its ideology.

8. Winand Callewaert, *The Hagiographies of Anantdas: The Bhakti Poets of North India* (Surrey: Curzon Press, 2000), p. 1.

9. Ibid., p. 32.

10. Ibid., p. 3.

11. R.G. Bhandarkar, *Vaisnavism Saivism and Minor Religious Systems* (New Delhi: Munshiram Manoharlal, 2001), pp. 66–7.

12. '*Shrimadagastyasamhitantargat Ramanand Janmotsva Katha Pandit Ramanarayndasji krit Bhashatikalankrita tatkirtabhahshtikayuta Shri Ramanand janmotsvashtakanch, tatkritamShriRamannadashtakanch'(the story* celebrating *the birth of Ramanand as found in the Agastya Samhita with a Hindi gloss by Pandit*

Ramanarayndasji also containing his Hindi gloss of the octave celebrating *the birth of Ramanand and his own Ramanand octave along with a Hindi gloss),* Mumbai, 1963 (Vikrama Samvat).

13. Sitaramsharan 'Rupkala', *Shri Bhaktamal* (Lucknow: Tejkumar Book Depot, 2001), p. 292.

14. I got this copy from the Goyanka Sanskrit Pathshala, Varanasi, with the permission of the deputy librarian, Pandit Indushekhar Tiwari. The National Library, Calcutta, also possesses a copy (call no.180.Jd.90.13) of this edition.

15. Mahavir Prasad Mishra, *Agastya Samhita—Purva Bhag* (Haridwar: Vidya Varidhi Granthmala, 1985), p. 3.

16. Hans Bakker, *Ayodhya* (Groningen: Egbert Forsten, 1986), part I, p. 67.

17. Ibid., p. 70.

18. Mishra, *Agastya Samhita*, p. 3 (footnote).

19. Bakker, *Ayodhya*, pp. 83–4.

20. Ibid., p. 68, fn. 1.

21. Pinuccia Caracchi, *Vita Di Ramanand* (Torino: Promolibri, 1989), pp. 10–13.

22. Ibid., pp. 11–12.

23. Balbhadradas, *Shri Vaishnava Matabaj Bhaskar Ramarchan Paddhati Sahit* (Jaipur: Mahant Ramakrishnanad Vikrami Samvat 1985, that is, 1928 CE), p. 243.

24. Bakker, *Ayodhya*, p. xv.

25. Ibid., p. xv.

26. Bhagwadacharya, *Swami Bhagwadacharya,* vol. III (Ahmedabad, Sri Rammandir, 1961), p. 104. 'Swami Bhagwadacharya' is the general title Bhagwadacharya gave to his own 'collected works' running into several volumes. The first of these, his autobiography, appeared from Alwar in January 1958.

27. Bhagwadacharya, *Shri Ramanand Digvijay* (Ahmedabad: Kashmira Society, 1967), p. 47.

28. Hazari Prasad Dwivedi, 'Kabir' in *Hazari Prasad Dwivedi Granthawali* (Collected Works), vol. 3 (New Delhi: Rajkamal Prakashan 1981), p. 70. 'Kabir' was first published in 1942.

29. Pitambar Dutt Barthwal, *Traditions of Indian mysticism based upon Nirguna School of Hindi Poetry* (New Delhi: Heritage Publishers,1978), p. 252.

30. *P.D. Barthwal, Ramanand ki Hindi Rachnayen* (Varanasi: Nagari Pracharini Sabha V.S. 2012, that is, 1955 CE), Introduction, p. 23.

31. Parashuram Chaturvedi, *'Uttari Bharat ki Sant Parampara'* (Allahabad, Leader Press, VS 2008 i.e. 1951 CE), p. 869.

32. Ibid., p. 228.

33. David Lorenzen, 'Traditions of Non-Caste Hinduism,' in David Lorenzen, *Who Invented Hinduism: Essays on Religion in History* (New Delhi: Yoda Press, 2006), pp. 79–80. This essay was first published in 1987.

34. John Stratton Hawley, *Three Bhakti Voices: Mirabai, Surdas and Kabir in Their Times and Ours* (New Delhi: Oxford University Press, 2005), p. 272.

35. David Lorenzen, *Kabir Legends and Ananta-Das's Kabir Parchai* (Delhi: Sri Satguru Publications, 1992), p. 11.

36. Abhilashdas, *Kabir Darshan* (Allahabad: Parakh Prakashak Kabir Sansthan, 1997), p. 89.

37. Sant Vivekdas Acharya, *Amarpur Desh Apna* (Varanasi: Kabir Vani Prakashan Kendra, 2006), p. 22.

38. P.D. Barthwal, *Ramanand ki Hindi Rachnayen* (Varanasi: Nagari Pracharini Sabha) 1955, Introduction, p. 1.

39. *The Sarvangi of Rajjab*, Shahabuddin Iraqi (ed.), (Aligarh: 1985), p. 490–1.

40. *The Sarvangi of Gopaldas*, Winand M. Callewaert (eds), (New Delhi: Manohar 1993), p. 166.

41. Ibid., p. 322.

42. Ibid., p. 424.

43. *The Sarvangi of Rajjab*, pp. 591 and 337.

44. Richard Burghart, 'The Founding of the Ramanandi Sampraday' in Lorenzen (ed.), *Religious Movements in South Asia*, p. 247.

45. Ibid., p. 231.

46. Bhagwadacharya, Swami *Bhagwadacharya,* vol. I (Alwar: Ramanand Sahitya Mandir, 1958), p. 79.

47. Ibid., p. 86.

48. *Swami Bhagwadacharya*, vol. III, pp. 31–2.

49. *Swami Bhagwadacharya*, vol. I, p. 596.

50. *Swami Bhagwadacharya*, vol. I, p. 118.

51. Ibid., pp. 486–9 and 574–5.

52. Burghart in Lorenzen (ed.), *Religious Movements in South Asia*, p. 231.

6. FIGHTING OVER KABIR'S DEAD BODY[1]

Linda Hess

It is a good story, one of the two most often told about Kabir. In fact it is so good that the Sikhs tell a similar story about what happened on the occasion of Guru Nanak's death.[2] The master passes on peacefully, but even before he draws his last breath, his followers (who have, as it turns out, been only temporarily united by his charismatic presence) begin fingering the hilts of their swords. As the warmth drains from his skin, their temperatures rise. Soon they are engaged, weapons drawn, in a full-scale confrontation. Over what? Ritual!

The Hindus want to cremate their beloved teacher to the soothing drone of mantras from the Vedas. The Muslims want to bury him while chanting verses from the Qur'an. The earliest known hagiography of Kabir, Ananta-Das's *Kabir Parachai*, says simply, 'The Hindus and Turks...formed...band[s]. One band said, "You should burn him." The other band said, "You should bury him"'.[3] Then it tells how his physical body disappeared amidst piles of flowers brought for the occasion. Later embellishments heighten the drama and give it a political tinge. Nawab Bijli Khan and Maharaja Virsingh Baghel gallop in with troops. A pitched battle is averted when someone discovers that Kabir's body is gone.[4] Tellers of the tale commonly add that, finding only flowers under the shroud, each faction took half of the flowers to bury or burn, as they pleased.

It is no coincidence that this story attaches to Guru Nanak and Kabir, and not to other poet-gurus of the period. Both Nanak and Kabir deliberately occupied an ambiguous space between Hindu and Muslim communities. In his enlightenment story, Nanak enters a river and emerges after three days with these words on his lips: 'There is no Hindu, there is no Muslim.' From that formula we can understand that there *were* Hindus, there *were* Muslims, they were often entangled in rivalries and conflicts, and Nanak wished to underline the deluded nature of their fighting as he offered a spiritual truth deeper than their precious religious identities.

Kabir is identified with Muslims by (for example) his name, his weaver caste, his Julaha parents, and the common appearance of 'Sahab' as a name for God. He is identified with Hindus by (for example) his guru Ramananda, his frequent use of yogic terminology, his apparent acceptance of reincarnation, and the common appearance of 'Ram' as a name for God. The poetry attributed to him features countless satirical jabs at the foolishness and hypocrisy of both Hindus and Muslims. It also condemns the general idiocy and viciousness of clinging to one's own sectarian identity while attacking others on the basis of theirs. In a famous poem that resonates with the story of Bijli Khan and Virsingh Baghel (as well as with murderous communal conflicts today), he says:

Saints, I've seen
the world is mad...
The Hindu says Ram
is the fountain of love,
the Turk says Rahman.
Then they kill each other.
No one understands.[5]

This first story of fighting over Kabir, like many to follow, has a special bite: the fighting devotees have to forget Kabir's central teachings in order to engage in the conflict.

A law of cultural politics everywhere is: collective entities will fight over possession of their heroes, origin stories, and histories; they will also fight over the proper ways to honour and reinforce their icons and narratives. These collectivities may be identified in terms of religion, caste, language, ethnicity, nation, or ideology (to name some obvious examples). When a sense of the sacred enters the discourse, some of the most interesting battles will take place on the fields of ritual and myth.[6]

In this essay we will learn about contestations in the late twentieth and early twenty-first centuries over narratives, doctrines, and rituals associated with Kabir. The famous story recounted above suggests that such debates may have started the moment he ceased breathing. Why are people still fighting? They are driven by considerations of both power and faith, and it is often difficult to disentangle the two. Institutional turf battles involve the usual types of power: control over many followers; accumulation of land and wealth; and wielding of political influence.[7] The faithful are driven by personal feelings of devotion; by loyalty to traditions and gurus; and by fear that they will be in trouble if they don't believe or behave as they have been told. In India, religious feelings are protected by law; people whose feelings are hurt can assert their rights as believers fairly aggressively, with some confidence that the law is behind them, as we will see below.

Two main points will emerge from this inquiry. First, studying how people fight over their heroes, doctrines, histories, and symbols provides valuable insight into the history of religion. Second, these contestations take place both publicly and privately, among leaders and followers. Usually we hear only about the public part. Here, we have the opportunity to see both institutional leaders and ordinary people getting into the fray. Should the followers of Kabir be doing rituals? Sectarian gurus will naturally express and enforce their views. But in this case, on the issue of the *chaukā āratī* ritual, I was also able to observe a dramatic unfolding of the debate among Kabir devotees in the Malwa region of Madhya Pradesh. Thus the story will be both top-down and bottom-up. We will see how the issues play out institutionally as well as on a more intimate level, among friends and family members.

KABIR RELIGION

If Hindus and Muslims were hotly contesting their claims to Kabir at the time of his death,[8] that situation soon changed. The Muslims seem to have lost interest, while Kabir's Hinduization proceeded rapidly.[9] Although he harshly criticized certain Hindu beliefs and practices (such as divine avatars, image-worship, and caste), there were also many positive references to Hindu tradition in his poetry.[10] On the whole, Hindus could easily accommodate Kabir in their diverse and flexible religious spaces. In the fluidity of oral tradition and the dynamics of sect formation, texts and practices that were compatible with Hindu forms and ideas flourished.

Soon there was a story to show that Kabir was not *really* the son of Muslims, but had been adopted. His true mother? A Brahmin widow, of course! Why not a Kshatriya, Vaishya, Shudra, or Untouchable? For the same reason that he could not be a Muslim. A great, holy, enlightened being, according to certain hegemonic views, should be a Brahmin. Today the story that the newborn Brahmin Kabir was set afloat on a pond at the edge of Varanasi, to be found and adopted by the Muslim weavers Niru and Nima, is widely believed by Hindus. Members of the Kabir Panth do not accept the story of the Brahmin widow; but most of them reject the idea that Kabir was the biological child of Muslim parents. He was, according to most Kabir Panthis I have spoken to, an avatar of God who appeared floating on a lotus pad on Lahartara pond on the outskirts of Varanasi. The Muslim Julahas Niru and Nima became his foster parents after finding and adopting the miraculous baby.[11]

The Hinduizing process gained momentum in a sectarian environment. In its symbols, rituals, and structures of authority, the Kabir Panth has used generally Hindu and particularly Vaishnav models and terminology: gurus and mahants, *āratī* and *sandhyā pāṭh*, *dīkshā* and *prasād*, *tulsī* beads, occasional Sanskrit chants, and a likeness of Kabir in the place normally occupied by a Hindu divine image.[12] But they have not imported all Hindu forms equally. Notably, they tend to refuse caste; their leaders often speak strongly against caste, and their institutions and functions generally appear free of caste distinctions. This social emphasis corresponds with their membership—the vast majority being from formerly 'untouchable' castes and poor agricultural classes in rural north India.[13]

The Kabir Panth was founded either prior to the master's death in 1518, or in the late sixteenth, or in the seventeenth century, depending on whose story you listen to and what evidence you find persuasive. Whenever it started, it gradually became heavy with authority, as religious institutions founded in the names of anti-authoritarian teachers are wont to do. Naturally, the Panth felt entitled to claim ownership of Kabir. They were the engine that produced his ongoing honour and glory, along with thousands—then hundreds of thousands, then millions—of disciples. They spread his teachings far and wide, kindling the lamp of awakening in the hearts of initiates. Inspiration from Kabir created the Panth. As time went on, the Panth created Kabir. After all, he could no longer create himself. He was dead. As he muses dryly in a poem: 'When you die, what do you do with your body? Once the breath stops, you have to put it away'.[14]

Here I will limit myself to a brief introduction of the Kabir Panth. For details, one can refer to the numerous articles by David Lorenzen, and for earlier research one can consult colonial scholars such as Wilson, Crooke, Westcott, and Keay.[15]

We don't know when or where the earliest version of the Kabir Panth began. There are today several 'seats' (*gaḍḍī*), also called branches (*shākhā*), which claim genealogies of gurus going back to Kabir. In this essay, I will refer only to the two largest and most influential traditions, which I will identify as the Kabir Chaura and the Dharamdasi or Damakhera traditions.[16] The word shākhā, literally 'branch', might give the impression that the two are related through some central organization, but that is not the case. They have independent histories, separate guru lineages, distinct literatures, and a relationship that is not necessarily friendly.[17]

The Kabir Chaura sect is headquartered at Kabir Chaura Math (monastery) in Varanasi, Uttar Pradesh, where Kabir himself lived. Its founding is attributed to Surat Gopal (or Shruti Gopal), a disciple of Kabir. The Dharamdasi sect is based in the village of Damakhera in Chhattisgarh, a linguistic and cultural region in central India which in 2000 became a state, carved out of the eastern side of Madhya Pradesh.[18] Dharamdas, revered in this branch as the most intimate and important direct disciple of Kabir, is believed to have started the Panth during Kabir's lifetime at the master's behest. The Dharamdasis also call their sect the '*bayālīs vaṃśa*' or 'forty-two generation' tradition. Kabir prophesied, they believe, that this sect would remain the authoritative source of his liberating teachings for forty-two generations of gurus in unbroken succession. Given that today, after more than five hundred years, they are only at the fifteenth guru, the prophecy suggests that their gaḍḍī will prevail for a very long time.

Both the Kabir Chaura and Dharamdasi sects have followers in widespread areas across northern India. Both believe that their tradition started first, and the other followed. Some Kabir Chaura spokesmen, following scholar Kedarnath Dvivedi, have asserted that

Dharamdas was not contemporary to Kabir but lived at least a century later.[19] Though both Panths accept the *Bījak* as Kabir's authentic composition, for Kabir Chaura the Bījak is the only sacred and authentic text. The Dharamdasis are ambivalent about the Bījak and place a much higher value on the *Anurāg Sāgar* ('Ocean of Love'), which they believe Kabir composed and Dharamdas wrote down. The two works are very different. The Dharamdasis also regard a number of other works as authentic—many of them having the word *sāgar* (ocean) in the title.

THE DANGERS OF DRAMA

Yogis say, 'Yoga's the top',
don't talk of seconds.'
Tuft of hair, shaven head,
matted locks, vow of silence—
who's gotten anywhere?
Brainy ones, gifted ones,
heroes, poets, benefactors
cry, 'I'm the greatest!'
The all go back where they came from
and don't take anything along.[20]

In 1987, the first episode of a serial on Kabir aired on Doordarshan, India's national television network. This was before the genre of religious serials on TV exploded with the unprecedented popularity of the epic *Ramayana,* which went on for over 100 episodes in 1988–9, and was followed immediately by the 96-episode *Mahabharata. Kabir* was a relatively low-profile enterprise, written and directed by Anil Chowdhary, a graduate of the National School of Drama who had worked in theatre before moving into the world of television and movies in Mumbai. Chowdhary was fascinated by Kabir. How did a poor, low-caste, uneducated member of a Muslim artisan family become such a powerful and popular figure in Brahmin-dominated Varanasi? Chowdhary read many books, spoke to academic and religious authorities, began writing a script, and shot the first episode in 1985. He loved the project and described himself as being in a state of *nashā* (drunken joy) while working on it.

But he was soon sobered by a series of lawsuits filed against him by followers of Kabir, most of them associated with a Gujarati tradition of the Panth. When I met him in 2003, he spoke of six initial cases—civil and criminal—filed in Ahmedabad, Surat, and Delhi. The main issue was that he had depicted Kabir as a human being, while these Kabir Panthis believed he was God. According to them, Kabir was not born but became an avatar when he manifested himself as an infant on Lahartara pond. They objected strenuously when the serial showed a non-miraculous birth and a normal family life, including a mother who slapped him when he misbehaved. Chowdhary described arriving at court hearings to find hundreds of Kabir Panthi men shouting and brandishing lathis (long sticks) at him.

Chowdhary's life became nightmarish. He was threatened and harassed. Describing a period when he was still trying to produce episodes, he spoke of spending two days shooting, two days editing, and two days in court. Ultimately becoming depressed and fearful, he cancelled the project after airing about a dozen episodes. He had to pay heavy legal expenses himself and suffered serious financial loss. Even in 2003, he was uneasy talking to me and asked me not to record the conversation. Later I heard that the number of cases had eventually multiplied beyond the initial six. Though he claimed that none of the cases had merit and all would have failed if brought to trial, his attackers were able to make his life a hell by continuing to file new cases.

It is important to mention that not all Kabir Panthis shared the viewpoint of those who sued and intimidated Chowdhary. Sant Vivek Das—today the acharya or top religious authority of the Kabir Chaura tradition, and at that time too an influential voice at Kabir Chaura—helped and supported Chowdhary through these struggles. (We will hear more of Vivek Das in the coming section on ritual.)

My conversation with Anil Chowdhary took place at the Mumbai residence of Shekhar Sen, a gifted classical singer, music director, and actor who had created a one-man play called *Kabir*. Sen's show has been very successful; at the time of this writing, he has done over 300 performances in India and abroad. But he too has felt the repressive hand of Kabir's true believers. In 2003, he organized a tour that was also a pilgrimage for him. It went from Kashi (Varanasi) to Magahar (near Gorakhpur in UP), places where Kabir is believed to have been born and died. Sen had scheduled performances in fourteen places along the way, shouldering most of the expenses himself.

But as he neared Magahar, a threatening headline appeared in a local newspaper: 'Rivers of blood will flow if Shekhar Sen brings his show to Magahar'. This time it was sadhus (initiated renunciant followers) of the Kabir ashram in Magahar, affiliated with Kabir Chaura in Varanasi, who objected to the way Kabir's life was depicted. The sticking point for them was that Sen showed Kabir as a married man with children. They insisted that Kabir never married and was a celibate sadhu. If the headline was to be believed, some devotees might be willing to kill for this point! Just before going to Magahar, Sen had performed to a very appreciative audience in the nearby city of Gorakhpur. A group of young men there suggested that they could accompany him to Magahar and beat up anyone who disturbed his performance, but Sen declined the offer.

Sen met with the mahant (religious head) of the Magahar ashram, along with other locals including sadhus and school teachers. They displayed books that stated that Kabir was celibate, never married, and of course never had children. Sen replied that he had read all these and more; that he had other sources that described Kabir's wife, Loi, and his son and daughter, Kamal and Kamali; and that one of the Kabir Panthi biographies which they were citing made absurd and even obscene claims.[21] He declared that Kabir belonged to all humanity, not just to the Kabir Panth, and he mentioned that his grandfather was Acharya Kshiti Mohan Sen—famed as a pioneering researcher of Kabir's oral and written poetry in the early twentieth century, the man who provided Rabindranath Tagore with the texts that were the source of Tagore's *100 Poems of Kabir*. Kabir, Sen asserted, was his heritage as much as the Panth's. Though the mahant at Magahar was an educated man and sympathetic to the artist's position, he emphasized the problem of dealing with believers who had little education and a strong faith in Kabir as their God. They couldn't help being extremely upset at seeing Kabir represented in a way that contradicted what they had been taught. Saying that he did not wish to cause grief to anyone, Sen agreed to remove offensive portions of his script in Magahar (but *only* in Magahar).

Was that the end of the story? No. In March 2006, Sen was to perform in Surat, Gujarat. He had been invited by one group of Kabir devotees; but another group sent a telegram stating that his drama was offensive and had to be stopped. He again offered to speak with them, but before that could happen he heard from an attorney associated with the friendly group. The outraged Kabir Panthis had gone to court to try to restrain him from performing. The friendly attorney was prepared to defend him. Sen sent photocopies of literary sources that supported his representation of Kabir.

At that point in the conversation I became exasperated and asked Sen why he bothered to defend himself at all. He was an artist and had a right to write his own script. What law had he broken? What could they do to him? He reminded me that in India, religious *feelings* are protected. Along with obvious offences such as injuring or defiling places of worship, disturbing religious assemblies, and trespassing with malicious intent, the law criminalizes insults, words, or even sounds that offend religious feelings.[22] Though a conviction would result only if the defendant was found to have injured feelings with deliberate intent, complainants can hound a person almost indefinitely with accusations and lawsuits. Anil Chowdhary's woes are a case in point.

Sen cancelled his *Kabir* performance in Surat and performed a show about Tulsidas.

THE IMPORTANCE OF RITUAL

Why bump that shaven head on the earth?
Why dunk those bones in the water?
Parading as a holy man,
You hide yourself, and slaughter.
Why wash your hands and mouth, why chant
with a heart full of fraud?
Why bow in the mosque, and trudge
to Mecca to see God?....
Does Khuda live in the mosque?
Then who lives everywhere?
Is Ram in idols and holy ground?
Have you looked and found him there?
Hari in the east, Allah in the west,

so you like to dream.
Search in the heart, in the heart alone.
There live Ram and Karim!
Which is false, Qur'an or Veda?
False is the darkened view.
It's one, one, in every body!
How did you make it two?[23]

Rituals in the Kabir Panth could be considered inherently controversial, because Kabir debunked rituals. In the poetry it is clear that his problems with rituals include the delusions and hypocrisies they encourage and the hard lines of status they reify.

But sects (like nations, families, individuals) require rituals. They need ways to solemnize membership, to conjure up the unseen founder, to renew their vows and symbolize their hopes, all the while invoking their communion with each other, their continuity with past and future members, their difference from non-members, and the differences in status and function among members. They need special times to get together and do their rituals. They also need structures of authority. Some people have special rights to interpret the master's words and tell his stories, initiate new members, represent the sect, and shape its policy. These special people also run the rituals and become the vessels of ordinary devotees' reverence and faith. They may be in a position to command obedience and receive material benefits.

Chaukā Āratī and Authority in Two Traditions of the Kabir Panth

Nearly all branches of the Panth regularly practise a ritual that they call chaukā āratī. 'Āratī' is a generic term for the most common kind of worship in Hinduism, involving various offerings to the divine, with some items being returned as blessed gifts to the worshippers. It culminates with the waving of burning lamps before the deity in Hindu settings, or before the guru or image of Kabir in the Kabir Panth. 'Chaukā' means square and refers to the specially adorned four-sided space that must be prepared for the rite as it is practised in the Panth.

In his article, 'The Rituals of the Kabir Panth', David Lorenzen describes the ritual life of Kabir Chaura sadhus and includes translations of key texts that participants recite and sing in their daily and occasional rites. Though he is well aware of the ironies of sects and rituals operating in Kabir's name, Lorenzen declines the easy critique and concludes that in some notable ways the form and content of these practices do reflect Kabir's teaching:

Kabir Panth rituals are not simply the product of an abject capitulation to the social and cultural pressures that foster Sanskritization, Hinduization, and socioreligious homogenization. In the first place, the rituals...are quite simple and inexpensive compared to those of more orthodox Hindu monasteries and temples. More important, however, is the fact that the Kabir Panth rituals express, in both actions and words, an implicit opposition to many of the accepted religious and social norms of more orthodox Hinduism at the same time that they incorporate the basic structure and many formal elements of more orthodox rituals.[24]

It is this question—whether the rituals give decorous expression to or make a mockery of Kabir's teachings—that will become a matter of heated controversy in the Panth leadership and among some devotees a few years after the publication of Lorenzen's article.

During the period of Lorenzen's fieldwork, 1976–94, chaukā āratī seems to have been an uncontroversial part of the lives of sadhus and lay followers at Kabir Chaura in Varanasi and its affiliates. Kabir Chaura recognizes two types of chauka: the *ānandī* ('joyful') and *chalāvā* ('custom[ary]'). The former is done on happy occasions such as initiation of new members; the latter is done when someone dies. In addition to these two, the Dharamdasi branch prescribes two more: *solah sut* (sixteen-son) chauka arati and *ekottarī* (101) chauka arati—the former to celebrate a birth or to produce progeny, and the latter a very large-scale version of the rite performed only when the supreme guru, the lineage holder, is present.

Gangasharan Das (Shastri), for many years the *adhikārī* or administrative head of Kabir Chaura Math, and for about a decade the acharya or religious head, wrote in a guidebook on administration and conduct in the Panth:

The chauka is done in a prescribed way by all Kabir Panth devotees, sadhus and mahants, similar to the way sacrifices (*yajñā*) and fasts (*vrat*) are done. If a Kabir Panth disciple or sadhu is ensnared in any difficulty, he should worship the Lord by means of chauka arati, and the trouble can be removed. Chauka arati is a pure form of worship (*sāttvik pūjā*), and everyone can do it. By organizing a properly performed chauka arati, a person can be released from all his sins, and his consciousness can be purified. Ultimately by the grace of the guru and the supreme lord (*parameśvar*), he can attain the state of *kaivalyā* ('singleness,' highest meditative state, enlightenment), and all the bonds of this world will fall away. Chauka arati should also be done on special occasions like births and weddings. At the time of death, chalava arati should be done for the peace of the [departed] soul....Chauka arati is not the worship of gods and goddesses (*devī deva*). It is worship of the lord through the medium of the guru. This is the source of human well-being.[25]

The last few sentences indicate the centrality of the guru in this ritual. In the western square marked as the consecrated seat, a human guru—usually an authorized mahant of the Panth—sits and receives the worship. He becomes the form of the lord.

Dharamdasi literature is more explicit about the origin and meaning of chauka arati. Kabir himself created the ritual and proclaimed that its practice should continue forever:

In the Kabir Panth, *ānandī chauka arati* is a widespread and universally respected method of worshipping the guru....In it, the visible and present guru is the very form (*svarūp*) of Satguru Kabir Saheb. Every devotee is moved to arrange this *pūjā* in his/her home, and they do it with great reverence on every happy occasion. This *pūjā* is the way to attain the manifest supreme being.[26]

The author—who is the acharya, the lineage holder, of the Dharamdasi sect—paraphrases a passage from the *Anurag Sagar* that describes the first performance of chauka by Dharamdas for Kabir, explaining the spiritual meanings of various physical actions:

Breaking the straw symbolizes rising above the three *guṇa*s [qualities of material existence]. The *kanthī* [*tulsi* bead worn around the neck] is dedication to *satyapuruś*. Taking the name is attaining the form of the swan (*haṃsa*), or opening the door of spiritual knowledge. And to receive the certificate is to attain liberation....This *pūjā* was held for the first time in the home of Dhani Dharamdas in Bandhavgarh. Satyapurush Sadguru Kabir Saheb himself designed it, and this very form has been preserved by the lineage-gurus and passed on to the faithful. This *pūjā* is a message of immortality in the world of death; it is the creation of Satyalok [the heavenly Realm of Truth] on this earth. The power to do it correctly rests only with lineage-gurus or with those *kaḍihār* ['helmsman', a term used in the Dharamdasi Kabir Panth for mahants] whom they select and authorize.[27]

This chauka origin story is part of a larger narrative of Kabir's becoming an avatar, selecting Dharamdas as the founder of his 'forty-two-generation lineage', ordaining that Dharamdas and his wife Amin-mata would produce the first occupant of the gaḍḍī in the form of their son, Muktamani Nam Sahab, and ensuring that all the other lineage gurus would emerge from the same family. These gurus are also called avatars:

Muktamani Nam Sahab himself is a portion (*aṃsa*) of Satyapurush[28] with a special form (*svarūp*), special qualities (*guṇa*), and special divine power (*śakti*). From him alone the forty-two lineage holders are created....Thus we see that a portion of Satyapurush takes avatarhood forty-two times in the family of Dharamdasji through the seed-lineage of Muktamani Nam Sahab, and from them alone living beings can get liberation. The duties of the lineage-seat holder and the burden of propagating the Panth are beyond the capacities of ordinary people. Therefore Kabir Sahab agreed to send a portion of himself in the form of the forty-two-generation lineage.[29]

From this, we understand that chauka arati is closely linked to maintaining the powerful authority of the Panth gurus in the Dharamdas tradition. At its centre is worship of the guru. During the chauka, the local mahant, the lineage holder of the Panth, Kabir, and God (Satyapurush) are conflated. In addition to being a medium for worshiping Guru-as-God and God-as-Guru, the chauka is supposedly able to deliver amazing practical results. Grindhmuni Nam Sahab—father and predecessor of the present lineage holder, Prakashmuni Nam Sahab—wrote of the centrality and incomparable power of the ritual:

In our lineage, chauka arati holds the first place among prescribed actions. Nothing else has been given as much importance as this....Chauka arati is a kind of scientific knowledge. In chauka arati the five elements are mingled in a scientific way, and a tremendous power comes forth from this....

*Chauka arati produces many authentic fruits.

*From chauka arati, a person's spirit becomes pure and long-term bad habits are destroyed.

*Mental problems diminish.

*Doing chauka arati sharpens your true intelligence; you can directly see Satyapurush. The spiritual joy that comes from doing chauka arati is of a world beyond this one. We call that world Satyalok....From chauka arati one is released from countless sins, and one attains the supreme being (*paramātma*). Without doubt, from chauka arati a person attains a peaceful and auspicious state.[30]

A KABIR PANTH CONVOCATION IN CHHATTISGARH

For five days in February of 2002 I attended the annual *melā* ('fair') in Damakhera, a village about two hours' drive from Raipur, the capital of Chhattisgarh. Aside from the big buildings in the Panth compound, the village appears ordinary. But once a year, it fills with countless devotees. People camp in tents, or under the huge canvas cover of the main assembly area, or in nearby fields. An immense kitchen operation provides two cooked meals a day to devotees who sit in rows as fast-moving volunteers ladle vegetables, *dāl,* and rice from stainless steel buckets and drop deep-fried bread on leaf plates. As hundreds finish their meal, hundreds more take their places.

The main organized activity at the mela is listening to discourses and songs that start in the morning and continue late into the night. Followers also form long lines to do homage, called *bandagī*, to the acharya of the sect, Prakashmuni Nam Sahab—often referred to as Huzur Sahab. Carrying coconuts and other offerings, they reach his presence after a long wait and enact an individual rite of devotion, bowing at his feet, looking into his eyes three times, touching the coconut to their bodies in a prescribed sequence, repeating '*Sāhab bandagī*', and leaving a monetary donation according to their means. Whenever Huzur Sahab emerges from his quarters, he is rushed by devotees who wish to touch his feet or make a gesture of homage. Those who can't get near, watch from stairways or other vantage points, drinking in the experience that Hindus call darshan—seeing someone or something holy. In the evening they eagerly await his arrival on the stage: the climax of the series of speakers and singers who have performed through the day. A rustle of anticipation and three blasts from a trumpet announce his imminent arrival. He sweeps in with an entourage including two grey-bearded guardians with embossed silver staffs who stand at attention to the right and left of the stage through his long presentation.

On my third night at the Damakhera mela, I witnessed ekottari (101) chauka arati, the grandest form of the ritual, in which the lineage guru officiates. I saw it again at a mela in Bandhavgarh two months later.[31] Manuals describe ekottari as requiring the materials of anandi chauka multiplied by 101, along with some extra items. These materials include coconuts, fruits, flowers, betel leaves and nuts, eight types of dried fruit, mango leaves, cloves, cardamom, saffron, perfume, crystallized sugar, camphor, sandalwood paste, vessels of silver, gold, and brass. The sung and recited texts are particular to ekottari.

The chauka space for the ritual was very large, the array of objects very elaborate. Scores of mahants in their special costumes including the compulsory tall cap, each with a set of paraphernalia, sat in rows in a roped-off square. Tens of thousands of devotees were crammed into the area, which became more and more impenetrable in the circles closer to the guru's seat. The excitement was tremendous. When Huzur Sahab entered with his entourage, it was only with great exertion that monitors could keep the narrow passageway clear and control the surge of bodies that wanted to move toward him. Singing continued throughout the ceremonies.

The most dramatic part was the lighting of over 800 ghee-burning lamps, each wick embedded in a base made of fresh wheat-flour dough. It took several men ten or fifteen minutes to light them all, and the job looked dangerous as more and more flames shot upward. I found the heat under the low canvas roof to be stunning, especially when I climbed onto a platform to see better. The temperature rose suddenly with the altitude, and I felt as if my head were on fire. From my vantage point about twenty yards away, the chauka area looked like a sea of fire. Smoke filled the air; only the open sides of the pavilion allowed us to keep breathing. For thousands of devotees, it was essential to approach the Acharya and do bandagī directly, one on one, before leaving the arati arena. This process went on for hours.

WITH KABIR SINGERS AND FRIENDS IN MALWA

I went to the melas in Damakhera and Bandhavgarh at the invitation of my friend, singing guru, and eventual *rākhī*-brother[32] Prahlad Singh Tipanya. Prahladji is a primary school teacher who lives in the small village of Lunyakheri, not far from the cities of Ujjain and Dewas in western Madhya Pradesh—a region known as Malwa. In the late 1970s, at the age of about twenty-four, he started playing the tambur, a simple five-stringed instrument, and singing bhajans for enjoyment. Like many men in Malwa villages, he often joined with others in a group, or bhajan *maṇḍalī*. But Prahladji's story became unusual. Singing in the melodious and vibrant Malwi folk style, though untrained, he displayed a musical talent and sparkling personality that made people want to hear more. By the time I met him in 2000, he was well known in the region and beyond, and much in demand as a performer. He had become devoted to Kabir in the 1980s and was always billed as a Kabir singer, though there was invariably a sprinkling of songs by other nirgun poets in his programmes.[33]

When I returned to India early in 2002 to work on Kabir oral traditions, Prahladji invited me to join him at the annual mela of the Kabir Panth in Damakhera, Chhattisgarh. There I discovered that he had a privileged place on the stage. He and his group were allowed to sing much longer than others. The acharya beamed at him when they were both present. He praised Prahladji's wonderful bhajans and sometimes requested favourites.

In the ensuing months I travelled with Prahladji and his group to many places where they were performing. The occasion might be a family celebration, a Hindu festival, a Kabir Panth function, a country fair. Most of the performances were in villages and small towns; but he was also invited to prestigious venues in Bhopal, Delhi, and Mumbai. He had a huge repertoire of songs and couplets by Kabir and other nirgun poets, an excellent ensemble to back him up, a delightful stage presence, and the ability to run a fluent commentary on Kabir's meanings, delivered with both earnest intensity and effortless humour, between and amidst his songs. Hosts and audience members treated him with great respect. Introductions featured effusive praise of his musical and spiritual gifts. At the end of a performance, people often crowded around and touched his feet. He responded to these tributes with gracious modesty, sometimes asking people not to touch his feet. But they persisted.

A PLATFORM FOR SINGING AND THINKING

To understand the controversy about chauka arati that unfolded in Malwa from 2002, we have to go back to the previous decade and learn about a programme that made the Kabir singers and devotees of the area a more cohesive and self-conscious group than they would otherwise have been. Eklavya, an educational NGO that had been active in Madhya Pradesh for some time, decided to organize a series of activities around Kabir. In 1990, with communal hostilities spiking in north India because of the campaign to remove a sixteenth-century mosque and build a grand temple to Lord Ram at his supposed birthplace in Ayodhya, Eklavya workers considered what popular and powerful religious figure might lend a voice to support communal harmony and undermine the efforts of those who promoted religious hatred. The obvious choice was Kabir.

After doing some research in villages, Eklavya experimentally launched a programme called *Kabīr bhajan evam vichār manch*: a stage/forum for singing and discussing Kabir. On the second of every month at their office in Dewas, they hosted singing sessions that became exceedingly popular and usually went on all night. Hundreds of Kabir bhajan groups eventually showed up; the programme continued, with monthly meetings as well as other activities, for about eight years. What was unusual about these sessions was their incorporation of *vichār*: thinking and discussion about the meanings of what participants were singing. Organizers of the manch emphasized Kabir's radical social commentary: his criticism of caste and other inequalities; his exposure of hypocrisy, greed, ostentation, and pretension, especially among the religious; his satirical jibes at both major religions, Hinduism and Islam, for their delusions and cruelties; his assertion of the immediate accessibility of truth and liberation to everyone, within the body, and therefore the non-necessity of temples, mosques, rituals, priests, and external objects of devotion. Eklavya leaders asked singers and listeners to discuss what Kabir's words might mean for them in their daily lives.

Gradually internal leadership developed. Prahladji was one of the natural leaders, as was Narayan Singh Delmia, a singer from Barendva village near Lunyakheri, and Hiralal Sisodiya of Ujjain city. Those who gathered on the second of the month spent countless hours singing and discussing Kabir. Their topics ranged from broad social issues to minute inquiry into the meanings of words. Some singing groups went on tours organized by state governments or non-governmental groups to promote communal harmony in those difficult times. It was during this period that Prahladji's star as a performer started to rise dramatically.

I interviewed a number of people about their experience of Eklavya's Kabir manch. Hiralal Sisodiya of Ujjain was a deep admirer of Kabir but not sympathetic to the Kabir Panth. He appeared to be in his sixties when we met in 2002 and told us he had studied up to the seventh grade. On being asked whether Kabir Panthi mahants came to the manch, Hiralalji said:

Yes, some gurus came. They wore their rosaries, caps, forehead marks, other marks. But their system, their way of thinking, was tied to ritualism. Fine, the Kabir Panthis give up drinking, give up intoxication. But so what, if there's no revolution of ideas? The most important revolution is in your ideas. When a revolution of ideas takes place within a person, his whole life is turned around. The person is transformed....In India there are many sects and schools which have caused all kinds of confusion. Kabir wanted a revolution of ideas. He wanted people to understand their own nature. Recognize yourself! The supreme being is not far away!

As far as I understand it, Eklavya's Kabir manch was a medium for this—the birth of a revolution in ideas in all human communities. The goal was to give all people some peace in their hearts and minds and to encourage the expansion of their imaginations....That's why I was so very happy to discover the *Kabīr bhajan aur vichār manch*, and that's why I went there so regularly....If someone becomes a Kabir Panthi and wears a rosary or a bead around his neck, does this mean he has become a good thinker, that his superstition and obscurantism have been erased?

Narayan Singh Delmia was quite radicalized by his experience with the Kabir manch. He had been a locally popular Kabir singer for many years, but after joining the manch, he realized that he was still in the grip of superstition and prejudice and was doing the very things that Kabir criticized. He had worshipped gods and goddesses and believed in their powers, and though a member of a formerly 'untouchable' caste himself, had accepted certain caste attitudes without thinking. He called a Brahmin priest to name his children; he looked down on castes below his in the hierarchy, treating them as untouchable. But under the influence of the manch, all this changed. Caste was no longer important. He saw all people as equal and bearing intrinsic dignity. He was deeply moved by the respect and love he received from the Eklavya staff, by their freedom from bias and pretension. He became critical of the Kabir Panth mahants, who seemed to be exploiting people, staging rituals to get money and assert their authority.

By all accounts, Prahladji had shared these kinds of ideas. Certainly since I had known him, he had always preached passionately against sectarianism, casteism, and other small-minded identities. He tried to undermine prejudice, and he emphasized the delusion of searching for truth in external forms and practices.

PRAHALADJI'S DECISION

By the time I started my research in Malwa, the Kabir manch had been over for four years. Prahladji had become a regional star, his cassettes enjoying vigorous sales, his recognition extending to highly placed people, his prosperity increasing. In April 2002, we went to the Bandhavgarh mela together. On the way home in the train, he surprised me with an announcement: 'I have become a mahant.' 'Surprised' is actually too mild a word. I was shocked. I was dismayed. The first thing I blurted out was, 'You're not going to wear one of those pointed hats!' He laughed. Of course he had received a pointed hat. He had also received a *panjā*, a lengthy official document granting permission to propagate religion (*dharma prachār karnā*) and setting forth his rights and responsibilities as a mahant.

A Dharamdasi Kabir Panth mahant is empowered mainly to do two things: to preside over the chauka arati ritual and to initiate disciples. He also pledges allegiance and obedience to the Panth and the Panth's guru. This did not fit the image of Prahladji that I wished to cherish. In that train rolling from Bandhavgarh to Malwa, we had the first of many discussions and debates on the subject. I was disappointed that he seemed to be buying into the ritualism and authority structure of the sect. I dreaded seeing him become more priestly and preachy. It made me gloomy to contemplate his energy draining from where I thought it belonged, in his unique calling as a singer, into humdrum sectarian functions that anyone could perform. He argued vigorously and cogently for his decision. First, he said, many people wanted him to be their guru, and in effect he *was* a guru. He had told me several dramatic stories about people insisting that he and he alone should initiate them. But he had no authority. He wanted a way to make it official. Then he argued that the Kabir Panth was doing good work in bringing Kabir Sahab's message to so many people. There was nothing wrong with rituals as long as one didn't propagate delusions about their purpose. Rituals were just a way of bringing people together to share understanding of Kabir and to encourage them to lead good lives.

For several years, Prahladji had hosted an annual Kabir festival on land adjacent to his house. On the full moon day in May 2002, in extreme heat, I was slowly moving around observing the preparations. Many people were at work. A boy was on a ladder in the simple temple that Prahladji had built, pasting bright paper flowers between painted verses of Kabir. A tall festive gateway had been erected. White triangular flags flapped from poles and rooftops, bearing the motto *satyanām* (true name). Huge tents without walls were set up to shelter the audience. Dozens of people were making food.

I saw Shantiji, Prahladji's wife, cleaning the wide front verandah of the house with a purifying solution made from cowdung. Then Kabir Panthi sadhus started extending cords, hanging strings of flowers, spreading cloth seats. Meanwhile, spectators and singers, sadhus and gurus, were drifting in. Prahladji was rushing from place to place, looking after arrangements and welcoming guests. He had slept very little in the past few days; his voice was hoarse. His family members were in the same condition.

In the late afternoon a crowd suddenly materialized near the house. I got there just in time to see events take a dramatic turn. This was the performance of Prahladji's first chauka arati. I was taken aback by how weighty and showy it felt. At one end of the crowd, two attendant sadhus were dressing him in special clothes—a long shirt, beads, and of course the pointed hat. Then he walked solemnly to the verandah, stepping on a cloth pathway, not at all his usual social self. He sat down on the gaḍḍī, the special seat in the chauka. I had heard that this was 'Kabir's seat'. Many devotees believed that the person who sat there became Kabir himself. I watched Pradladji being worshipped by a series of people starting with his wife, then his son and daughter-in-law (the married women with their faces completely covered, as is customary in this community), and other family members, waving the tray that contained flaming wicks.

Prahladji and his attendants went through the order of the chauka, chanting, gesturing, moving things around according to the rules. At the heart of the event, dozens of individuals went before him one at a time, knelt at his feet, offered a coconut and some money, and went through a routine of looking up at his eyes, then down again, three times, while placing their joined hands in right, left, and centre positions. I did it too. He appeared to be very concentrated, acknowledging no one in a personal way.

Eventually those who wished to 'take the name', or be initiated by him, did so, one at a time. He whispered the mantra in each one's ear and gave them a kanthī, a single tulsī bead on a string to wear around their neck. His feet were washed and the water distributed as *charaṇamrit*, a holy substance. Then prasād was distributed, as usual in a Hindu rite of worship—cut-up fruits and little sugar balls. Everybody wants prasad. It transfers the holy essence of the rite in a concrete form, conferring blessings. By that time I had retreated to one of the rooms off the verandah, as the crowd had become suffocating. Prahladji's wife came in, smiling broadly, offering prasad. 'Take this,' she said, 'It's a ticket to Satlok.' Was she serious? Satlok was the Kabir Panth's version of heaven.

Later that night, as he introduced the singing programme, Prahladji gave a speech. Once again he said what I'd heard him say so often: that it doesn't matter whether you wear white clothes or red clothes or no clothes; if you're not pure inside, if your way of living, your thoughts and deeds, aren't right, then all your appearances are just a show, a sign of your pride. Then he said: 'May it never happen that I think like this—I am a great bhajan singer or a mahant or somebody who holds a high position. May that never happen. If you see me with that kind of pride, you should understand that I have fallen.' His voice started to crack as it often did, but this time realized that he was crying. He was praying and crying, on that day when the pomp of mahantship had begun for him and he'd passed the mantra to his first crowd of initiates, praying that he wouldn't get lost.

THE DEBATE

For the next three years, my Kabir-connected friends in Malwa were debating Prahladji's decision to be a mahant and to do chauka arati. Hiralal Sisodiya said, 'For all those years in the Kabir manch he was with us, criticizing pomp and pretension, mahants and rituals. Now look! He's a mahant himself, and he's doing chauka arati. What's going on?'

Hiralalji told stories about his own habit of publicly challenging mahants and their followers. He described this exchange at a chalava arati, the ritual for the dead:

> There was one *divānjī* [ritualist]...his name was Kashinathji. In chalava chauka arati, they say they are bringing peace to the soul of the deceased. So I said to him: Do you have any proof? Kabirji says [quoting a couplet]:
>
> 'Everyone goes from here, carrying heavy loads.
> No one has come from there. Have you found anyone to ask?'
>
> The soul of this person to whom you're bringing peace has gone somewhere else. Did he send you a letter saying I'm peaceful or not peaceful, hungry or thirsty, happy or unhappy? Have you gotten any proof? That guru got angry with me! He said, you only want to criticize Kabir's teachings, nothing more. I said, I'm not criticizing Kabir, I'm talking about his philosophy. Kabir's philosophy is very pure, and you're ruining it, turning it into a shopkeeper's business. That's not acceptable to me.

Narayan Singh Delmia, who had known Prahladji for many years, had often sung with him, and was related by marriage, was disturbed and critical. In the 1990s he had come to believe that the Kabir Panth mahants did more harm than good. He had seen evidence that some of them were corrupt, that their positions of authority in local communities could easily bring out the worst in them. He and Hiralalji both described chauka arati as a kind of business (*vyāpārī*) or setting up shop (*dukāndārī*) to get money and gifts. They felt it exploited poor people and encouraged superstition. Panth gurus and official writings promised that people would be delivered from their sins or would attain heaven or final liberation by participating in chauka arati. What could be farther from Kabir's real teaching? It led people astray and sent the wrong message to the next generation.

Narayanji also said with a smile that had a tinge of disgust, 'They are drinking the water that they use to wash his feet.'

I was not neutral. I had become close to Prahladji and the whole family. In August of 2002, during the annual festival of *rakshā bandhan* that celebrates brother-sister relationships, I had ritually become Prahladji's sister with corresponding ties to everyone else in the family. This gave me freedom to argue with him. Being his *elder* sister, I actually had the right to criticize and make jokes about him—which the rest of the family, conventionally tied to deference and obedience to the male head of household—found quite enjoyable.

In 2003, a new urban friend joined our circle. Shabnam Virmani, a filmmaker based in Bangalore, was making a series of films on Kabir music and culture in which Prahladji would figure prominently. From Malwa to Damakhera, from Delhi to New York, Shabnam and I would spend countless hours with Prahladji and his singing group, along with other friends and relatives. Here is a brief summary of our endless discussions about his decision to become a mahant and perform chauka arati.

When challenged, Prahladji did not back down but gave arguments for the value of ritual that students of religion will find familiar. Ritual creates community. It is necessary for initiation, giving and receiving the name, an act by which people make a commitment to join Kabir's tradition. Kabir's teachings communicate on many levels, and most people aren't ready right away to understand the highest teachings. Ritual helps them to begin the process. If abuses or delusions have developed in the way ritual is practiced, a wise leader can remove them. Prahladji made a point of telling participants that the chauka arati had no magic powers and that receiving the name in itself would not transform their lives. They had to change their behaviour and deepen their knowledge. They should never think that the Kabir Panth was the only true religion and never shrink the greatness of Kabir down to narrow sectarian attitudes.[34]

Of course there were many people who accepted the forms and structures of the Panth and did not criticize Prahladji's mahantship. Many wanted to be his disciples.

Prahladji felt the pressure from former comrades in Eklavya's Kabir manch as well as from me and other urban friends. Occasionally he would laughingly admit defeat in a discussion and resolve not to do chaukā āratī anymore. But then he would do it again. He would say that he was helpless, that people insisted that he do it, and he couldn't say no. Eventually he introduced innovations in the chaukā. He stopped sitting in the ritual square dedicated to Satguru Kabir. Leaving it empty, he sat to the side. He forbade distribution of the charanamrit or water from his own foot-washing. He told people that showing reverence to the guru was fine, but they shouldn't be bowing and scraping to him excessively. He refused take money, or allowed only a symbolic offering of a rupee or two. He stated that mahants should not expect to get their income from ritual activities but should earn a living from their own work, as Kabir did. Doing satsang, *nām-dān* (giving the name, initation), and chaukā āratī, should be a service, without pecuniary rewards. He defined the guru-disciple relationship as one in which there is no *len-den* (giving and taking), a relationship where participants freely give knowledge and respect, not money and goods.[35]

News of these innovations reached the sect leadership in Damakhera. They were not pleased. They did not like his presumption that he could unilaterally change the established form of the chaukā. They did not like the imputation of corruption among mahants.

IRE OF THE ACHARYAS

Prahladji liked meeting different gurus. He had taken initiation in several nirgun sects over a period of twenty-five years, including the Nath Panth, Radhasoami, the Damakhera Kabir Panth, and the Parakh Panth of Abhilash Das.[36] Though he was now sure that he wouldn't deviate from the Kabir Panth, he still respected the gurus of different branches and sometimes visited leaders of traditions other than Damakhera. He had a dream that all the sectarian groups might get past their differences and unite in the larger cause of serving Satguru Kabir. When in Delhi, he often went to the Kabir Bhavan, a new centre built by Vivek Das, the religious head of the entire Kabir Chaura network.

Vivek Das became the Acharya in 2000. In his early youth, by his own account, he had been a Naxalite, or member of a revolutionary Maoist movement that organized violent uprisings in the pursuit of justice for the poor and disenfranchised. Coming to understand the futility of violence, he became a Kabir Panthi. He was a young sadhu when I first visited Kabir Chaura in 1976. After the death of the elderly Acharya Amrit Das in 1988, I had heard there was some jostling for leadership. For over ten years the more conservative Gangasharan Das—who at a certain point had begun to call himself Gangasharan Shastri, indicating his wish to take on a more Brahminic identity—had held the position of Acharya. But after some wrangling and deal-making, Gangasharan had moved to a temple on the bank of the Ganges, and Vivek Das had assumed leadership.

Gangasharan Shastri supported the long observed tradition of chauka arati. He also unhesitatingly called himself a Hindu and a Vaishnav.[37] Soon after taking leadership, Vivek Das came out strongly against chauka arati. In a conversation in 2002, he told me he was urging his followers not to do it, though he wasn't strictly forbidding it. He also said that he was about to publish an aggressive critique of the Dharamdasis, who in his opinion did not deserve to be called Kabir Panthis. Having just enjoyed the hospitality of the Dharamdasis, I challenged Vivek Das on the usefulness of attacking rival factions of the Panth. I pointed to the title of a book he had edited, *Dhāī akśar* (two-and-a-half letters). In a famous couplet of Kabir, those letters spell *prem*, love, which is said to contain more wisdom than all the holy books of the pandits. If this is so, I asked, then why spend your time attacking other people who are devoted to Kabir? Don't you have better things to do? Vivek Das replied, 'I do many other things, but this is important too. Kabir was aggressive. He attacked deluded people. If people are on the wrong road, Kabir would not hesitate to say, "You're on the wrong road."'

In two books published in 2003, Vivek Das invokes the radical Kabir who stood against conventional religion, questioned authority, satirized pretension and superstition. He attacks a tendency in the Panth that he calls *paurāniktā*, meaning doctrines, stories, texts, and practices that seem to mimic the Sanskrit Puranas and the Vaishnav traditions associated with them. The number one offenders are the followers of Dharamdas:

In the middle of the seventeenth century, pauranikta swept into the Panth like a storm. Dharamdas was the leader of this. Dharamdasji was a Vaishnav devotee who accepted the Kabir Panth after coming under the influence of a Kabir Panthi *sant*. As soon as he arrived, there was an influx of pauranikta so overpowering that a question mark was placed over all the actual facts about Kabir. In the false form of dialogues between Kabir and Dharamdas, dozens of books were composed (Anurag Sagar, Bodh Sagar, etc.). Because of these Puranic writings, ordinary people were led far from Kabir's true wisdom. In these 'ocean' (sagar) volumes, buckets full of insults and filth were unloaded on Kabir's contemporary disciples. The *Bijak*, Kabir-sahab's basic work, is the universally revered religious text in the Kabir Panth. But in these Puranic 'ocean' books, the *Bijak*'s wisdom is referred to as the worms in the *guler* fruit, and the composer of the *Bijak* is called the messenger of death.[38]

Vivek Das criticizes the Dharamdasis' propagation of an avatar theory, not only about Kabir, but also about the progeny of Dharamdas who ascend to the leadership of their 'forty-two-generation' lineage. He criticizes the notion that Kabir's closest disciple was an extremely wealthy merchant. He brands the 'ocean' literature as 99 per cent lies. And he underlines the fact that all these books promote chauka arati.

In a volume called *Ghat kā Chaukā* ('The Chauka in the Body'), Vivek Das attacks the chauka ritual and the centrality it has assumed in the lives of Kabir Panthis. The main text is based on a lecture that he gave to Kabir Panthis in Trinidad-Tobago on the occasion of a chauka arati they had organized for his visit on the full moon of the month of Kartik. He scolds them heavily for doing so. His language is vivid, his condemnation unequivocal:

> Kabir-sahab opposed these phony forms of worship (4).
>
> Kabir gave a great message of awakening, and today his followers have joined the Idiot Panth, the Puranic Panth (20).
>
> Worshiping through the chauka arati is a powerful assault on Kabir's revolutionary ideas.[39]

Vivek Das sarcastically dismisses the priestcraft, the expense, the greed for offerings, and above all the delusion that makes people believe that they will avoid death by breaking coconuts or achieve liberation by writing a mantra on a betel leaf and then eating the leaf. He declares that these delusions are destroying the Kabir Panth. After cataloguing the sorts of external practices that Kabir rejected, he says, 'To know the spiritual self within your own body is the essence of all worship.'(7) His title, *Ghat kā Chaukā*, recalls the earliest reference to the chauka in the ritual texts that Lorenzen studied.[40] There seems to be an understanding, rooted in early layers of the Panth, that the outer chauka is only a symbol of an internal process of transformation:

> The chauka that Kabir-sahab wanted to tell us about is the chauka inside every human being. That is what we need to know, that is the light we need to kindle and spread. Only then can we break the head of the lord of death. Without that, even if we break a thousand coconuts, even if we perform not just 101 but thousands of chauka aratis, we'll get no benefit (29).

In this essay too, Vivek Das emphasizes that the worst offenders, the greatest purveyers of ritualized delusion, the leaders in turning the Kabir Panth into a Puranic fools' Panth, are the Damakhera-based Dharamdasis.[41]

In the Dharamdasi melās that I had attended, Prakashmuni Nam Sahab also criticized rival branches of the Panth. Though he did not single out Kabir Chaura in 2002, he spoke sharply against dissident groups of Dharamdasis that split off from the mainstream, and he strongly underlined the authenticity and sole authority of the forty-two-generation lineage. The crucial importance of the chauka arati ritual cannot be questioned in the Dharamdasi Panth.

Perhaps failing to appreciate the seriousness of their differences, or hoping despite everything to bring them together, in 2004, Prahladji invited both Acharyas to grace the occasion of the annual Kabir celebration that he hosted in his village. But he went one step further: in published announcements of the event, he indicated that both would actually be there. Later he said that this was a mistake, that he had only meant to mention both as sources of inspiration. But he was severely upbraided in phone calls from Damakhera for publishing such a claim without getting Huzur Sahab's permission. That same year, at the annual mela in Damakhera, the climate changed dramatically for Prahladji. Huzur Sahab was not only chilly. He made critical remarks about Prahladji when they were seated on the stage before tens of thousands of people.[42]

Things came to a head in June 2005, when Acharya Vivek Das asked Prahladji to perform on Kabir Jayanti (Kabir's birthday) at his centre in Delhi. Prahladji agreed and the publicity was circulated. When Acharya Prakashmuni Nam Sahab heard of it, he summoned

Prahladji to appear before him in Chhattisgarh, hundreds of miles away from Delhi, on the same day. Prahladji refused, citing his prior commitment. There was a showdown in which Prahladji defied the command of his Panth guru, stating that his loyalty is only to Kabir, not to any Panth. He stayed away from the required annual meeting of mahants in Damakhera. Later that year, a gathering of mahants convened by the acharya took disciplinary action. Pradladji's panja, or authorization to be a mahant, was revoked. The days of wearing the pointed hat and conducting chauka arati were over.

'Isn't it ironic,' I asked Prahladji one day in his village house, 'that you had dreams of bringing together all the different Kabir Panths—you thought you'd unite Vivek Das, Prakash Muni Nam Sahab, Abhilash Das, and the rest—and now you seem to have aroused even more enmity and factions?'

'What did I know,' he replied, 'when I took diksha from Abhilash Das in 1994? I thought the Kabir Panth was all one thing, not Varanasi and Damakhera and Allahabad and Kharsiya and on and on.' He laughed and walked out of the room.

CONCLUSION

Popes wear tall hats, observant Jews wear yarmelkahs, pious Muslim men wear beards, Sikhs never cut their hair, the Dalai Lama shaves his head. Tibetan Buddhists, while teaching non-attachment and emptiness, practise some of the most elaborate rituals on the planet. Taking a break from my research in Malwa one year, I went to Dharamasala where the Tibetan government-in-exile is based. There I witnessed a 'long-life ceremony' for the Dalai Lama, who had recently recovered from a serious illness. Monks in rows droned hallowed verses. Bells and long-necked trumpets resounded. A virtual mountain of offerings rose on one side of the sacred space—foodstuffs and other items symbolizing nourishment and life. The Dalai Lama himself received the community's good wishes, so complexly bodied forth in physical form, with his usual smiling grace. Euro-American guests in a special reserved section (myself among them) seemed happy and respectful. I have never heard admirers of Tibetan Buddhism seriously criticize the Tibetan penchant for ritual in light of the Buddha's simple lifestyle and teaching of emptiness.

Why did a controversy over ritual erupt among Kabir devotees in Malwa and elsewhere in the early 2000s? Why did I feel invested in it? Did I help to cause it? How was this controversy related to the fights over whether Kabir was born in a lotus or from a woman's body, and whether he was celibate or had biological children? What was at stake?

Everyone concerned had a stake in the representation of Kabir: the central leaders and local authorities of the Panth; the singers; the devotees; the script-writers for stage and screen; the scholar-translator; the filmmaker. Some of us, while deeply admiring the character and poetry of Kabir, believing in the value of his contributions to humanity, also receive material gain and worldly recognition from our association with Kabir. Devotees who don't make a profit from the master still build their identity around him. No one is disinterested.

Like all organized religions, the Kabir Panth has found ritual indispensable in maintaining itself institutionally. Ritual creates solidarity, distinction, authority. It provides symbols and concepts that are easy to understand, even if there are also claims of deeper meanings. It gives people something to do.

The Dharamdasi Kabir Panth has followed one well-travelled road in the history of religions by claiming that the founder of the religion actually founded the ritual and enjoined its performance. They show this founding moment in a sacred text that was, they affirm, dictated by Kabir. Going even further, they claim divinity not only for the master but also for the lineage of gurus he established. The ritual specifically enacts worship of the guru and his duly named representatives, reinforcing authority and obedience. In the normal course of human affairs, the ritual becomes a source of income for some mahants.

The Kabir Chaura branch of the Panth has used chauka arati in the usual ways—to solidify the community, to provide followers with symbols and prescribed acts, to promote guru-devotion, to get donations. But since Kabir Chaura believes in only one authentic book of Kabir's compositions, the Bījak, and since the Bījak says nothing of the ritual, they don't claim that Kabir commanded its performance. They also don't have father-to-son succession in leadership of the lineage, or any claim to avatarhood of the acharyas.

Vivek Das has taken another well-precedented course in the history of religions, that of the reformer. Harking back to the 'original' teaching and spirit of Kabir, he excoriates the accretion of ritual, superstition, and mythology. He notes that the main rival branch of the Panth has tried to delegitimize his branch by insulting and demoting the Bījak. He comes back with harsh arguments that serve to delegitimize the rival, at the same time promoting reform within his own organization.

On the ground, all these things look much more personal.

Coming from a very poor rural family and a very low-status caste, Prahlad Singh Tipanya achieves fame, prosperity, and respect as a Kabir singer and teacher. But he still longs for the legitimacy of institutional affiliation, the authority of conventionally sanctioned guru-hood.

His family members support his decisions; they don't have much choice. But some express discontent, saying he should not have become a mahant and should not be doing chauka arati.

Prahladji's old comrades from the Kabir manch criticize him based on their understanding of Kabir's message. They are convinced he has taken the wrong path, which they find all the more regrettable as he has become powerful and influential. But there are other layers in this conversation. Some people (not the ones named in this article) resent his success and his seeming to turn away from them. Some who speak of Kabir also have issues that are more local and personal.

Linda, the American scholar-translator of Kabir, and Shabnam, the filmmaker from Bangalore, play their roles. Whether actively taking a position or simply witnessing as the camera rolls, they are not taken lightly. They are impressive and well funded; they are enthusiastic and warm; they sing, laugh, and debate, they become friends, sisters, aunties. Both are highly educated, politically secular and left-leaning; both are inspired by what they see as Kabir's non-sectarian spirituality, remarkable independence, and social radicalism; both have their educated urban constituencies to think about.

Then we have to remember the *Kabir bhajan evam vichār manch*. It is conceivable that this controversy would never have occurred at all had it not been for Eklavya's sponsorship of the manch in the 1990s. We can never know for sure how crucial Eklavya's role was, but it was certainly important.

In these concluding remarks, the top-down observations (about sect leaders, institutional motives, historical patterns in religion) come across as more cogent than those that reflect bottom-up movements, global crosscurrents, and personal relationships. Fragmentary glimpses of people's lives and interests do not add up to a clear conclusion. But I sometimes think that fragments reflect reality better than perfectly cogent arguments.[43]

THE LAST LAUGH

Kabir says, when I was born,
the world laughed and I cried.
Let's hope that when it's time to go,
the world will cry and I'll laugh.

Everyone knows the main meaning of this popular couplet. Babies are born crying while their families celebrate. Kabir hopes to live a good life—in which case, people may be sad to see him go. And he hopes to be so free of attachment to this life, so fearless, that he'll go out with a smile while others cry in sorrow.

Kabir was quite serious, but he also had a great sense of humour. The matters we have been discussing are both serious and funny. With his sharply penetrating insight, did Kabir know that his followers would fight over his dead body? Was the decision to have a good laugh an alternative to despair? Do we, his followers and admirers, keep reconstructing his body and then arguing over how to dispose of it? Is he still laughing?

NOTES

1. Special thanks to David Lorenzen, who responded to my inquiries with a stream of information and materials that helped me to complete this article. David has been a reliable (and forgiving) friend and colleague since we first met in Varanasi in 1976.

2. Here is a version of this well-known story from a Sikh website: 'Feeling his end was near, the Hindus said we will cremate you, the Muslims said we will bury

you. Guru Nanak said; 'You place flowers on either side, Hindus on my right, Muslims on my left. Those whose flowers remain fresh tomorrow will have their way.' He then asked them to pray and lay down covering himself with a sheet. Thus on 22 September 1539 in the early hours of the morning Guru Nanak merged with the eternal light of the Creator. When the followers lifted the sheet they found nothing except the flowers which were all fresh. The Hindus took theirs and cremated them, while the Muslims took their flowers and buried them.' (http://www.sikhs.org/guru1.htm) (2007)

3. David N. Lorenzen, *Kabir Legends and Ananta-das's Kabir Parachai* (Albany: State University of New York Press, 1991), p. 125. Lorenzen dates this text at around 1600. Ibid., pp. 10–13.

4. Ibid., p. 41. A song chanted regularly in Kabir Panthi rituals refers specifically to this episode. David N. Lorenzen, 'Rituals of the Kabir Panth', in David N. Lorenzen (ed.), *Praises to a Formless God: Nirguni Texts from North India* (Albany: State University of New York Press, 1996), p. 251.

5. *Bījak* shabda 4, translated in Linda Hess and Sukhdeo Singh, *The Bijak of Kabir* (New York: Oxford University Press, 2002 [1983]), p. 42. (I have slightly changed my own translation here.)

6. By 'myth' I mean not falsehood, as in common parlance, but sacred narrative—the stories communities tell to convey the deepest truths about their founders, histories, and understanding of reality. See Alan Dundes, *Sacred Narrative: Readings in the Theory of Myth* (Berkeley: University of California Press, 1984).

7. According to the official state website in 2007, Chhattisgarh's population includes 44.7 per cent Scheduled Castes and Tribes. Thus these communities are indispensable for politicians. The site notes that religious reform movements stressing equality have been important in Chhattisgarh, and it provides a paragraph on the Kabir Panth. http://chhattisgarh.nic.in/profile/corigin.htm#mainhistory (2007) At the two melas I attended in Damakhera and Bandhavgarh in 2002, the then Chief Minister of Chhattisgarh, Ajit Jogi, made conspicuous appearances, and the speeches included warm mutual praise from the leaders of the Panth and the state government.

8. Usually given as 1518. See Lorenzen, *Kabir Legends*, pp. 9–18.

9. David Lorenzen, 'The Kabir Panth: Heretics to Hindus', in David N. Lorenzen (ed.), *Religious Change and Cultural Domination* (Mexico, El Colegio de Mexico, 1981a), pp. 151–71.

10. When I say that 'Kabir' was critical or positive or emphasized certain points, I refer to themes that are common across all the important collections attributed to him.

11. David Lorenzen notes that not all members of the Kabir Chaura believe Kabir was an avatar who manifested himself on Lahartara pond. In particular, he says that Vivek Das does not believe this (e-mail, 3 July 2006).

12. All these terms pertain to Hindu forms of ritual and authority. A mahant is the head of a temple or sectarian religious branch. Āratī is the common form of Hindu worship. Sandhiyā pāṭh is morning and evening chanting, dīkshā is initiation by a guru; tulsī is a bush regarded holy from whose pranches beads are made and used for religious purposes.

13. Caste distinctions are notoriously entrenched in Indian society, and a particular outpost of the sect will only be as enlightened as its leadership. The Chhattisgarh website cited in n. 7 above states: 'The Kabir Panth does not believe in caste hierarchies. However in contemporary times the Panth has been divided along caste lines. The only time that they do not adhere to caste hierarchies is in the presence of the Chief Guru on the birth anniversary of Kabir.' Keay observed in 1931 that Kabir's attempts to preach against caste 'met with little success' and that separate chauka arati rituals were arranged for different castes. F.E. Keay, *Kabir and His Followers* (Calcutta: Association Press [YMCA], 1931), p. 109. Lorenzen finds the Kabir Chaura ritual practices quite free of caste distinctions. Lorenzen, 'Rituals of the Kabir Panth', pp. 249–50. I have heard Acharya Prakashmuni Nam Sahab speak vigorously against the caste system and was told that he had arranged high-profile marriages, including that of his own brother, across castes.

14. Hess and Singh, *The Bijak of Kabir*, p. 61.

15. H.H. Wilson, *Religious Sects of the Hindus* (Calcutta, Sushil Gupta, 1958 [1861]); William Crooke, *The Tribes and Castes of the North-Western Provinces and Oudh*, 4 vols (Calcutta: Asian Education Services, 1999 [first published 1896]); G.H. Westcott, *Kabir and the Kabir Panth* (Varanasi: Bharatiya Publishing House, 1974 [1907]); F.E. Keay, *Kabir and His Followers* (Calcutta: Association Press [YMCA], 1931).

16. David Lorenzen has been a mine of information on the various Kabir Panth traditions for many years. During the writing of this article, he pointed out to me that one important tradition, the 'Parakhi' sect headed by Abhilash Das, are atheists who seem to have considerable Jain influence. 'He is said to be a Brahmin of a family somehow related to Ram Chandra Shukla' (e-mail, 6 July 2006).

17. For a summary of stories about Kabir's disciples and the Panths they founded, see Lorenzen, *Kabir Legends and Ananta-das's Kabir Parachai*, pp. 55–65. Recent historical accounts in Hindi of the Kabir Panth with its various branches have been written by Rajendra Prasad, *Kabir Panth ka Udbhav Evam Prasar*, Damakheda, Shri Sadguru Kabir Dharmdas Sahab Vanshavali Pratinidhi Sabha, third edition, 1999, who is affiliated with Damakhera; and Vivek Das, Acharya of Kabir Chaura. See Vivek Das, *Kabir ka Sach* (Varanasi: Kabirvani Prakashan Kendra, 2003a).

18. A rival faction of Dharamdas-following Kabir Panthis is based at Kharsiya in Chhattisgarh.

19. Lorenzen, *Kabir Legends*, p. 60.

20. Hess and Singh, *The Bijak of Kabir*, pp. 53–4.

21. Some Kabir mythology claims that he had five penises.

22. 'Chapter XV of the Indian Penal Code: Of Offences Relating To Religion 145[295A].Deliberate and malicious acts, intended to outrage religious feelings of any class by insulting its religion or religious beliefs

Whoever, with deliberate and malicious intention of outraging the religious feelings of any class of 146[citizens of India], 147[by words, either spoken or written, or by signs or by visible representations or otherwise], insults or attempts to insult the religion or the religious beliefs of that class, shall be punished with imprisonment of either description for a term which may extend to 148[three years], or with fine, or with both]....'

[http://www.helplinelaw.com/bareact/bact.php?no=15&dsp=ind-penalcode &PHPSESSID=cf79e2d637bbaa65e271dd8bd3a3913a]

23. Hess and Singh, *The Bijak of Kabir*, pp. 73–4.

24. Lorenzen, 'Rituals of the Kabir Panth', p. 248.

25. Gangasharan Shastri (Das), *Aahar Samhita* (Varanasi: Kabirvani Prakashan Kendra, 1983), p. 8.

26. Prakashmuni Nam Sahab (eds), *Ashirvad: Shatabdi Granth*, Damakheda, Chhattisgarh, Shri Sadguru Kabir Dharamdas Sahab Vanshavali, Pratinidhi Sabha, 2004. (*Most pages unnumbered.)

27. Ibid.

28. This is the name used in the Damakhera Kabir Panth for the supreme being who sends forth avatars in each of the four ages. Satyapurush is like Vishnu for Vaishnavs.

29. Prakashmuni Nam Sahab (ed.), *Ashirvad*, p.'0'.

30. Ibid., pp. 201–03.

31. Bandhavgarh is a remote spot in the far north of Madhya Pradesh, known today for its tourist-attracting wild animal reserve. It is important in this branch of the Kabir Panth as the home of Dharamdas, the wealthy merchant who gave his money to his guru Kabir and became the founder of the Panth. They believe that Dharamdas spent years with the master in a cave at the top of a high cliff, receiving teachings and preparing to establish the true lineage of Kabir's followers. The teachings would be written down in the form of the *Anurag Sagar*, this sect's most cherished sacred text. Acharya Prakashmuni Nam Sahab had organized the mela at Bandhavgarh for the first time in April 2002, saying it was a long-time dream of his to bring the Kabir Panthis to this spot and lead a pilgrimage through the forest and up the cliff to the sacred place of origin.

32. Raksha Bandhan, a festival celebrated around August in much of India, is devoted to the special relationship between brothers and sisters. A sister ties a decorative thread called a rakhi on her brother's arm, and he gives her gifts. The holiday is often used to create ceremonial brother-sister relationships between people who are not biologically related.

33. Nirgun = without qualities, indicating devotion to a supreme being beyond form.

34. These views are summarized from several video conversations filmed by Shabnam Virmani.

35. One weakness in Prahladji's argument was that he was well-off, having a government job as a school teacher as well as a substantial income from his success as a singer. Other mahants were likely to be poorer and to have fewer choices.

36. See n. 15.

37. Lorenzen, 'The Kabir Panth: Heretics to Hindus', p. 162. Gangasharanji made the same statement in a 2003 conversation with me.

38. Das, *Kabir ka sach*, Preface.

39. Vivek Das, *Ghat ka Chauka* (Varanasi: Kabirvani Prakashan Kendra, 2003b), p. 25.

40. 'The earliest reference to the chauka seems to be that of the above translated '*Jñan gudari*' ('Quilt of Knowledge'), which states:

He disperses all his egotism and pride,/ as he lights his body's chauka.// Making mind the sandalwood, intellect the flowers,/ welfare his bow of respect, he finds the root.// Making faith the flywhisk, love the incense,/ he finds the pristine name, the form of the Lord.

...the date of the 'Jñān gudarī' is unknown...The oldest manuscript...is dated...1838 CE...The presence of the '*Jñān gudarī*' in the *Sandhyā pāṭh* booklets of almost all branches of the Kabīr Panth, however, suggests that it is an old composition, perhaps older than the split of the Kabīr Panth into its Kabīr Chaurā and Dharmdāsī branches. This split cannot be dated with any assurance either, but it is probably took place over 300 years ago'. Lorenzen, 'Rituals of the Kabir Panth', p. 238.

41. In a 2007 update, based on his visit to India in January, David Lorenzen informed me that Vivek Das had compromised with other leaders who wanted to keep the chauka. They had started to describe it as 'guru puja', keeping the forms almost identical but eliminating references to Satyapurush (the supreme being who, especially for the Dharamdasis, is seen as the source of Kabir's four avatars in the four ages). Vivek Das's attack on the Dharamdasis had grown even sharper. In a 2006 book, *Vaṃśa Kabīr kā Aṃśa?* (Varanasi: Kabirvani Prakashan Kendra), he goes so far as to refer to them as 'cockroaches' (e-mail, 30 January 2007).

42. I did not attend this mela, but got a report from Shabnam Virmani, who caught these comments by Huzur Sahab on video.

43. The power of fragmentary evidence has been forever impressed on me by Gyanendra Pandey's brilliant article 'In Defense of the Fragment: Writing about Hindu-Muslim Riots in India Today', *Representations*, vol. 37 (Winter 1992); reprinted in Ranajit Guha, ed. *Subaltern Studies Reader, 1986–1995* (Minneapolis: University of Minnesota Press), pp. 1–33.

REFERENCES

Crooke, William, *The Tribes and Castes of the North-Western Provinces and Oudh*. 4 vols (Calcutta: Asian Education Services, 1999 [1896]).

Das, Vivek, *Kabīr kā Sach* (Varanasi: Kabirvani Prakashan Kendra, 2003a).

____, *Ghat kā Chaukā* (Varanasi: Kabirvani Prakashan Kendra, 2003b).

____, *Vaṃsa Kabīr kā Aṃsa?* (Varanasi: Kabirvani Prakashan Kendra, 2006).

Das, Vivek and Krishna Kalki (eds), *Ḍhai Akśar* (New Delhi: Kabir Bhavan, 1998).

Barari, Mahant Sukritdasji. 1980 [1947]. *Chaukā-chandrikā, Arthāt Kanḍihārī Bhed.* Kharsiya, Madhya Pradesh.

Dehalavi, Mahant Sudhadas (ed.), *Chaukā Paddhatī, Arthat Kaṇḍiāri Gutakā.* Damakheda (Madhya Pradesh: Vansh pratap gaddi, Kabir Nagar, 1970).

Dundes. Alan, *Sacred Narrative: Readings in the Theory of Myth* (Berkeley: University of California Press, 1984).

Hess, Linda and Shukdeo Singh, *The Bijak of Kabir* (New York: Oxford University Press, 2002 [1983]).

Keay, F.E., *Kabir and His Followers* (Calcutta: Association Press [YMCA], 1931).

Lorenzen, David N., 'The Kabir Panth: Heretics to Hindus', in David N. Lorenzen, ed., *Religious Change and Cultural Domination* (Mexico: El Colegio de Mexico, 1981a), pp. 151–71.

——, 'The Kabir Panth and Politics', *Political Science Review* [Jaipur], vol. 20, pp. 263–81

——, 1987. 'The Kabir Panth and Social Protest', in K. Schomer and W.H. McLeod (eds), *The Sants: Studies in a Devotional Tradition of India* (Delhi: Motilal Banarsidass, 1981b), pp. 281–303.

——, *Kabir Legends and Ananta-das's Kabir Parachai* (Albany: State University of New York Press, 1991).

——, 'Rituals of the Kabir Panth', in *Praises to a Formless God: Nirguṇī Texts from North India* (Albany: State University of New York Press, 1996).

——, 'Traditions of Non-caste Hinduism: The Kabir Panth', in David N. Lorenzen, *Who Invented Hinduism? Essays on Religion in History* (New Delhi: Yoda Press, 2006), pp. 264–83.

Pandey, Gyanendra, 'In Defense of the Fragment: Writing about Hindu-Muslim Riots in India Today', in *Representations*, vol. 37 (Winter 1992); reprinted in *Subaltern Studies Reader, 1986–1995*, ed. Ranajit Guha (Minneapolis: University of Minnesota Press, 1997), pp. 1–33.

Prakashmuni Nam Sahab, (ed.), *Āshīrvād: Shatābdī Granth* (Damakheda, Chhattisgarh: Srī Sadguru Kabīr Dharamdās Sāhab Vanṣāvali, Pratinidhi Sabhā, 2004) (Most pages unnumbered.)

Prasad, Rajendra, *Kabīr Panth kā Udbhav Evam Prasār*, third edition (Damakheda: Srī Sadguru Kabīr Dharmdās Sāhab Vanṣāvali Pratinidhi Sabhā, 1999 [1981]).

Russell, R.V., 'The Tribes and Castes of the Central Provinces of India.' '*Kabirpanthi*,' vol. 1, 1916, pp. 233–45. Available online: http://www.gutenberg.org/files/20583/20583-h/20583-h.htm#d0e6746 (2007)

Shastri, Gangasharan, *Achār Samhitā* (Varanasi: Kabirvani Prakashan Kendra, 1983).

Westcott, G.H., *Kabīr and the Kabīr Panth* (Varanasi: Bharatiya Publishing House, 1974 [1907]).

Wilson, H.H., *Religious Sects of the Hindus* (Calcutta: Sushil Gupta, 1958 [1861]).

7. ORIENTALIST MUSEUM

ROMAN MISSIONARY COLLECTIONS AND PRINTS

Ines G. Županov

When Paulinus a S. Bartholomaeo arrived in Pondicherry aboard *L'amaible Nannette* on 25 July 1776, the scene was set for another missionary life in south India.[1] As he described two decades later in his *Viaggio alle Indie Orientali*, for thirteen years, he worked hard in his mission among the Syrian or St Thomas Christians, travelled in the Malabar region, met people from the lowest fishermen to Dutch administrators and the kings of Travancore.[2] Written with hindsight, of course, *Viaggio* documents as much Paulinus' achievements as his desires and deceptions. The choice of Italian, instead of a scholarly Latin of his numerous books written and published upon return to Europe, is undoubtedly a sign that he tried to reach a wider audience. In the same way, the title he chose pointed to a particular genre of writing—a travelogue—developed in the course of almost three centuries during which Italians and other Europeans travelled to and came back with stories about the Orient.

A missionary life, if one studies prosopographies and hagiographies of the Catholic missionaries in the early modern period, consisted of two or three stages. The first is the stage before entering the order or leaving for a mission. In the hagiographies it is a time of evangelical preparation endowed with premonitions, miracles and prophetic dreams, and the visions of future. The life in the mission is a heroic period of intense social interaction, politics, learning languages, a holy fatigue and an eventual martyrdom. For some, but not all, there is a third stage of return back to Europe or to some quiet place with a possibility of writing down the recollections and reflecting on the mission fieldwork.

Paulinus a S. Bartholomaeo returned to Europe via Brest only to find that after a difficult trans-oceanic passage he had to deal with another 'evil', the French Revolution. In his opinion, it was at that point, while travelling through the devastation in France during the Revolution that he started 'thinking about countries and nations that [he] saw and comparing them with Europeans, my dear compatriots'.[3] In a melancholic statement, Paulinus both condemned and extolled Europe's achievements. For him, China and India were regions with gentile and gentle people governed by simple laws. With stable governments, their religion and customs remained unchanged. Europe on the other hand was 'inconstant' and politically volatile, part of which he attributed to the influx of the ferocious Scythians from the cold climates.[4] The originary inconstancy was responsible for multiplication of laws and the fact that 'people are easily duped' by novelties (*novità*) and liberty (*libertà*), 'the two new idols'.[5] One of the consequences of this unbound mobility of the Europeans who also became conquerors of the rest of the world, and thus developed excellent armies, was that they acquired 'one little advantage' compared to Asia. 'This advantage lies in arts and sciences'.[6] And yet, Paulinus tried to prove in all his texts that these arts and sciences came originally from India.[7] The Europeans only perfected them. His mission was, therefore, to rescue the ancient wisdom of the Indian arts and sciences from the forces of historical corruption (and oblivion) and to save the Indians from the 'darkness of ignorance' in which they continue to live without the Christian message.

Paulinus' predicament lies right here. In what follows I will try to show that, from what we can discern in his published books written upon return to Rome, Paulinus was torn between two opposing tasks. On the one hand, he was a professional missionary even when he worked as a professor of oriental languages at the mission seminary of the Propaganda Fide (Collegio Urbano) in Rome and published books for the use of the future missionaries.[8] In addition, he also considered himself a scholar and an Orientalist. The problem was that he felt, and rightly so, that his expertise was not taken all that seriously by his peers, especially by the British and French students of Indian languages and culture. In a way, he was at the end of the line of a series of the Catholic 'missionary Orientalists', from the learned Jesuits who arrived in the sixteenth century to the Discalced Carmelites,

Capuchins, and the French of the Société des Missions-Étrangères in the eighteenth century.

By the early nineteenth century a new kind of professional, the colonial scholar-administrator, entered the Orientalist scene and captured it for the next century and a half. The formation of the Asiatic Society in 1784 that organized scientific discussions and lectures, which were then quickly published in the *Asiatic Researches* became the arenas in which one's scholarly worth was measured and evaluated. The founding of the College of Fort William in 1800 gave a new educational dimension to the study of Indian languages and culture. Thomas Trautmann called it a 'titanic shift of authority'.[9]

As all scientific societies and institutions, especially those on the rise, the Asiatic Society and its members were exclusionary and filtered out everything and everybody who did not comply with the established or imagined rules, paradigms, and norms of 'scientificity'. Paulinus, obviously, did not fit and knew it. He did not fit because he was a Catholic missionary and because his 'Indological' sources were from south India. Upon his return to Europe, through publication of his books and in his ample correspondence, Paulinus fought against the British Orientalists and their authority in the field of Orientalist studies. He was, in particular, angry with William Jones who was, he must have sensed, his scholarly doppelgänger.[10] It has been remarked that he never mentioned Jones by name in any of his works, although he quoted liberally from his texts, until 1795.[11] For example, in *Systema Brahmanicum*, he quoted Govardhan Caul (Kaul) and failed to mention that it was Jones who 'officially' translated the text from Sanskrit.[12] However, after Jones's death in 1794, Paulinus miraculously resurrected his name and it gained in honorific titles with each of Paulinus' new publications. By 1799, Jones was extolled as 'famous' and as the 'President of the Calcutta Academy'.[13] Paulinus was himself quite keen on displaying his own scholarly titles. They appear on the front page of all his printed books. On the *Monumenti indici del museo Naniano,* printed in Padua in 1799, we read that in addition to being *Carmelitano Scalzo,* he was *Professore di Lingue Orientali, sindico delle Missioni Asiatiche et Socio Academico di Velletri, e di Napoli.*[14]

In Rome, his incredible erudition and expertise in Indian languages did not sit all too well with the fact that he was a monk and a former missionary. From a letter written by the Secretary of the

Propaganda in 1790, Paulinus was described as a very learned man, but a bad character and even bad 'religious' character. The Secretary (Giulio de Carpineo) decided not to send him back to India, in spite of Paulinus's ardent desire, but to let him publish his works all the while keeping him under surveillance.[15] It was, nevertheless, a former secretary of the Propaganda, Cardinal Stefano Borgia, who provided the best possible venue for Paulinus's scholarly ambitions. He was invited to organize the Indian collection in Borgia's Museum in Velletri.[16] As an editor, archivist, and museum curator, Paulinus single-handedly invented and practised his own Orientalist 'sciences'. Without learned Brahmans to sit by his side, as they did sit by the side of the Calcutta Orientalists, Paulinus listened to his museum archives full of manuscripts and objects brought from India by his missionary predecessors and by himself. These codices and objects were the authorities on which he relied and this is why he spent a great amount of time and energy on trying to preserve, describe, classify, and publish them.

COLLECTING *NECESSE EST*

Arrival in India was for most of the missionaries, Paulinus included, a breaking point in their life and in their life narratives (autobiographies and hagiographies). Besides cultivating the mission field, collecting curious objects and manuscripts, taking notes and writing letters were also considered an important part of their missionary tasks. Paulinus was from the beginning a diligent collector and writer.[17] In the department of rare manuscripts of the Biblioteca Nazionale Vittorio Emmanuele in Rome there are numerous boxes and folders (*scatole* and *buste*) of Paulinus's various letters and notes. Some are written in his own hand, some are by anonymous scribes, and there are cut-outs from printed books or other manuscripts. These notes are in various languages. Some are exercise notebooks of Chaldean, Armenian, Arabic, Tamil, Malayalam, and Grantha alphabets. Some of these documents were written for the local use and consumption such as Christian catechetical and pious texts in Malayalam or Manipravalam for his parishioners and charges as well as, perhaps, to convert local literate castes. He also wrote a grammar-manual for learning English through Malayalam and Portuguese. Paulinus was commissioned to write it by the king of Travancore, Rama Varma.[18]

Good relations with the kings of Travancore, Martanda Varma and his son Rama Varma, and with the Dutch in Kochi were crucial for the survival of the Verapoly (Varapuzha) mission of the Propaganda Fide and the Discalced Carmelites. Until the seventeenth century, all Catholic missions in India were part of the Portuguese royal patronage network (*padroado*).[19] However, with the establishment of the Congregation for the Propagation of Faith (Propaganda Fide) in 1622, the Papacy took over under its own wing all the territories *in paritibus infidelium* left uncovered by the Portuguese padroado. Since the missionaries sent by the Propaganda Fide were recruited in Rome and from missionary orders that had no allegiance to the Portuguese king, the Estado da Índia and the Portuguese authorities in Goa often treated them as enemies.[20] The Discalced Carmelites came to India in order to replace the Jesuits who were the first missionaries sent to work on the reformation of what was considered as schismatic liturgy and customs of the St Thomas or Syrian Christians in Kerala.[21] When the Dutch captured Kochi in 1662, all Catholic missionaries were expelled and even the first Carmelite Giuseppe di Santa Maria Sebastiani had to leave after appointing as his successor a Syrian Christian priest, Parambil Chandy alias Alexander de Campo. Upon his return to Rome, Sebastiani inaugurated the first in a series of publications by the missionaries of his order in Kerala.[22] In addition, the Propaganda Fide supported all missionary projects by way of its polyglot printing office.[23] The access to the printing press is a crucial element in Paulinus's Orientalist enterprise in Rome.

For their passage to India, the Propaganda missionaries used French carriers and this is why Paulinus's *Viaggio* starts in Pondicherry, the capital of the French colonies in India and ends in the French harbour of Brest thirteen years later.[24] Although he never travelled to Goa, Paulinus did have contacts with the rival padroado missionaries and collected manuscripts and notes written by the Jesuits who were the first 'missionary Orientalists' in India. His most precious manuscript was the Sanskrit grammar written by a Jesuit, Johann Ernst Hanxleden.[25] When it was suggested that he had plagiarized Hanxleden's work, he responded in his *De manuscriptis codicibus indicis* printed in Vienna in 1799, that they both used the same Sanskrit sources.[26]

Most of the early Propaganda Fide missionaries in Kerala were keen students and collectors of manuscripts and of natural objects.[27]

Possessing and collecting nature was part and parcel of the late Renaissance and Baroque culture that defined the civil space of the Italian elite. The members of the religious orders in Rome participated in this common enterprise of unveiling the secrets of natural history.[28] Before ending on display or in the drawers, chests, and boxes of the cabinet of curiosities, the objects had to be collected through travel, exchange, or purchase. The missionaries were among the agents employed in this enterprise. Besides objects themselves, what they often brought were their representations (pictures, descriptions) or remains and traces of the natural objects (*horti secchi*, dried plant or flower specimens, for example).

Vicenzo Maria di Santa Caterina da Siena (alias Antonio Murchio) wrote a travelogue called *Il Viaggio all'Indie Orientali* with a long excursus in the Book IV on the Malabar plants.[29] Another missionary Matteo di San Giuseppe who remained in Malabar until his death in 1691, collected during his lifetime in India information on plants, seeds, and medicinal remedies.[30] His expertise must have been well known in Kochi and it attracted the attention of a Dutch amateur natural scientist and a commissioner general of the VOC (the Dutch East India Company) in Malabar, Hendrik Adriaan van Rheede tot Drakenstein (1637–91). The result of their collaboration was Van Rheede's monumental *Hortus Indicus Malabaricus* published in Amsterdam between 1678 and 1703, and a grant of a church in Chatiath (Vaduthala) for the Carmelites.[31]

Just like Jesuits before them, Discalced Carmelites were sent into their missionary field as general experts in 'conversion' and pastoral care. However, some of them cultivated on the side other type of skills. For example, Matteo di San Giuseppe was an Arabist, botanist, and a good draughtsman. Before his arrival to Kerala, Paulinus studied oriental languages in Rome. That the study of nature and of languages in India was an important part of the Carmelite mission enterprise in Kerala is evident from the titles of the books the missionaries printed upon return to Europe and from the manuscripts they left unpublished in the archives. In this respect they were not unique, since most of the Orientalists in the eighteenth century were interested both in botany and in languages. Moreover, the study of nature and the study of languages followed the same line of reasoning, at least in terms of understanding morphological and etymological structures.[32] William

Carey, a Baptist missionary, Orientalist, and a professor of Oriental languages in the Fort William College in Calcutta was also an amateur botanist who edited and published William Roxburgh's *Flora Indica; or Descriptions of Indian Plants*.[33]

William Jones was also interested in botany, which was his 'principal amusement' together with 'the conversation with the pundits, with whom I talk fluently in the language of the Gods'.[34] The two contemporaries—Paulinus a S. Bartholomaeo, a Catholic missionary in Kerala and William Jones, an enlightened Orientalist in Calcutta—each within their own cultural milieu, were therefore chasing the same scientific paradigm and the same Christian teleology. They both tried to preserve their vision of the Christian world guaranteed by the Bible and the structure of the Mosaic ethnology.[35]

One of the crucial differences between these two early scholars of India was the manner in which they handled and organized their 'research' data and material evidence, and in the cultural and social context in which the constituted data were available for scholarly consumption. For Jones and the other Orientalists, the newly conquered Bengal and its capital Calcutta provided a fertile space for setting up all the institutions indispensable for scholarly activities—a learned society, a journal, a college, and an informal, ever growing pool of local literati ready to be employed.[36]

Paulinus a S. Barthlomaeo, on the other hand, rarely had the opportunity of enjoying and profiting from a closely-knit scientific community during his stay in India. Residing in India resembled more a fieldwork period in which he collected materials rather than studying them in depth. In a way, he was collecting specimens for his future museum, presumably somewhere in the European Catholic world. Knowledge of India was, therefore, to be constituted outside of its borders. In Paulinus's case—in a fixed and framed public space of the Papal court.

MUSEUM IN PRINT

It was upon his return to Europe in 1789 that Paulinus had a chance to put his notes in order and think about a larger picture for his scholarly ambitions. For the next seventeen years he published twenty-six (or more) books and articles on a wide variety of topics, from catalogues of various museum collections, learned treatises and grammars to short polemical papers in comparative linguistics.

Paulinus sifted through, classified, pruned, and prepared for print documents and materials from his prodigious manuscript collection, including his fieldwork diaries. Within the five years that he spent in Rome as a professor of Oriental Languages at the Propaganda Fide Mission seminary, he had managed to publish eight books: a Sanskrit grammar, *Sidharubam seu Grammatica Samscrdamica* (1790), a synthetic treatise on religious and civil organization in Brahmanic India, *Systema Brahmanicum Liturgicum, Mythologicum, Civile, ex Monumentis Indicis Musei Borgiani Velitris, Dissertationibus historico-criticis* (1791), a history of Christianity in India, *India Orientalis Christiana* (1794), a few works on various South Asian alphabets and proverbs, and two catalogues/inventories of Oriental manuscripts and objects, one for the Propaganda Fide and the other for the Museum in Velletri.

What used to be scattered, though copious notes from the mission took shape under various titles and topics. *Viaggio alle Indie Orientali* was not simply an effort at capturing a larger public, but also a way of quickly storing information that Paulinus probably knew he would not have enough time to organize in the near future and that may thus be forgotten in the archives. Publishing *Viaggio* was also a way of inscribing himself onto a long list of travelogue writers about India, and to remind his readers of his first-hand authority in things Indian.

Describing the Indian climate, illnesses, plants, and remedies was an authenticating topos in most of the travel literature on India. The hot and humid 'torrid zone' had a reputation, often copied from one printed book to another, of crushing Europeans under its weight. At the same time, it was also considered as extremely rich in remedies and medicinal plants. Just like his predecessors, Vincenzo Maria di Santa Caterina da Siena, Matteo di San Giuseppe, and others, Paulinus collected a huge amount of medical and botanical information and included only a part of it in his *Viaggio*, a museum in print.

In one of the most dramatic opening scenes of the *Viaggio*, the readers are compelled to witness and ponder over a somewhat ironic episode in which printed books, dangers of Indian climate, and the utility of Indian remedies are brought together in an exemplary fashion. When he was still in Pondicherry before reaching his mission in Kerala, Paulinus encountered the famous white ants or termites responsible for the widespread and indiscriminate destruction of wood, textile and paper:

I kept my stuff in my room in a chest. One day after lunch I opened it to take a book that I wanted to read, and as soon as it was open, I saw an infinite throng of small white animals that the Tamils, that is the inhabitants of *Ciòlamandala* call *Carea* and the Malabars *Cedel*.[37]

Not without a tinge of amusement, Paulinus admitted that among the things he had lost to the ants were some of his clothes and a theological book by Padre Gazzaniga.[38] The story of white ants called immediately another story, a story of the earwig or millipede (*una centipeda o centogambe*). While the ants attacked things, the earwig menaced human beings by getting into the ear and 'biting its way out, and without finding one, heading straight in'. The servant attacked by the insect was so much in pain that he 'hit his head and his feet against the floor, screamed, and went around in frenzy'.

This dramatic scene, however, ends happily since a certain Signor Jallaber applied a small spoonful of *droga amara* (bitter drug) and cured the servant. Paulinus is obsessed with recording and collecting factual information. Thus he gives the exact contents of the preparation with measures in ounces. 'For one pitcher of 24 French bottles, it is necessary to take 24 ounces of *Resina*, or *Calafonia*, 12 ounces of incense, 4 ounces of aloe, 4 ounces of *Mirra,* and 4 ounces of Calumba'. The mixture, according to Paulinus was an excellent remedy for all kinds of illnesses that come from corruption such as indigestion, wounds, labor pains, ulcers, worms, scurvy, et cetera.[39]

However, properly assembled and condensed data on Indian botany and medicine is gathered in one place at the end of the book, in chapter eleven of the second part. While the first part of the book resembles, at least in the beginning, a travel narrative, the second part is mostly structured as a museum credenza or a filing cabinet. Thus we find eleven chapters discussing birth and education, marriage customs, laws, classes and tribes, ministries and tribunals, languages, religion and gods, Indian 'hieroglyphs', division of time, calendar and festivals, music, poetry, architecture, and finally climate, botany, and remedies.

There is nothing surprising in this particular division of topics since it has been worked out in detail and with variations during the two centuries of missionary writings about the manners and customs of the peoples they encountered in the whole world. Within each category of phenomena, there were further subdivisions in more or less pronounced order of importance. In between his direct comments, anecdotes, and opinions, we find long lists of various things that can be listed. Paulinus's favourite game throughout the *Viaggio* as well as in his other printed works and in his correspondence was to castigate careless, imprecise, and ignorant authors writing about India. His belligerent and self-righteous tone antagonized some of his readers, especially those whom he mercilessly ridiculed. It is no wonder that the Orientalists, especially the British, returned fire with the same scornful words. Thus, J.R. Forster, who translated into German two of Paulinus's books—*Systema Brahmanicum* and *Viaggio*—mentioned that he had to correct some unclear Latin sentences in the first and factual errors in the second book. Knowledge about India was, obviously contested and with each new publication, new mastery over Indian *realia* and *spiritualia* was claimed from various Orientalist camps. As long as one was a target of such scholarly attacks, one counted for something in the Orientalist circles. The end of the line for Paulinus was probably the publication of the French translation of his *Viaggio*. Translated from Italian by a mysterious Mr M., the text also contained comments by J.R. Forster, by Anquetil Duperron who died before completing the annotation of the manuscript, and by Antoine Isaac Silvestre de Sacy who had a final word on all authors.[40] By the time the *Voyage aux Indes orientales* appeared in 1808, Paulinus had been dead for two years.[41]

Although Paulinus rooted his authority, as most missionaries did, in his direct experience of what he saw 'with his own eyes' during his travels and residence (1776–89) in South Asia, in the chapter on Indian botany and medicine he makes a special mention of the manuscripts and books that he consulted or had in his possession. It is this material on paper, either manuscripts or 'many paintings from Malabar made by a Malabar physician', that Paulinus proudly puts forward as the ultimate basis and a guarantee of his narrative. 'I have [a text of the] Brahmanical Medicine translated from Sanskrit by Father *Giovanni Alvarez* and enlarged by Father *G. Ernesto Hanxleden*, a Jesuit.'[42]

In one of the *scatole* (boxes) full of Paulinus' manuscripts preserved today in the Biblioteca Nazionale Vittorio Emanuelle (Rome), there is a folder (*busta*) called *Botanica Malabar*. The largest and the best preserved document in the folder is a notebook in Portuguese describing Indian plants and their medicinal properties.[43] The entire text (about sixty pages) is written in one hand with corrections in another ink. The corrections were only made for names in Malayalam script. It is possible that this was the manuscript Paulinus referred to in the *Viaggio*. But next to it in the same folder, there are his chaotic notes, clippings from books or printed sheets, a crude drawing of a palm tree on a transparent white paper. The pieces are of all sizes and some of them bear signs of earlier calamities such as water, humidity, and fire. A printed sheet in French reads, 'Les Vértus d'une eau de mélisse composée...., par le carme dechaussé de Paris,...contre l'apoplesie et les vapeurs.'[44] Another printed page in Italian is entitled, '*Balsamo Samaritano*'. There is also a handwritten recipe for preparing the droga amara concoction. We can glimpse from the contents of this folder—and it is only one folder in one of the numerous boxes—at the insatiable interest in knowing and collecting. What he really and passionately collected were not things, nor medico-botanical specimens, but words, especially words that could take one back in history to the very source of human civilization.

SANSKRIT

Sanskrit, the scholarly language (*la lingua dotta*) of the Indians became Paulinus's obsession, as it became for most of the Orientalists and Indologists in the nineteenth century. By the time he returned to Europe, he was already an accomplished Sanskritist in spite of unfriendly and unfair remarks by some British Orientalists who denounced him as a fraud. Alexander Hamilton thought that Paulinus's Sanskrit dictionary was 'a dictionary of the Malabar idiom, which bears the same relation to the Sanscrit that Italian does to Latin'.[45] It is clear today that the misunderstanding came from the fact that Paulinus transcribed Sanskrit words from the Grantha script and under the influence of Dravidian phonology, and into the Italian orthography. As for the British Sanskritists in Calcutta, they were taught by the Bengali pundits and transliterated Sanskrit into English.[46]

Paulinus was perfectly aware that the transcription and transliteration of Indian languages remained a problem.

The Europeans, Arabs, Persians, Greeks who do not understand Indian language, try to pronounce or write Indian words with the same corruption as dictated by their spirit (*genío*) and secondly according to the pronunciation of their country (*patria*) which leads to another corruption that changes and transforms and corrupts in everything and in part the true native Indian name.[47]

Paulinus, of course, intended to correct all the names bastardized by the foreigners (*stranieri*) and travellers (*viaggiatori*) and to standardize their pronunciation according to the Italian orthography. Thus, he claimed *Coromandel* should be spelled *Ciòlamandala*. Taking up William Jones's opinion that '[our] English alphabet and orthography are disgracefully, and almost ridiculously, imperfect', Paulinus adds his own more devastating appraisal.[48] 'The English alphabet is not only imperfect but plainly ridiculous when it comes to expressing Indian nouns, they horribly corrupt them when writing them in that alphabet.'[49] But, of course, the way history unfolded, these linguistic decisions were not left to the Italians.

In his Sanskrit grammar, *Sidharuban seu Grammatica Samscrdamica* printed only a year after his return to Rome in 1790, Paulinus wrote a veritable panegyric to 'this language of the ancient sages of India'. For Paulinus, Sanskrit was a kind of *omnimedium* for storing and generating culture. First of all, it 'possessed all conceivable words', it had 'unlimited abundance of nouns and verbs' and it was 'the most adequate medium for discussing any subject whatsoever'.[50] He was not the first Catholic missionary who admired Sanskrit and dreamt of making it a perfect receptacle for the Christian message, often called a 'local Latin'.[51] In south India, Roberto Nobili (1577–1656) in the early seventeenth century started writing Christian literature in Sanskrit and in Sanskritized Tamil.[52] Independently, Heinrich Roth (1620–68), a Jesuit missionary at the Mughal court, was equally enthusiastic and tried to enlist to the cause of Sanskrit the famous Jesuit polyhistor Athanasius Kircher in Rome. Kircher received bundles and bundles of information from all over the world and some made it into his printed works. While he included five plates with Sanskrit alphabet into his *China Illustrata*, the main text of Roth's Sanskrit grammar remained lost in the archives of the Collegio Romano.[53] William Jones, who looked down on Catholic missionaries and their conversion methods, unknowingly agreed with them when he stated that the *Muselmàns* and *Hindus* could be easily converted if certain biblical chapters such as the Prophets, 'particularly of Isaiah' and one of the Gospels were translated into Sanskrit and Persian. Such translations may cause 'a great revolution [read conversion]'.[54]

Sanskrit was, therefore, a repository and a witness of the Brahmanical high 'learning, cultivation of sciences and arts... multiplicity of philosophic and religious sects, a variety of castes and trades, a refinement of life, and a most intensive study of logic and metaphysics'.[55] It is also a mother language of all Indian vernaculars such as, according to Paulinus, *Ceilanica, Tamulica, Malabarica, Canara, Maràshda, Telinga, Bengalina, Devanagirca, Guzaratica, Nepalese*, and of two languages that migrated out of India such as *Zendica (*in Persia) and the *Gypsy* vernacular (in Europe).[56] In the same way, Paulinus continued, Latin is the mother of Italian, French, Spanish, and Portuguese. In addition, Paulinus proved in numerous convoluted etymological derivations that Sanskrit had also at one point or another penetrated 'Greece and Latium'.[57] Here again, Paulinus takes a combative stand, in spite of the fact that his own conclusions that India, not Egypt or Greece, was the most antique civilization was not so different from, neither irreconcilable with, other scholars and writers such as William Jones whose texts he knew well. By 1798, Paulinus's comparative method produced one of the first studies on the kinship of Indo-European languages.[58] In his *De antiquitate et affinitate linguae Zendicae, Samscrdamicae et Germanicae dissertatio*, Paulinus juxtaposes linguistic forms in Sanskrit, Avestan, and German in order to prove the existence of kinship between these languages.[59] In fact, Paulinus set out to prove with examples the famous claim made by Jones in 1786 of the common origin of Greek, Latin, and Sanskrit, but it was not until 1802 that he finally came up with a decisive pronouncement on the issue. Thus, he wrote in his *De latini sermonis*, both Sanskrit, Zend, and Latin possess between them 'an intimate affinity' and resemble as 'one egg to another'.[60]

Sanskrit was, as most of the learned Orientalists would agree with Paulinus on this—a language-museum in which all true meanings were contained and often hidden behind 'fables' and 'corruption'. In particular, the origin and the truth of Indian religious and philosophical ideas were to be obtained by carefully learning Sanskrit and reading ancient books. In *Sidharubam*, Paulinus presented the Brahmanical view of the origin of Sanskrit, simultaneous with the creation of the world. According to the story, the supreme power *Ishvara* became inflamed by the power of his own imagination, and a woman he longed for, *Shakti*, came out of his back. As he proceeded to create all the things in the world he said to Shakti, '*Hum*, i.e., the interrogative 'Will you?' to which the Goddess replies: *Om,* or *ām,* both of which means: 'Indeed, definitely, I do, so be it, amen'.[61] From these two 'particles or vowels', insisted Paulinus, the Brahmans explained the creation of all things and the twenty-five characters ('basic ones') of the Sanskrit alphabet.[62]

Paulinus compiled this particular creation story from the works of two of his Carmelite predecessors in the Verapoly mission, Clemens a Iesu (Peanio) and Ildephonsus a Praesentatione B. Mariae Virginis.[63] What he did not know is that the story was taken from an anonymous manuscript, which has been later attributed to a Jesuit Jacome Fenicio, written in the early decades of the seventeenth century.[64] What is interesting is that Fenicio's text portrayed the fable of the divine creation as a kind of divine debauchery and fornication. Thus, Ixora (Īśvara) grew a long lingam, ' which is a male member (*membro uiril)*', because of his desire for woman, and ploughed the world with it and created mountains and seas. The same desire then grew into a form of a woman on his back. To his question '*om*, which means do you desire (*quereis*)...the woman responded *am*, which means I desire (*quero*)'.[65]

However, in Paulinus' text there is not a trace of the divine pornography so dear to Fenicio. It is possible that the obscenities were already ironed out by his source, Ildephonsus a Presentatione B. Mariae Virginis.[66] Whatever the case, Paulinus was after proofs of Sanskrit antiquity and the first conversation between Ishvara and Shakti reminded him of something other than sex. The particles Hum and Om 'entirely correspond to the text of Genesis: God said: let there be...., and so it was, and...it is this text which has been corrupted, deformed and mixed up with fables.'[67] Having thus connected Christianity and Brahmanism at the very source of the divine revelation, Paulinus tried to prove that Indian gods were nothing but natural phenomena: Brahma is earth, Vishnu water, and Shiva fire.[68]

In spite of his missionary duties, it is these relics of the past that Paulinus tried to preserve, if only in his books and in his museum. In fact, the preservation of the ancient Indian life and wisdom was the prime task of the Brahmans. They were ready to give life in this effort.[69] In a way similar to some of the Jesuit missionaries of the seventeenth century, Paulinus also strove to replace the Brahmans. The first stage in this process was to take control of their learned language and their books.

REPLACING BRAHMANS

The first to take professional interest in Indian 'pagan' books were Jesuits. They were also the first to learn and teach vernacular languages. It became clear very early to the Portuguese in Goa that books considered sacred were kept by the Brahmans who treasured them and kept them hidden from all intruders. The way to procure such books was usually by theft, plunder, or by converting the Brahmans. A well-known Jesuit writer Luís Fróis, famous for his *História de Japam*, wrote of one such incident while he was still in Goa in 1559.[70] A learned young Brahman not only converted to Christianity, but he led the viceroy's army to a house of a Sanskrit pandit who had a whole library of old books. With these books in his possession, the converted Brahman who took a Portuguese name of Manuel d'Oliveira, translated 'in a few days all the main things'. This particular pattern of acquiring Indian 'sacred' books was quite common in Goa in the sixteenth century. It was not until the end of the seventeenth and in the eighteenth centuries that Europeans noticed that these books were also for sale.[71] Paulinus bought manuscripts from a person who was entrusted with safekeeping a library left by a Brahman fleeing the army of Tipu Sultan.[72] That books and manuscripts were a cherished booty is seen from a letter by Charles Wilkins who hoped that the library of Tipu Sultan, defeated by the British in 1799, would be given to the Orientalists in Calcutta.[73] Catholic missionaries in Pondicherry and Chandernagor were encouraged to acquire and send manuscripts, paintings, books, and other curious objects for the Royal Library in Paris. The Propaganda Fide missionaries were also supposed to collect texts and objects for the display in Rome. With the rise in demand and good amounts of money offered in cash for such commodities, more books, paintings, and other objects became available for sale. Anybody with money and interest could buy and sell in, what Muzaffar Alam and Seema Alavi call, the 'oriental book bazaar' of the eighteenth-century north India.[74] This bazaar was not merely about commercial transactions. It was a space of intellectual sociability in which pandits and Persianate scholars came into direct contact with European and, most importantly, British administrators. With the collapse of indigenous patrons, various kinds of oriental literati offered their services and books to the English Company and its new breed of Orientalist administrators.

While the local literati could move to Calcutta or to other centres of learning set up by the British, many books and material objects moved directly to Europe, sometimes even without being read or copied in India. In one of the comments printed in Paulinus' French edition of *Viaggio*, Anquetil Duperron provides an interesting history of a large collection of the Zend Avesta manuscripts, 'hundred and thirty-seven volumes in all', purchased by Samuel Guise from the widow of a Parsi scholar, Destour Darab, who was Anquetil Duperron's Persian and Zend Avesta teacher in Surat.[75] Paulinus may have met Samuel Guise who was a surgeon in Anjengo, the first English East India Company settlement in Travancore, between 1783 and 1784.[76] In his *Examen Historico-criticum,* Paulinus listed Guise's collection of oriental manuscripts among one of the four most important collections in Europe (that he knew of).[77] This lead Anquetil Duperron to exclaim with some indignation and a lot of irony, 'it is England now rich in Zend and Pahlavi works'.

All European merchants, collectors, and Orientalists dreamt of nothing else but repatriating Asian riches to Europe. William Jones desired to 'transfer to Europe all the sciences, arts, and literature of Asia'.[78] He also deplored the fact that his official duties as a court judge in Calcutta prevented him from working in leisure on his translations and research. A missionary in India was not less busy with his everyday duties and obligations, but, of course, could not complain about it. Even when Paulinus came back to Rome, he was certainly not a 'leisured gentleman' scholar. He was teaching, preparing various books for print, compiling catalogues, and participating in an ever-complicated political life in Rome.[79] He could not even dream, as William Jones did, of retiring to a quiet life of an independent scholar in England.[80] Paulinus was certainly in agreement with Jones that time was, indeed, in short supply[81] if one were to invest it in learning Indian sciences, but he also presumed that what was needed were 'subjects (*soggetti*) who know the language' and money.[82] The missionaries were chronically lacking money and technically did not have 'subjects (soggetti)' but pastoral 'charges'. In addition, Paulinus's 'learned charges' were not necessarily Sanskrit scholars since they were St Thomas Christians.

From Anquetil Duperron's perspective of a scholar who was neither a colonial administrator nor a missionary, 'the English have time and money' and human resources to prepare and publish a book on Indian botany.[83] He insisted in particular on the fact that there were already enough British administrator-scholars who knew Sanskrit. Paulinus was quite consistent in underestimating and ridiculing his contemporary Orientalists in Calcutta. He slashed Wilkins's translation of the Bhagavad Gita[84] 'How can a European have courage to translate from Sanskrit without grammar, without Sanskrit syntax that demands at least twelve years of study?' In fact, he was suspicious of all translations from Sanskrit in particular. 'There are so many ridiculous things printed in Europe', he exclaimed, instead of original Indian works. Anquetil Duperron agreed to a point with Paulinus since he also thought that without Sanskrit grammars and dictionaries printed, 'Europe will remain completely ignorant of all Indian things'.[85] What exactly Paulinus meant by 'original Indian works' is, however, ambiguously unclear, since he himself printed only translations, his own translations. From what follows in the text, it seems that what he meant by 'original' may be expressed by another epithet—authentic. Indian authenticity was its antiquity since India was, according to Paulinus, the only 'antique' nation that preserved 'until today' its old language, books, poetry, rites, and customs.

Excessive eagerness to find ancient books made Europeans vulnerable to frauds. Paulinus denounced the book, the *Ezour-Vedam*, that impressed Voltaire so much and armed him with deist arguments against the Catholic Church. He claimed as did Pierre Sonnerat in his *Voyage aux Indes Orientales et à la Chine*, published in 1782, that it was a work of a Catholic missionary, and therefore, neither ancient nor Indian.[86] If the Jesuits or one of their converts tried to dupe Europeans, the Brahmans were even more dangerous falsifiers according to Paulinus.[87] He quotes a work in Persian, *Azret hisù & Azret musa*, written by a Brahman against Christian teaching in north India that fell into the hands of the Capuchin Tibetan mission.[88] Indian reactions to missionary presence in India in terms of written books with refutation of Christianity were, unfortunately for historians, rather rare, almost non-existent in the sixteenth and the seventeenth centuries. In the southern Jesuit missions the only pamphlets and published texts that opposed their methods and their teaching came from the Lutheran camp in Tranquebar.[89] Especially the learned Brahmans were insistently silent on Christianity that gained some ground among the lower echelons of the society.

The early Jesuit Orientalists such as Roberto Nobili whose method of conversion inaugurated the Malabar rites controversy, tried to work out a way to replace the Brahmans as the cultural, religious, and intellectual leaders of society. The principle of the 'accommodation' means displacement through imitation or partial strategic mimesis. Through his learning of languages (Tamil, Telugu, and Sanskrit), he wanted to change from inside—according to the famous Ignatian formula, *entrar con el otro y salir consigo*—all the books pertaining to religious and theological precepts of the Brahmans in order to bring them closer to Christian theology.[90] Missionary 'pseudo-Vedas' or the 'pseudo-puranas' were intended deliberately to replace existing 'heathen' narratives and stories. Hence, they were designed to correct certain key ideas in the Brahmanical religious 'system' in order to bring out from the 'heathen material' the pristine (i.e. Christian) meanings hidden away by the cunning and avaricious religious specialists.

Compared to Nobili, Paulinus is already far from this kind of militantly corrective 'missionary Orientalism' and closer to his contemporaries, Orientalists in Calcutta. He did write, however, one major work in Malayalam, *The Life of St. Theresa* (*mar tresiya punyastriyude caritram*). It is equally true that Paulinus' printed texts—such as his Sanskrit dictionary and grammar, and his *Systema Brahmanicum*—were potentially useful to future missionaries and were written for them, but they were also texts inspired by the *Asiatick Researches*, by Anquetil Duperron and by other Orientalist scholars in India and Europe. One of the characteristic practices of the new Orientalists was to dissociate the traditional keepers of the texts, the Brahmans, from the 'ancient texts' of their tradition. The 'antiquity' of the Indian literary or sacred texts dis-authorized, in the Orientalist view, those who were merely their transmitters. It was often repeated that the Brahmans who knew by heart the Vedas and were able to recite them did not understand their meanings.

THE END OF CATHOLIC MISSIONARY ORIENTALISM

In the nineteenth century, a purely 'ocular' authority of the travellers and missionaries was on the wane in terms of its capacity to shore up a new type of 'scientific' episteme englobing the Orient. Being there and seeing with one's own eyes was not a prerequisite for acquiring the new type of knowledge based on linguistic expertise. Paulinus is aware of this, although at times he uses this older type of authority to bash his critics. Thus he treated those who travelled through and stayed in India for years without learning even a vernacular language as 'ambulant suitcases (*bauli ambulanti*)'.[91] Those who did not know Sanskrit were equally uninformed. For example, Paulinus described a ritual of *yajña,* or as he called it, *il sagrifizio Yàga*, unknown to the Capuchin missionary Marco della Tomba who called it a hoax, '*impostura*'.[92] Paulinus explained that if Marco never heard of it, the reason was that he did not know Sanskrit and never read *Amarasinha.*[93] Therefore, to 'discover' this major Vedic sacrifice, it was sufficient to read authentic books in original languages in Europe, without ever visiting India.

The Calcutta Orientalists were, of course, based in Bengal, but for them as well, authority was not located in being there but in reading the right type of books and in avoiding being duped by avaricious interpreters. The production of knowledge moved further and farther away from the sites and people involved in 'data collection'. 'The centers of calculation', as far as Indological sciences were concerned, moved to the nineteenth-century Europe.[94]

Well, Paulinus obviously also moved in the right direction, but not the right capital, or not quite. In terms of materials produced on India, from the Jesuit collections of letters and treatises, to manuscripts and books published by travellers and by the missionaries of the Propaganda Fide, Rome was probably one of the richest European capitals. However, many of the documents were not easily accessible for various reasons.[95] On the other hand, the latter part of the eighteenth century was the period in which museums and collections of antiquities and curiosities came into fashion, supported by patrons who were some of the richest and the most influential Papal officials.

Stefano Borgia was an emblematic figure combining in his person all qualities of an eighteenth-century Roman mecenae. He was from a rich aristocratic family, himself an amateur antiquarian and historian as well as a talented Papal administrator. On his family property in Velletri, Borgia founded a museum of antiquities and relics of the 'ancient' civilizations such as coins, manuscripts, and artwork. It was with Borgia's encouragement and protection, since he was an influential member of the Propaganda Fide that Paulinus was able to work on his publications. Paulinus's comparative perspective was further developed through the access to materials and scholars working on Coptic, Egyptian, Greek and Roman archeology, and literature. His printed books are full of references to various Velletri collections and catalogues.

Paulinus belonged, therefore, to a certain community of scholars, all of whom belonged to Stefano Borgia's patronage network. It is clear that their common interest and expertise in antiquities and classical learning defined the topics and agreed-upon set of procedures.[96] For example, the *lingua franca* of their enterprise was Latin, rather then the vernacular Italian. 'Borgia's' scholars were also often employed in cataloguing, ordering, classifying, and describing the items in the collections rather then 'speculating' about larger philosophical and theological issues of the day such as the origins of language, comparative religion, and ethnography. They were not prevented from writing scholarly articles on whatever topic they chose, but their work in the Velletri Museum was mostly antiquarian research.

Ancient, primitive, and exotic were closely linked in the eighteenth century antiquarianism, especially when applied to non-European 'antiquities'. For Paulinus the whole Brahmanical civilization was a relic of a past and thus worth studying in its entirety. In spite of excellent material provided by the Roman libraries and archives, Paulinus did not have a sufficiently numerous community of Indologists in Rome and in Italy in general. In a hostile comment, Anquetil Duperron remarked that for Paulinus 'all his science comes from the Propaganda Fide library, Museum of Cardinal Borgia, from F. Hanxleden [the Sanskrit grammar] and from *Asiatick Researches* in Calcutta, whether he understands it or not.'[97] It seems that some other scholars from

Borgia's network felt the same lack of intellectual stimulation. Jakob Georg Christian Adler wrote in his *Kurze Übersicht seiner bibl.-krit. Reise nach Rom* (Hamburg-Altona 1783) that in Rome there were excellent libraries for learning Oriental languages, but that there were no scholars among the Orientals.[98]

Knowledge in Rome was stored in the libraries, museums, and books accessible to the scholars who had permission to use them.[99] Finally, all knowledge about the past and about other peoples was part of an 'ecumenical' and universal Catholic mission of which Borgia and some other 'enlightened' cardinals dreamt on the eve of the French Revolution.

Paulinus's archival and comparativist work was, therefore, torn between two differently articulated projects. For Borgia and his Catholic universal mission, Paulinus was a 'conservationist' or curator of documents and objects that were to prove what the Church already knew, and to prevent theories that would argue against the basic Catholic dogmas. A wide variety of opinions was allowed within this fixed framework. Thus Paulinus could exchange punches with Father Antonio Giorgi on the meaning of Brahmanical religion or write against Anquetil Duperron, Jones, and Voltaire. At the same time, as an Orientalist, Paulinus 'belonged' to an international community of scholars who worked on the same or similar texts and issues. This Orientalist community in Bengal and Europe was also Christian, but it prided itself on scientific, secular epistemologies and mistrusted in particular Catholic missionaries in India. Paulinus felt snubbed by the British and French Orientalists, but he also often agreed with their conclusions and even invited them to come and consult his books in Rome.[100]

None of the Orientalist came to Rome, very few read his books and after his death in 1806 and the dispersal of the Borgia Museum in 1814, Paulinus's Orientalist treasures sank into oblivion. Rome became a backwater on the map of the nineteenth-century Orientalist scholars. With a loss of political autonomy through French invasion and the internal 'revolutions', the patronage network for missionary Orientalists disintegrated. A new kind of professional Orientalists such as Count Angelo de Gubernatis in the late nineteenth century and Giuseppe Tucci in the twentieth had more in common with

British, German, and French Orientalists than with their immediate Catholic missionary predecessors like Paulinus.[101]

NOTES AND REFERENCES

1. This essay has been presented as a paper at the conference on *Misiones católicas y producción de saberes entre América y Asia en la edad moderna*, in Puebla, Mexico, 4–6 March 2005. I thank the organizers—Centro de Estudios de Africa y Asia, El Colegio de México, and Bibliotheca Franciscana y Centro de Estudios Humanísticos Fray Bernardino de Sahagún, Universidad de las Américas, Puebla—for inviting me. For thoughtful comments my gratitude goes to all the participants, especially to David Lorenzen, Thomas Cohen, Elisabeta Corsi, Eugenio Menegon, Norma Duran, and Pedro Gil. The research on Paulinus a S. Bartholomaeo has been partly supported by the project 'Kulturno-povijesne veze Hrvatske i Indije', Ministarstvo za Znanost Republike Hrvatske. My gratitude goes to the director of the project Zdravka Matišić, Professor of Sanskrit at the University of Zagreb.

2. Paulinus a S. Bartholomaeo, Carmelitano Scalzo, *Viaggio alle Indie Orientali, umiliato alla Santita di N.S Papa Pio Sesto Pontefice Massimo,* Roma 1976, with 12 copperplates [henceforth *Viaggio*]. For the sake of uniformity, I will be using the Latin version of the name, which is Paulinus a Sancto Bartholomaeo. A 'secular' name of this missionary born to a Croat family in Austria was Filip Vesdin.

3. *Viaggio*, pp. 391–2.

4. Paulinus a S. Bartholomaeo, *Scitismo svilupato in risposta alla lettera del signor Conte Gastone della Torre di Rezzonico su' monumenti indici del Museo Borgiano di Velletri,* Roma, 1793, p. 24. In his response to the Count Gastone della Torre di Rezzonico Paulinus rejects the theory of the Scythian origin of the Indian civilization.

5. *Viaggio*, p. 391.

6. Ibid., p. 392.

7. On the development of 'Indophilia' among the eighteenth-century Catholic Orientalists see Sylvia Murr, 'Les conditions d'émergence du discours sur l'Inde au siècle des Lumière', *Purushartha*, vol. 7 (1983), pp. 251–4.

8. Giovanni Pizzorusso, 'I satelliti di Propaganda Fide: Il Collegio Urbano e la tipografia poliglotta; note di ricerca su due instituzioni culturali Romane nel XVII secolo', *Mélanges de l'Ecole française de Rome, Italie et Méditerranée,* tome vol. 116, no. 2, 2004, pp. 471–98.

9. Thomas Trautmann, *Aryans and British India* (Berkeley: University of California Press, 1997), p. 30.

10. Just like William Jones, Paulinus left behind a whole library of printed works.

11. Paulinus a S. Bartholomaeo, *Dissertation on the Sanskrit Language*, translation and introduction by Ludo Rocher, Amsterdam: John Benjamins B.V, 1977, p. xiv. The dissertation is the introduction to Paulinus' Sanskrit grammar, the first Sanskrit grammar printed in Europe. *Sidharubam seu Grammatica Samscrdamica, cui accedit Dissertatio historio-critica in linguam samscrdamicam, vulgo Sanscret dictam, in qua*

hujus linguae existentia, origo, praestantia, antiquitas, extensio, maternitas ostenditur, libri aliqui ea exarati critice recensentur, et simul aliquae antiquissimae gentilium orationes liturgicae paucis attinguntur et explicantur, 188 pp., typis S.C. de Prop. Fide, 1790 [1791].

12. Trautmann, *Aryans and British India*, p. 32. Rocher, *Dissertation on the Sanskrit Language*, p. xxiii,

13. Rocher, *Dissertation on the Sanskrit Language*, p. xxiii.

14. Paulinus a S. Bartholomaeo, P., *Monumenti indici del museo Naniano illustrati dal P. Paulino a S. Bartolomaeo, Carmelitano Scalzo, Professore di Lingue Orientali, sindico delle Missioni Asiatiche et Socio Academico di Velletri, e di Napoli*, XXVIII, Typ. Seminarii, Padova, 1799.

15. 'A Monsignor Luigi Maria di Gesù Vescovo Usuliense Vicario Apostolico del Malabar: Verapoli, 6 Ottobre 1790', in 'Lettere della Sacra Congregazione dell'Anno 1790, (vol. 258, ff. 697b–699a), Historical Archives of the Congregation for the Evangelization of Peoples or 'De Propaganda Fide', Rome. I owe this information to David Lorenzen Sbrega who found this letter in the Propaganda archives. He presumed that the letter was written by Stefano Borgia. It seems unlikely since Borgia must have been on good terms with Paulinus, while the letter shows quite a bit of personal animosity on the part of the writer.

16. As a curator of the Indian collection for Stefano Borgia's museum in Velletri, Paulinus catalogued all the manuscripts and objects—sculptures in metal and wood representing Indian gods, paintings on paper, votive objects and two painted home 'oratories'. In *Viaggio*, he calls these oratories in the Velletri museum '*altarini mobile*' in Italian or *sacelli* in Latin. See his *Musei Borgiani Velitris codices avenses, peguani, siamici, malabarici, indostani, animadvesionibus historico-criticis castigati et illustrati. Accedunt monumenta inedita et Cosmogonia indico-tibetana*, auctore pp. xvii+266, 3 figures, Romae, 1793, in -4°. See articles by Rosa Maria Cimino, 'L'Italia e il collezionismo d'arte indiana', and Rossana Muzii, 'Un recupero e un restauro al Museo di Capodimonte: I disegni indiani della collezione Borgia', p. 276, in *Le quatro voci del mondo: arte, culture e saperi nella collezione di Stefano Borgia, 1731–1804,* Marco Nocca, ed. Naples: Electa Napoli, 2001, pp. 268, 276.

17. About how he collected information while he was travelling along the Coromandel Coast, Paulinus writes in this *Viaggio*, 'I wrote every evening in my diary what I have seen and what the inhabitants told me, when there was nothing else to see, I left'. *Viaggio*, p. 50.

18. Ibid., p. 126.

19. Francisco Bethencourt, 'A Igreja', in *História da Expansão Portuguesa*, Bethencourt, Francisco and Chaudhuri, Kirti, (eds) (Lisbon: Circulo de Leitores, 1998), vol.1, pp. 369–86.

20. *Viaggio*, p. 50.

21. See my article 'One Civility, but Multiple Religion: Jesuit Mission among St. Thomas Christians in India (16th–17th centuries)', *Journal of Early Modern History*, vol. 9, nos 3–4, 2005, pp. 284–325.

22. Giuseppe di Santa Maria Sebastiani (1623–89), *Prima speditione alle Indie Orientali* (Rome, 1666), *Segunda speditione alle Indie Orientali* (1672). Technically,

the first Carmelite travel narrative on India was published by Philippe de la Très Sainte-Trinité (1603–71) in Latin, *Itinerarium Orientale* in Lyon in 1649.

23. Willi Henkel, 'The Polyglot Printing-office of the Congregation, The press apostolate as an important means for communicating the faith', in *Sacrae Congregationis de Propaganda Fide Memoria Rerum*, 1622–1700, J. Metzler (ed.), vol. I, no. 1 (Rome, Freiburg, Wien: Herder, 1972), pp. 335–50.

24. Paulinus's diary during the sea passage from France to Pondicherry, written in German, remains unpublished. See Ivan Slamnig, 'Ivan Filip Vesdin (1748–1806), pionir evropske indologije i komparativne filologije', *Rad*, JAZU, vol. 350 (1968).

25. Hanxleden (born near Osnabrück in Germany, 1681; died at Palayur, Kerala, 1732) is locally known as Arnos Paathiri. He was a Malayalam/ Sanskrit poet, grammarian, lexicographer, and philologist.

26. Paulinus a S. Bartholomaeo, *De manuscriptis codicibus indicis R.P. Joan. Ernesti Hanxleden epistola ad R.P. Alexium Mariam a S. Joseph Carmelitam Excalceatum*, Vindobonae anno MDCCXCIX (1799).

27. For Paulinus' naturalist writing see Ines G. Županov, 'Amateur Naturalist and Professional Orientalist; Paulinus a S. Bartholomaeo in Kerala and Rome (18th–19th)', *Os viajantes europeus e o mundo natural asiático (séculos 16 a 18) I, [European travellers and the Asian natural world (16th–18th centuries)–I]*, ed. Rui Loureiro, numéro special de *Revista de Cultura/ Review of Culture*, 20 (Macau, 2007), pp. 77–101.

28. Paula Findlen, *Possessing Nature, Museum, Collecting, and Scientific Culture in Early Modern Italy* (Berkeley, Los Angeles, London: University of California Press, 1994).

29. Vicenzo Maria di Santa Caterina da Siena (alias Antonio Murchio) visited Kerala in 1657 with Giuseppe di Santa Maria Sebastiani. They were sent by the Propaganda Fide in order to take over the mission territory among the Syrian or St Thomas Christians administered until then by the Jesuits.

30. He was a member of the first Discalced Carmelite expedition. He joined Sebastiani and Muchio in Banda, north of Goa.

31. Donald Lach, *Asia in the Making of Europe* (Chicago, London: The University of Chicago Press, 1993), vol. III, no. 2, p. 926. Matteo di San Giuseppe wrote and sent to Europe his own botanical work entitled *Viridarium Orientale*. Županov, 'Amateur Naturalist', p. 99.

32. Paul B. Salmon, 'The Beginnings of Morphology; Linguistic Botanizing in the 18th century', *Historiographia Linguistica*, vol. 1, no. 3, 1974, pp. 313–39.

33. William Carey edited and published Dr William Roxburgh's *Flora Indica; or Descriptions of Indian Plants*, in the Serampore Press in 1820 (vol. 1) and in 1824 (vol. 2).

34. Quoted in Rosane Rocher, 'British Orientalism in the Eighteenth Century', in Carol A. Breckenridge and Peter van der Veer, (eds), *Orientalism and the Postcolonial Predicament; Perspectives on South Asia* (Philadelphia: University of Pennsylvania Press, 1993), p. 232.

35. Trautmann, *Aryans and British India*, pp. 28–61.

36. The factors behind the success of the Orientalist scholars in inaugurating the tradition of modern Indological research compared to missionary Orientalist

failure is discussed in David Lorenzen, 'Marco della Tomba and the Brahmin from Banaras: Missionaries, Orientalist and Indian Scholars', *Journal of Asian Studies,* vol. 65, 2006, pp. 113–41.

37. *Viaggio*, p. 7.

38. Pietro Maria Gazzaniga (born in1722 in Bergamo, died in 1799 in Vicenza) was a Thomist theologian. He published, among other works, the *Praelectiones theologicae habitae in Vindobonensi Universitate, nunc vero alia methodo dispositae, emendatae et auctae*, 9 vols., Bologna, 1788–93.

39. *Viaggio*, p. 8.

40. Jean Pierre Abel-Rémusat (1788–1832) mentions the name Marchena. In the copy of the French edition in the Bibliothèque National de France in Paris, Marchesan is added in handwriting.

41. Paulin de Saint-Barthélémy, *Voyage aux Indes orientales du père Paulin de Saint-Barthélémy*, Paris, 1808, 3 vols.

42. *Viaggio*, p. 355.

43. *Botanica Malabar*, Biblioteca Nazionale Vittorio Emmanuele, Rome, Documenti rari e manoscritti, Fondi Minori, Santa Maria della Scala, scatola 36, G.

44. 'The virtues of the lemon balm...by a Discalced Carmelite in Paris,...against apoplexies and vapors'. This work is quoted in *Viaggio*, p. 362.

45. Trautmann, *Aryans and British India*, p. 36. (Alexander Hamilton, *Review of Asiatick Researches*, vol. 6., 1802, pp. 30–310)

46. Trautmann, *Aryans and British India*, p. 36.

47. *Viaggio*, p. 17

48. [William Jones], 'A dissertation on the Orthography of Asiatick Words in Roman Letters by the President', *Asiatic Researches*; or, *Transactions of the Society Instituted in Bengal, for Inquiring into the History and Antiquities, the Arts, Sciences, and Literature of Asia,* volume the first, Calcutta, printed in 1788. London reprinted, for Vernor and Hood, no. 1, Poultry, 1798, p. 13. In Paulinus's *Examen Historico-criticum Codicum Indicorum Bibliothecae Sacrae Congregationis de Propaganda Fide,* Romae, 1792, p. 80, p. 6.

49. Rocher, *Dissertation on the Sanskrit Language*, p. 92.

50. Ibid., pp. 102–3.

51. A Jesuit dream of finding a perfect language receptacle for the Christian message made the missionaries interested in all languages cultivated by the learned non-Christian literati. The Jesuits at the Mughal court singled out Persian while those in China thought that Mandarin qualified to become the language of the Mass for the Chinese.

52. Ines G. Županov, *Disputed Mission, Jesuit Experiments and Brahmanical Knowledge* (*17th c.*) (New Delhi: Oxford University Press, 1999).

53. Roth's grammar was discovered in Bibioteca Nazionale Vittorio Emmanuele in Rome in 1976 by Arnuld Camps, O. F. M, see Lach, *Asia in the Making of Europe*, vol. III, no. 2, plate 129. Athanasius Kircher, *China monumentis...illustrata*, Amsterdam, apud Jacobum à Meurs, 1667.

54. [William Jones] 'On the Gods of Greece, Italy and India, written in 1784, And since revised by the President', *Asiatic Researches*; or, *Transactions of the Society*

Instituted in Bengal, for Inquiring into the History and Antiquities, the Arts, Sciences, and Literature of Asia, volume the first, Calcutta, printed, reprinted in London for Vernor and Hood, no. 1, Poultry, 1798, p. 275.

55. Rocher, *Dissertation on the Sanskrit Languages*, p. 103.

56. *Viaggio*, *Dissertation on the Sanskrit Languages*, pp. 258–63.

57. Rocher, p. 113.

58. Milka Jauk-Pinhak, 'Some Notes on the Pioneer Indologist Filip Vesdin (Paulinus a Sancto Bartholomaeo)', *Indologica Taurinensia*, vol. XII, 1984, Torino, p. 136

59. Paulinus a S. Bartholomaeo, *De antiquitate et affinitate linguae Zendicae, Samscrdamicae et Germanicae dissertatio*, Typis seminarii, Padova, 1798 [1799]

60. Jauk-Pinhak, p. 136. *De latini sermonis origine et cum orintalibus linguis connectione dissertatio, Romae apud Antonium Fulgonium*, 1802. A ten page manuscript copy of the article with slight differences can be found in Rome, BNVE, Rari e manoscriti, Fondi minori, Santa Maria della Scala, box 36 (C), p. 2. The date on the manuscript is 1801. There is another copy in box 34, pp. 58–77.

61. Rocher, *Dissertation on the Sanskrit Languages*, pp. 107–9.

62. Ibid., p. 109.

63. Clemens a Iesu (Peanio), (1731–82), published *Alphabetum Grandonico-Malabaricum Sive Samscrudonicum*, Typis S. Congregatione de Propaganda Fide, Rome, 1772. See, Ambrosius a S. Teresia OCD, *Nomenclator Missionariorum Ordinis Carmelitorum Descalceatorum, Romae*, 1944, p. 94–5. Ildephonsus a Presentatione B. Mariae Virginis (1724–90), who was a prolific writer, never published any of his works. They are preserved in manuscript form in the Archives of the Discalced Carmelites in Rome. See in particular, *Collectio industriosa omnium Dogmatum et Secretorum, ex Puranis, seu libri canonicis...*, see Ambrosius, p. 186–9.

64. For the history of the authorship attribution and the abridged published version of the text, see Jarl Charpentier, (ed. and intro.), The Livro da Seita dos Indios Orientais *(Brit. Mus. Ms. Sloane 1820) of Father Jacobo Fenicio, S.J.*, Uppsala, 1933 [henceforth Fenicio].

65. Fenicio, p. 8. See also, Ines G. Županov, *Missionary Tropics, Jesuit Frontier in India (16th-17th century)* (Ann Arbor: University of Michigan Press, 2005), pp. 179–80

66. Paulinus provided a short summary and a negative 'evaluation' of Ildephonsus' text in his *Examen historico-criticum*, pp. 72–3. The text was written, according to Paulinus, in a bad style, with many repetitions, with frequent exclamations and digressions, and a tendency to vilify the Brahmans.

67. Rocher, *Dissertation on the Sanskrit Languages*, p. 110.

68. Ibid., p. 130.

69. Ibid., p. 117.

70. Joseph S.J. Wicki, (ed.), *Documenta Indica* (henceforth DI), Rome, 1956, vol. IV, pp. 334–5.

71. Dr Giuseppe Barone, *Vita, Precursori ed Opere del P. Paolino da S. Bartolommeo (Filippo Werdin), Contributo all storia degli studi orientali in Europa,*

Napoli, Cav. Antonio Morano, 1888, p. 18. *Sidharubam*, p. 22, *Systema Brahmanicum*, pa. XII, *Alaphabetum grandonico-malabaricum*, p. 7.

72. A similar story is told by Marco della Tomba. The raja of Bettiah 'consigned' four big chests of books to the Capuchin missionaries in 1762 before being taken prisoner by the army of the Nawab Casmalican [Kasim Ali Khan]. Quoted from David N. Lorenzen, 'Marco della Tomba and the Brahmin from Banaras, Missionaries, Orientalists and Indian scholars', *Journal of Asian Studies*, vol. 65, 2006, pp. 113–41.

73. Muzaffar Alam and Seema Alavi, *A European Experience of the Mughal Orient, The I'jāz-i Arsalānī (Persian Letters, 1773–1779) of Antoine-Louis Henri Polier* (New Delhi: Oxford University Press, 2001), p. 35. For the larger claims about the connection between the practice of collecting and imperial expansion, see Maya Jasanoff, *Edge of Empire; Lives, Culture, and Conquest in the East, 1750–1850* (New York: Vintage Books, 2006).

74. Alam and Alavi, *A European Experience*, p. 32.

75. Paulin de Saint-Barthélémy, *Voyage aux Indes orientales du père Paulin de Saint-Barthélémy*, Paris, 1808, vol. 3, p. 138 footnote, *Viaggio*, p. 72. *A Catalogue of Oriental Manuscripts, collected in Indoostan.* By Mr Samuel Guise, Surgeon to the General Hospital at Surat, From the Year 1777 till 1792 (printed) pp. 1–32. Biblioteca Apostolica Vaticana, Rome, Borg. Lat 529, pp. 1–18.

76. Paulinus also stayed in Anjengo for two years. Anjuthengu (Anjengo) is situated 40 km, north of Thiruvananthapuram along the sea coast. It was the first settlement of the English East India Company on the Malabar Coast, established in 1764. It was a diocese belonging to the Vicariate of Verapoly in Paulinus's time.

77. The other three were in the Royal Library in Paris, the library of the Propaganda Fide, and the Museo Borgiano in Velletri.

78. [William Jones], 'The Design of a Treatise on the Plants of India', *Asiatic Researches; or, Transactions of the Society Instituted in Bengal, for Inquiring into the History and Antiquities, the Arts, Sciences, and Literature of Asia*, volume the second, printed verbatim from the Calcutta Edition, in Quarto (London: Printed for Vernor and Hood, in the Poultry, 1799), p. 345.

79. Slamnig, *Ivan Filip Vesdin*, p. 8.

80. His dreams did not come true. William Jones died in Calcutta in 1794. Trautmann, pp. 28–9.

81. [William Jones], 'The Design of a Treatise on the Plants of India', *Asiatic Researches; or, Transactions of the Society Instituted in Bengal, for Inquiring into the History and Antiquities, the Arts, Sciences, and Literature of Asia*, volume the second, printed verbatim from the Calcutta Edition, in Quarto (London: Printed for Vernor and Hood, in the Poultry, 1799). Jones: 'Give me time, we may say, for our investigations, and we will transfer to Europe all the sciences, arts, and literature of Asia', p. 345.

82. *Viaggio*, p. 365.

83. Paulin, *Voyage*, vol. 3, p. 486, (quoting page 462, line 23; Italian edition of *Viaggio*, p. 365). 'The English have promised...that they would give us Indian Botany,

but I do not have much confidence in these promises, because to do it, one needs men who know local languages, time and money'. (Paulinus quoted *Asiatic Research*, vol. II). Anquetil Duperron added his own gloss to this statement, 'Father Paulinus's remark is easily refuted. The English have the *time* and the *money* necessary for such an enterprise : and when they will want to choose their subjects, they will have no lack of their own to learn the languages of India'. William Carey posthumously edited and published Dr William Roxburgh*'s Flora Indica; or Descriptions of Indian Plants*, in the Serampore Press in 1820 (vol. 1) and in 1824 (vol. 2).

84. *Viaggio*, p. 331

85. Paulin, *Voyage*, vol. III, p. 401 (quoting p. 207, *Viaggio*, p. 263).

86. *Examen Historico-criticum,* pp. 42–50. Paulinus's most elaborate attack on *Ezour-Vedam* is in his *Systema Brahmanicum*, pp. 315–17.

87. According to Paulinus, the Jesuits in Masulipatnam produced *Ezour-Vedam* in Tamil in order to refute paganism. He does not speculate as to how this manuscript in Tamil (Paulinus only thinks of a Tamil original, not Sanskrit) got into the hands of the French traveller Conte de Modave after passing through a translator in Pondicherry. Or was this the text that was translated into Tamil and Sanskrit? The Sanskrit text was found together with the French 'translation' by Sir Alexander Johnston in the Jesuit College in Pondicherry. This particular Sanskrit text was examined by Francis Whyte Ellis, who decided that the work was written by Roberto Nobili. Rocher, *Ezour-Vedam*, p. 18. Ellis's article is published in *Asiatic Researches*, vol. 14, 1822. The Jesuit College in Pondicherry possessed many more similar catechetical works. August Wilhelm von Schlegel reviewed the *Asiatic Researches* (vol. 14) in his journal *Indische Bibliothek*, vol. 2, p. 50–6 and called *Ezour-Vedam* a pious fraud ('*ein frommer Betrug*'). Ludo Rocher's arguments that the *Ezour-Vedam* was originally written in French appears to be conclusive. Ludo Rocher, *Ezour-Vedam, A French Veda of the 18th century* (Philadelphia: University of Pennsylvania Press, 1984).

88. He quotes a manuscript in the Museum Borgianum in Velletri, written by a Capuchin, Marco della Tomba, *Osservazioni sopra le relazioni che fa Monsieur Holwell Inglese*. Marco della Tomba himself deposited the text in the Museum before returning to India in 1775. *Examen Historico-criticum*, p. 6.

89. There were controversies between Protestant missionaries such as Bartholomaeus Ziegenbalg in Tranquebar and a Jesuit Giuseppe Constanzio Beschi in Madurai. See Stuart Blackburn, *Print, Folklore, and Nationalism in Colonial South India* (Permanent Black: New Delhi, 2003), pp. 43–65.

90. See Županov, *Disputed Mission*, pp. 74, 115.

91. *Viaggio*, p. 306.

92. Ibid., *Systema Brahmanicum*, p. 1. Paulinus did not indicate in which text Marco della Tomba issued this opinion. According to David Lorenzen, most of his extant writings were left in Rome before he left for India (1783) for the second time. Apart from a few letters during his second stay until his death in 1803, no other texts seemed to have survived. David N. Lorenzen, 'Europeans in Late Mughal South Asia: The Perceptions of Italian Missionaries', *The Indian Economic and Social History Review*, vol. XL, no.1, January–March, 2003, pp. 1–32.

93. Paulinus printed the first part of this oldest Sanskrit dictionary (AD 6th c.), which he called erroneously by the name of its author Amarasinha instead of by its title, *Amarakośa*. Paulinus a S. Bartholomaeo, *Amarasinha. Sectio prima, de Coelo. Ex tribus ineditis codicibus indicis manuscriptis*, figures, Roma, 1789. See also *Amarakosa: With the Commentary of Mahesvara / Ramakrishna Gopal Bhandarkar*. Revised enlarged edition (New Delhi: Cosmos, 2004).

94. For the notion of 'centers of calculation' see Bruno Latour, *Science in Action* (Cambridge, Mass.: Harvard University Press, 1987).

95. Jesuit documents were filtered out by the Jesuit censors and only the acceptable part was published and disseminated. With the Jesuit order abolished, many documents were either hidden by the Jesuits or taken over by other ecclesiastical agents who blocked access to them or simply neglected them.

96. Paula Findlen described a similar situation in her article on the emergence of natural history as a discipline from the perspective of community formation. 'The Formation of a Scientific Community: Natural History in Sixteenth-century Italy', Anthony Grafton and Nancy Siraisi, *Natural Particulars, Nature and the Disciplines in Renaissance Europe* (Cambridge, Mass. and London, England, The MIT Press, 1999), pp. 369–400.

97. Paulin, *Voyage*, vol. 3, p. 439.

98. Paola Orsatti, *Il Fondo Borgia della Biblioteca Vaticana e gli Studi Orientali a Roma tra Sette e Ottocento* (Città del Vaticano, Biblioteca Apostolica Vaticana, 1996), p. 12

99. Stefano Borgia was known for his 'liberal' attitude towards circulation of books while he was a Prefetto della Sacra Congregazione dell'Indice, but he was a staunch opponent of revolutionary ideas, just as was Paulinus. Stefano Borgia was jailed when the Jacobites took hold of Rome. Paulinus wrote a pamphlet against the Republicans.

100. Rocher, *Dissertation on the Sanskrit Languages*, p. 165.

101. De Gubernatis, Angelo, *Matériaux pour servir à l'histoire des études orientales en Italie*, Paris, 1876. See an interesting view of his « Italian » Orientalist predecessors. While he rejected Paulinus (whom he mistakenly and sneeringly designated as « italianised hungarian »), he extolled some other 'pure' Italian travellers-Orientalists and missionaries, such as Filippo Sassetti (16th c.) and Marco della Tomba (18th c.).

8. THE MISSIONARY AND THE ORIENTALIST

Thomas R. Trautmann

David Lorenzen's recent research has been on Italian missionaries in early modern India, and out of it has come a splendid piece, first aired at the University of Wisconsin South Asia Conference in 2003 at a panel he organized and I had the pleasure of taking part in and since published in the *Journal of Asian Studies*.[1] Under the title 'Marco della Tomba and the Brahmin from Banaras: Missionaries, Orientalists, and Indian Scholars', David proposes a comparison between the knowledge about India produced by missionaries and Orientalists. He puts it in the form of a question: How do we explain 'the slow growth of European scholarly knowledge about literate Hindu culture' under scholar-missionaries over the long period from about 1500 to 1770, and 'the exponential growth of such knowledge among British scholar-administrators' thereafter, especially with the founding of the Asiatic Society in 1784? The question is built around a surprising truth. Although Christian missionaries had been in India for two and a half centuries before British trade in India morphed into British empire, and although both Christian missionaries and British colonial rulers needed knowledge of Indian languages, beliefs, and conduct, the production of European scholarly knowledge of India by missionary-scholars was, on the whole, and granting that there are exceptional works of great intellectual distinction, comparatively poor, limited, and non-durable.

It *is* a surprising truth. One thinks of the missionaries as especially given to the learning of Indian languages and the writing of grammars and dictionaries, compiling ethnographies of gentiles and analysing heathen religions—and of giving a lead to other Europeans in these endeavours. Indeed, as David's comparison implies, wherever

Orientalists went, missionaries had been there first. Thus in some degree the knowledge of British-Indian Orientalists was better because it *built upon* the pioneer works of missionaries. On that account alone the Orientalist-produced knowledge of India after 1770 *should* have been an advance upon the missionary-produced knowledge of before 1770, because it had the advantage of these prior works. Nevertheless, and making generous allowance for this Orientalist advantage, I believe after reading David's article that when one looks closely, as David does in his study of Marco, it remains true that the knowledge-production of missionaries prior to 1770 was rapidly overtaken and superseded by the much more voluminous, effective, and durable knowledge produced by Orientalists in British India.

I have been thinking of David's argument in relation to my own recent researches into the beginnings of Orientalist knowledge in south India, specifically Madras, at the start of the nineteenth century, and it is clear to me that his position is true for the south as well as the north, and is confirmed by early colonial sources. We can take the measure of the prior missionary knowledge of south India from a report to the government of Madras undertaken by a committee headed by F.W. Ellis, Collector of Madras and the leading Orientalist of his time in south India. In the run-up to the creation of the College of Fort St George (1812) to instruct arriving junior civil servants in the languages of south India, Ellis and his committee made a survey of existing works for these purposes, that is, missionary-produced works, almost all of them in manuscript, which gives us a baseline for comparison.[2]

For Tamil there were the grammars and dictionary, in Latin, of the missionary Constantius Beschi, which were highly revered; the committee proposed they be printed by the college for its students. Beschi is *the* outstanding exception at this period to Lorenzen's rule. In this notable counter-instance, the Company Orientalists actively used the work of the missionary and burnished his memory; there is now a statue of Beschi for his contribution to Tamil literature on the Marina in Chennai. For Telugu, on the other hand, the committee found that there was a passable missionary grammar in French, and a Telugu, Sanskrit, and French dictionary, but judged these works not serviceable for students. A new grammar for Telugu was soon written by A.D. Campbell with the help of Udayagiri Venkatanarayana, drawing, not upon those missionary works, but on older grammars in Telugu. Similarly, for a Telugu dictionary the committee looked to the recently compiled work of Mamadi Venkaya, a Komati trader-scholar of Masulipatam, and Campbell later composed a Telugu-English dictionary that the College published. For Kannada and Malayalam the Madras Orientalists had no missionary precursors, and John McKerrell of the Company service eventually wrote the first grammar of Kannada in English, relying on Indian grammars, not missionary ones. Thus for Kannada and Malayalam there were no missionary grammars and dictionaries, and for Telugu those that existed did not come up to the mark. As for the ethnography of south India, a later project to translate a work of this kind by the Abbé Dubois, missionary in Mysore, at the College was pre-empted by the Court of Directors in London; but it is clear from discussions of the project in the colonial records that when Ellis looked closely at the text of Dubois he found that as an account of the caste system of south India it was deficient and would need to be augmented by notes from Company servants, who had acquired better knowledge. Max Müller, in the preface to an edition of the English translation,[3] remarked on the sense of antiquity and out-of-dateness that one felt in reading the Abbé's work, and how it seemed to belong to the period before the great Orientalist work that commenced at Calcutta in the 1770s—which fits David's point very well. Without knowing it, Max Müller had hit the nail on the head; for Sylvia Murr has shown in our own time that the Abbé Dubois borrowed the substance of his text, and much of the words, from an earlier work of Father Gaston-Laurent Coeurdoux, eighteenth-century Jesuit missionary of Madurai.[4] Finally, I may note that Father Coeurdoux himself is important in having recognized similarities between Sanskrit and Latin at the same time, more or less, as the famous pronouncement by Sir William Jones in the *Asiatic Researches* published at Calcutta; but Coeurdoux's recognition was only published in 1808, after Jones' work had become widely read in Europe and stimulated great interest in Sanskrit and its relations with European languages, and after Coeurdoux and Jones had died.[5] In other words, the significance of Coeurdoux's work was only appreciated retrospectively, in the light of the published work of Jones. All in all, as this examination of the south Indian situation confirms, the new Orientalist knowledge from British India was of a higher quality and had greater effect, both in the short and the longer run. In the short run it provoked a wave of Indomania among European intellectuals; in the long run it formulated and consolidated scientific ideas about language classification, including the concept of the Indo-European language family, that have continued to be in use as scientific categories to this day.

David's explanation of the Orientalist advantage over the missionary is in three parts. First: the education of the missionaries and the Orientalists, he believes, was not so very different in substance; but the secular and Enlightenment-tinged character of Orientalist research made for greater openness to India and Indian religion. Missionary accounts of India could always be construed as sympathy for false religion by narrow-minded readers back home, and were produced, therefore, under an inhibiting fear of committing doctrinal incorrectness and with considerable pre-emptive censorship at source. Second: but by far and away the major factor, according to David, was the Orientalist advantage in manpower and money. Missionary establishments in India were small and poorly funded; correspondence with the authorities back home regularly included appeals, more or less piteous, for money and more missionaries. Moreover, little of the knowledge-production of missionaries made it into print, outside of the famous series, the *Lettres édifiantes et curieuses*, or *Jesuit relations* as they are often called. Most missionary works remained in manuscript form and had limited readership. Some have reached print only in recent times for their interest as historical documents, not as contributions to knowledge of India. All of this contrasts greatly with the conditions under which the Orientalists of British India worked. They had secure and well-paid employment, the resources of an empire, the encouragement of learned societies at Calcutta, Bombay, and Madras and the publishing opportunities of their journals. That empire promotes knowledge, much as war promotes science and engineering, is scandalous but true, however one might wish it were otherwise. Third: finally, the missionaries lacked, for the most part, direct and prolonged access to Indian scholars. This lack was in part a combination of the first two factors, anti-Enlightenment religious inhibition and lack of resources and institutional support. All of these points of David's argument seem exactly right to me. To them I would add that the engine propelling the Orientalist project was the Indian people themselves, whose taxes paid the large salaries of the East India

Company servants and financed the institutions that supported Orientalist research, while the missionaries had to rely upon financial transfers from Europe. Most Orientalist scholars employed by the East India Company had salaries that enabled them to maintain Indian scholars as assistants, and sometimes those establishments were large, maintained by the huge difference between British and Indian salaries. While these sordid facts are not the whole story of the Orientalist advantage, they are a very large part of it.

Thus, in brief, David Lorenzen's statement accounting for the imbalance of knowledge-production, favouring the Orientalist of British India after *c.* 1770 over the missionary of the time before. I believe this is a very important statement, one that contains more than this précis indicates. Moreover the implications are very great, and extend far and wide. For example, if we take the two terms, 'missionary' and 'Orientalist' and put them in different chronological and comparative framings, we may see that the significance of David's comparison is very large indeed. I see five ways in which we might configure the contrast between the missionary and the Orientalist to follow out further implications of David's most interesting and persuasive argument.

THE MISSIONARY BEFORE 1770, THE ORIENTALIST AFTER 1770

This is David's own framing. In this comparison, the year 1770 stands for the beginning of the British Empire in India, and with it, of (later British-Indian) secular Orientalist scholarship as opposed to the (earlier) Catholic missionary work allied to the Portuguese regime in Goa or the French one at Pondicherry, and the Lutheran missionaries of Halle working out of Danish Tranquebar.

BRITISH ORIENTALISM BEFORE AND AFTER 1770

But, of course, the British merchant companies had been in India for a century and a half before the transformation into empire. So the question may be asked, what about *British* knowledge-production about India *before and after* 1770, that is, while it was confined to mercantile factories along the coast, compared to when it became a governing power over masses of Indians in the agrarian interior? I believe the contrast is even more stark than the one David established, that is, British knowledge of India before 1770 was if anything poorer and less durable than that produced by the missionaries of whom David has written, and it contrasts even more unfavourably with the Orientalism of British India after 1770. Indeed there is hardly anything that can properly be called Orientalism among the British in India before the coming of empire caused it to spurt forward and build solid structures. This way of framing the comparison brings to the fore even more emphatically the element of empire as a force for knowledge-making. What empire brought was not so much a greater *demand* for knowledge as more effective *means* for its production, including especially the financing of it. Equally important, perhaps, is that the transformation of the British presence in India from a mercantile one to a governing power, brought with it a flow of more highly educated civil, judicial, and military personnel to British India, people with scholarly and scientific interests and some of them with university education.

PORTUGUESE, FRENCH, DANISH, AND BRITISH KNOWLEDGE-PRODUCTION IN INDIA

Another way of looking at European production of knowledge about India would be to compare the knowledge-producing regimes of the various European imperial projects in India. Here, flattening the difference between the missionary and the Orientalist and holding the fact of empire constant (though with much variation of extent, chronology, and so forth), we might seek to explore the differences among European empires.

THE MISSIONARY AND THE ORIENTALIST IN BRITISH INDIA AFTER 1770

Of course, missionary production of knowledge did not end in 1770, even in British India where the government tried to exclude missionaries and succeeded in doing so for quite some time. In this framing we hold empire constant and focus on the missionary/Orientalist difference. I will take up this framing of the comparative question and examine it at some length below.

INTERACTIONS OF INDIANS WITH THE MISSIONARY AND THE ORIENTALIST

Since all European knowledge-production about India begins with interactions between Indians and Europeans, we might learn much by examining these relations comparatively, as between missionaries and Orientalists, examining further David's point about the better working relations of British-Indian Orientalists with learned Indians. What is at issue is the paradox of this kind of knowledge, that it is made by Europeans but its authority in the end rests with Indians; and this inescapable truth is a problem for the authority-claims of such knowledge. In turn, missionary and Orientalist projects stand in different relation to Indians, and have different receptions and effects in India, which could be objects of comparative study.

In this essay I should like to take up David's invitation to comparative study by examining the missionary and the Orientalist in British India, number four in the discussed list of permutations. For although British India was for a time missionary-free, eventually there were *both* Orientalists *and* missionaries; and so, instead of comparing later Orientalists with missionaries of an earlier age, we ask instead, what were the relations of the Orientalist and the missionary in British India, and what was the nature of the knowledge of India they produced? What follows is a sketch of what a comparative programme of this kind might look like, and some of the results we might reach.

The matter is by no means straightforward, which is good, because that is what makes it interesting and worthwhile to think about, using David's comparison in a new application. On the one hand, the difference between the Orientalist and the missionary was strongly marked both discursively and in policy in British India; on the other hand, many missionaries were Orientalist scholars and many Orientalists had strong Christian beliefs, putting the very terms of comparison in doubt at the outset. Given such intermediate cases we need to understand that the missionary and the Orientalist are ideal types that flow into one another in practice. But they remain conceptually distinct for the principals. We will find that the missionary versus Orientalist contrast is a paradoxical social fact of early British India that ought to be highly unstable but is not, a solid that ought to be a fluid. Social and political forces of the moment conspire to maintain the conceptual distinction even in the face of their intermixture.

Perhaps the most illustrious example from British India of a missionary who was also an Orientalist is Bishop Robert Caldwell, whose *Comparative Grammar of the Dravidian or South-Indian Family of Languages* (1856)[6] was a work of enduring scientific value that is still in print and is much cited by linguists. The pioneering work of the Reverend John Stevenson discriminating the Sanskritic and non-Sanskritic element in modern Indian languages in lengthy articles of the 1840s and 1850s constituted an important contribution, even though it was surpassed by later scholars.[7] One may also mention the first missionary-Orientalists of British India, the Baptists Carey, Marshman, and Ward, who published grammars of Indian languages for English speakers and translations of Indian works while working toward the translation of the Bible into the modern languages of India. William Carey was made a professor of Bengali and Sanskrit at the College of Fort William at Calcutta, and a member of the Asiatic Society.[8] There are other such category-blurrers, some of whom produced Orientalist scholarship of lasting value.

On the other side of it, most Orientalists were at least nominally Christian, and some were fervent. Sir William Jones certainly considered himself a Christian. His intellectual make-up combined a strong proportion of Enlightenment rationalism with Christian belief, and as a result the character of his religious belief was itself highly rationalized. He had convinced himself rationally of the truth of Christianity, the proof being that the prophesies of Isaiah were fulfilled in the Gospel. In many ways the Orientalist programme of Jones was to give a reply, on rational grounds, to Voltaire, whom he admired but whose attack on Christianity he opposed; and Sanskrit literature served this purpose by giving outside confirmation of the truth of the Bible in what he construed to be its version of the flood of Noah. As I have said elsewhere, Jones made Hinduism safe for Anglicans.[9]

But even before Jones' premature death in India the tide of English opinion was turning away from Enlightenment values, seen to be implicated in the French Revolution and its increasingly alarming after-effects, including the spread of atheism, and toward a more enthusiastic, warmer and socially reformist type of Christianity in the Evangelical movement, which was far more critical of Hinduism. One of the adherents of the new movement was John Shore, Lord Teignmouth, protégé and biographer of Jones, sometime governor-general of British India and an Orientalist in his own right. In Shore's biography of Jones we see the changed moral vision at work, in the light of which Jones' Christianity appeared too tepid, even Deist, and his Orientalism too sympathetic to Hinduism.[10] The biographer, therefore, had to do some fancy work of reinterpretation to rescue Jones' reputation as a Christian before the new generation with its more stringent criteria for being counted a Christian. In those circumstances, Orientalism itself was becoming religiously dubious.

Even so, there were committed Christians in Orientalist ranks in the generations after Jones. I mention two of them, John Leyden and C.P. Brown.

John Leyden, whose ambition it was to surpass Sir William Jones in Orientalist scholarship, was denied it by an early death. He left a vast collection of papers on Indian languages, now in the British Library, from which we can say that, had he lived, his scholarly contribution would have been formidable. He had been licensed to preach in the Scottish church before doing a medical degree and coming to India as a surgeon. We see the inhibiting effects of his religious belief in his strongly negative, not to say slanderous, statement concerning Hinduism:

> The moral character of the Hindus—'the blameless, mild, patient, innocent children of nature,' as they are ridiculously termed by gossiping ingnoramusses, who never set eyes on them—is as utterly worthless and devoid of probity, as their religion is wicked, shameless, impudent, and obscene.[11]

C.P. Brown, whose scholarly work on Telugu remains a valued legacy among Telugu scholars in India, was the son of a Company chaplain who, Schmitthenner says,[12] was an Evangelical and Orientalist, though increasingly critical of Orientalists. Bishop Caldwell gives a long character assessment of C.P. Brown, in which he probes the missionary/Orientalist difference in respect of Christianity; Brown, who was a strong contrarian, doesn't fit the Orientalist mould, as Bishop Caldwell is pleased to find. Of this contrarian streak he says, in this remarkable passage,

By a resolute denial of the things that are 'most surely believed' by all other people, a man is certain to attract notice, if he does not win admiration, and with some characters to be marked out, and wondered at is the summit of earthly honour. It is necessary, however, to mention distinctly that this skepticism [of Brown toward received views] is not extended to [Christian] religion, though Indian scholars of eminence are generally freethinkers, and though one would have expected that a mind in other respects sceptical would have been sceptical with regard to this matter too. Yet I am happy to say in this respect Mr B. is, as usual, of a different opinion from those with whom he has intercourse. His literary friends are many of them infidels. No tendency towards their way of thinking is apparent in him. Sir William Jones for a considerable period of his life was a sceptic; and even in his later writings there are certain passages of a doubtful character. While Colbrooke, Wilkins, Wilford and Wilson, who have taken up and carried onward the study of Sanscrit literature, are Brahmins, if anything. Wilkins told Mr Brown some time ago that 'he thought in another century Christianity would be worn out.'

Wilson, the Sanskrit Professor in Oxford, actually advised an individual who was going out to India as an official to use his influence in favour of Hindooism. And Colbrooke, who was by general confession the deepest and most extensive of Sanscrit scholars, was well known to be of no religion. Hence one might have expected that a zealous disciple would have followed these 'Western Brahmins' even in their free-thinking. But such has not been the result [in C.P. Brown]. He seems to have a sincere, thorough, and well-grounded belief in Christianity as a system, and a very low opinion, I may say a contempt, of Hindooism: not a surprising thing after all when his education is kept in mind; when it is remembered that, beside others of a similar cast who were met with later in life, he was once intimate with Buchanan, Martyn, Thomason and the missionaries of Serampore.[13]

I give this passage at length because it comes from an outstanding missionary-Orientalist, insisting on the difference between the missionary and the Orientalist (freethinker, infidel, sceptic, western Brahmin), in such extreme terms, praising Brown not only for his faith in Christianity but his contempt for Hinduism. Brown himself certainly disapproved of Hinduism, and yet he maintained a 'college' of Brahmin scholars at his own expense to aid his researches, and in many ways held them in high regard. Nevertheless, for both Leyden and Brown their Christian commitment caused significant inhibition in the study of Hinduism, and the scope of their Orientalist work suffered this limitation. Contrast these attitudes with this passage about the Madras Orientalist F.W. Ellis, a contemporary and friend of Leyden, by another friend of both, William Erskine, Orientalist of Bombay:

He [Ellis] was remarkable for the proficiency he had made in the various languages of Southern India, and for his thorough acquaintance with the manners, customs and literatures of the Hindus. He is said to have written the Tamil with great elegance, and was a poet in that tongue....He was eager to improve the condition of the natives, but had perhaps too high an opinion of their literature and acquirements... He lived much among the natives & had a perfect knowledge of their habits of thinking.[14]

It was doubtless because of Ellis' generous estimation of the value of Indian literature and society that the Reverend William Taylor virtually called him a non-Christian, further testimony of the polarization of the types of the missionary and the Orientalist in British India in the nineteenth century. In his *Catalogue raisonné* of the College library manuscripts he says, of Ellis' edition and translation of the *Tirukkural*,

Mr Ellis was a learned, and laborious editor; but not a fit editor; as allowing his own prepossessions, and prejudices to appear prominent on almost every page. Apparently, his views were not based on the alone foundation of true morality' [that is, Christianity].[15]

Thus although there are all possible gradations of intermediate cases the types of the missionary and the Orientalist remain distinct at a deep level; they are, indeed, forcibly held apart conceptually in spite of their frequent mixture in fact. What draws them together has mostly to do with the study of Indian languages; what holds them apart is the matter of sympathetic engagement with Indian culture, especially Indian religion, which, with exceptions such as Leyden and C.P. Brown, was typical of Orientalists such as Jones and Ellis. The missionary and the Orientalist are not just ideal types in a field of variation, but real types in the minds of the British.

That sharp opposition between the type of the missionary and the type of the Orientalist has a history. I have already invoked the growing force of Evangelicalism in Britain and its unsympathetic gaze upon Hinduism and the Indian past. No one put it more forcefully than Charles Grant, who declared the Indians 'a people exceedingly depraved', and prescribed the light of European civilization and Christianity the cure of the darkness in which they lived.[16] This was at the same time an attack upon the Orientalist ideology of sympathetic engagement with Hinduism.

There were other striking differences between the missionary and the Orientalist, beginning with their legal status in British India. In its earliest policies the government of British India sought to exclude missionaries completely, along with European colonists of all kinds, in the interest of reducing the irritation foreign rule inevitably causes to those upon whom it bears, and strictly patrolled its borders, to the degree that the first American missionaries to arrive in India from New England after the War of 1812 were clapped in jail at Madras and had to shift their attentions to Burma. There, outside the empire, Adoniram Judson wrote—what else?—a Burmese-English dictionary that has become a classic.[17] William Carey had to confine his missionary activities to Danish Serampore, near Calcutta, and leave off when going to his job in British Calcutta as professor of Sanskrit and Bengali at the College of Fort William. It was only after intense lobbying of Parliament at the renewal of the East India Company charter in 1813 that missionaries were finally admitted. Until then, with the exception of the Serampore missionaries, Orientalists in British India were non-missionaries by law, so to say, and the only religious specialists allowed in were chaplains to the Company servants, civil and military; while missionary activity was perforce confined to places outside British India, such as the Danish enclaves at Tranquebar and Serampore, and the remains of Portuguese India on the west coast. In the mean time, British-Indian policies and institutions took on a consistently Orientalist cast. The government sought to respect Indian institutions of family and religion, acquiring knowledge of Hindu and Muslim law and dispensing it in its law courts; the Asiatic Society (1784) promoted Orientalist learning; and the College of Fort William (1804) taught the languages of India to arriving civil service recruits. Government, courts of law, learned societies, and the bodies educating civil servants became the institutions through which Orientalist knowledge was formed, consolidated, applied, and propagated at Calcutta, and, on the model of Calcutta, at Madras and Bombay.

Once the missionary lobby in England succeeded in gaining admission to British India, the era of Orientalism without missionaries came abruptly to an end. Thereafter, the debate over the practice of sati greatly mobilized Christian opinion in England in the direction of missionary-led critique and reform of Indian society, and against the Orientalist policy of keeping hands off Indian custom. This mobilization brought increasing friction between missionary and Orientalist.

The other great debate pitting the gathering strength of the missionary against the established strength of the Orientalist was the culture war fought over education in English. The Anglicist position lead by Charles Trevelyan and brilliantly articulated by Thomas Babington Macaulay, had strong religious and missionary roots in the Evangelical movement, which joined reinvigorated Christian belief with deep commitment to social reform and education. The Orientalist position, led by the Sanskritist H.H. Wilson and others, believed that social reform and education in European knowledge would best take hold in India if it were grafted upon the root stock of the existing high learning of India, in Sanskrit, Persian, and Arabic. At some level, the two positions profoundly disagreed over whether Hinduism was essentially pernicious and an obstacle to reform and modernization, or was on the whole benign and had to reform itself from within. On another level, the two positions agreed that European learning and social forms were India's future, differing over how to get there.

The increasing polarization of missionary and Orientalist reached its peak in the early 1830s, the age of reform both in Britain and in British India. The Evangelicals' programme joined Christianity with social reform and education. Utilitarianism under James Mill pushed for parliamentary reform at home and an aggressively reformist policy in British India. These forces had some inherent affinities, perhaps, but they were sharply divided, too. Mill had been licensed to preach in the Scottish church, like Leyden, but he seems to have lost his faith and replaced it with faith in Jeremy Bentham's Utilitarian philosophy. Macaulay, grandson of a famous Evangelical reformer, had published a scathing critique of Mill's 'Essay on government', a major statement of Utilitarianism, trashing it so thoroughly that one could not have expected Mill and Macaulay to become allies in the reform era as, to a degree, they did. Religiously tinged social reform, and social reform that was the secular expression of a certain kind of post-Christian subjectivity, converged for a time and wrought great changes in India and in Britain. During that convergence, Orientalist scholarship continued apace but it lost its major political battles; we might say indeed that while Orientalist scholarship was foundational for government policy in the era before the missionaries, it ceased to be so as a result of losing those battles, and was rendered antiquarian and disconnected from current political debates.

Whether the generalizations offered in this sketch will stand up to closer investigation I leave it to others to determine. But I have recently had occasion to do research among the papers of H.H. Wilson, and because he was unquestionably the leading Orientalist of British India in his generation I wish to take a look, in this connection, at the form taken by the conflict between the missionary and the Orientalist in Wilson's election to become the first Boden Professor of Sanskrit at Oxford, in 1832. In some ways it was the perfect storm, in which the opposed interests and philosophies of the missionary and the Orientalist met in a vortex of great intensity. Richard Gombrich, a recent Boden Professor, has told the story well in his inaugural lecture, and the University Archives fill in the details.[18]

What precipitated the clash was the will of Joseph Boden, lieutenant colonel in the Company's army, who left the bulk of his estate to Oxford for a professorship of Sanskrit,

> being of opinion that a more general and critical knowledge of that Language will be a means of enabling my Countrymen to proceed in the conversion of the Natives of India to the Christian Religion, by disseminating a knowledge of the sacred Scriptures amongst them more effectually than all other means whatsoever.[19]

This seemed to call for precisely an amalgam of the two types, a missionary who was also an Orientalist, or at least an Orientalist who was devout. However, the regulations drawn up for the Boden Professorship did not incorporate the founder's goal of the conversion of Indians to Christianity or the translation of the Bible into Sanskrit, but merely listed, among grounds for dismissal, the holding and teaching of doctrines contrary to the Established Church of England and Ireland, and gross or habitual immorality.[20] Framing the regulations in this way did not prevent the strife between missionary and Orientalist from intruding and, indeed, taking center-stage.

There were eight candidates for the Boden Professorship, which was to be decided by vote of Convocation, that is, Oxford faculty and graduates holding masters' degrees and present at the election meeting on 15 March 1832. The leading candidate was Horace Hayman Wilson, in Calcutta. Wilson had gone out to India in 1809 as a surgeon, but soon entered the service of the mint under the Orientalist John Leyden, and became assay master when Leyden died in 1811. He threw himself into Oriental studies even before his arrival, studying Hindustani on the ship to India with an Indian fellow passenger, and quickly took up Sanskrit after his arrival. He became secretary to the Asiatic Society in 1811 until his return to England, and was toward the end of that tenure its president in fact if not in name. By the time of his candidacy he had published a translation of Kalidasa's *Meghadūta* (Wilson 1813), the first Sanskrit-English dictionary (1819), translations of Sanskrit drama (2 vols, 1827), and lots of articles, including the book-length treatise modestly called 'A sketch of the religious sects of the Hindus' (1828) and other specialized works.[21] It was widely agreed that in the matter of Sanskrit scholarship—which after all was *the* criterion according to the regulations that were the legal framework for the election—Wilson was by far and away the best qualified. Other candidates could only succeed by appeal to other criteria than scholarship alone.

As the day of election drew near the other candidates withdrew, leaving Wilson and the Reverend William Hodge Mill as the only two remaining. Mill, who had come out to India on the ecclesiastical service of the East India Company[22] was principal of Bishop's College in Calcutta and author of an exposition of Christian doctrine in Sanskrit, called *Christa-sangítá*.[23] He combined in his person the missionary and the Orientalist, the ideal candidate, perhaps, if Boden's statement about propagating Christianity and translating the Bible had been included in the regulations; but even though they had not, the founder's intentions as expressed in the words of the will were frequently appealed to in the electioneering that ensued.

The electioneering became intense and, because Wilson's superior Sanskrit scholarship was unassailable, inevitably focused upon Wilson's character and religion. The worst of it was a pair of letters by a former professor of Bishop's College, one Just Henry Alt, printed and disseminated a few days before the election. He stated that shortly after arriving in Calcutta he and Mill, being students of Oriental matters and so desirous of meeting Wilson, presented letters of introduction and were invited to breakfast; but 'certain equivocal appearances excited uneasiness' and their suspicions were afterwards confirmed when they learned that Wilson was 'living in a state of notorious concubinage'.[24] For this reason the missionaries ceased attempting to make a connection with the Orientalist. Further, Wilson's religious opinions were reported to be questionable on good authority. Further still, he was a supporter and actor in the Calcutta theatre,

another circumstance conveying but a melancholy notion of his moral character, from his presumed association with certain extravagant and immoral persons among the actors, and particularly with the actresses, who were principally the wives of common European soldiers.

Another letter printed in the same circular, by Frederick Holmes, a senior professor in Bishop's College, alleged that Wilson had some eight or nine illegitimate children, and that he was 'little in the habit of attending Church' until his marriage to Sarah Siddons, a few years back. Holmes had heard it on good authority that Wilson was 'at best indifferent about the Christian religion, and inclined to prefer the Hindu morals to those of the Gospel.' He continued,

I look on the whole of his Sanscrit career as one series of efforts to support and render respectable the Brahminical system, as in preference and opposed to Christianity; and I consider him one of the most active and able adversaries to the diffusion of that blessed religion in Bengal; strictly and mainly connected with the institutions there by which it is endeavoured to cultivate the intellect of the Hindus without the cooperative aid of Christian instruction and morality.[25]

This alludes to Wilson's connection with Hindu College, in some sense the opposite of Bishop's College, to which both Alt and Holmes were connected. It scandalized missionary opinion that Christianity was kept out of the curriculum at Hindu College, and could be encountered only outside the classroom, in the College library, at the desire of the Hindu philanthropists whose benefactions created the College in the first place. Wilson, as Secretary for the Committee of Public Instruction, was also connected with the Sanskrit colleges in Calcutta and Benares, the Madrassah in Calcutta, and the colleges for Hindus and Muslims at Delhi and Agra, maintained by the government. Holmes assured the electors that he would not have gone public with such matters 'if I did not think that the cause of Christianity in India at stake in this election for the Boden Chair'.[26]

Supporters of Wilson's election countered with letters asserting that although he had fallen in with the regrettable but then customary practices of young Company servants in India (concubinage, that is), he had changed his ways; that the number of children of the former union had been wildly exaggerated, and was only two; that lady and children had been properly provided for; that he had since married and his religious practice was without blemish.[27] Indeed, one writer, the Reverend J. Lightfoot, a cleric who evidently did not think that the cause of Christianity in India was at stake, cited the testimony of two ladies from India 'who would be shocked at the very idea of countenancing the pretensions of anyone liable to the slightest imputation on the score of Irreligion' in evidence of Wilson's church attendance and of reading the liturgy to them when weather or illness kept them from church.[28] It was a mitigating defence, one that conceded the main point but put it in the past. On the matter of education, his defenders painted Wilson as an agent of government policy, not its maker. This no doubt was disingenuous; the crisis over education in India was underway and would reach its climacteric a few years hence; and Wilson was, even in his absence from Calcutta, considered the leader of the Orientalist party, opposed by the famous Anglicist minute of T.B. Macaulay of 1835.

In the event the vote for the first Boden Professor of Sanskrit in Oxford was very close: 206 for Wilson, 200 for Mill. Had four votes for Wilson gone the other way, Mill would have been the first Boden Professor. It is highly likely that Wilson would have won by a larger margin but for the raising of these questions about his morals and his religion. They were raised just at this point because of the growing conflict over education in India, which directly implicated religion. Wilson and Mill were not merely symbols of that conflict but were seen to be leading players in it.

Wilson's success in the election confirmed his status as the leading British Sanskrit scholar of his generation. But the fact that the election was close and the airing in public print of his personal life cannot have made the highly clerical Oxford a congenial climate for himself or for his wife. The election was nearly as public and equally seamy as a contest for a seat in Parliament, and the things said in public or printed and circulated must often have lingered. One of the partisans of the missionary side, the aforementioned Holmes, for example, avowed that many in Calcutta, 'and no one to my knowledge more than the young lady's mother', were surprised that Wilson's bride had consented to marry someone a good deal older than her own father.[29] It is painful to think what must have been the effect upon Mr and Mrs Wilson when they read the printed circular in which this was made public. It is hardly a surprise, then, that when the librarianship of the East India Company's headquarters in London became vacant by the death of Charles Wilkins, Wilson went for the job and moved his family to London, travelling to Oxford seasonally to fulfill the minimum requirements attaching to the Boden Professorship. He continued to be highly productive in scholarship till his death in 1860, whereupon Oxford, in an even more acrimonious contest between Monier Williams and Max Müller, reversed the earlier result by voting in, by a large margin, the lesser scholar, who had promised to direct his scholarship and teaching to the founder's wishes. Monier Williams was not a missionary, but he publicly associated himself with the founders' wish to promote Christianity in India through the cultivation of Sanskrit in Oxford, in order to gain an advantage over Max Müller that his scholarship did not give him. Added to this was an undercurrent of antipathy for the foreigner. Monier Williams won the election and the chair that, on the merits, should have been Max Müller's.

Returning to Wilson and Mill, the Orientalist and the missionary, we need to resist falling in with the backers of their election and assuming a deep chasm of dislike and difference between the two men themselves, and resist, too, the gravitational pull of the missionary/ Orientalist opposition to get the true measure of them, especially of Mill. To begin with, Alt made it clear that he was speaking for himself and had had no contact with Mill since leaving India. May we trust Alt's account of Mill's reaction to Wilson? Even if we can, it did not prevent Mill, some time after this supposedly distasteful encounter, from inviting Wilson's help in a book establishing proper Sanskrit equivalents for theological terms, 'with a view to uniformity in translations of the Holy Scriptures', and in printing Wilson's comments upon the terms proposed by Mill—such tricky and highly important concepts as the Holy Ghost, Trinity, and the like.[30] Wilson took the charge seriously and gave quotations from Sanskrit works such as the Mahabhārāta and the Purāṇas to illustrate usage.[31] Thus for 'Son of God, one, only begotten' Wilson suggested avoiding compound terms as they are liable to be mistaken for proper names or tribes or individuals, and use of *sutah* rather than *putra* as the latter suggests etymologically the one who redeems his father from the hell to which the childless are condemned (thinking, no doubt, of the definition of 'son' in Manu), which is not appropriate here, whence *devasya sutah*. Mill had proposed *ekamatrah*, but Wilson thought that perhaps *ananyaja* or *advitiya* would be preferable, adopting the phraseology of the Vedanta to advantage; say, *devasya suta eka evadvitiyah*, 'The Son of God, one only without second.' That Mill sought such assistance, and that Wilson complied so fully, allows us no room to suppose that they were personally at loggerheads. Moreover Wilson evidently respected Mill's Sanskrit scholarship, for he expressed the hope that if he did not get the Boden Chair, Mill should.

Mill, besides cultivating a knowledge of Sanskrit for the propagation of Christianity in India, was also an active contributor to the Orientalist project and its leading institution, the Asiatic Society, of which he was a member since 1821,[32] during Wilson's reign as secretary and virtual president, and after Wilson won the Boden Chair and left India, till Mill left India in 1837. In Kejariwal's fine study of the Asiatic Society we learn a lot about Mill, whom he puts in the company of the greats of the society, namely William Jones, Charles Wilkins, H.T. Colebrooke, H.H. Wilson, George Turnour, and James Prinsep, but also among those who 'seem at this distance of time merely shadows with little said or written about them'.[33] It is a surprise to learn that the greatness of Mill upon which Kejariwal insists is based, among other accomplishments, in Mill's having deciphered the Gupta genealogy in the Allahabad Pillar Inscription of Samudra Gupta and the Bhitari inscription. Prinsep considered that Mill had discovered 'a dynasty before wholly unknown to the Indian historian', namely that of the Guptas, no less.[34] Reading Kejariwal's chapter five on the collective effort under the leadership of James Prinsep which resulted in the decipherment of the Brahmi script and the reading of the Aśokan inscriptions, it is clear that it was a process to which many Indian and British scholars contributed, and that W.H. Mill was one of the major players through his work on the Gupta inscriptions and coins. It is abundantly clear that Mill was no dilettante on the Orientalist side of his endeavour, but a major contributor to the work of the Asiatic Society of which he and Wilson were both active members, with very substantial scientific work to his credit, even though it has been more or less wholly forgotten.

Thus the Orientalist and the missionary persist in the minds of contemporaries as distinct and opposed types even when there is plenty of evidence that the two types were not watertight compartments and that some missionaries were also Orientalists and some Orientalists contributed to the missionary project. The typological opposition kept getting asserted even though, as appears to be the case of Mill and Wilson, the principals refused it or, as was certainly the case of Caldwell, the principal embraced it against the evidence of his own life and work. The sharpness of the opposition was certainly caused by a very specific conjuncture of the missionary with support for government-imposed social reform, that is, a policy of aggressive Westernization, and of the Orientalist with support for the social status quo in India and an unforced Westernization that did not impose itself through government action. No doubt this typologizing against the evidence was at its height in the education controversy which culminated in 1835, after Wilson's departure from Calcutta; no doubt after the Revolt of 1857, which many (including Wilson) attributed to the forced march of government-imposed change, it declined. But throughout British rule we cannot truly draw a sharp distinction in knowledge-production of the missionary and the Orientalist in British India, because they were much the same, certainly so in the matter of grammars and dictionaries, but also to a degree in the production of knowledge about religion, manners, and customs, in spite of a felt distance between the missionary and the Orientalist in those days, above all on the part of the missionaries and the Orientalists themselves.

David Lorenzen's programme of examining the Italian Christian missionaries in early modern India is an invaluable contribution from a ripened scholar ideally equipped with the skills and interpretive judgment and patience in the decipherment of difficult manuscript materials to make it a success. It is an outstanding scholarly achievement, yielding an eye-opening and convincing comparison of missionary scholarship with that of the Orientalists of British India. The comparison itself is so very striking, so very rich in suggestion and promise, that it seems to overflow and expand. Putting the missionary and the Orientalist together as David has done to such good effect, contains abundant possibilities for ways by which this splendid work may live and grow.

NOTES AND REFERENCES

1. David Lorenzen, 'Marco della Tomba and the Brahmin from Banaras: Missionaries, Orientalists, and Indian Scholars', *Journal of Asian Studies,* vol. 65 2006, pp. 115–43.

2. Tamil Nadu State Archives, Madras Public Consultations, 10 December 1811, paras 38–58.

3. Abbé J.A. Dubois, *Hindu Manners, Customs and Ceremonies*, third edition, tr. Henry K. Beauchamp, with a prefatory note by F. Max Müller (Oxford: Clarendon Press 1906), pp. v–vii.

4. Sylvia Murr, *L'Inde philosophique entre Bosuet et Voltaire.* 2 vols; vol. 1 Moeurs et coutumes des Indiens (1777); vol. 2: L'Indologie du Père Coeurdoux: stratégies, apologétique et scientificité. Publications de L'École française d'Extrême-Orient, vol. 146 (Paris: École francaise d'Extrême-Orient, 1987).

5. For details see Thomas R. Trautmann, *Aryans and British India* (Berkeley, Los Angeles, London: University of California Press, 1997), chapter 2, and Thomas R. Trautmann, *Languages and Nations: The Dravidian Proof in Colonial Madras* (Berkeley, Los Angeles, London: University of California Press, 2006), chapter 1, pp. 13–21.

6. Robert Caldwell, *A Comparative Grammar of the Dravidian or South-Indian Family of Languages* (London: Harrison, 1856).

7. Discussion and references in Trautmann, *Aryans and British India*, pp. 155–8.

8. David Kopf, *British Orientalism and the Bengal Renaissance: The Dynamics of Indian Modernization 1773–1835* (Berkeley and Los Angeles: University of California Press, 1962).

9. Trautmann, *Aryans and British India.*

10. John Shore, Lord Teignmouth, *Memoirs of the Life, Writings, and Correspondence of Sir William Jones* (Philadelphia: William Poyntell, 1805).

11. John Leyden, cited in James Morton, (ed.), *The Poetical remains of the late Dr John Leyden, with memoirs of his life* (London: Printed by Strahan and Spottiswoode, for Longman, Hurst, Rees, Orme and Brown, 1819), p. lxv.

12. Peter L. Schmitthenner, *Telugu Resurgence: C.P. Brown and Cultural Consolidation in Nineteenth-century South India* (New Delhi: Manohar, 2001), pp. 37–41.

13. Caldwell, cited in J.L. Wyatt, (ed.), *Reminiscences of Bishop Caldwell* (Madras: Addison and Co., 1894), pp. 18–19.

14. National Library of Scotland, Erskine Papers, Mss 35.1.5, f. 21.

15. William Taylor, *A catalogue raisonnée of Oriental manuscripts in the library of the (late) College, Fort St. George* (title varies) (3 vols) (Madras: Fort St George Gazette Press, United Scottish Press, 1857–1862), vol. 3 p. 19.

16. Charles Grant, *Observations on the state of society among the Asiatic subjects of Great Britain.* Printed as Appendix I in Report from the select committee on the affairs of the East India Company 1831–32, pp. 3–92. Facsimile reprint, Irish University Press series of British Parliamentary papers. vol. 5: Colonies: East India. Shannon: Irish University Press, 1970.

17. Adoniram Judson, *A Dictionary, Burmese and English* (Maulmain: American Baptist Mission Press, 1852).

18. Richard F. Gombrich, *On being Sanskritic* (Oxford: Clarendon Press, 1978, and Oxford University, University Archives Shelfmark N.W. 16.2).

19. Oxford University, University Archives, the same, folio 1.

20. Ibid.

21. Horace Hayman Wilson, *The Mégha dúta; or, Cloud messenger; a poem, in the Sanskrit language, by Cálidása; translated into English verse, with notes and illustrations* (Calcutta: L. Pereira, 1813); *A dictionary, Sanscrit and English translated, amended, and ed. from an original compilation prepared by learned natives for the College of Fort William* (Calcutta: L. Pereira, 1819); *Select specimens of the theatre of the Hindus, translated from the original Sanscrit.* 3 vols (Calcutta: V. Holcroft, 1827); 'A sketch of the religious sects of the Hindus', *Asiatic researches*, vol. 16 1828: pp. 1–136; 17 1829: pp. 169–314. See Paul Courtright, Wilson, Horace Hayman (1786–1860), *Oxford dictionary of national biography*, 2004. http://www.oxforddnb.com/view/article/29657, accessed on 27 May 2006.

22. O.P. Kejariwal, *The Asiatic Society of Bengal and the Discovery of India's Past 1784–1838* (New Delhi: Oxford University Press, 1988), p. 171.

23. William Hodge Mill, *Christa-sangítá, or the sacred history of Our Lord Jesus Christ, in Sanskrit verse*, second edition, Calcutta: Bishop's College Press, 1842.

24. University Archives, ibid., f. 119.

25. Ibid.

26. Ibid.

27. Ibid., f. 26.

28. Ibid., ff. 70–1.

29. Ibid., f. 119.

30. William Hodge Mill, *Proposed version of theological terms, with a view to uniformity in translations of the Holy Scriptures &c. into the languages of India.* Part

the first—Sanscrit....With remarks upon the rendering proposed by Dr Mill, by Horace Hayman Wilson, Esq., Secretary of the Asiatic Society (Calcutta: Bishop's College Press, 1829).

31. Horace Hayman Wilson, 'Remarks upon the rendering in Sanscrit of theological terms, as proposed by The Rev. W.H. Mill, D.D.'. In Mill 1829, pp. 25–37.

32. Kejariwal, *The Asiatic Society of Bengal*, p. 132.

33. Ibid., p. 122.

34. Cited in Kejariwal, *The Asiatic Society of Bengal*, p. 202, from the preface to the journal for 1836.

9. WITNESSING LIVES

CONVERSION AND LIFE HISTORY IN COLONIAL CENTRAL INDIA

Saurabh Dube

This chapter discusses the interplay of conversion and life history, embedded within processes of evangelical entanglements between Euro-American missionaries and central Indian people.[1] It explores distinct autobiographies and biographies of converts to Christianity in the Chhattisgarh region of central India, especially accounts written between the 1920s and the 1940s. At first, these slender manuscripts and slim typescripts, writings pertaining to native evangelical workers, can appear as being wholly formulaic in nature. Yet, careful attention to the very ordinariness and precise details of the texts reveals how they constitute key registers of evangelical entanglements. Indeed, by sieving such writings through the critical filters of an ethnographic sensibility, including reading them alongside materials collected during fieldwork in Chhattisgarh among Indian Christians, it becomes possible to unravel how materials of life history imbue notions and narratives of conversion to Christianity with their own salience.[2]

STIPULATIONS OF CONVERSION

Terms of conversion are intimately intertwined with conceptions of lives, notations of history. Immaculately imagined, the event of conversion is widely understood as intimating a singular life and indicating an exclusive history for the convert, individually and collectively. Consider here authoritative conceptions of conversion: from representations that depict it as the collective search for meaning in the face of modernization to understandings that present conversion as the personal exercise of self-determination among competing faiths;[3]

and from readings that project conversion as symptom and substance of bad faith in the body of the nation—a violent view that has wide prevalence in India today—through to Gauri Viswanathan's recent, radical rewriting of the concept-entity as 'the subversion of secular power' in front of modernity.[4] The point is that in these distinct understandings, conversion serves to plot the narrative of the life and the history of the convert in a literal fashion, a distinct manner, envisioning it variously yet exclusively as individual autobiography of religious transference and/or collective biography of secular transformation.

Clearly, such accounts carry force. Their co-ordinates are clear and commanding. Their story lines are simple and seductive. Their familiarity invites belief and elicits agreement. None of this should be surprising. From the presence of the self-determining actor to the resonance of universal history, the stipulations of the subject and the norms of narrative articulated by these understandings variously form the very basis of the modern condition and the contemporary world. Indeed, it is possible to argue that the clarity and seduction, the familiarity and simplicity of such tales often animate the politics of hate against the figure of the convert, through the phantasm of conversion, including in India today. For these different reasons, the terms of these accounts bear rethinking.

The problem is at once wide ranging and quite simple. Authoritative academic conceptions and pervasive everyday understandings of conversion—as a primarily individual event or a broadly collective endeavour—are marked by two overlapping difficulties. They remain grounded, albeit in different ways, in common sense European connotations of the category. And they discretely turn conversion into a self-contained analytical apparatus and a self-generative descriptive domain. Thus, conversion becomes at once too limited a concept and too large an arena, also raising questions regarding its adequacy to capture the terrain and temporality, the terms and textures of evangelical entanglements.

Recent writings on Christianity and colonialism have followed connected pathways: they have pointed to the acute contradictions at the heart of evangelical endeavours, underscoring that the missionaries and their projects elaborated and questioned imperial power in frontier sites and metropolitan locations;[5] and they have revealed that such processes of contention and contradiction within colonial cultures further shaped patterns of vernacular Christianity.[6] Drawing on these perspectives, it seems to me, that evangelical entanglements in central India are best understood as lying at the intersection of two overlapping processes: the contradictory location of the mission project in the fabrication of colonial cultures; and the intricate interleaving of missionary proposals and convert practices in the fashioning of a vernacular Christianity. Not only were these twin processes inherently enacted in the quotidian key, but they involved the contending yet conjoint energies of the Euro-American evangelists and the central Indian converts in discrete yet overlaying arenas. All of this suggests distinct possibilities for discussing the construction of autobiographies and biographies of converts within evangelical entanglements.

The autobiographical and biographical materials explored in this chapter narrate the life histories of individual converts to the Christian faith in colonial India. On the one hand, all too often, particularly in social science literature, Christian conversion in non-western contexts appears as an essentially collective endeavour, opposing it to the image of the solitary Saul who sees the light in understandings of conversion in western arenas. Here modular understandings construe conversion as a search for meaning in front of the onslaught of modernization/modernity in remote non-western theatres. One of the problems with such schemes lies in their tendency to bracket the distinct apprehensions of particular persons of the events and processes of conversion, including the notions of lives and histories these entail. On the other hand, Pauline propositions and psychological prototypes regarding conversion tend to present it as an exclusively individual act, also intimating a solitary trajectory. Here the lone seeker transfers to a new, primary religious affiliation through a judicious choice among distinct and competing faiths, and then acts upon this choice through sincere personal belief and committed membership of community in Christ. At the basis of such understandings are meta-historical and meta-cultural assumptions regarding action and apprehension, conversion and Christianity, which tend to overlook the diversity and distinction that underlie transference of faith and transformation of religion, ever embedded in discrete pasts and different cultures. Through their shared reliance on the overriding opposition between collective logic and individual choice and their mutual dependence upon divergent yet singular teleological terms underlying conversion, these two apparently opposed orientations can incline toward discounting what is salient and specific about life histories in the wake of conversion.

Most conversions to Christianity in colonial central India came about through networks of extended kinship, further entailing bonds of caste-sect and the prospects of a better life under the paternalist economies of mission stations. Yet, people also converted in other ways, variously negotiating ties of kith and kin, caste and sect. What is more, even those Christians whose conversion was effected through conduits of kinship were not simply figures of a singular, collective logic. In each case, conversion provided a resource for the distinct plotting of lives, the different telling of histories. This is revealed by the writings discussed in this chapter, which were at once shaped by colonial frames and marked by vernacular forms. As noted earlier, such accounts are apparently formulaic in nature. Yet, it is important to stay with their routine ordinariness and everyday attributes. For prudent attention to the critical details of these tales reveals how they engage and exceed the underlying *telos* of authoritative narratives of conversion to Christianity, imbuing these exclusive story lines with their own notations.

GROUNDS OF WITNESS

In 1868, the Reverend Oscar Lohr of the German Evangelical Mission Society initiated evangelical work in Chhattisgarh. Over the next three decades, Lohr and his evangelical brethren toiled the field, sowing the seeds of faith.[7] The halting enterprise of conversion in the region gradually grew through ties of kinship, often within the confines of the paternalist economy of mission stations. During this time, there was also the expansion of evangelical, educational, and medical endeavour in four posts of the German Evangelical Mission Society in Chhattisgarh. By the turn of the century, missionaries of other denominations—the American Mennonites, the General Conference Mennonites, the Disciples of Christ, and the Methodists—had joined the members of the German Evangelical Mission Society. Now the evangelical enterprise extended to several communities. Yet these converts to Christianity continued to understand missionary injunctions and to interpret evangelical truths through the grids of quotidian cultures. Drawing in the energies of their western benefactors as witting accomplice and hapless victim, these peoples participated in the making of a vernacular and a colonial Christianity.

From the very beginnings of the missionary project, lowly, native workers of the mission played a critical role in the expression of evangelical entanglements. I have discussed elsewhere that the early Euro-American evangelists were pressed for time and strapped for money.[8] Hesitant in the primary language, Hindi, they were unsure of the regional vernacular, Chhattisgarhi. Here trained native Christians provided the way forward for the evangelical enterprise. Yet, the perceptions and practices of the Indian evangelical workers could also exceed the interests and expectations of the missionaries, critically shaping patterns of evangelical entanglements, including the designs of a vernacular Christianity. It is the writings concerning such Indian evangelical operatives that are the subject of this essay.

The first Indian workers of the mission arose from among the ranks of the original lower-caste converts in Chhattisgarh, taught and trained by the missionaries.[9] At the same time, for the work of evangelism, the other means of acquiring workers—primarily preachers, later pastors—consisted of drawing in the energies of the occasional, often upper-caste, literate convert to Christianity within the region.[10] This was the case with Simon Ramnath Bajpai, a Brahman convert, who began his vocation as a teacher, then became an evangelist, and was finally ordained into the Ministry. The mission also engaged the services of trained employees of missions outside Chhattisgarh. This was the case with Pandit Gangaram Chaube, a 'native evangelist' with the Church Missionary Society in Jabalpur, who was brought to the village of Bisrampur as a catechist of the German Evangelical Mission Society in April 1872.[11] Gangaram Chaube was to be followed by other catechists and pastors, such as M.M. Paul and Johann Purti, trained at different missions in north India and then recruited to work in Chhattisgarh. Such were some of the preconditions for the work of witness and the labour of life history of, among others, Ramnath Balpai and Johann Purti, which are unravelled in the account ahead.

AN EXEMPLARY CONVERT: A MISSIONARY'S WITNESS

Let us begin, then, with two biographical accounts of the Reverend Ramnath Simon Bajpai, one written by his son David Bajpai and the other drafted by the missionary, Theodore C. Seybold.[12] The two narratives, which exist as typescripts, show particular overlaps but they also reveal critical differences. In reading them, my focus will be on their distinct descriptions of the formative years of Ramnath Bajpai, particularly the divergent portrayals of the conversion of this Brahman, an exemplary figure who worked as an evangelist for many years and was ordained to the Ministry two years before his death.

Here is how the missionary opens his account:

One of the earliest entries in the baptismal registry in the archives of the Evangelical and Reformed Mission in Raipur, C.P., India, reads as follows: Ramnath Simon Bajpai, about 22 years old, baptised May 6 1882, by Andrew Stoll. Thus started the Christian life and the Christian ministry of a man...whose life was demonstrated for the first time in the Central Provinces of India that the Church of Christ is a living organism which welds together people who throughout the history of India have never been able to unite. Ramnath the Brahmin became, as a follower of Jesus Christ, a member of the Church and served to win many, mostly Untouchables, with whom formerly he could never have so much as associated; now those from among them who became Christians became with him fellow-members of the body of Christ.[13]

The very singularity of the life of Ramnath Bajpai is inextricably entwined with the history of the evangelical mission in Chhattisgarh, the one luminously reflecting the other. Inserted into the living organism that is the Church, the exemplary figure of this Brahman convert to the Christian faith renders asunder the dead past of India, which has separated the upper-caste from the untouchable, pointing to the horizon where the unity of India's peoples lies.

The authoritative terms of the missionary narrative are next carried forward through an invocation of the trials and tribulations faced by the young Ramnath Bajpai.

Small wonder that the conversion of Ramnath, the Brahmin, upset the thinking of his fellow-Brahmins and other caste people and caused consternation throughout the city. He was persecuted, despised, ridiculed.

In fact he was forcefully prevented from visiting his missionary friend for several days while pressure was being brought upon him to recant and betray his Master. His sons were persuaded to leave him...

The chief hurdles in the path of Ramnath are imposed by the burden of caste, denying him paternal bonds and fraternal ties, quotidian kinship and Christian affinity. Kith and sons forsake him. Attempts are made to separate him from his only friend, the lone missionary, and his spiritual father, the one Master. Ramnath's story is envisioned in the mirror of the Apostles. Indeed,

...he himself confessed that the pressure was so great that at one time he almost yielded; and he would then humbly say: 'How very appropriate that the name of Simon was given to me, for like Simon Peter I was tempted to deny my Lord. But God saved me from this great sin.'

Like Simon Peter, Ramnath Bajpai stands at the head of his flock.

If this story line is framed by the living presence of the Church, the dead hand of caste, and the struggles endured by the Apostles, the narrative as a whole is animated and articulated by the critical trope of conversion, a transformation of faith that comes with its own twist. Theodore Seybold does not equate the conversion of Ramnath with his institutional acceptance of the Christian faith, the event of his baptism. Rather, the missionary locates it long, long before, in the phenomenal transformation that came upon Ramnath, when he miraculously met the pioneer missionary in the Chhattisgarh region.

At the time of his conversion Ramnath was a student in a normal school in Raipur as he wanted to become a teacher. While there he and other students came to hear of a missionary who had come into the area and who seemed to be fulfilling the prophecy of an old Indian leader who predicted that a white teacher would come to them and lead them into an understanding of the truth. So he went to visit this missionary, the Rev. Oskar Lohr, and was very much impressed by what he heard and by what he read in the tracts and booklets given him by his new friend.

Note that the missionary unequivocally situates Ramnath's conversion at the time when he was a student in school. The conversion came about when he met the missionary Oscar Lohr, 'who seemed to be fulfilling the prophecy of an old Indian leader who predicted that a white teacher would come to them and lead them into an understanding of the truth.'

Theodore Seybold's simple statement carries immense import. A tale current in the late nineteenth and early twentieth centuries in Chhattisgarh told of how Ghasidas, the first guru of the Satnami caste-sect, had prophesied that he shall be followed by a *topi-wallah sahab* (hat wearing white man) who would deliver the Satnamis. This story became salient lore for the Euro-American missionaries and Indian Christians in the region, and an article of faith for the Satnami converts to Christianity. Elsewhere, I have shown how this tradition was shaped through the pooled resources of Satnami myths, missionary stories, and converts' tales, authoritatively inscribed in official histories of the mission and the Church in Chhattisgarh.[14] My point here is that if the missionary Seybold seized upon this myth to imbue it with a distinct resonance this was precisely because the story carried critical connotations for his narrative of an exemplary convert, his account of the formative conversion of Ramnath Bajpai.

In the lore of Christian communities and evangelical missionaries in Chhattisgarh, the extraordinary prophecy of Guru Ghasidas and its miraculous fulfilment by Oscar Lohr constituted the motive force behind the first conversions in the region. Such was the strength of this lore that the missionary Theodore Seybold could not escape its implications while writing in the mid-twentieth century of an early and exemplary convert to Christianity. To plot the life of a pioneer upper-caste convert, a connection had to be made between an ancient prophecy, Oscar Lohr, and Ramnath Bajpai. It followed that in the missionary's account the story regarding the prophecy was robbed of its specificity, simultaneously widening and narrowing its range of address. The palpable figure of Ghasidas was rendered simply as 'an old Indian leader'. The prophecy itself did not concern just the Satnami community, but all the people of Chhattisgarh. At the same time, the divination really came true with the consummate convert, Ramnath Bajpai.

We have noted that singular understandings of conversion tend to overlook distinct processes of the making of myths, the fabrication of histories, and the construction of narratives that are constitutive of evangelical entanglements. In the testimony of Theodore Seybold, the conversion of Ramnath was exclusive in nature, based on the image of the solitary Saul who saw the light, intimating a novel trajectory of faith and life. At the same time, in this account the very terms of an immaculate conversion were acutely forged through the force of rumour and the strength of prophecy—in other words, distinctive entailments of myth, history, and narrative—that broke upon the missionary's description of Ramnath's life history. Thus, a most singular rendering of conversion was yet enacted through the wide-ranging formations of meanings embedded in the evangelical encounter.

The initiation of conversion behind him, Ramnath Bajpai was all set to embark upon his Christian vocation. Considering that 'at that time Rev. Lohr was the only missionary in the area, and lived 37 miles from the city of Raipur', it was not easy for Ramnath to visit him. And so,

> We can appreciate his joy when a few years later the Rev. Andrew Stoll, D.D., opened work in the city of Raipur itself and brought with him an evangelist, Pandit Gangaram Chaube, who himself was a converted Brahmin and thus had an experience similar to Ramnath's. Through this contact Ramnath came in touch with the few Christians that had moved to Raipur as Government employees and he frequently attended the little chapel in which services were then held.
>
> When the Rev. Mr Stoll began work in Raipur he opened a little school and requested Ramnath to become its headmaster, which he did. He served in this capacity for the two years from 1880 to 1882. This gave him an opportunity to spend much time with the missionaries and with the books which they gave him. These contacts gave him the answers he had sought to his questions and he soon came to realize that Christ would give him the inner peace and assurance for which he yearned. Thus he was prepared for the first great step that was so utterly to change his life and he received baptism on May 6, 1802, and from then on rejoiced in the beauty of the fellowship in which he lived with his master.[15]

Two points stand out. On the one hand, this passage underscores that in Theodore Seybold's account of Ramnath Bajpai's life, conversion was the first intimation of a sharp change in spiritual orientation. Driven by a prophecy and shaped as a miracle, the transformation primed and prepared the Indian enquirer for the events that lay ahead, plotted in a manner that led from one inexorable step to another irresistible step. From the Reverend Stoll opening a mission station in Raipur to Ramnath's encounters with Gangaram Chaube and the Christian community in the town, his employment in a little school, the spiritual convert-enquirer's further meetings with missionaries and their books, and his eventual and unstoppable baptism. On the other hand, the manner of Ramnath's fulfilment of his destiny mirrors the growth of the mission and the church in Chhattisgarh. From the fledgling beginnings of mission work in Raipur by a missionary and a catechist, to the tiny community of Christians and their 'little chapel' in the town, to the 'little school' of which Ramnath is the headmaster, to the widening of the evangelical enterprise in strength and numbers. The conversion of Ramnath Simon Bajpai was complete.

AN EXEMPLARY CHARACTER: A SON'S TESTIMONY

Let us turn now to the account of Ramnath's life that was written by his son, David Bajpai.[16] At first, this typescript of 16 pages, completed in 1945, more than two decades after the death of the commendable Christian, seems to resemble the missionary's writing, emphasizing the centrality of the conversion of Ramnath. 'It required considerable courage on the part of my father to act according to his conscience and conviction when he became a Christian. He was not only the first Brahmin in Raipur to take this step, but he also knew what it would involve.' (p. 1) But after this opening statement, David Bajpai's account follows a different direction from the missionary's narrative.

> Before making the decision he [Ramnath] met another Brahmin, Pandit Gangaram Chaube, who showed him a large scar on his head. Several years previously when he [Gangaram] decided to become a follower of Christ his father became so furiously angry that he struck him on the head with an iron rod causing a deep wound. His wife and child were taken away from him; and as persecution continued he sought refuge (1873) in Bisrampur with Rev. O. Lohr, the first pioneer missionary in Chhattisgarh. Missionaries and other friends who knew my father very well verify the fact that he was brave and fearless. (p. 1)

Unlike the central connection between the conversion of Ramnath and the history of the mission, including the arrival of Oscar Lohr, that governs the narrative of the missionary Seybold, the critical figure in David Bajpai's account of his father is the Brahman, Gangaram Chaube. This should not surprise us. The meeting of Ramnath the enquirer with Gangaram the convert intimates the paths of two Brahmans, strewn with obstacles, which each fearless character faces with equanimity. Working in tandem, the lives of these two Brahman converts to Christianity stand apart from those of other, early, mainly lower caste converts in the Chhattisgarh region.[17]

Indeed, David Bajpai's account reveals his family's pride in its uncommon ancestry.

He [Ramnath Bajpai] was born June 25, 1849 in Bambda District where his father, Kusipari Din Bajpai, had joined the army. Due to faithful work he was soon promoted to a higher rank. Later he was made Subedar in a Madras regiment. In our home was a sword which father guarded proudly, for it was a valuable gift he had inherited from his father. We children always regarded it with deep respect after hearing about our grandfather who had carried it so many years. (p. 1)

Added to the twin determinants of an ancestry that was at once priestly and martial, Ramnath Bajpai's own qualities of intelligence distinguished him even further. And so it was that Ramnath came to Raipur with his mother who wanted to live in her natal home. In the town, he started attending school at the age of seven, passing 'from class to class without difficulty.' Next, he joined the Government Normal School at Raipur, and after completing the course of study there he became a teacher in the government primary school.

We have seen that the life of the mission and the growth of the Church, the obstacle of caste and the trope of conversion orchestrated the missionary Seybold's biographical sketch of Ramnath Bajpai. In contrast, David Bajpai's account of the life of his father seems to follow another blueprint, that of the biography of an exemplary character, itself inflected by the lore of the learned Brahman. The former narrative was underwritten and overwritten by Ramnath's breach with caste and Hinduism. The latter story was hardly embarrassed by Ramnath's initial immersion in the rites and passages of Hinduism and caste:

He [Ramnath] was especially proficient in Hindi and Sanskrit. Among the religious books of the Hindus he had particular preference for the Ramayan, and could repeat long portions of it from memory. Hindus invited him to their homes in order to have him read the shastra to the group assembled there. Prominent and wealthy Hindus would grant him gifts of money and cloth for serving them in that way. His way of reading the Ramayan was so pleasing that Zamindars and Rajas in and around Raipur would also invite him...Thus his fame reached beyond the borders of Raipur. It was a happy event in his life when the Raja of Dondi Lohara sent for him to visit his palace. (pp. 1–2)

Here the narration draws upon classical images and popular representations of the scholarly Brahman who is feted by the famous and the wealthy, to be eventually discovered by a royal patron. Now, it followed inevitably that the raja of Dondi Lohara was greatly impressed with Ramnath, and soon invited him to become the *raj-pandit* (head priest). After repeated requests, Ramnath agreed. The diwan of Dondi Lohara was jealous of the young man (only recently arrived) who was being accorded such importance, but in front of the raja's desires he was unable to throw a spanner in the works at hand. At any rate, the diwan soon died. Ramnath Bajpai became the new diwan.

In David Bajpai's account, his father was not merely successful as a learned Brahman. Rather, Ramnath's remarkable scholarly capacities were equally accompanied by an incipient spiritual orientation. The one fed the other.

Near the palace [in Dondi Lohara] was a beautiful garden in which the Raja took much pride. The trees and flowers as well as the supervision of the garden received his personal attention. Often he called my father to accompany him on his evening walks through the garden and along the bank of the tank so that they could carry on discussions on various subjects undisturbed. On one particular evening the Raja was indisposed and informed father that he would not take the customary walk, hence he went alone. At the time of sunset brilliant rays of the setting sun were reflected on the bright flowering trees in a most beautiful manner making the impression that they were expressing their approval of him with their colourful smiles. Approaching a particular tree in all its glory and beauty he was overcome with joy at the sight of the beauty and the fragrance of the flowers. This magnificent scene was to him like a 'darshan' (vision of the gods), and caused him to enter a state of serious meditation, deeply pondering what it could all mean.

Ramnath does not remain content as a 'state-servant'. His 'sensitive nature' is offended by 'transactions of a shady and questionable character', which are entailed by his office. And so Ramnath leaves his position as soon as possible without creating 'any ill-feeling' with the raja.

The place and the time set the scene for Ramnath's intensely spiritual experience. The garden receives the raja's personal attention. It is especially beautiful, a space for shared exchanges and mutual confidences between the raja and Ramnath. But on one evening it so transpires that Ramnath must go into the garden alone. At sunset, nature in its resplendent glory smiles upon him, transporting him into ecstasy. On the one hand, this experience paves the way for the further spiritual quest of Ramnath, which will lead him toward Christianity, particularly as he ponders 'what it all could mean'. On the other hand, the structure of his feeling and the nature of his vision are defined not by the religion that he will embrace, but rooted in the past and the present of the faith he practices, 'a darshan (vision) of the gods'.

Put differently, in this account, Ramnath's preparation for his eventual religious transformation is not governed by a rupture with caste, a break with Hinduism, an encounter with a missionary, a spiritual experience in the image of Christian conversion. Much of this will happen, but only rather later, in ambivalent ways. Instead, a distinct narrative propels Ramnath toward his encounter with Christianity. This story is based upon Ramnath's already distinguished ancestry, at once Brahmanical and martial, as also his own intellectual prowess as a student. This portrayal is rooted in the widespread lore of the learned Brahman conquering all with his liturgical abilities and scholarly propensities, finding high office in the court of a king, and in Ramnath's own spiritual experience envisioned in the mirror of Hindu *darshan.* This tale concerns an upright character, unable to countenance questionable transactions, a sensitive soul, incapable of usual blandishments, who leaves the palpable seductions of high office. Indeed, only after he is thus primed, does Ramnath Bajpai sally forth to consummate his manifest, Christian destiny.

Not surprisingly, in the account that follows, David Bajpai's description of his father's 'change of faith' is less the litany of a miraculous spiritual transformation and more the mapping of an everyday religious turn. The narrative recounts the arrival in Raipur of the pioneer missionary Oscar Lohr and his family after travelling 180 miles from Nagpur in ox-carts, a scene that was witnessed by many inhabitants of the city. It recalls that soon 'the report was spread that the Satnamis of the area considered his [Oscar Lohr's] coming the fulfilment of the prophecy of their Guru Ghasidas to the effect that: "After my death a white topi-wala will appear to liberate you and bring you definite news of Satnam, namely the Truth about God."' (p. 3) At the same time, despite the account's staging of the pioneer missionary's arrival, the rehearsal of the lore regarding Ghasidas, Oscar Lohr, and the Satnamis, and the Christian appropriation of *satnam*, in it Ramnath Bajpai himself remains a curious observer of, rather than an active participant in, these processes. As a student in the Normal School his interest is piqued by these events, but he does little to embrace them as part of his life history.

Actually, Ramnath's missionary link lay elsewhere. David Bajpai explains that before going off to Dondi Lohara, his father had taught Hindi to a missionary, the Reverend J. Frank, in Raipur. On his return to Raipur, Ramnath once more went to visit his 'missionary friend', but he was 'sorry to discover' that Frank had returned to the United States. It was now that his curiosity and his interest led Ramnath to walk 37 miles to the village of Bisrampur. Here he met Gangaram Chaube who narrated to the young Brahman the trials that followed his decision to accept Christianity, but a completely undeterred Ramnath continued to enquire about the new faith, buying a Bible and several pieces of Christian literature that he read ardently. Ramnath also met Oscar Lohr and Andrew Stoll in Bisrampur, and the 'sincere friendliness and uprightness of the missionaries captivated him and awakened a sympathetic response in his heart, for he himself was of a sincere and upright nature.' And it was in the first Christian village in Chhattisgarh that Ramnath was 'impressed with Rev. Lohr and the philanthropic work he was doing to [up]lift the Satnamis and Chamars of that area'. Indeed:

During his visit to Bisrampur one matter continually rose uppermost in his mind: 'Why should the missionaries accord such kind treatment to the low caste people whom all others so deeply despised?' He saw these Untouchables welcomed in the Mission school, he saw them being trained as printers, carpenters, and stone masons. Could it be possible, he argued in his mind, that this high and noble type of character revealed and demonstrated by the missionaries is the fruit of a high and noble religion? (pp. 3–4)

Note that at each stage, at every step, Ramnath Bajpai reveals an independent mind and critical judgement. He revels in the challenge represented by the Brahman Gangaram Chaube's conversion to Christianity, finds an affinity of character with the missionaries, and is genuinely surprised and impressed by the missionaries' 'philanthropic' effort to raise the status of the untouchables. Far from predicating Ramnath Bajpai's change of spiritual orientation upon a miraculous meeting with a pioneer missionary, David Bajpai's account locates the transformation as an outcome of his father's own abilities and propensities.

Significantly, Ramnath's visit to Bisrampur spells the end of his curiosity about the missionaries. Rather, his enquiries now come to centre on the Bible—as the source of 'noble character', as the means of discovering 'the truth for himself'.

Until his visit to Bisrampur he always held the conviction that being a learned Brahman and knowing his Hindu Scriptures so well, he could refute the claims of all other religions. He felt convinced that no other representative of another religion would be able to stand up against him in an argument regarding the truth of the Hindu religion. But now he found himself sympathetically interested in the Bible, began to read it with a critical, yet open mind. Many of the previously held Hindu beliefs gradually began to fade away and eventually were completely discarded. The Truth of the Gospel enlightened him and won his heart as well as his head. (p. 4)

Closely conjoint, barely distinct, the one folded into the other, there are two critical movements here. On the one hand, Ramnath is presented as the ideal convert who judiciously compares between competing faiths to discover the truth for himself. If the encounter with the Gospel reveals the limits of Ramnath's anterior religious certainties, he nonetheless reads the Book with a 'critical, yet open mind.' On the other hand, Ramnath's breach with Hinduism is founded upon the Bible, quite literally. In a context where the missionaries at once cast native converts as 'equals in the Kingdom of God' and yet treated them as children, struggling to grasp rational thought, a surplus of belief in the Bible was often an article of faith for literate Indian Christians. My point here is that the two movements outlined above undergird David Bajpai's description of his father's religious transformation. Taken together, Ramnath's commitment to the Gospel builds upon his prior propensities and draws in his present faculties, enlightening and enthralling the enquirer, compelling him to reason while capturing his emotions, winning 'his heart as well as his head'.

Ramnath is not just a mimic man or a pale reflection, an acute double or a dark silhouette, simply envisioned in the evangelical mirror, in front of the likeness of the missionary. In David Bajpai's account, Ramnath's sincere character and self-commitment to the Bible put him on par with the missionaries, while distinguishing his persona from their personalities. This is revealed by the very terms of Ramnath's pleasure in the fellowship of the four Indian Christians in Raipur, and his joy at working among, indeed '[up]lifting', low-caste people a few miles out of the city in Khandwa, a village owned by a Christian, where he undertakes employment as the headmaster of a school. The narrative is carried forward further by the manner of Ramnath's eventual conversion to Christianity

Once it became known that Ramnath, the learned Brahman, the 'well-known Ramayan-reader', was 'continually reading the Bible and Christian literature and associating with Christian people so frequently', pressure was brought upon him from all sides. A wealthy, Brahman landowner and a Brahman inspector, both of Raipur town, 'called him to their home[s] and during many hours of private discussion sought to persuade him to sever all connections with the Christians.' There was more to follow. News of his orientation toward Christianity reached the raja of Dondi Lohara, who summoned Ramnath and 'appealed to him not to leave Hinduism and to give up the idea of identifying himself with such a group that also admits low caste people into their organisation.' Ramnath's 'former Hindu friends' sought to dissuade him from visiting the missionary Andrew Stoll, and when arguments failed, they pelted him with stones. Most of these reactions were borne of the utter ignorance of the people of Raipur regarding the Book, their notions of Christianity based rather upon hearsay and rumour, including the belief that only poor people converted for material again.' And so it was that when Ramnath 'went to the market to make purchases' people would 'follow him and call out in disgust: "Hello, you Christian! Hello, you Christian!" and on two occasions impertinent youth tore his dhoty.' Indeed, when it became evident that Ramnath was not going to forsake his inclination toward Christianity, 'the Brahmins and other Hindu people held a meeting', now forcibly preventing him from reaching the missionary bungalow, constantly keeping a watch over him, while continuously harassing, insistently insulting, the enquirer. (pp. 5–6)

What was Ramnath's response? Undeterred by the arguments of the Brahman worthies of Raipur town, he also proved equal to the raja of Dondi Lohara.

Both [the raja and Ramnath] were determined to win. My father contended that having fully and thoroughly weighed the teachings of Hinduism and the truth of Christianity he must follow his conscience, whichever way it might lead him. The Raja finally replied: 'Do anything and go anywhere, but do not go the way of Christ.' Father deliberated in silence for a long time. As he remained in deep thought so long, the Raja concluded that he was wavering in is resolve to become a Christian, but was shocked when he was given the firm reply: 'Once the seal of Christ is impressed upon the heart of a seeker, who can eradicate it?' This ended the interview. (p. 5)

A 'meek disposition', a resolute unwillingness to quarrel, and a complete lack of 'ill will against those who were once his friends and had now turned against him', equally accompanied Ramnath's fearless and forthright character. Instead of getting angry and retaliating against those who harassed him in public spaces by reporting their actions to the police, Ramnath bore all insults patiently, using such 'occasions as opportunities' to inform his assailants of the truth of Christianity. Rather more than in the case of the missionary Andrew Stoll, who was also pelted with dust and dung when preaching in the bazaar, Ramnath's 'silent suffering' spelled no small success. Now, 'even his opponents had to admit that his motive was born out of honesty and sincerity', and several of his 'erstwhile enemies gradually became his friends again', some of them even agreeing to study the Bible for themselves. (pp. 6–7)

Only after the final assault launched by his Brahman kith and his immediate kin, did Ramnath realize that 'such unjust treatment would make it impossible for him to remain at home among his family and relatives.' It dawned on him that 'like other converts before him, he would not long be tolerated among his own people, would be disinherited and put out of caste.' He asked himself: 'Where shall I go? Where shall I eat?' Now Ramnath 'felt compelled to seek a place of refuge among the Christians.' His fears were assuaged by the assurance of Andrew Stoll that so long as the missionary had something to eat, so would Ramnath. On 6 May 1882 Ramnath was 'received into the Christian Church by baptism and given the name Simon.' (p. 7)

In front of the missionary Seybold's linear account of Ramnath's change of faith, David Bajpai's narrative of his father's conversion traverses a jagged trajectory. In the former story, a single string binds Ramnath's conversion with his baptism—his formative change of spiritual orientation with his formal entry into the Christian Church—where each step is marked by a breach with the past. The latter tale exceeds the life of the convert as a reflection of the history of the mission. On the one hand, Ramnath's upright character and his self-commitment to the Word—on par with the missionary, yet innately different—seemingly surmount all obstacles in his path to conversion, leading inexorably toward his entry into the community of Christ through baptism. On the other, binds of caste and kin constitute more than hurdles that are deftly overcome by the enquirer-into-convert. Rather, they also bear a distinct gravity, a discrete force. It is Ramnath's realization of the rupture with these ties and the fear this engenders that lead him to seek refuge among Christians, unto his conversion through baptism, as a last step, a final resort.

The question arises: writing their biographical accounts of the same man, who had read whom? Did the son David Bajpai peruse first the missionary Theodore Seybold's account of Ramnath Bajpai? Or was it the other way around? Or did the two write simultaneously, comparing notes, the one with other? Fortunately, we do not need to speculate. A passage at the end of David Bajpai's account tells us that he wrote after the missionary. Clearly, as an instance of an inter-textual transaction, David Bajpai's writing did not merely supply details to a prior blueprint provided by the missionary. Rather, it populated the narrative of his father's life with a different resonance, underscoring thereby how two stories of one life reveal the divergent conjunctions between conversion and life history.[18]

DRAMA, DISCONTENT, AND DISTINCTION: A TALE OF AN ADIVASI CHRISTIAN

Despite their differences, both the narratives that we have discussed were founded on the mutual premise that the life they were recounting embodied distinction, which barely required discovery, but acutely demanded description. At the same time, few autobiographical accounts embedded in the evangelical encounter could similarly take for granted the distinctiveness of their own lives. Here the uncommon and the unremarkable had to be conjured and construed; the distinctive and the routine had to be reckoned with and sorted out. Such is the case with the writings of native evangelical workers, elicited by missionaries in the 1920s and 1930s, possibly for publication, and the life stories of Indian Christians, which I collected in the 1990s, for the purpose of research. Mired in the common and the quotidian, in various ways these narratives dramatized the ordinary as the remarkable and pursued the uncommon in the everyday. I will focus on the 'Life Story of Johann Purti', a typescript of three-and-a-half pages, first drafted by J. Purti and then typed by a missionary in April 1934, while keeping in view other autobiographical accounts, written and recounted in the past and the present.[19]

Here is how the 'Life Story of Johann Purti' begins:

Sandu Purti was a Munda farmer in Kotna village 7 miles East of Khanti Sub-Division and Police Station in Ranchi Station. After Sepoy Mutiny in 1857 he became a Christian and was named Samuel Purti in baptism when he was a young man. He had three children Kushalmay, Yakub and Boaz. I am the youngest son of his oldest son Kushalmay Purti. My grand father possessed some farms in Ulihatu too, 12 miles East from Kotna. I was born in 4th April 1890 in Ulihatu and was brought up in the same village. (p. 1)

At the beginning, through an emphasis upon exactness of geographical detail and historical chronology, Johann Purti establishes his ancestry and the fact that he was born a Christian. Here there is no rhetorical rhapsody or tortured tale of religious transformation. A simple sentence suffices: 'After Sepoy Mutiny in 1857 he [Purti's grandfather] became a Christian and was named Samuel Purti in baptism.'[20] Next, the account quickly describes Johann Purti's initial lack of interest in attending school, his appreciation of learning upon moving to a boarding, and his return home in the middle of the last year of high school after discovering that his father was borrowing money for his education.

None of this is remarkable, hardly preparing us for the change of note that now follows.

After leaving school my father asked me to join the Theological Seminary but I refused, telling him that one who wanted to be a padre should join because I looked down on the padres. Then my father asked me to learn the work of petition writer in the court but I said to him that one who would tell a lie and would rob the poor, should go to the court. Then my father asked me to get a position in the Railway or in the Forest Department. I answered him that one who wanted to be a vagabond should join these two lines. Then my father asked me what should I do. I told him I would be a farmer. Outwardly he assented but inwardly he wanted that I should change my mind. So he began giving me very hard works. I was working with servants as servants. I was working so hard that it changed my mind. I went to a relative who was a doctor with the intention to learn the work of a compounder but I was not satisfied and wanted to go to a great hospital for which I asked a recommendation from the Principal of my school. (pp. 1–2)[21]

This unusual passage introduces us to the critical devices shaping Johann Purti's autobiographical account, which together constitute a curious amalgam. First, the narrative is entirely cast as that of a life seeking an occupation, an existence stalking a vocation. Second, recalcitrance toward paternal authority, refusal of paternalist power, runs through the text. Third, a perpetual note of dissatisfaction afflicts the protagonist of this story, which is also the basis of his recalcitrance. Fourth, the sources of this discontent often lie in the nature of the occupation ahead of Johann Purti, and in the hardships such work entails, which teach him a lesson. (Consider, respectively, the responses of the protagonist to his father when the latter asks him to take up a position in the law courts, the railways, or in the forest department, and Purti's change of mind after his father gives him hard work in the fields.) Yet, the roots of this discontent equally constitute an existential condition. Fifth, abrupt changes of mind as much as God's guidance lead our protagonist in his choices of career. Finally, such tropic designs—the salience of occupation, the place of recalcitrance, the presence of dissatisfaction—pattern the entire narrative, driving it toward its resolution. Here the critical forms are the vocation of a padre and the work of a compounder. Yet, like the narrative itself, the resolution too is unstable.

Having pre-empted the nature of the narrative ahead, let us cycle back to the nitty-gritty of Johann Puri's life story. After receiving Johann's letter, the principal sends him a letter of recommendation, also inviting him back to the school, offering to pay for the former pupil's education 'if desired again'. When Johann goes and meets the principal, the benevolent, paternalist figure provides the assurance that he would personally write to the civil surgeon of the 'great hospital' about a compounder's position, and in the meanwhile gives Johann 'a light work of clerk in his office'. Presumably Johann Purti had refused the principal's offer of returning to school, but now another opportunity presents itself, of resuming education to enter God's work: 'One day he [the principal] asked me placing his hand on my shoulder "Well you dear chap, learn Theology?" Johann's recalcitrant response is characteristic: 'I threw his hand away say "no." From that day he never asked me like again.' Soon after Johann refuses his Christian calling, a letter comes from the civil surgeon stating that there is no vacancy for a compounder in the hospital. But such is Johann's investment in the idea of becoming a compounder that he even considers training for the position at the Leper Asylum in the town of Purulia, a place of hardship, a far cry from the 'great hospital', a consideration that he does not put through into practice. (p. 2)

Instead, not much later, Johann returns to the principal, once more with the thought of asking him to write a recommendation letter, now to the civil surgeon of the Government Hospital in Ranchi. But on his way a change comes upon Johann's 'mind' quite by itself, explained only by the direction it points to: 'I told him that I would read in the seminary.' The astonished principal asks him to return in a few hours, when he reminds Johann that he would have to 'learn 4 years in the Seminary'. But Johann is equal to the challenge: 'I replied I would learn for 7 years. From that day I began studying in the Seminary.' At the same time, Johann's education toward the service of God does not lead to his own happiness. When he finishes at the seminary, it is 1915, the Great War has begun, the German missionaries have been sent away from India, and there is no work for the seminary-trained Johann in his own church. Only after reading an advertisement in his church newspaper, more than a year later, at the end of 1916, does Johann find employment as a catechist in Bisrampur.

Johann remains at the pioneer mission station in Chhattisgarh for four years, but we can only wonder if he is actually satisfied with his life there. For as soon as he comes across an advertisement for the position of a compounder in the service of the National Missionary Society in the princely state of Rewa, something happens: 'My mind again revolted and I went way and joined the N.M.S. [National Missionary Society].' Yet, joy and content are not to be had by him even now: 'sorry I was not made a componder but was made a private tutor and pedagogue of the Prince of Sohagpur. In their company I spent five year[s]. I suffered a great loss there. Within the course of 3 years there I lost my 3 dear children.' (pp. 2–3)

Soon the National Missionary Society is forbidden to conduct 'public Christian work' in the region by the ruler of Rewa. Johann is once more 'placed in a dilemma': 'The N.M.S. called me for work in Jharsaguda and Dr J. Gass [of the American Evangelical Mission Society] called me for work in the Kalahandi State.' What is Johann's way out of his predicament? 'I submitted myself to God for guidance and he sent me back to Raipur.' While in Raipur, the missionary J. Gass informs him that the congregation at Bisrampur wants him as their pastor. Not unlike his answers to his father and the school principal when they ask him to learn theology, Johann tells Gass that he is 'not willing' to take up the position. The missionary suggests that Johann 'pray and think over it then to reply.' Now, a mellow Johann comes home and decides that he would do 'what God wished.' (pp. 3–4)

The moment of revelation, the most dramatic event in his discontented life, is upon Johann Purti.

I opened the Bible and 2 Tim. 2 came out to my eyes and I began reading. I thought the book opened by itself, it is not of any great consequence. I closed it. Second time I decided that this time whatever may come out I must abide. This time 1 Tim. 4: 12 came out. I sat silent and said 'O God, Thou art victorious.' Next day I told Dr J. Gass that I would go to Bisrampur. I was licensed as a pastor in 1927 and ordained Feb. 23, 1930. I am now a compounder of the greatest physician Jesus. (p. 4)

How are we to read this resolution, which of course bears upon the entire, prior narrative? The fact that Johann Purti's story follows a pattern of constant struggle leading to an eventual realization in the Truth of Christ suggests that it perhaps reflects the life of a saint, or that it possibly follows the tale of an exemplary Christian figure. However, after talking with scholars of Christianity, delving into the hagiographies of the Early Christians and the Church Fathers, I have yet to make the connection. Indeed, the closest related narrative that I chanced upon was during fieldwork in Chhattisgarh in early 2001.

In late January of that year, conducting interviews among Indian evangelists and pastors in the neighbouring town of Champa and Janjgir in eastern Chhattisgarh, one afternoon I found myself in front of a newly built yet plain structure, a Pentecostal place of worship. My companion and guide around Champa, Dr Singh, a senior lecturer in the local college, introduced me as a 'foreign Professor' researching history and culture to two men standing outside the church. This capacious introduction was hardly necessary. No sooner had Dr Singh left, the moment we were inside the church, one of the two men, the padre it turned out, a person in his twenties, asked me if I wanted to hear his *gavahi*, his witness. Needless to say, I was interested. What followed was the story of the padre's life. The details of this account constitute a tale within the tale, which are better recounted elsewhere. My point here concerns the structure of the story:

Born into a Roman Catholic family, once he came of age, the padre's early life was wholly undistinguished, marked by listlessness, marred by discontent. Though not depraved, he sinned in thought, word, and deed. Tired of his existence, he thought several times of ending his life. One night, utterly disconsolate, he was on the verge of suicide, when a voice within led him to pick up the Bible. He opened it and a passage mentioning the Pentecost, asking the notional Catholic to find a new life in Christ, swam before his eyes. Unconvinced, he opened the Book again. The very passage appeared once more. How could this be, he asked himself? In front of God's command, he began to pray, which he did till the next morning, when he went out and joined the Pentecostal Church. Growing from strength to strength in spirit and faith, he was now the padre of the small Pentecostal congregation in Champa.

Johann Purti's tale and the Pentecostal padre's story bear resemblance. In both cases, discontented lives morph into meaningful spirits through a miraculous encounter with passages of the Bible, the Book opening by itself to guide the two men to the work of the Lord. Yet, this is also where the similarity between these accounts ends, intimating thereby the divergences that often attend varieties of tales of evangelical transformation. In the Pentecostal padre's story, the passage of the Book that opens before him calls upon him to make a complete break with the past. Indeed, later when I tentatively asked the Padre about where in the Bible—on which page, in what part of the Gospel—the passage occurs, he did not answer the question directly. Rather, he emphasized again that the Word itself had guided him to new life, a new faith. This was the moral of the story. In contrast, the identifiable passages from 1 Timothy and 2 Timothy that open in front of Johann Purti actively bind together his history and his here-and-now, providing an explanation of his past as much as offering guidelines for his future.

Recall that when he first opens the Bible, trying to decide whether he should become a pastor, Johann's eyes alight upon 2 Timothy 2:

You then, my son, be strong in the Grace that is Jesus Christ. And the things you have heard me say in the presence of many witnesses entrust to reliable men who will be also qualified to teach others. Endure hardships with us like a good soldier of Christ Jesus. No one serving as a soldier gets involved in civilian affairs—he wants to please his commanding officer. Similarly, if anyone competes as an athlete, he does not receive the victor's crown unless he competes according to the rules. The hardworking farmer should be the first to receive a share of the crops.[22]

Now, the messages to be 'strong' and to bear the truth to 'reliable men' carry immense import for Johann's vocation ahead as a pastor. At the same time, the advice to 'endure hardships' and to be 'hardworking', the admonition against getting 'involved in civilian affairs', and the injunction to play according to the rules seem to speak poignantly not only to Johann's possible future but also to his discontented past. This was a past that extended from Johann's recalcitrant nature to his quest to become a compounder, which led to constant dissatisfaction, abrupt moves, and several hardships in the story of his life.

Yet, this is not all. For a little later, under the description of 'A Workman Approved by God', immediately after learning of the need to cleanse oneself of ignoble purposes in life, Johann would have read:

Flee the evil desires of youth, and pursue righteousness, faith, love and peace, along with those who call on the Lord out of a pure heart. Don't have anything to do with foolish and stupid arguments, because you know they produce quarrels. And the Lord's servant must not quarrel; instead, he must be kind to everyone, able to teach, not resentful.[23]

It is hardly surprising that both the poignancy and prescience of these words startled Johann. And so he opened the book again, where 1 Timothy 4: 12 told him:

Don't let anyone look down on you because of you are young, but set an example for the believers in speech, in life, in faith and in purity.[24]

Taken together, these passages possibly directed Johann to confront his past of 'foolish and stupid arguments' (and of the consequent 'quarrels', both inner and outer), to come to terms with his (young?) life of 37 years, and to go forth into pastoral labour.[25] Unlike the end of the witness of the Pentecostal padre that simply shook off his past, the resolution of the testimony of Johann Purti struggled and reckoned with his history, intimating and endorsing his future. Indeed, Johann's past and future stood conjoined in the declaration that he was 'now a compounder of the greatest physician Jesus', his own worldly desire spiritually realized, the prior wishes of his father, the school principal, and the missionary J. Gass—that their ward serve the Lord—finally fulfilled.

Yet, it would be much too facile to present Johann Purti's narrative as 'all-of-a-piece'. Mindful of a warning issued by Arthur O. Lovejoy more than fifty years ago, this will be to ignore the 'inner tensions—

the fluctuations and hesitancies between opposing ideas or moods' that run through Johann's account. Of course, such attributes are no monopoly of Johann's tale, finding discrete expression in several of the writings explored in this chapter. At the same time, 'inner tensions' do appear more strikingly in Purti's story. This should not surprise us. After all, Johann's attempt was to revealingly dramatize the very commonness of his life. Such dramatization provided the narrative with an end, but it could not resolve the 'fluctuations and hesitancies' at the heart of the story and the finish of the tale. Indeed, the dramatization was itself propelled and contained by the constitutive tensions of the account.[26]

At every step, Johann's narrative juxtaposes contrary ideas and images, contending thoughts and tendencies. He is wrong and right, quarrelsome and correct, discontented and honest. Recall that at the beginning Johann is not interested in school, but upon his move to a boarding he not only succeeds at school but also selflessly sacrifices his education because he does not want his father to go into debt. In his exchange with his father about his future occupation, Johann is mistaken when he abruptly dismisses the vocation of a padre. Yet he is astute in his refusal to rob the poor by becoming a petition writer in the law court or to lead the life of a vagabond by joining the railway or the forest department. He learns a lesson when made to undertake hard work as a farmer, but this only leads to him toward his obsessive desire to become a compounder. Johann rejects the school principal's suggestion that he learn theology. Yet a little later he himself gives up on his desire to become a compounder and goes off to study in a seminary. He completes the course of education at the seminary, but he does not find a job in his own church. Johann wrongly leaves the post of a catechist in Bisrampur, yet is himself clearly wronged when the National Missionary Society does not appoint him to the position of a compounder, and when he loses his three children in the course of three years, working in Sohagpur. Johann returns to Raipur following God's guidance, but also unequivocally refuses the proposition that he serve as a pastor, a proposal made by the congregation at Bisrampur, an offer conveyed by the good missionary Gass.

And what of the end of Johann's story? It is not only that the transformation that follows Johann's encounter with passages of the

Book loses some of its motive force because obedience to God's command had also characterized his life earlier. (Compare Johann's account with that of the Pentecostal padre.) It is also that the resolution itself—Johann's becoming a compounder of the greatest physician Jesus—is not simply joyous, but equally accompanied by a note of discontent. For at the very moment Johann makes this declaration, he also recalls that he was 'willing to be persecuted in Kalahandi which means black earthen pot.' Similarly, now in Bisrampur there are 'difficulties and persecutions not only from non-Christians but even more from Christians who are not loyal and do want to listen to the admonitions of Gods Word.' (p. 4) It bears mention that these difficulties are tied to the struggle launched over the early 1930s by the Bisrampur congregation against the missionaries and their pastor, Johann Purti. This struggle, conducted in an evangelical idiom, had its beginnings in a 'case' of adultery between Rebecca, a 'virgin Christian girl of Bisrampur', and Boas Purti, Johann's uncle and the *lambardar* (official in charge of landed property) of the mission-owned village of Bisrampur. Equally, such persecution is betokened by the pointlessness of arguments and quarrels described by the fragments of the Book that Johann faces. Yet, my point is that the appearance of 'difficulties and persecutions' at the very moment of the resolution of Johann's tales are bound as well to the contrary moods and textures that characterize his entire narrative.[27]

To be sure, the pointed nature of Johann's story of a life in search of a vocation are very much those of a Christian in colonial India. Born into an adivasi family that had converted to Christianity in the mid-nineteenth century, Johann's acquisition of education leads him to negotiate the choices of occupation that were open to an Indian Christian in the early twentieth century. At the same time, this should not obscure two inter-related points. On the one hand, the decisive commonness of Johann's autobiography, including his attempts to dramatize his life story that only underscore its pathos, militate against the melodrama implied by authoritative versions of conversion. On the other hand, the acute contrariness that run through Johann's narrative, the opposing tendencies that underwrite the tale, these 'inner tensions' escape and exceed the exclusive life of the convert insinuated by dominant conceptions of conversion.

CONCLUSION

Discussing the autobiographies, biographies, and other writings of Indian evangelical workers, this essay has sought to show the limitations of authoritative apprehensions and commonplace conceptions of conversion, which imbue lives and histories of subjects of religious change with relentless singularity. At the same time, I have not proceeded by sharply separating the vernacular attributes of an Indian Christianity from its colonial connections, barely discussing, for example, the continuities between prior faiths and an indigenous Christianity. Such connections and differences are ever salient, but they never constitute pristine, pure verities. Indeed, to imagine and institute an unsullied, heroic, minority faith is to share ground with propositions regarding radical rupture as constitutive of conversion, already given, always there. Mere oppositions assiduously reverse yet acutely reflect the objects of their critique. As an alternative, in this chapter I have focused on the details and the dynamics of accounts of Indian Christians, their drama and their divergence, their exact surplus of faith in the Book and their own renderings of the Word. My analytical wager concerns ways of reading that explore the distinction and difference of these narratives, at once vernacular and colonial, simultaneously contrary and common.

As a word, conversion carried exclusive connotations mainly in the writing of the missionary, Theodore Seybold. Yet, even this most singular rendering of the conversion of the Brahman Ramnath came with its own twist, split and shaped by the force of the wide-ranging making of myth and narrative, history and legend at the core of evangelical entanglements. As an event, conversion was described in inherently different ways in the narratives explored in the essay. As a resource, conversion—to be born into or to become the member of a new faith—allowed life stories of Indian Christian to be plotted in distinct ways, quite as these accounts usually remained rooted in the common and the quotidian. On the one had, the precise diversity, difference, and distinction at the heart of these tales exceed the singularity of lives entailed by dominant designs of conversion. On the other hand, the very commonness of these life stories, including efforts to dramatize their constitutive terms, militate against the melodrama implied by inherited imaginings of conversion.

NOTES AND REFERENCES

1. The issues explored here intersect with several questions explored over the years by David Lorenzen, including especially those of life stories and missionary entanglements. David has himself provided valuable suggestions on the chapter. I would also like to thank David Arnold, Stuart Blackburn, Martha Elena Venier, Manuel Ruiz, and Rowena Robinson for their comments on the materials explored here. The chapter forms part of a larger project on the evangelical encounter in central India and North America in the nineteenth and twentieth centuries.

2. Much archival material dealing with life histories of native Christians in central India is slim in size or fragmentary in character. The most substantial collection of such writings is to be found in Eden Archives and Library, Webster Grove, Missouri (henceforth, EAL), the repository for the records of the German Evangelical Mission Society, which later changed its name to the American Evangelical Mission. These accounts form the core of this chapter. In writing the essay, I also consulted other materials from EAL and from two archives of Mennonite missionaries in Goshen, Indiana, and Newton, Kansas. But these writings were either very fragmentary or they consisted of obituaries, missionary-authored 'autobiographies' of Indian converts, or 'life sketches' of Christian women and men written by missionaries that reported on the conduct and character of Indian evangelical operatives. While useful in providing a context for the questions discussed in this chapter, these accounts did not prove important for its central arguments.

3. These conceptions of conversion are discussed in detail in Saurabh Dube, 'Conversion to Translation: Colonial Registers of a Vernacular Christianity', in Saurabh Dube (ed.), *Enduring Enchantments*, a special issue of *South Atlantic Quarterly*, vol. 101, no. 4, 2002 and in Saurabh Dube, *Native Witness: Colonial Writings of a Vernacular Christianity*. Manuscript of book in progress. This section and parts of the next one draw upon these writings.

4. Gauri Viswanathan, *Outside the Fold: Conversion, Modernity, and Belief* (Princeton: Princeton University Press, 1998).

5. See, for example, Ussama Makdisi, 'Reclaiming the Land of the Bible: Missionaries, Secularism, and Evangelical Modernity', *American Historical Review*, vol. 102, 1997, pp. 680–713; John Comaroff, 'Images of Empire, Contests of Conscience: Models of Colonial Domination in South Africa', *American Ethnologist*, vol. 16, 1989, pp. 661–85; Jean Comaroff and John Comaroff, *Of Revelation and Revolution: Christianity, Colonialism, and Consciousness in South Africa*, vol. 1 (Chicago: University of Chicago Press, 1991); John Comaroff and Jean Comaroff, *Of Revelation and Revolution: The Dialectics of Modernity on a South African Frontier*, vol. 2 (Chicago: University of Chicago Press, 1997); Saurabh Dube, *Stitches on Time: Colonial Textures and Postcolonial Tangles* (Durham: Duke University Press, 2004); and David Scott, 'Conversion and Demonism: Colonial Christian Discourse on Religion in Sri Lanka', *Comparative Studies in Society and History*, vol. 34, 1992, pp. 331–65. See also, Ann Stoler, 'Rethinking Colonial Categories: European Communities and the Boundaries of Rule', *Comparative Studies in Society and History*, vol. 31, 1989, pp. 134–61; and Vicente Rafael, *Contracting Colonialism:*

Translation and Christian Conversion in Tagalog Society under Early Spanish Rule (Ithaca: Cornell University Press, 1988).

6. See, for example, Birgit Meyer, *Translating the Devil: Religion and Modernity among the Ewe in Ghana* (Trenton, NJ: Africa World Press, 1999); Pier M. Larson, '"Capacities and Modes of Thinking": Intellectual Engagements and Subaltern Hegemony in the Early History of Malgasy Christianity', *American Historical Review*, vol. 102, 1997, pp. 968–1002; Geoffrey White, *Identity through History: Living Stories in a Solomon Islands Society* (Cambridge: Cambridge University Press, 1991); Dube, *Stitches on Time*; Paul Landau, *The Realm of the Word: Language, Gender, and Christianity in a Southern African Kingdom* (London: Heinemann, 1995); *Conversion to Christianity: Historical and Anthropological Perspectives on a Great Transformation*, ed. Robert Hefner (Berkeley: University of California Press, 1993); Comaroff and Comaroff, *Revelation and Revolution*, vol. 2. See also, Rafael, *Contracting Colonialism*; Derek Peterson, 'Translating the Word: Dialogism and Debate in Two Gikuyu Dictionaries', *The Journal of Religious History*, vol. 23, 1999, pp. 31–50; and Diane Austin-Broos, *Jamaica Genesis: Religion and the Politics of Moral Orders* (Chicago: University of Chicago Press, 1997).

7. Fuller details of the processes described in this section are contained in Dube, *Stitches on Time*; Saurabh Dube, 'Travelling Light: Missionary Musings, Colonial Cultures, and Anthropological Anxieties', in Raminder Kaur and John Hutnyk (eds), *Travel Worlds: Journeys in Contemporary Cultural Politics* (London and New Jersey: Zed Books, 1999), pp. 29–50; and Dube, *Native Witness.*

8. Dube, *Native Witness.*

9. M.M. Paul, *Chhatisgarh Evangelical Kalasiya ka Sankshipt Itihas* (Allahabad: Mission Press, 1936), pp. 8–9; Theodore Seybold, *God's Guiding Hand: History of the Central Indian Mission 1868–1967* (Philadelphia: United Church Board for World Ministeries of the United Church of Christ, 1971), pp. 28–9.

10. Paul, *Chhatisgarh Evangelical Kalasiya*, p. 9.

11. The missionary Andrew Stoll was later to write of him: 'Still very active at 60 years of age, he preaches in the villages and in the city day after day. Once a proud young Brahmin, the Spirit of Christ has transformed him into a friend and a brother of the lowliest of the low. His example has often strengthened my faith.' Andrew Stoll, cited in Seybold, *God's Guiding Hand*, p. 29.

12. Theodore Seybold served as a missionary in Chhattisgarh between 1913 and 1958. For nine years he frequently met Ramnath Bajpai: Seybold lived for a long time in the home of the Missionary Jacob Gass; Ramnath was the head catechist working under Gass, and was often present in the missionary's home. Few biographical details are forthcoming about David Bajpai.

13. Theodore Seybold, 'The Reverend Ramnath Simon Bajpai', typescript, n.d., 84–9b Bio 52, EAL, p. 1. Except when indicated, all the quotations from this text are from the first page.

14. Saurabh Dube, *Untouchable Pasts: Religion, Identity, and Power among a Central Indian Community, 1780–1950* (Albany: State University of New York Press, 1998), pp. 76–7, 193–204.

15. Seybold, 'The Reverend Ramnath Simon Bajpai', pp. 1–2.

16. David Bajpai, 'My Father—Rev. Simon Ramnath Bajpai', typescript, 1945, 84–9b Bio 52, EAL. All citations of page numbers of this account will appear in parenthesis in the text itself.

17. Indeed, converting to Christianity from a Brahman background carried critical distinction. Thus, M.M. Paul, a native evangelist, spent the most part of his own 'autobiography' describing the circumstances and events of the conversion of his father and uncle who were from a poor but priestly Brahman family. His account reveals that M.M. Paul was at once proud of this ancestry, but as a catechist he also felt compelled to criticize the superstitious beliefs of his family prior to its conversion. Similarly, the narrative shows a certain ambivalence about how the members of the family came to eat meat and fish, which are presented as Christian habits, but the pride in being vegetarians once is not entirely absent here. At the same time, as I show below, even this account did not dramatize the conversion of his family. M.M. Paul, 'Autobiography of M.M. Paul, Head Catechist at Mahasamund', typescript, 84–9b Bio 52, EAL, pp. 1–2.

18. The two accounts also followed divergent trajectories in their description of the later life of Ramnath. While the missionary Seybold once more envisioned it in the mirror of the growth of the mission, David Bajpai described his father's life rather as that of an honest and fearless worker with a keen sense of humour, entirely in keeping with his character, ever on par with the missionaries.

19. Johann Purti, 'Life Story of Johann Purti', typescript, 1934, 84–9b Bio 52, EAL. Once more, the citations of page numbers of this account appear in parenthesis in the text.

20. Indeed, conversion does not appear as a dramatic or miraculous event in any of the life histories written or narrated by Christians in central India that I consulted for this chapter. This is true of various autobiographical accounts of women and men in Chhattisgarh today. It also holds for narratives written in the colonial period. If contrary tendencies characterize David Bajpai's story of his father's conversion and Johann Purti narrates the event of his grandfather's becoming Christian as an undramatic fact, even those accounts in which conversion was accorded centrality told the tale in rather low-key ways. For example, consider the life story of the catechist Loknath Timothy, written in the late 1920s. Loknath's family were among the earlier converts to Christianity in Chhattisgarh, and the first of his two-page narrative concerns these times. At the beginning he tells us: 'In a village 12 miles from Bisrampur, Jangir I was born 12 July 1864. Father's name (after Baptism) Adam, mother's name Eve.' After this Loknath describes the networks of kinship that led his entire family, Satnami by caste, to move to Bisrampur, the land they were given to settle there, and their eventual 'confirmation' as Christians by the missionary Oscar Lohr. On the one hand, there is no rancour or persecution that greets Loknath's family when they decide to move to Bisrampur. Rather, the proprietor of their ancestral village entreats them not to leave their land, promising them a comfortable life there. On the other hand, in addition to the strength of kinship, the family's turning to Christianity appears as a consequence of the contented community that was to be found in Bisrampur. Taken together, there is nothing theatrical about this narrative of conversion, and its unremarkable representation speaks for itself. Similarly, in the

autobiography of M.M. Paul—a native evangelist, later a 'national' missionary—the conversion of his father and uncle, 'Tiwari Brahmin[s]', is a critical part of the narrative, occupying more than a page of the one-and-a-half page typescript. Yet, the circumstances and the event of conversion are not described as a magnificent melodrama of religious transformation. Instead, they are presented in an entirely matter-of-fact manner as a story of gradual change of faith, from the meeting of the two poor but religious Brahmans with itinerant Christian speakers, to their sustained contact with missionaries, to the bitterness they face from their own community, to their escape to a big city and their conversion there, all rendered in a quotidian key. Loknath Timothy, 'Autobiography of Old Catechist Loknath (Hindi idioms retained)', typescript, 1928, M.P. Davis Papers, EAL, p. 1. M.M. Paul, 'Autobiography of M.M. Paul, Head Catechist at Mahasamund', typescript, 84–9b Bio 52, EAL, pp. 1–2.

21. A compounder is a doctor's assistant, who mixes and distributes medicine. After the dominance of medicines produced by large, often multinational, pharmaceutical corporations, the compounder of the past is now rarely found in India.

22. *The Holy Bible* (East Brunswick: International Bible Society, 1978), p. 1248.

23. Ibid., p. 1249.

24. Ibid., p. 1245.

25. The passages of the Book that opened before Johann also carried critical connotations for him given the context he was writing in, a point discussed below. Later, I propose to explore the specific significance of the Book of Timothy as articulating Johann's account.

26. The precise terms of its dramatization and the exact form of its contrariness distinguish Johann's tale from other life histories within the evangelical encounter. Here the contrast with the writings of Theodore Seybold and David Bajpai is abundantly clear. Equally, other accounts often represented the distinction of a life by seeking out the remarkable in the common. Whether it was Loknath Timothy establishing in his life story that he was an earlier convert to Christianity in the region and describing a fight in which the missionary Andrew Stoll and he were both injured. Or it was M.M. Paul highlighting the conversion of his Brahman father. Or it was older, Mennonite women—met during fieldwork—telling their tales as a succession of life-stages. Birth, childhood in a home or an orphanage, courtship under the supervision of the missionary 'mama', marriage solemnized by the missionary 'papa', employment, and the death of the husband, all punctuated by extraordinary events such as famines and floods. Even when there were attempts to dramatize the narratives, these followed the rehearsals of Mennonite principles or Christian codes being upheld at different moments of lives and stories.

27. For a detailed reading of the conflict mentioned above see Saurabh Dube, 'Paternalism and Freedom Encounter in Colonial Chhattisgarh, Central India', *Modern Asian Studies*, vol. 29, 1995, pp. 171–201.

10. SPEAKING OF CASTE?
COLONIAL AND INDIGENOUS INTERPRETATIONS OF CASTE AND COMMUNITY IN NINETEENTH-CENTURY BOMBAY

Frank F. Conlon

'The knowledge imposes a pattern, and falsifies
For the pattern is new in every moment.'
'Four Quartets', T.S. Eliot

A familiar trope in contemporary South Asian studies is the invocation of 'invented traditions'—the view that many institutions often described as characteristic of Indian civilization, are, in fact, 'inventions' arising from the activities of British colonial authorities.[1] At first blush, the interpretation seems plausible given the considerable powers associated with 'the Raj'. On the other hand, this assertion by modern scholars of colonial hegemony seems to deny agency to generations of Indians who lived both in colonial times and before. Among the many scholarly contributions of David Lorenzen, one that I have most appreciated has been his unwillingness to accept the 'invention' theory uncritically, and his explorations of how, in the case of Hinduism, there may be seen to be many fathers and mothers, rather than a small coterie of colonial administrators and 'Orientalist' scholars.[2]

In this essay I wish to briefly visit the scholarly problem of the 'colonial invention of tradition' in an analysis of India's social and cultural history, taking the Bombay region as an arena for exploration during the seventeenth to nineteenth centuries. I am concerned to re-examine the contexts within which 'caste' and 'community' were generated and popularly used by both Indians and their British colonial rulers. Perspectives of colonial administrators, Christian missionaries, Indian social reformers and religious revivalists are examined, revealing a pattern of social description and analysis rather more complicated than would be suggested by the model of 'invention of tradition' as an artefact of a colonial project.

Not long ago I was visited by a colleague from another discipline who was 'hoping to get caught up' on the social history of modern India. Thinking about the myriad aspects of that topic, I asked 'what have you read about caste?' 'Caste?' my visitor exclaimed, 'I thought that was all an invention of the British!' My colleague, it transpired, was vaguely familiar with some writings of Bernard S. Cohn and Nicholas Dirks from which an impression had been gained that caste was an 'invented tradition'—an artefact of 'the colonial project'.[3] I never discovered the specific source of my colleague's opinion; perhaps that does not matter. It was clear that what I may call the 'tradition of invented tradition' was once again in play. The term 'invention of tradition' was popularized by an influential collection of essays edited under that title by Eric Hobsbawm and Terence Ranger, published in 1983, containing six critical case studies that demonstrated certain 'ancient traditions' had, in fact, been created in modern times, in response to varying requirements.[4] Hobsbawn, in his introduction, explained that

> 'Invented tradition' is taken to mean a set of practices, normally governed by overtly or tacitly accepted rules and of a ritual or symbolic nature, which seek to inculcate certain values and norms of behaviour by repetition, which automatically implies continuity with the past. In fact, where possible, they normally attempt to establish continuity with a suitable historic past....However, insofar as there is such reference to a historic past, the peculiarity of 'invented' traditions is that the continuity with it is largely fictitious. In short, they are responses to novel situations which take the form of reference to old situations, or which establish their own past by quasi-obligatory repetition.[5]

Hobsbawm conceded that there was probably no time and place which had not seen the 'invention' of tradition, arguing further that invented traditions emerged more frequently at times of rapid social transformation when 'old' traditions were disappearing. Therefore, he reasoned, it might be expected that an especially large number of 'new' traditions would be invented over the past two centuries, in both 'traditional' and 'modern' societies.[6]

No contemporary student of non-Western cultures would dispute that the 'invention of tradition' has become a touchstone for many scholars, but at least one skeptical critic observed that

> for a long time now, historians have treated the work of Eric Hobsbawm and his anthology *The Invention of Tradition* as something approaching Holy Writ, and the mention of it is guaranteed to certify oneself as a deep thinker, a critical mind, a properly educated person who is not rube [slang expression for an innocent and gullible person] enough to be taken in by nationalist sentimentalities and packaged nostalgia.[7]

Of course in practice no Manichean-like choice between primeval 'tradition' and human invention is required, nor observed by academicians. However, as my colleague's viewpoint would indicate, a simple, easily remembered point has staying power never equalled by nuanced or subtle explanations of difference.

Approaching this question from the perspective of my own research and writing, I am of the view that caste is 'real enough' to merit survival in the academic discourse of South Asian social and cultural history. Yet within the limited power of human perception, 'caste' has been real enough for centuries in the subcontinent. Also, from a personal perspective, I had published an exploration of the history of a caste from its pre-colonial formation to modern times.[8] Reading pre-colonial histories of India, I kept finding references to castes and caste identities. Had everyone been misled? Or was the issue rather that modernity in the form of colonial rule had seized upon 'caste' and had, in effect, frozen it into a conventional knowledge by which one could know India? And, was it all a product of naughty orientalism and colonialism? Or, were we scholars overlooking the invocations and uses of 'tradition' by Indians not merely for promotion of self-interest, but also as a medium of resistance? Even if caste were 'invented' as my visitor had assumed, did it follow that that which was 'invented' could also be 'not real?' The fact that some of the most recent 'crystallization of concepts and institutions' occurred in the colonial period may lead to an over-imagined agency and power of the colonial rulers.[9]

In truth, I wondered too at 'the colonial project.' Having long before been alerted to the problems of 'orientalist essentializing', it appeared now that 'the colonial project' amounted to a bit of 'post-colonial essentializing,' thus becoming like 'globalization', a term which was being used to explain everything, and thus, perhaps, to explain nothing.[10] There was little question that the British colonial governments in India had some role in shaping caste in colonial times, but as for 'invention' I felt doubts.

Perhaps T.S. Eliot had it right; knowledge 'freeze frames' the subject producing a snapshot which then becomes a baseline for imagining or measuring 'change'. Or ought I to say 'inventing' change? Yet when Eric Hobsbawm turned the now well-known phrase of 'invention of tradition,' perhaps scholars have been too willing to see that 'invention' as a hegemonic means by which powerful forces imposed upon weaker or exploited, even 'subaltern' peoples, or at the very least an invocation of a symbol of inside knowledge by a member of a 'guild'.[11]

When considering India and the 'invention of caste' it is striking that a well-rounded, essentialized, conception of caste understood as a by-product of a collaboration of 'orientalism' and the 'colonial project' appeared relatively late in the day. This is a particular consideration in an era when some students demonstrate a remarkably limited sense of historical contingency. Having been educated to detect and denounce bias in received accounts, they do not turn the eye on themselves or on the received canon.

In one of his seminal essays, which appeared in a special issue of *Representations* titled 'Imperial Fantasies and Postcolonial Histories', Nicholas Dirks opens with these words: 'When we think of India it is not hard to think of caste'.[12] He had earlier argued that 'The Invention of Caste' had been the work of British colonial knowledge. 'Caste' had been constructed as the religious basis of Indian society, a cultural form that became viewed as a specifically Indian form of civil society.'[13] Virtually as soon as this highly quotable term had entered the discourse, Dirks began to qualify the statement, noting that 'caste—now disembodied from its former political contexts—lived on...appropriated and reconstructed by the British.' He stated that the British were 'Paradoxically...able to change caste only because caste in fact continued to be permeable to political influence.'[14] Caste institutions, customs, and autonomy had, of course been a subject of pre-British political influence as well, presumably without the malign influence of 'the colonial project.'[15] But such qualifications often get overlooked in a quick read. Later Dirks stated that he did not wish 'to imply that that [caste] was simply invented by the too clever British'[16] As Nels Brimnes usefully pointed out, Dirks presented 'his basic argument in surprisingly uneasy terms: 'I hope to weave an argument far more complicated than that the British invented caste, though in one sense this is precisely what happened.'[17] The 'sound bite' is easily remembered, and often misconstrued. I found that an eminent colleague in sociology had glossed Dirks' work too readily. An online syllabus from his seminar in the University of Washington's Department of Sociology suggested readings on:

'malign consequences' of 'imposed' institutions. Edward Said's, *Orientalism*, appeared without comment, followed by James C. Scott, *Seeing Like A State* ('social engineering necessarily falters when it fails to appreciate the cultural context in which intervention occurs'), Yale 1999 and Nicholas Dirks, *Castes of Mind* ('how the British imperial state led to the caste system in India'), Princeton 2001.[18]

Dirks was not alone. At about the same time, one of his teachers, Ronald Inden, was writing a trenchant critique of 'orientalism' and all other modes which had 'essentialized' India.[19] Identifying and critiquing colonial ethnographies as foundations of British imperial rule in India has become a common theme for historians and anthropologists. In the aftermath of Edward Said's *Orientalism* and the related turn to re-examination of the sociology of colonial knowledge, the idea of caste, and indeed much of 'traditional India' having been a colonial construct or invention grew to be a neo-canonical norm, or, perhaps less charitably, a cliché.[20] Even if a cliché is merely a truth that's been stated too often, the issue of caste's 'invention' calls for reexamination.

If 'invention' is the appropriate term, and 'caste' does constitute a discursive realm, it should be useful to explore the issue by a preliminary examination of how 'caste' was 'used' in a specific arena over the years leading up to the apogee of colonial rule. Because of my prior research experience, I have Bombay/Mumbai and its hinterland as the arena in which to explore how 'caste' was discussed or imagined. It appears that various authors and speakers, European and Indian, described, or invoked, 'caste' quite variously, depending upon the context or their interests. It may be obvious that European knowledge of 'caste' and other aspects of India's society were gained incrementally over time leading to such collective culminations as the Ethnographic Survey of India publications which, along with various census volumes, appear to be the principal sites where the normative 'invented' caste was defined.[21] May it also be proposed that knowledge of 'caste' similarly was acquired over time by Indians, particularly those occupying the historically marginal coastal zones such as Bombay and its surrounding Konkan region? I decided to return to my old haunts and to explore and rethink the issue of caste (and community) in the Mumbai that was Bombay.[22]

From the European perspective in Bombay in the seventeenth century, caste (or community) had salience insofar as it might be used to recruit population to the new port to promote its economic development, traders and weavers and some other functionaries were required. Relations between rulers and merchants in the ports of Gujarat provided a model wherein East India Company officers sought to find leaders of communities or castes, through whom members of their respective groups could be encouraged to contribute to the growth and prosperity of the Company's trade.[23] During the eighteenth century, caste was employed as a category to which the East India Company's Indian subjects belonged, and through which some measure of governance and maintenance of order might be obtained. By the opening of the nineteenth century, these views had become somewhat routinized, and were reinvoked by Mountstuart Elphinstone and his compatriots in the Deccan settlement following the defeat of the last Peshwa, Baji Rao II in 1818.[24] At about the same time, the revisions of the East India Company charter gradually opened India's door to Christian missionaries. Newly arrived evangelicals readily appropriated 'caste' as a fundamental symbol of the backwardness of Indian culture. The prominent Baptist missionary in William Ward saw it as a significant pathology of the Hindu tradition; he characterized caste as the equivalent to the bound foot in China.[25] While it may have suited missionary minds to regard caste as unchanging, other interests of entirely different perspectives also embraced the idea of caste's 'changeless' nature—namely Brahman informants whom the British consulted regarding laws and usages of Indian society. That these articulations of caste's static nature occurred in the time of colonial intrusion and extensive political and social change, meant that a simultaneous counter development was occurring as new economic and cultural opportunities led other Indians to explore and experiment with caste institutions and ideas to suit the changed circumstances.

The British encounter with western Indian society evolved in a lengthy historical process commencing in the seventeenth century when East India Company factory at Surat and outstations at places such as Broach, Rajapur, and Karwar.[26] At Surat, which was a Mughal possession, the Company's concerns were commercial and centred upon relations with merchants and artisans. The prominence of merchant castes in Surat's life was critical to trading opportunities and clearly made an impression upon the minds of British officers.[27] When, following the transfer of Bombay island from the British crown to the Company in 1668 and the determination to shift activities to the new site, East India Company officers sought both to understand and use concepts of caste and community for the improvement of their new port of trade.[28] Efforts were made to recruit suitable merchants, artisans, and labourers to Bombay, and to further this effort, the Court of Directors suggested that the Company officers should recognize the rights of communities to enjoy a limited autonomy of self-regulation, considering:

> that it is a great encouragement to the Banians in severall places that they have a little power for the ordering of themselves and for the hearing and determining of small controversies that arise from amongst them; and though wee thinck it not convenient to erect a judicature that should clash with our government, yet it may very much obteine our end in drawing them to Bombay that you permitt them to choose out certaine persons among themselves as a kind of moderators or superintendents over them.[29]

Gerald Aungier, the governor of Bombay, specifically sought to transfer to the town of Bombay a model of organization based upon his understanding of the trading *mahajans* or merchant guilds of Surat. He and his council proposed to concede official recognition of significant social distinctions:

> In order to preserve the Govern^t^ in a constant regular method free from the confusion wch a body composed of so many nations will be subject

to, it were requisite y^t y^e severall nations at $pres^t$ inhabiting or hereafter to inhabitt on Island Bombay be reduced or modelled into so many orders or tribes & that each nation may have a Cheif or Consull of the same nation appointed over them by the Govr and Councell whose duty & office must be to represent y^e grievances wch Moors of any said nation shall receive.[30]

The Company subsequently issued a proclamation decreeing that each caste or community in Bombay should have established a *panchayat* (village council).[31] These panchayats were to adjudicate disputes with their respective groups as well as making representations to the governor on matters of group concern.[32] The panchayats were to function as autonomous bodies serving at once to provide means for dispute settlement in accordance with the laws and customs of their own constituencies and to create a basis for an inexpensive preservation of civil order within the town of Bombay. It appears that several years passed before some of the castes and communities actually convened panchayats. It may be speculated that this in part rested in the fact that many of the groups in Bombay were segments of larger communities residing on the Indian mainland, up and down the coast.

Aungier's policy, set in the 1670s, appears to have been continued well into the eighteenth century. Documents from that century provide scattered references to the working of panchayats in the town of Bombay, but no connected history is, as yet, possible. Indeed, one of the better-documented groups, the panchayat of the Parsi community, appears to have flourished, atrophied, and flourished again, in relationship to the rising fortunes of the community and power and influence of specific families.[33] Urban growth and economic change introduced new dynamics into the social spectrum. In many instances, caste and community members long settled in Bombay faced the entry of cousins come lately to pursue their fortunes. Usually these newcomers entered at the lower rungs of the economic scale and were cast into the roles of 'dependents'. Yet even in that condition, they might resent domination by their more well-established 'betters'. With the rise of wealth came expectations of participation in community affairs. However 'traditional' the English rulers of Bombay might choose to consider their Indian compatriots, the growing port city offered opportunities for mobility.

Geographically, Bombay was linked most readily with adjacent coastal regions and coastal castes were predominant in the locality. Early nineteenth century annexations of Gujarat districts brought more Gujarati Hindus and Muslims into the city. Subsequent to the British conquest of the Deccan in 1818 many inhabitants of the *desh*, in particular Brahmans began to come to Bombay for education and employment, thus linking up territories which had been administratively separate for some time.[34]

Pre-colonial Indian rulers, both Hindu and Muslim, had adjudicated disputes between or within castes involving properties, ritual rights, social relations, and status.[35] The Honourable East India Company's officers were unqualified, if not reluctant, to play such traditional kingly roles with relation to issues of caste precedence and disputes. Nonetheless, when required, the 'state' would adjudicate caste questions. In 1778 the aforementioned Parsi panchayat requested Governor William Hornby to confirm that the panchayat had authority to punish those of the community (described as 'some Low Parsees') by 'shaming them...by beating them with a few Shoes, agreeable to their crime.'[36] The governor concurred, noting that they were also sanctioned to exclude offenders from caste feasts. There was little interest in undermining the accepted authority by which a caste or community governed itself.

In the early years of the nineteenth century, the Bombay officials saw positive advantages in keeping caste issues at a distance. No censorious moral judgments were being passed; rather, there was merit in allowing caste authorities to internally exercise punishments for maintenance of order. In 1811, the Bombay Advocate General, S.M. Thriepland argued that:

> On grounds of publick policy nothing can be more obvious than that the jurisdiction which is exercised by casts in this country ought as little as possible to be interfered with. It is a power which experience does not prove to be liable to much abuse, and its proper exercise is of such eminent utility in the prevention of misconduct on the part of our native fellow subjects, that whatever tends to weaken its authority must be accounted an evil of considerable magnitude.[37]

Further, he emphasized that caste discipline should increase the chance that a party guilty of a criminal act who gained acquittal in a

British court still would be subject to the pains and penalties of the caste panchayat.[38] In fact, by 1827, the Bombay authorities explicitly excluded 'caste questions' from court jurisdiction.[39] Recently, Hiroyuki Kotani has revisited the question of the 'caste autonomy' which was followed in the Bombay Presidency in contrast to the patterns in Bengal and Madras.[40]

On the other hand, the Bombay authorities discovered that individual litigants bringing suits in the new British courts made claims upon the customary legal and social usages of their particular caste. While judges could consult translations of *Dharmashastra* that had been compiled in Bengal by Jones and Colebrooke, the general nature of these works did not provide insights into western Indian practices. Accordingly two Bombay civil servants, Arthur Steele, and Harry Borradaile were ordered to collect and assemble an inventory of laws and customs of castes of the Deccan and Gujarat.[41] Steele put queries to groups representing varying castes, but also convened groups of Brahmans and consulted pandits at the Poona Sanskrit school. This Brahmanical tilt was very much aligned with a wider reliance by the colonial rulers upon elite Hindu informants.[42] Steele found, however, that most of his informants agreed on matters of intercaste marriage, inheritance, adoption, and family property. However, Steele reported that he was surprised at 'the great variety of castes and sects' and equally varied usages, but anticipated that the intention of

> separating and classifying the rules binding on all Hindus from those which are observed by particular castes only, or by the local varieties of the latter would be accomplished and eventually a clear guide to points of law and custom would be available in English and in Marathi.[43]

Steele's investigations in the Deccan territories recently conquered from the Marathas reflected the British perception that the desh of Maharashtra was different from the coastal Konkan region, a distinction reinforced by separation of judicial systems. Elphinstone and his successor, William Chaplin, had been confident that respectable Brahmans of the Deccan would not repair to Bombay for education where 'there is such a mixture of classes and inhabitants of various nations that all distinctions of caste are in a great degree confounded.'[44] In fact, however, the conquest of 1818 not only opened the desh to Bombay; it opened Bombay to the desh.

In the Deccan territories, the Maratha rulers had adjudicated caste questions, both with reference to intracaste excommunications and intracaste disputes.[45] The arrival of British rulers did not end the pre-colonial disputes among castes, including claims to recognition of status and access to Vedic ritual. In general the administration of the Brahman peshwas stood firm against upward claims of status made by castes deemed inferior by the elites.

One such case involved claims by the Pancal Daivadnya Sonars (goldsmiths) to Brahmanical status and rights to perform rituals. The opening of the new connection to Bombay provided additional support for the dispute since the claim could be supported by an influential and well-to-do Sonar merchant of the city, Jagannath Shankarshet. When a Brahman panchayat in Poona rejected Sonar claims, William Chaplin reassured the wealthy Bombay citizen that since Bombay and the Deccan were two distinct legal jurisdictions, no Sonar (or more accurately Daivadnya Brahman) claims in Bombay would suffer, but the fact of British control of both coast and Deccan plateau, meant that Chaplin's assurances provided no comfort.[46] In this context, the British sought to remain aloof to caste disputes, but could not ignore potential sources of unrest. Caste here was an administrative problem, whereas for Nana Shankarshet, it was a matter of collective identity in which he and his urban friends were investing their new-found wealth for the benefit of themselves and for their rural cousins beyond the Bombay locality.

From the mouths and pens of Christian missionaries, 'caste' was an unmitigated evil, a sign of the inferiority of the Hindu religion as against Christianity. Following the East India Company charter revisions of 1813 and 1833, missionaries could establish their operations in Company territory and commence the evangelical work of bringing India to Christianity.[47] 'Caste' was generally condemned as illustrative of the cruelty of Hindu society, and most mission tracts criticized the invidious distinctions among social groups, with particular attention given to the claims of Brahmans to prestige, and the degraded status of the lower orders of Hindu society.[48]

John Wilson, a prominent missionary, educator, and scholar, conceded that 'pride of ancestry, of family, of personal position and occupation, and of religious pre-eminence, which is...the grand characteristic of "caste", is not peculiar to India.' The capacity of the high to look with contempt upon the lowly is found throughout the world.[49] But Wilson observed that

it is among the Hindus...that the imagination of natural and positive distinctions in humanity has been brought to the most fearful and pernicious development ever exhibited on the face of the globe...Indian Caste is the condensation of all the pride, jealousy and tyranny of an ancient and predominant people dealing with the tribes which they have subjected, and over which they have ruled, often without the sympathies of a recognized common humanity.[50]

Yet to a significant degree, examination of missionary tracts and newspapers in Bombay suggests that 'caste' mattered far less than issues of the nature of truth, of manifestations of divinity and critiques of the Puranic lore of Hinduism. Brahman arrogance could be condemned, but 'caste' was largely discussed in terms of invidious social distance and distinction. At times it would appear that missionaries were more excited by the prospect of conversion of a single Brahman than of a dozen lower caste persons, but that reflected the perception of the priestly caste as fundamental to the view of how Hinduism was sustained.

Some Indian writers accepted the critique of caste, or at least that critique of Brahman arrogance and inhumanity. Gopalrao Hari Deshmukh, who wrote under the name 'Lokahitavadi', a reformer and government servant, who began a career as an essayist in 1848, saw caste as contributing to the weakness and decline of Indian society, hindering national unity and creating obstacles to tapping the capacity of the majority.[51] He suggested that varna had been displaced by the 'caste system', and that a flexible social order had been rigidified.

Perhaps because missionaries gave more attention to the four-fold varna scheme than trying to understand the complexities of regional caste arrangements, most of the defenders of Hinduism who wrote and spoke against them, similarly did not put emphasis on justification or explanation of 'caste' or *jati*. Morobhat Dandekar's 1831 critique of missionaries, was not drawn to any extensive discussion of caste.[52] Conversion to Christianity was more than a matter of caste, it was, for orthodox Hindus, akin to death and all that that implied. Conversion and caste collided in a controversy of 1843–5 over readmission of a Brahman boy who had lived with Christians, but sought to return to his caste.[53] Caste rules and identity served as a foil for disputes within and among castes of Bombay and Maharashtra.

In the 1850s, Vishnubawa Brahmachari, a newly emerged defender of Vedic dharma, criticized Christian missionaries and Christianity.[54] Vishnubawa, however, in his public talks, debates, books, and tracts, was prepared to propose reforms to strengthen Indian society which were not too dissimilar from those suggested by Lokahitavadi, that is, a recognition of a reconceived varna system as a basis for social renewal.[55] In his *Vedoktadharmaprakash* Vishnubawa offered a characteristically idiosyncratic view of caste, both as a means to preserving dharma and morality, but also as a moral concept not tied to issues of kinship or blood. He sought to curtail in his criticism of various 'immoral' activities, such as the bawdy performances of:

> *tamashas* with the accompaniment should not be presented, and poems describing obscene love between man and woman and songs narrating immoral exploits should not be sung or read; if anyone sings or reads them, or paints obscene pictures or sells or even looks at them or gets them printed, etc., he must be punished by the government.[56]

Beyond the power of the state, Vishnubawa added, such a sinner should be excommunicated by his caste as required by rules of religion, and he should be rendered helpless and ineffective so that morality is protected.[57] Discrimination against Mahars could cease if Mahars would cease to eat the meat of dead cattle. 'Then they will be pure and clean and will be eligible to enter the temple.'[58]

Vishnubawa accepted the idea of a caste system, although his prescriptive writings favoured recapture of a fourfold varna social organization. He suggested that only a small minority of the people should truly be viewed as inferior shudras:

> Those who have the best qualities are called Brahmans. It is their duty to study and know Vedas and become gurus of those who should be taught. The next are with fair qualities and are named Kshatriyas; they may study Vedas but should not become gurus to teach others because their duties are of middling quality; if they are made gurus they will create chaos of opinions. The third are inferior in qualities and are grouped together to be described as Vaishyas. They may read Vedas, but should

not become teachers because their intellects are dull. Now the small number of people left out of these three classes, in whom laziness and stupidity of the most extreme type prevails, cannot think and have no skill to pursue any profession, and to whom knowledge cannot be imparted, should be termed shudras. Vedas should not be taught to them because they are heavy of tongue and cannot recite Vedas. But the general sense of the Vedas should be told them in such a shrewd manner that the sense will sink into their heavy skulls. If this varna system is not strictly maintained, there will be confusion of castes (*varasamskara*) through inter-caste marriages. That would mean that people would not remain in distinct categories: the best, the middling, the inferior and the stupid, and all would become barbarous. Therefore every individual should act or live in his own caste. This is his Vedic religion, but if he strays into other caste's duties or work or action, his natural primordial nature will be sullied. And if he does the duties of a caste not his own, such as a Brahman doing work as a kshatriya, it will lead to a terrible catastrophe. Therefore it is right and proper to act, work and live by one's own caste's division of work, and follow the teachings of the Vedic religion.[59]

Varna could be justified if people were classified according to their true qualities (*gunas*) born of their nature. In a later publication on his prescriptions for an ideal government and state, Vishnubawa invoked the Hindu tradition of the king as maintainer of caste, but with a twist.

men are not all endowed with the same kind and extent of taste, and are consequently not habituated to the performance of the same kind of duties. Hence, the king, after examining the natural bent and qualifications of each of the subjects, whether male or female, on their first being delivered over to his care at the age of five, should bring them up in the subjects for which they may naturally evince the best powers. Now, this would become evident from the turn of thought or actions of boys and girls when they come to the age of five years.[60]

Yet reinstating the varna system was recognized as difficult. So long as studies of *shastra* were neglected and people consumed meat and alcohol, it would be difficult to restore this mode of social organization based on true qualities and actions. But until that time, 'caste should be determined on the basis of family of birth and should be accepted. This is true and based on shastras.'[61]

In this abbreviated survey of usages of 'caste' and deployment by both European and Indian actors, I believe we glimpse the multi-faceted nature of the 'caste' concept as deployed in Bombay over the course of 200 years. Was 'caste' being invented? Was the construction of the descriptions of 'caste' the collaboration of European officers and Brahman informants, imposing a specific unity on the complexities of Indian society? May we consider the Indian contributions to this definitional initiative to be an act of collaboration with or of resistance to, colonial rule?

If by invention, one means introduction of new meanings and applications, the answer may be a qualified yes. However, it is not clear that the impetus for this arose predominantly from colonial agency. Is it possible to settle the matter? I think not. Susan Bayly's comment that the British did not invent caste merits reiteration. As she puts it, the social reality of caste existed beyond the acknowledged influence of the British. Western 'constructions' of caste did have an effect on Indian life 'especially where such views were shaped by contributions from Indians themselves'.[62] David Lorenzen, in his meditation 'Who Invented Hinduism?' quotes a Hindi critic Purushottam Agrawal's quip: 'We Indians may well have been denied the capacity to *solve* our own problems, but are we so incapable that we could not even *create* them on our own?'[63] . As the anthropologist Declan Quigley put it recently: 'If ever there was a Pandora's box, caste is it.'[64]

And here is an example. During my graduate training, I spent some time at the Deccan College in Pune (where I met David Lorenzen). Back in America I had learned that Indian language sources would be more 'authentic' and 'representative' of the indigenous traditions. So, when I discovered a Marathi book *Mumbai Ilakhyantila jati* ('Castes of the Bombay Province') full of information on the castes of Bombay, written by one Shri Kalelkar, I dedicated my waking hours to its translation.[65] Some months later, I met N. Kalelkar, a distinguished professor of linguistics at the Deccan College. In our conversation, he mentioned that his father had written the work on which I had devoted my energies.

'Yes,' he said, 'my father was the PA (Personal Assistant) to Sir Reginald Enthoven. Sir Reginald was so pleased with my father that he permitted him to make a translation into Marathi of the ethnographic volume edited by Enthoven, *Tribes and Castes of Bombay*!'

My feelings at that moment were more readily acknowledged than described.

From this rather short excursion through the local history of 'caste' in and near Bombay over the course of two centuries, it would seem clear that 'caste' had a variety of manifestations and meanings. Colonial rulers tried to use it, as had pre-colonial powers. Members of groups that thought themselves to be 'castes' were using it as well. The term 'invention' itself carries meanings including fabrication, falsehood, fantasy, or fiction. Possibly the imagined powers of caste as invented by British ethnography could be so described. Could all of the circumstances reported above be so described also? It seems to me that it is time we moved on, for so long as we reactively dwell only upon the powerful role of the 'colonial project' we may fail to recognize the autonomy and agency of Indians in their own history.

NOTES AND REFERENCES

1. An earlier version of this paper was presented at the 16th European Conference on Modern South Asia, Edinburgh, 7 September 2000. I wish to acknowledge the useful criticisms of that version by members of the History Research Group of the University of Washington, Department of History.

2. David Lorenzen, 'Who Invented Hinduism?' *Comparative Studies in Society and History*, vol. 41 (October, 1999), pp. 630–59.

3. For example, see Bernard S. Cohn, *Colonialism and its Forms of Knowledge: The British in India* (Princeton: Princeton University Press, 1996); or Nicholas B. Dirks, 'The Invention of Caste: Civil Society in Colonial India', *Social Analysis*, vol. 25 (September 1989) pp. 42–52. Subsequent to the publication of Dirks' first piece on the subject, he began to qualify the idea of caste as 'invented' in later publications, and by the time of his book on the subject, he stated that he did not wish 'to imply that that [caste] was simply invented by the too clever British' (Dirks, 2001, p. 5). As Neil Brimnes, 'Caste between Essentialism and Constructivism', *Nordic Newsletter of Asian Studies*, no. 4 (2002) points out, Dirks 'presents his basic argument in surprisingly uneasy terms: 'I hope to weave an argument far more complicated than that the British invented caste, though in one sense this is precisely what happened'. Perhaps my visitor, like others apparently, absorbed the 'idea' of 'invention' without taking on board Dirks' qualifiers. I did not have to look far for a characteristic misreading of Dirks as I shall soon discuss.

4. Eric Hobsbawm and Terence Ranger (eds), *The Invention of Tradition* (Cambridge: Cambridge University Press, 1983).

5. Ibid., p. 1.

6. Ibid., pp. 4ff.

7. Wilfred M. McClay, 'Tradition, History, and Sequoias', *First Things*, vol. 131, (March 2003), pp. 41–7.

8. Frank F. Conlon, *A Caste in a Changing World: The Chitrapur Saraswat Brahmans, 1700–1935* (Berkeley and Los Angeles: University of California Press, 1977).

9. Brian K. Pennington, *Was Hinduism Invented? Britons, Indians, and the Colonial Construction of Religion* (Oxford: Oxford University Press, 2005), p. 167. Perhaps, in the aftermath of Edward Said's promotion of a critical view of 'orientalism' it should not be surprising that the influence of colonial officials, Christian missionaries, and 'Orientalist' scholars would be viewed as complicit in the emergence of the forms of belief and practice which have been perceived in modern Indian life. The imposition of a new foreign rule, the introduction of new forms of religion—most notably evangelical Protestant Christianity, of European educational practices and ideas, and of new technologies, notably those of print, all contributed to an intensification of change. cf Lorenzen, 'Who Invented', Vasudha Dalmia and Heinrich von Stietencron, eds, *Representing Hinduism: The Construction of Religious Traditions and National Identity* (New Delhi: Sage Publications, 1995), and Gauri Vishwanathan, 'Colonialism and the Construction of Hinduism', in Gavin Flood, ed., *The Blackwell Companion to Hinduism* (Malden, MA: Blackwell, 2003).

10. Edward Said, *Orientalism* (New York: Random House, 1978).

11. Apart from my own 'friendly curiosity' on the matter, I am also influenced by Alain Babadzan, 'Anthropology, Nationalism and 'The Invention of Tradition', *Anthropological Forum*, vol. 10, no. 2 (November 2000), pp. 131–55 [esp. 'Who has read Hobsbawn?' pp. 133–5. and Gaurav Desai, 'The Invention of Invention', *Cultural Critique*, no. 24 (Spring, 1993), pp. 119–42.

12. Nicholas B. Dirks, 'Castes of Mind', *Representations*, vol. 27 (Winter 1992) p. 56.

13. Dirks, 'The Invention of Caste', p. 45.

14. Ibid., pp. 45–6.

15. Narendra Wagle, 'A Dispute between the Pancal Devajna Sonars and the Brahmins of Pune regarding Social Rank and Ritual Privileges: A Case-Study of the British Administration of *Jati* Laws in Maharashtra', in N.K. Wagle, ed., *Images of Maharashtra* (London: Curzon Press, 1980), pp. 131–6.

16. Nicholas B. Dirks, *Castes of Mind: Colonialism and the Making of Modern India* (Princeton: Princeton University Press, 2001), p. 5.

17. Brimnes, 'Caste between Essentialism and Constructivism', pp. 3–4.

18. Michael Hechter, *Sociology*, vol. 590, 'The Politics of Culture: Alien Rule and Its Discontents' University of Washington *Spring 2005* URL: (consulted 15 March 2006) http://www.soc.washington.edu/users/hechter/The%20politics%20of%20culture.pdf

19. Ronald B. Inden, *Imagining India* (Oxford: Blackwell, 1990).

20. Inden, *Imagining India*, p. 58; Bernard S. Cohn, 'The Census, Social Structure and Objectification in South Asia' in Bernard S. Cohn, *An Anthropologist among the Historians* (New Delhi: Oxford University Press, 1987) pp. 224–54; for a general survey of how caste was quantified, see Frank F. Conlon, 'The Census of India as a Source for the Historical Study of Religion and Caste', in N.G. Barrier, ed., *The Census in British India: New Perspectives* (New Delhi: Manohar Publications, 1981), pp. 103–17.

21. For a masterful overview of the caste issue in modern India, see Susan Bayly, *Caste, Society and Politics in India from the Eighteenth Century to the Modern Age: New Cambridge History of India:* IV, 3, (Cambridge: Cambridge University Press, 1999); and for a critique on the same subject see Inden, *Imagining India*, pp. 58ff. The culmination of the Ethnographic Survey of India project in Bombay was a three-volume compendium, compiled under the direction of Sir Reginald E. Enthoven, *The Tribes and Castes of the Bombay Presidency*, 3 vols (Bombay: Government Central Press, 1920–2).

22. Or the Bombay that is Mumbai. The official name was changed in English to Mumbai on 22 November 1995. It had always been Mumbai in Marathi and Gujarati. Here I will utilize the traditional English language usage.

23. Frank F. Conlon, 'Caste Community, and Colonialism: The Elements of Population Recruitment and Urban Rule in British Bombay, 1665–1830', *Journal of Urban History*, vol. 11 (February 1985), pp. 181–208.

24. Kenneth A. Ballhatchet, *Social Policy and Social Change in Western India, 1817–1830* (London: Oxford University Press, 1957), pp. 31–7.

25. William Ward, *A View of the History, Literature, and Mythology of the Hindoos* (London: Kingsbury, Parbury & Allen, 1822).

26. Charles Fawcett, *The English Factories in India*, vol. I (New Series) *The Western Presidency: 1670–1677* (Oxford: Clarendon Press, 1936); Charles Fawcett, *The English Factories in India*, vol. III (New Series) *Bombay, Surat and Malabar Coast* (Oxford: Clarendon Press, 1954).

27. Ashin Das Gupta, *Indian Merchants and the Decline of Surat: c.1700–1750* (Wiesbaden: Steiner Verlag, 1977); Lakshmi Subramanian, *Indigenous Capital and Imperial Expansion: Bombay, Surat and the West Coast* (New Delhi: Oxford University Press, 1996).

28. Conlon, 'Caste, Community and Colonialism'.

29. William Foster, *The English Factories in India: 1668–1669* (Oxford: Oxford University Press, 1927), pp. 239–40.

30. George Forrest, ed., *Selections from the Letters, Despatches and Other State Papers Preserved in the Bombay Secretariat: Home Series*, vol. I (Bombay, Government Central Press, 1887), The distortions, p. 54.

31. The details of the scheme are in Bombay Government Consultation of 24 July 1674 (India Office Records: *Factory Records for Bombay*, I, ff. 66–9); Fawcett, *First Century*; Pherozeshah M. Malabari, Behramji M. Malabari, *Bombay in the Making: being mainly a history of the origin and growth of judicial institutions in the Western Presidency, 1661–1726* (London: T.F. Unwin 1910) p. 125.

32. Charles Fawcett, *First Century of British Justice in India: The first century of British Justice in India; an account of the Court of Judicature at Bombay, established in 1672, and of other Courts of Justice in Madras, Calcutta and Bombay, from 1661 to the latter part of the eighteenth century* (Oxford: Clarendon Press, 1934), p. 135.

33. Dosabhai Framji Karaka, *History of the Parsis* (London: Macmillan, 1884); vol. I, 217ff.; J.J. Modi, *Mumbaini Parsi Pancayatni Tavarikha* (Mumbai: Parsi Panchayat, 1930); cf Christine Dobbin, 'The Parsi Panchayat in Bombay City in the Nineteenth Century', *Modern Asian Studies*, vol. 4 (1970), pp. 149–64; Jesse S. Palsetia, *The Parsis of India: Preservation of Identity in Bombay City* (Leiden: E.J. Brill, 2001).

34. This point about post-1818 linkages with the ex-Maratha *desh* was first suggested to me in a conversation by A. John Roberts in 1971.

35. Hiroshi Fukazawa, 'The State and the Caste System (Jati)', in Hiroshi Fukazawa, *The Medieval Deccan: Peasants, Social Systems and States: Sixteenth to Eighteenth Centuries* (New Delhi: Oxford University Press, 1991), pp. 91–113.

36. Modi, *Mumbaini Parsi Pancayatni,* p. 157.

37. Harry Borradaile, *Reports of Civil Causes adjudged by the Court of Sudur Udalut for the Presidency of Bombay* (Bombay: printed at the Courier Press, 1825) p. 40.

38. Borradaile, *Reports of Civil Causes*, p. 42.

39. Raymond West, *Acts and Regulations of the Legislature in force in the Presidency of Bombay, 1827–1866* (Bombay: Education Society's Press, 1868); L.T. Kikani, *Caste in Courts* (Rajkot: author, 1912).

40. Hiroyuka Kotani, 'The 'Caste Autonomy' Policy in the Nineteenth-Century Bombay Presidency' in Hiroyuka Kotani, *Western India in Historical Transition* (New Delhi: Manohar, 2002), pp. 86–111.

41. Arthur Steele, *The Law and Custom of Hindoo Castes within the Dekhun Provinces subject to the Presidency of Bombay* (London: W.H. Allen, 1868), [1827]; Harry Borradaile, *Gujarat Caste Rules. Published from the Original Answers of the Castes with the sanction of Her Imperial Majesty's High Court of Judicature, Bombay*, edited by Mangaldas Nathoobhoy, 2 vols (Bombay: editor at Nirnaya Sagar Press, 1884–87). Steele's work was published in English, whereas Borradaile's compilation was published in Gujarati, reflecting the intended audience of its editor, in the approximate time of the '*invention*' of caste.

42. Steele, *Law and Custom*, pp. vi–ix. Topics covered included marriage, widowhood, parentage, adoption, guardianship, community of property, partition, inheritance, contracts, and evidence. Ibid., pp. 23–76.

43. Ibid., p. xviii.

44. Ballhatchet, *Social Policy*, p. 268.

45. Fukazawa, 'The State and the Caste System'.

46. Wagle, 'A Dispute', pp. 131–6.

47. G.A. Oddie, *Social Protest in India: British Protestant Missionaries and Social Reforms, 1850–1900* (New Delhi: Manohar, 1979).

48. Duncan Forrester, *Caste and Christianity: Attitudes and Policies on Caste of Anglo-Saxon Protestant Missions in India* (London: Curzon Press, 1979); Geoffrey

Oddie, 'Constructing 'Hinduism': The Impact of the Protestant Missionary Movement on Hindu Self-Understanding', in R.E. Frykenberg (ed.), *Christians and Missionaries in India: Cross Cultural Communication since 1500* (Richmond: Curzon, 2003) pp. 155–82.

49. For early mission activity see George Smith, *The Life of John Wilson*, second edition (London: John Murray, 1879), pp. 32–6.

50. John Wilson, *Indian Caste*, 2 vols (Bombay: Times of India Press, 1877) I, pp. 9–11.

51. Vasant K. Kshire, *Lokahitwadi's Thought: A Critical Study* (Poona: University of Poona, 1977).

52. John Wilson, *An Exposure of the Hindu Religion in Reply to Mora Bhatta Dandekara* (Bombay: American Mission Press, 1832), and John Wilson, *A Second Exposure of the Hindu Religion in reply to Narayana Rao of Satara* (Bombay: n.p., 1834).

53. N.K. Wagle, 'Readmission of Sripat Sesadri: Dharmasastra vs. Public Consensus, Bombay 1843–45', in A.R. Kulkarni and N.K. Wagle, eds, *Region, Nationality and Religion* (Mumbai: Popular Prakashan, 1999), pp. 130–56.

54. Frank F. Conlon, 'The Polemic Process in Nineteenth Century Maharashtra: Vishnubawa Brahmachari and Hindu Revival', in Kenneth W. Jones ed, *Religious Controversies in British India* (Albany: State University of New York Press, 1992), pp. 5–26.

55. Vishnubawa Brahmachari, *Shri Vedoktadharmaprakasha* (Mumbai: Ganpat Krishnaji's Press, [1859]). I wish to acknowledge the assistance of the late Professor M.A. Mehendale, M.G. Desai, M.V. Ghaskadbi, and the late B.R. Sunthankar in understanding Vishnubawa's massive work. They are not responsible for my errors of translation or interpretation.

56. Vishnubawa, *Vedokta*, p. 930. *Tamashas* were a form of musical dramatic entertainment often involving risqué or lewd language and gesture.

57. Ibid., p. 934.

58. Ibid., p. 104.

59. Ibid., pp. 259–60.

60. Vishnubawa Brahmachari, *Sukhadaayak Raajyaprakara Nii Nibandha* (Mumbai: Indu Prakash Printing Press, 1867), p. 17; Vishnubawa Brahmachari, *An Essay in Marathi on Beneficent Government*, translated by Captain A. Phelps. (Bombay: Oriental Press, 1869), p. 16; *Bombay Guardian*, vol. 13 (n.s.), 18 May 1867, p. 90.

61. Vishnubawa, *Vedokta*, p. 323.

62. Bayly, *Caste, Society*, p. 97. Intersections of judicial decisions and caste or community identities may also be discovered among Muslim groups, see J.C. Masselos, 'The Khojas of Bombay: The Defining of Formal Membership Criteria During the Nineteenth Century', in Imtiaz Ahmad (ed.), *Caste and Social Stratification among the Muslims* (New Delhi: Manohar, 1973), pp. 1–20; 1978 reprint edition, pp. 97–116.

63. Lorenzen, 'Who Invented Hinduism?', p. 659; see also, David Lorenzen, *Who Invented Hinduism? Essays on Religion in History* (New Delhi: Yoda Press, 2006), p. 35.

64. Declan Quigley, *The Interpretation of Caste* (Oxford: Clarendon Press, 1993) p. 158. Quigley here refers to the wide number of variables which appear to provide the underpinnings of caste. (Perhaps some day that noted Hindu revisionist, P.N. Oak, will claim that 'Pandora's Box' was really the 'Pandava's Box.')

65. Govinda Mangesha Kalelkar, *Mumbai Ilakhyantila jati* (Mumbai: A.A. Moramkar, 1928).

11. SANĀTANA DHARMA AS THE TWENTIETH CENTURY BEGAN[1]

TWO TEXTBOOKS, TWO LANGUAGES

John Stratton Hawley

In his powerful essay 'Who Invented Hinduism?' David Lorenzen argued that no clear line of demarcation could be drawn between understandings of Hinduism that emerged in the British colonial period and those that were in place earlier, even if the latter were yet to be designated by the name 'Hinduism'. Yet at the same time he drew a clear line of demarcation of his own. He distinguished between two opposing camps: scholars whose view of this subject made them 'constructionists' and those who had rejected such a view. By constructionists he meant those who would argue that 'Hinduism was constructed, invented, or imagined by British scholars and colonial administrators in the nineteenth century and did not exist, in any meaningful sense, before this date.'[2] Somewhat to my discomfort, David placed me in the first group on the basis of an essay I had written called 'Naming Hinduism'—actually, 'The European Naming of Hinduism' before the editors of the *Wilson Quarterly* shortened it without my knowledge.[3] David located himself, of course, in the anti-constructionist camp. This was not the first or the last time that David found pleasure in a scholarly disagreement, and we all owe him a great debt for his willingness to take sides so that the truth would emerge more clearly.

The thoughts that follow may well be read as an attempt to continue this argument, but on somewhat different terrain. At issue this time is not Hinduism but Sanātana Dharma, one of its closest kin. I can well imagine David's reading me as again putting forward a constructionist claim, still blinded by the brilliance of the nineteenth century. If so, I must plead guilty, but with the important caveat that only God, as they say, is able to construct something out of nothing. Anyone else's edifices require pre-existing models, plans, and bricks.

* * *

In *Modern Religious Movements in India,* published in 1915, J.N. Farquhar, who was the Literary Secretary of the National Council of Young Men's Christian Associations, India and Ceylon, takes aim at one of his least favourite competitors. This was the Bharat Dharma Mahamandal, an organization founded in Hardwar in 1887 to coordinate the work of the various Sanātana Dharma Sabhās that had been established across north India to defend *varṇāśramadharma* from critics both outside and in.[4] Farquhar was little impressed with any aspect of that purpose, but what especially galled him was the way it was presented in the first issue of the *Mahamandal Magazine.* He quotes the following passage:

> But the Sanatan Dharma is not marked by any such spirit of narrowness or exclusiveness. It is not a particular *creed* promising salvation to its followers alone; it is the universal Dharma for all mankind.[5]

Farquhar objects that it is an 'extraordinary spectacle' to hear such talk from an organization 'created for the express purpose of defending the religion which in all its own sacred books is expressly restricted to the four highest castes.' For Farquhar, this 'Hindu system' could not rightly claim any sort of universality.[6] For one thing, as he made plain in his most widely read work, *The Crown of Hinduism*, he was reserving that honour—that crown—for a certain carpenter of Nazareth.

Yet Farquhar was in many ways an astute observer. He noted that 'the foundation of such an organization [was] in itself almost a portent,' since 'Hinduism has never in the course of its whole history been a single organization.' Being a sociologist at heart, its no wonder he put things in these terms. It was his way of plunging the knife into the eternality of 'the Sanātana Dharma, the Eternal Religion, as they call it.'[7] Though he did not wish to deny Hinduism a long history of 'natural growth', he thought it was only 'the pressure of the modern spirit and of Christian criticism to-day' that had produced this Sanātanist claim to eternality.[8] In broad outlines, many of us would share his assessment. However long-lived the Hindu tradition may be, it became 'eternal'—and eternal in a way that would last—only toward the end of the nineteenth century. That was the moment in time when it became Sanātana Dharma.

But how? Farquhar may have overemphasized the impact of 'Christian criticism to-day'. The indigenous challenge posed by the Arya Samaj and other Hindu reformist groups was also a major factor. Perhaps these were expressions of what Farquhar called 'the pressure of the modern spirit.' In that light, it was not so much the ancient origins of Sanātana Dharma that mattered—that turf the Arya Samajis claimed even more eagerly—but its uninterrupted persistence through time. That persistence, that continuity of practice, became a central aspect of Sanātanist ideology. Who can forget Śraddhā Rām Pillaurī's riposte to Kanhayā Lāl Alakhdhārī as he attempted to found a Nīti Prakāś Sabhā (Society for Moral Enlightenment) in Ludhiana in the early 1870s:

Mr Alakhdhari who is against Shruti and Smirti and who does not keep a knot on his head and does not wear the sacred thread which is essential for the Vaishya and who hates to have cow dung paint in the kitchen and uses a dining table and calls *Bhōjan* as *Khānā* and thinks all the caste system is useless, then how is it possible that Hinduism can spread and prosper through his efforts?[9]

Here its the 'livedness' of dharma that makes it count as *sanātan,* but it was a livedness that had to be not only sustained but (as we are so fond of saying these days) produced. And one of the most important realms in which it was produced—or reproduced, if you follow the diction of Sanātanists themselves—was the classroom, especially when that classroom expanded its walls through public oratory and print. In this essay I want to visit two Sanatanist classrooms, or rather, the texts they produced. One is the *pāṭhśālā* operated by Pandit Gurusahāy in Shahjahanpur, between Bareilly and Lucknow. The textbook Gurusahāy produced is called *Sanātanadharmamārttaṇḍa* ('The Sun of Perennial Religion'); it was published in Banaras in *vikram saṃvat* 1934, that is, AD 1878.[10] The other classroom is the one established by Annie Besant and her Theosophical colleagues when they created the Central Hindu College and Collegiate School at Banaras in 1898. The basic text that they produced to structure their work was called

Sanatana Dharma: An Elementary Textbook of Hindu Religion and Ethics, first published by the College itself in February, 1903.

These classrooms and their associated texts are quite different from one another—to begin with, they operate in different languages—but they share an explicit devotion to the cause of Sanātana Dharma. Neither work, neither classroom produced the eternality of Sanātana Dharma single-handedly, but if we think about the terrain they marked out together, we may be in a good position to ask how we came to inherit the sort of Sanātana Dharma that is now regularly offered as the best Indic-language translation for 'Hinduism'. I do not mean to be contentious by putting matters that way, and I certainly don't want to repeat Farquhar's mistake. I don't want to assume that what happened in the metropole, in English, in the developing discourse of comparative religion, or under the implicit patronage of the British colonial state determined what Sanātana Dharma was going to mean. It's inescapable that Sanātana Dharma as a named entity and specific historical force emerged on the British watch, but it didn't just happen in one way. That's the point in looking at these two rather different texts individually.

Let us begin with the one that is better known if still, nonetheless, largely forgotten. This is the *Sanatana Dharma* of Annie Besant. The cover and table of contents of the 1910 edition are reproduced here (Figs 11.1 and 11.2), but as I say, the book originally appeared in 1903. Annie Besant's name cannot be seen on the title page, but in his preface to a subsequent edition, her collaborator Bhagavan Das tells us that it was indeed she, the President of the College and the main force behind its creation, who drafted the text. This happened in Srinagar from the middle of May to the middle of July 1901 when Mrs Besant was a guest of Maharaja Pratap Singh of Kashmir, and it happened in English.[11] As the preface explains, she was working with 'Saṃskṛt texts, English translations, and other material' supplied by Indian members of the subcommittee established to produce this central curricular text, together with 'other learned scholars'.[12] The subcommittee believed they were providing the basis for 'systematic instruction...in those principles of Hinduism ("Sanātana-dharma") which may be regarded as common to all its many sects.'[13] The book sold 130,000 copies in the first four years of its life, generated separate versions that were simpler and more advanced, was translated into

Benares. Central Hindu college

SANĀTANA ḌHARMA

AN ELEMENTARY TEXT-BOOK

OF

HINDU RELIGION AND ETHICS

Twentieth Thousand

PUBLISHED BY THE BOARD OF TRUSTEES
CENTRAL HINDU COLLEGE,
BENARES

1910

Price Ans. 12, boards. Re. 1, cloth. Postage 1½ Anna.

Fig. 11.1: Annie Besant *et al.*, *Sanatana Dharma: An Elementary Text-book of Hindu Religion and Ethics* (Benares: Central Hindu College, 1910 [originally 1903]), title page

CONTENTS.

PART I.

Fig. 11.2: Besant *et al.*, *Sanatana Dharma*, Table of Contents

several Indian languages,[14] and has stayed in print for more than a century. To my knowledge, it is the first textbook on Hinduism to have been produced in English for classroom use on the part of Hindus themselves.[15] One could even consider the hypothesis that it was the first such book in any language, but more of that later.[16] For now, let me just express wonderment at the fact that this book has not been better remembered as the revolutionary text it was.

Consider its organization. The first and most obvious fact is that, contrary to what Śraddhā Rām might have urged, its first priority (part I) is doctrine or theology, not practice, which follows in part II. Such a sequence would have been standard in British texts geared to the instruction of young Christians: first belief, then practice.[17] The book then proceeds to a third area, ethics (part III), enacting a distinction that was enshrined in its title and was also found commonly in other works of the time, for example, in the *Encyclopaedia of Religion and Ethics* edited by James Hastings and published toward the end of the decade in question (1908). So for all the Sanskrit texts and glosses that she had at hand, not to mention her Indian collaborators, it seems that Annie Besant framed her task substantially from a European point of view.

One sees this not just in the book's overall organization but in the way its author/editor structures and sequences the chapters she designs. She begins with the unity of God—'The One Existence', she calls it—and uses that as a way to approach the issue of 'The Many'. From the battlefront of polytheism and idolatry, then, she proceeds to the next set of issues that had captured the European imagination when confronted with Indian religion: metempsychosis and karma. Only when all that has been managed does she turn to sacrifice, which is a key element in the dharma that she herself was arguably most interested in propounding. As she says in the first paragraph of chapter 5, the kind of sacrifice about which she is concerned is not 'the idea of 'offering sacrifices' [which] is very familiar in India.' Rather, 'a student needs to understand the principle which underlies all sacrifices, so that he may realize that everyone should sacrifice *himself* to the good of others....'[18] This is what it means to be a *jīva,* she says—to recognize one's parentage, one's

identity in nature with Īshvara....As a man lives in such thoughts of his non-separatedness from younger Selves, he begins to feel more really his non-separateness from elder Selves and from the Universal Parent, Īshvara. Slowly he realizes that his true function is to live for others, as Īshvara lives for all....Then every action becomes a sacrifice to Īshvara, and actions no longer bind him. Thus the law of sacrifice becomes also the law of liberation.[19]

Mrs Besant does refer to the Puruṣa Sūkta in introducing all this, and she includes a story from the Mahābhārata, but the text from which she quotes constantly, especially in this crucial first part of the book, is the Bhagavad Gītā.[20]

Does this sound familiar? Two decades later a group of Marwari Agrawals living in Gorakhpur would establish a press they intended to be 'the mouth of Sanātana Dharma' and would take the Bhagavad Gītā as its emblem: Gita Press. One can trace the lineage back to the Central Hindu College through one of their closest associates, Pandit Madanmohan Malviya, who succeeded in transforming the Hindu College into the core of his new Banaras Hindu University. Bhagavan Das, who was no great friend of Malviya, was also an Agrawal. So this gathering Gītā-ism with its *baniya* context is definitely worth our notice.[21]

But despite Mrs Besant's preference for the Gītā, she was careful to inaugurate her textbook by arguing that its authority rested on a wider foundation. In her very first sentence she explains that 'Sanatana Dharma means the Eternal Religion, the Ancient Law, and it is based on the Vedas....'[22] She then parses out the various 'portions' of the Veda—*mantra, brāhmaṇa, upaniṣad,* and *upaveda* or *tantram* (glossing the last as 'science,' what else?)—and she goes on to explain about the 'Smriti or Dharma Shāstra' and the Purāṇas and Itihāsa. She depicts Śruti as the foundation of Sanātana Dharma, Smṛti as its walls, and the Purāṇas and Itihāsa as its buttress-like supports.[23] The whole edifice comprises 'the Religion that was given to the first nation of the Aryan race', who settled Āryavarta. It is 'the oldest of living Religions...but unless you grow up worthy of it,' she cautions, 'this great and holy Religion will do you no good.'[24] She does not mention the Bhagavad Gītā in the elaborate initial list of texts that render Sanātana Dharma secure, but especially in the first part of the book it emerges time and again as the *sine qua non*, evidently the best resource for a student 'growing up worthy' of the Aryan heritage. References to Manu increase in the second part, and the epics become very important in the third.

But before we become swamped in the Sanātana Dharma that was to be produced in the Central Hindu College, let us turn to the *Sanātanadharmamārttaṇḍa* of Pandit Gurusahāy and his *pāṭhśālā* in Shahjahanpur (Fig. 11.3).[25] Here we enter quite a different world—a world not just in Hindi, but of it. In his preface Gurusahāy explains that his whole purpose is to make available to Aryans[26] who can no longer read in Sanskrit the content of their own religious heritage, their own dharma. Like Mrs Besant, his sources will be the Veda and Smṛti at large, and he too regards one text more than any other as his principal authority. This time it is not the Gītā but the *dharmaśāstra* of Manu. Every chapter of Annie Besant's *Sanatana Dharma* concludes with a string of Sanskrit verses translated into English; these round out the expository text and were presumably intended to be committed to memory by students using the book. Gurusahāy's text shows us the milieu in which this sort of procedure arose. Not only does he give us a roster of such verses, but he thoroughly interleafs exposition and quotation. Or rather, quotation and exposition: text creates the pretext for comment, and not the other way around.

From the very outset, Gurusahāy quotes a Sanskrit verse, translates it into the *deś bhāṣā*, and proceeds to unpack it further if he wishes. After he gives the proper citation for the original verse (*Manusmṛti* 2.6.10 and so forth), he assigns it an additional number, indicating its location in the gathering pile of verses he assembles so as to comprise any given chapter of his *Mārttaṇḍa.* What we get is a sort of thematic commentarial text—a *nibandha,* you could say—and with the single exception of the invocatory verse with which it begins, it is a nibandha on Manu. Pandit Gurusahāy does occasionally quote verses from other texts—including the Gītā, by the way—but when he does so, he stops short of according these ancillary *ślokas* a position in his sequential account. His real text is Manu. It is Manu who authorizes his commentary.[27]

When he has finished this exposition, all twelve chapters of it, Gurusahāy shows us in another way that the world in which he is operating is measurably different from that of Annie Besant. This is a printed text, to be sure, but the manuscript on which it is based remains a manuscript nonetheless. When he comes to the end of his work, Pandit Gurusahāy supplies a colophon, just as if he were writing a manuscript to be archived as a handwritten document. In

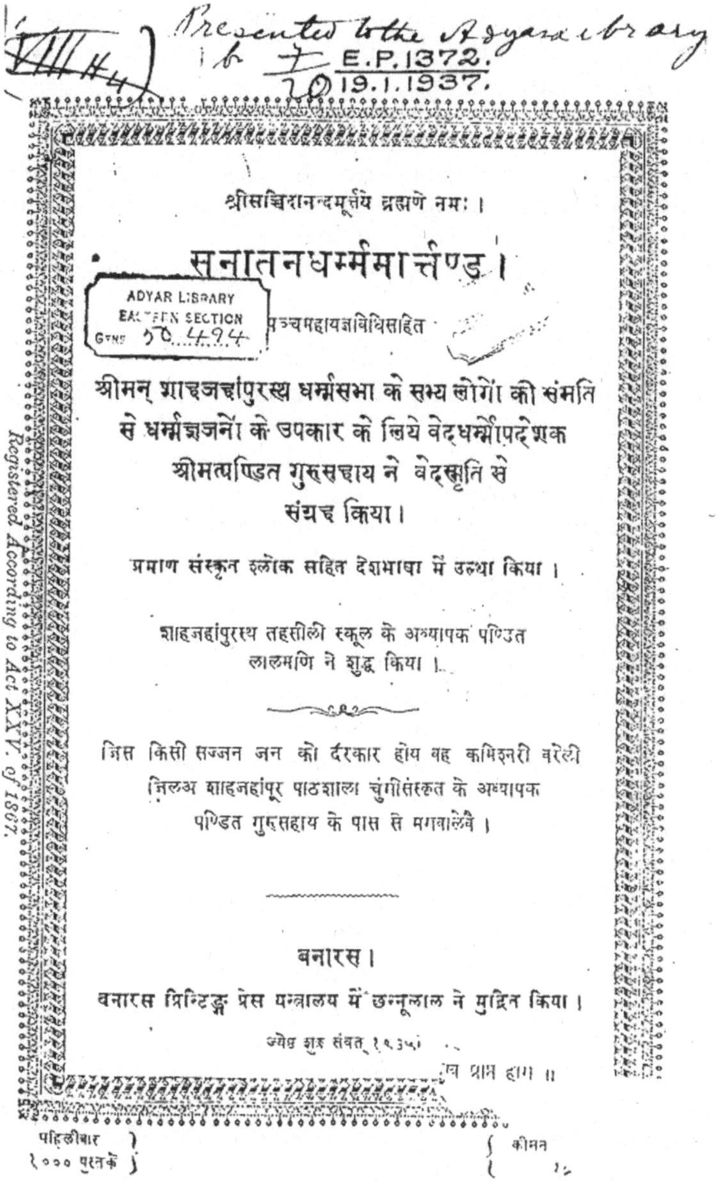

श्रीसच्चिदानन्दमूर्त्तये ब्रह्मणे नमः ।

सनातनधर्म्ममार्त्तण्ड ।

पञ्चमहायज्ञविधिसहित

श्रीमन् शाहजहांपुरस्थ धर्म्मसभा के सभ्य लोगों की संमति से धर्म्मज्ञजनों के उपकार के लिये वेदधर्म्मोपदेशक श्रीमत्पण्डित गुरुसहाय ने वेदस्मृति से संग्रह किया ।

प्रमाण संस्कृत श्लोक सहित देशभाषा में उल्था किया ।

शाहजहांपुरस्थ तहसीली स्कूल के अध्यापक पण्डित लालमणि ने शुद्ध किया ।

जिस किसी सज्जन जन को दरकार होय वह कमिश्नरी बरेली जिलअ शाहजहांपूर पाठशाला चुंगीसंस्कृत के अध्यापक पण्डित गुरुसहाय के पास से मगवालेवै ।

बनारस ।

बनारस प्रिन्टिङ्ग प्रेस यन्त्रालय में छन्नूलाल ने मुद्रित किया ।

ज्येष्ठ शुक्ल संवत् १९३५

त्व प्राप्त हुआ ॥

Registered According to Act XXV. of 1867.

पहिलीबार १००० पुस्तकें

कीमत ।)

Fig. 11.3: Pundit Gurusahāy, *Sanātanadharmamārttaṇḍa* (Benares: Channūlāl, V.S. 1934 [AD 1878], title page

his case, given his own sense of status and mission, this demands not one colophon but two—first in Sanskrit and then in Hindi. Here is the latter:

On Friday, the first day in the waxing half of the month of Pauṣ, in the year 1934, this book was completed. This book was drawn together by Agnihotra Pandit Gurusahāy, a resident of Shahjahanpur. Thus concludes the twelfth chapter of 'The Sun of Sanatana Dharma', which describes the views of people who distort the Veda. The book is at an end.

The conventions of the British classroom and its literature were evidently second nature to Annie Besant—we are told she was able to draft her book within the space of two months—and the same was true for the pāṭhśālā world of Pandit Gurusahāy. That was entirely his medium, and there he stayed. We don't know to what extent he himself was involved in the project of bringing it into print. The title page confers that honour on one Channālāl at the Banaras Printing Press, who was presumably either the head of the factory or the patron responsible for financing the project. We are also told that the text had been passed under the nose of Pandit Lālmaṇi, *adhyāpak* in the Tahsīlī School ('school', not pāṭhśālā) of Shahjahanpur before it went to print. People interested in obtaining copies were told to order them from Pandit Gurusahāy, so he cannot have been entirely removed from the printing process, but it is striking that the book he produced was of its own idiom, nonetheless. When a series of mantric verses were added at the end—*sandhyā, agnihotra, tarpaṇa, valivaiśyaveda,* and rites appropriate to guests, women, and *śūdras*—they were simply allowed to follow the colophon, as so often happens in manuscripts. If pages remain blank, the book can grow to fill them out.

But now, what is this Sanātana Dharma that Pandit Gurusahāy expounds? A copy of the book's contents (Fig. 11.4) as they appear in the table of contents *(sūcīpatram)* that follows its preface, but readers may still find it a little hard to get their bearings. This is because while Pandit Gurusahāy's chapters are enumerated there, they are accompanied by subheadings and appendices as well. Therefore I offer a supplementary table of contents—in English—in which are listed the chapters as he marks and names them in the text itself (Fig. 11.5). It reveals quite clearly that Sanātana Dharma as conceived by Pandit

अथ सनातनधर्म्ममार्त्तण्डस्य सूचीपत्रम्।

सूचीपत्रम्	पृष्ठ	पंक्ति	सूचीपत्रम्	पृष्ठ	पंक्ति
धर्म्म का उपदेश	१	१	गुरु शुश्रूषा	९३	२१
धर्म्म के दश लक्षण	४	६	ब्रह्मचारी का धर्म्म	९६	१७
सत्य का धारण	४	२०	ब्राह्मण का गृहस्थ धर्म्म	१०४	४
धृति अर्थात् सन्तोष का करना	६	२५	पंचमहायज्ञ और श्राद्ध का विधान	१०८	१७
क्षमा का माहात्म्य	८	१८	महादेव और शालिग्राम पूजा विधि	१२३	६
दम का लक्षण	१०	१३			
अस्तेय अर्थात् न्याय से जीविका करनी	१२	२६	प्रतिमा पूजा विधान	१२५	१७
			क्षत्री का धर्म्म	१३९	१५
शौच वा भक्ष्याभक्ष्यज्ञान	१९	२०	वैश्य का धर्म्म	१४५	७
इन्द्रियनिग्रह	३१	२६	शूद्र का धर्म्म	१५०	६
धी का वर्णन	४१	१	स्त्री का धर्म्म	१५५	२०
विद्या का माहात्म्य	४९	३	जन्ममरण शौच विधि	१६७	१७
अक्रोध का फल	५७	२०	पाप से छूटने की विधि	१७०	४
दानधर्म्म	६८	१	तीर्थों की उत्पत्ति	१७३	१८
दानपात्र का लक्षण	६९	१	वाणप्रस्थधर्म्म	१७६	८
अन्नादि वस्तु दान फल	७०	१	संन्यासधर्म्म	१७७	१०
दान के तीन प्रकार	७२	१	वेदविरुद्धधर्म्म	१८५	१५
इष्ट पूर्त्त का विधान	७४	४	सन्ध्या	१९७	१
अतिथिसत्कार	७५	६	अग्निहोत्र	२०१	२१
सृष्टि की उत्पति	८२	१८	तर्पण	२०४	१९
गर्भाधानादिदेह संस्कार विधि	८४	२२	बलिवैश्वदेव	२०७	१७
			अतिथि पूजन	२१०	१
गायत्री का माहात्म्य	८७	७	स्त्री शूद्रों की संख्या	२१०	१७
ब्रह्मचारी का सन्ध्यादि कर्म्म	९०	६			

Fig. 11.4: Gurusahāy, *Sanātanadharmamārttaṇḍa*, Table of Contents

Sanātanadharmamārttaṇḍa – Alternate Table of Contents

Chapter 1.	An exposition of universally shared (*sāmānya*) dharma	1
Chapter 2.	Gift-giving (*dāna*)	68
Chapter 3.	A description of the student's life as expressed in Veda and Smṛti	82
Chapter 4.	The description of a Brahmin's life	104
Chapter 5.	The dharma of a Kṣatriya	139
Chapter 6.	The dharma of a Vaiśya	145
Chapter 7.	The dharma of a Śūdra	150
Chapter 8.	The dharma of a woman, as determined by the fourfold *(cāturvarṇya)* dharma	155
Chapter 9.	Cleansing impurities and sins *(āśaucapāpaśuddhi)*	167
Chapter 10.	An examination of the dharma of one who has departed for the wilderness *(vānaprastha)*	176
Chapter 11.	The dharma of a renouncer *(sannyāsadharma)* as ordained in Śruti and Smṛti	177
Chapter 12.	A description of the views of people who distort the Veda *(vedaviruddhapākhaṇḍamata)*	185

Fig. 11.5: Alternate Table of Contents for Gurusahāy, *Sanātanadharmamārttaṇḍa*, based on the summary information provided at the end of each chapter

Gurusahāy is structured around the core of *varṇa* and *āśrama*, the former being framed by the latter. One sees the names of the four varṇas in chapters 4–7, and Chapter 8 tells how the order of womanhood relates to all that. (Is it accidental that a chapter on pollution follows directly afterward?) And all this is cross-referenced to the stages of life: the student in Chapter 3, the householder in all the chapters we've just mentioned, and the person getting ready to renounce society, in Chapters 10 and 11.

Yet as far as the number of pages is concerned, that is only half the book. Most of the rest—the bulk comprising Chapters 1 and 2—is concerned with expositing a *sāmānya* or *sādhāraṇ dharma*, the commonly shared dharma that Gurusahāy regards as comprising the most basic elements required for an elaboration of *sanātan dharma* (1, 67).[28] Its kernel and structure he finds in the *daśa lakṣaṇa* expounded in *Manusmṛti* 6.92. This is 'the ten-point law', to adopt Patrick Olivelle's translation:

Resolve, forbearance, self-control, refraining from theft, performing purifications, mastering the organs, understanding, learning, truthfulness, and suppressing anger: these are the ten points of the Law.[29]

Efficacious and perennial as these qualities may be, what's really interesting is why Pandit Gurusahāy felt they needed so desperately to be rearticulated in the late 1870s. This he tells us bluntly in his preface. He observes that the English teach the New Testament in the very process of teaching their children the alphabet, and that Muslims do the same with the Qur'an.[30] So the kids get it no matter whether they specialize in such matters or not. He goes on:

These are the people who have called the Aryas Hindus and who say they are slaves *(gulām)*. It's a terrible shame that up until now Aryans have forgotten their dharma and name and don't read Veda and Smṛti. All Aryans should teach their children the alphabet and this *Sanātanadharmamārttaṇḍa*. That way, before long, they will know their own dharma and won't do anything against it or believe what the perverts *[pākhaṇḍī]* say. This book follows the actual Dharma, Veda, and Smṛti of the four castes and all humans. People who know dharma will be pleased to see this book, and the perverts, if they'll really examine their consciences, will understand that I have put it into common speech from only the highest motives.[31]

Who are these perverts, these *pākhaṇḍīs,* who are so much on Pandit Gurusahāy's mind? The list he gives in his twelfth and concluding chapter spells it out in torrential detail: anyone who ever started a sect or lineage of his own, from Rāmānuja right down to the present—and by the way, he reminds us, that includes a lot of people who came from the contemptible echelons of society.[32] These are the people who broke apart the golden unity of the Vedic age, and it is tragic because only the boat of the Veda is capable of fording life's raging sea. For Śraddhā Rām it was the Brahmo Samājīs and the Ārya Samājīs and their imitators who posed such a palpable threat; for Pandit Gurusahāy it was anyone who ever dared challenge pure Vaidik ways. Thank goodness for the enlightened policies of Empress Victoria and the other rulers who have contributed to the increase of proper education![33] If those perverts had been able to get in the way, they would not have allowed funds to be donated in support of pāṭhśālās such as his.[34]

So here we have a real traditionalist, a Sanātanist Farquhar would surely have disliked—someone dedicated to, as he said, 'full defense of the old religions.'[35] And now we must ask: was his the Sanātanism that became eternal as decade led to decade, or was it Mrs Besant's variety instead?

If in looking forward we are thinking of the sort of Sanātana Dharma that is conscious of its position on the stage of 'world religions', is accustomed to being known to outsiders as Hinduism but recognizes an interior landscape that is somewhat different, and represents itself without protest in English, then there is no question which of these two *Sanātana Dharmas* we must choose—Annie Besant's.[36] Despite the resistance with which it was greeted on the part of most Banarsi pandits at the time, Mrs Besant's programme was a hardy hybrid better suited to much of the weather that lay ahead than that of Pandit Gurusahāy. True, certain of its aspects did not survive in widening Sanātanist discourse. Her final chapters explaining how 'virtues and vices' should be calibrated in relation to superiors, equals, and inferiors, for example, tended to fall by the wayside.

And consider what happens when Mrs Besant comes to the doctrine of God in her *Sanātana-Dharma Catechism,* first published in 1902. She asks the children,

> *Q.* 10. What are we taught to believe about the Supreme Being, God?'
> *A.* That there is one Boundless Eternal Being, 'One only without a second'....
> *Q.* 11. Can we know that Eternal Being?
> *A.* Only when revealed as Īśvara, the Lord, the loving Father of all the worlds, and of all the creatures who live in them.

This sounds inordinately Christian,[37] and later English-language manuals of Sanātana Dharma tended to abandon that idiom, without necessarily abandoning the catechetic format in which it is embedded. Many readers will have seen Ed Viswanathan's *Daddy, Am I a Hindu?*, first published by Bharatiya Vidya Bhavan in 1988 and now, hundreds of thousands of copies later, simply called *Am I a Hindu?*[38] This book was written as a dialogue between a father and his fourteen-year-old son, living in New Orleans. The catechetical form remains, but its Christian baggage—even its responsibility to convey a 'religion'—is self-consciously shed. We do not find in Mrs Besant the doctrine that takes front billing in Viswanathan's book: 'Hinduism is not a religion, but a way of Life [sic].'[39]

So it's not that every segment of the Central Hindu College discourse survives. But it is surprising how much does, how well the programme persists. In *Am I a Hindu?* we find an immediate prioritizing of the Gītā, just as back in Banaras, and we find an even more immediate insistence on Sanātana Dharma as 'the religion forever' or as Viswanathan later says, 'Righteousness Forever...That which has no beginning or end.'[40] As for Mrs Besant's up-front monotheism, if we look at Sitansu Chakravarti's much read *Hinduism, A Way of Life*, written in Toronto and published in Delhi in 1991, the first chapter deals with 'God: The One in Many'. This is even before he gets to the paragraph on Sanātana Dharma as such. The first sentence of the book proper reads, 'Hinduism is a monotheistic religion which believes that God manifests Himself or Herself in several forms.'[41] Annie Besant's exposition of the One expanding to the Many—Puruṣa and Prakṛti, Brahmāṇḍa and Brahmā, Brahmā and the *devas*, Vishnu and his avatars—is not far in the background, though Chakravarti prefers a more Smārta approach. I was pleased to see that an early reader of the copy of *Sanatana Dharma* I checked out of the Burke Library at Union Theological Seminary had come to the passage about Brahmā emanating the devas from his mind and had scribbled in the margin: 'like angels'.[42]

There is, however, one important aspect of latter-day Sanātanist teaching that can be found more easily in Pandit Gurusahāy's text than in Mrs Besant's. This is the affirmation that Sanātana Dharma is universal—the very thing that drove Farquhar up a tree. Of course, the discourse is rather different nowadays. Take, for example, the book called *Hindu Dharma,* published by Bansi Pandit in 1996 from B & V Enterprises of Glen Ellyn, Illinois and now adopted for distribution by the Hindu Temple Society of North America, that is, the great Ganesha temple in Flushing, Queens, New York. Bansi Pandit tells us in his first paragraph that 'The original name of Hindu Dharma is *Sanātana Dharma,* or "universal religion"'[43] (7) and goes on to expound the theme as follows:

> All religions have some universal aspects, but all aspects of Hindu Dharma are universal. The reason for this difference is that Hindu Dharma does not derive its authority from the teaching of a single person or book. The spiritual experiences of numerous sages and saints of yore form the basic foundation of Hindu Dharma.[44]

This sounds like Swami Vivekananda, but the roots go back farther—to people like Pandit Gurusahāy and the sorts of institutions where they laboured. Bansi Pandit tells us in that first paragraph that 'Hindu Dharma is also known as *Vaidika Dharma,* meaning 'religion of the Vedas,' the ancient Hindu scriptures.' Its authenticity depends on its authorlessness, the fact that it is collective. As Gurusahāy says (following *Manusmṛti* 4.238), it's like ants building up an anthill.[45] There is nothing he so dislikes as those Rāmānujas and Rāmānandas and Lakṣmaṇ Bhaṭṭs and Vallabhas and Rādhāramaṇvāllās and Pīpās and Nānaks—all those people who have tried to scoop out some segment of the anthill, cart it off, and 'circulate it under their own name' (*apne apne nām jārī kiye haiṅ*).[46] He uses a word that also connotes adultery. These are the 'perverts' he cannot stand—pākhaṇḍīs, 'hypocrites' who deserve that title because they misrepresent the collective, universal, ageless nature of the dharma they propose to teach. He, by contrast, claims the Veda as his basis (*ved hī dharm kā mūl haiṅ*); there's nothing new (*navīn*) in what he propounds.[47] And he begins his exposition with a sense of the whole—the *sādhāraṇ dharma* that is most sanātana—before he sketches out its various parts.

Later Sanatanists of many stripes would have to reconcile this universalist vision with an expanded religious universe. Bansi Pandit is one example, but there are many others. Among the most influential of these is doubtless the Shankaracharya of Kancipuram, who in 1932–3 delivered a series of lectures in Madras (Chennai) that were later translated into English as *The Sanātana Dharma, or the Hindu View of Life*. He grants that the term Sanātana Dharma has come into its current usage only recently and 'cannot be said to be the strictly traditional name of our religion'. That, rather, is 'the Dharma', and the fact that it is otherwise nameless is the seal of its authenticity or, as he says, its grandeur.[48] It points to its universality, as well. The Shankaracharya adduces a series of testimonies from around the world to show that the religion of 'our forefathers' was once practiced globally. He says, for example, that

> ...one of the charges against Jesus which made the Jews crucify him was that Jesus drank water from a well intended for the lower classes. Does this not imply the existence of a caste system even before Jesus's time?[49]

This fully articulated sense of the universal, anchored in primordial time, is well ahead of anything Pandit Gurusahāy found it necessary to articulate. He knows there are others out there—Muslims and Christians with their independent systems of dharmic formation—but he doesn't feel the need to integrate them into his text, his world. They lurk there in the preface, observed but not observing. Instead, when he looks to the encompassing body, the great universe, he finds it in the deś—a nation and land that both precedes and supersedes the nation-state. He sees his task as reconstructing the wholeness of a whole that has been destroyed from within.

Two decades later, the Trustees of the Central Hindu College—read Annie Besant—would say in the preface to *their* Sanātana Dharma textbook that they did not want to be misunderstood. They too were worried about sectarianism, but it seems they saw Sanātanism itself as potentially bearing that stigma. They said:

The name of this series, *Sanātana Dharma*, was chosen after full discussion, as best representing the idea of the fundamental truths presented. It has become somewhat of a sectarian name in some parts of India, but it is here taken only as meaning the eternal religion.[50]

They wanted to represent 'the religious and ethical instruction [that] all Hindus can accept', but they were aware that in doing so, they were featuring 'the special teachings which mark out Hinduism from other religions.'[51] Or to put it in a political frame, they aimed to produce 'citizens of their Motherland and of the Empire.'[52] The Motherland, for all its glory, had become a part of a larger whole: that's how Annie Besant got there in the first place.[53]

For Gurusahāy, this Empire could be a useful frame; it could be a source of patronage. But the *sāmānyatā* of his Sanātana Dharma—its universality, its eternality—really only concerned the Motherland. He didn't need to respond to someone like Farquhar. His pākhaṇḍīs were provided by the evolution (or devolution) of Bhārat Khaṇḍ itself; they figured more or less in his own discursive world. If he had been propelled thirty or forty years forward and forced to hear what Farquhar said, he might have responded by saying that Farquhar just didn't understand. What Farquhar saw as restrictions—the varṇas and āśramas—were really just aspects of an ideal amplitude, now threatened and debased. This was the view from the top of the anthill, and it wasn't appealing to everyone. Too sanātana for some, and for others, not sanātana enough.

When I discovered the *Sanātanadharmamārttaṇḍa* in the Adyar Library in Chennai, I thought I might have come upon an important vernacular prototype for the textbook on Sanātana Dharma by which children were to be educated in the English-speaking Theosophist institution in Banaras. I wondered if the *Mārttaṇḍa* had been in Annie Besant's private library. After all, she died in 1933; it was accessioned in 1937. The staff of the Adyar Library have informed me, however, that Pandit Gurusahāy's work did not come into the library by this route. Nothing indicates the *Sanātanadharmamārttaṇḍa* ever belonged to Mrs Besant's collection.

Seeing what we have seen, this comes as no surprise. If Pandit Gurusahāy's book did indeed form part of the canvassing process that preceded the Kashmir summer when Annie Besant put pen to paper, the *Mārttaṇḍa's* sense of what could be universal and eternal was nonetheless largely superseded at that moment. It was 1901 and a new century had begun—at least the way Annie Besant had been taught to count the years.

NOTES AND REFERENCES

1. I am grateful to Brian Hatcher for helpful bibliographical tips as I prepared this essay, and to Laura Shapiro, as ever, for its editing. Different versions of the essay have been presented orally on four occasions: in a panel on 'Constructing Sanatana Dharma' organized by Diana Dimitrova for the annual meeting of the Association for Asian Studies, Chicago, 2 April 2005; as a lecture sponsored by the Center for Sikh and Punjab Studies at the University of California, Santa Barbara, 20 May 2005; as a talk at the South Asia Center of the University of Wisconsin-Madison on 3 November 2005; and as a lecture called 'Inventing the Eternal Religion', given on 31 March 2006 at the invitation of the Department of Religious Studies of Illinois Wesleyan University. I have benefited from questions and comments from persons present at all these events, particularly Jose Cabezon, Vasudha Dalmia, Donald Davis, Monika Horstmann, Gurinder Singh Mann, Velcheru Narayana Rao, Tracy Pintchman, Ben Schonthal, and again Brian Hatcher.

2. David N. Lorenzen, 'Who Invented Hinduism?', *Comparative Studies in Society and History*, vol. 41, no. 1 (1999), pp. 630–59. The passage quoted appears on the opening page.

3. John Stratton Hawley, 'Naming Hinduism', *The Wilson Quarterly*, vol. 15, no. 3 (Summer 1991), pp. 20–34.

4. A portrait of its work and that of its primary founder, Pandit Din Dayalu Sharma, appears in Kenneth W. Jones, 'Two *Sanātan Dharma* Leaders and Swami Vivekananda', in William Radice, ed., *Swami Vivekananda and the Modernization of Hinduism* (New Delhi: Oxford University Press, 1998), pp. 232–8; also Kenneth W. Jones, *Socio-Religious Reform Movements in British India* (Cambridge: Cambridge University Press, 1989), pp. 77–82.

5. J.N. Farquhar, *Modern Religious Movements in India* (New Delhi: Munshiram Manoharlal, 1977 [originally 1915]), p. 321. Farquhar's reference is to *Mahāmaṇḍal Magazine*, vol. 1, no. 1 (n.d.), p. 8.

6. Farquhar, *Modern Religious Movements in India,* p. 321.

7. Ibid., p. 320.

8. Ibid., pp. 320–1.

9. Tulsī Dev, *Śraddhā Prakāś* (Lahore: Punjab Economical Press, 1986), pp. 30–1, as translated by Kenneth W. Jones, *Arya Dharm: Hindu Consciousness in 19th-*

Century Punjab (Berkeley: University of California Press, 1976), pp. 27–8. A later, slightly revised translation by Jones appears in Radice, ed., *Swami Vivekananda and the Modernization of Hinduism*, p. 229.

10. Pandit Gurusahāy, *Sanātanadharmamārttaṇḍa* (Benares: Channūlāl, V.S. 1934 [AD 1878]).

11. Sri Prakash, *Bharat-Ratna Dr Bhagavan Das Remembered by his Son* (Meerut: Meenakshi Prakashan, 1970), pp. 37–8.

12. Annie Besant *et al.*, *Sanatana Dharma: An Elementary Textbook of Hindu Religion and Ethics* (Adyar: The Theosophical Publishing House, 1939), preface by Bhagavān Dās, viii.

13. Annie Besant *et al.*, *Sanatana Dharma*, p. vii.

14. I have seen records for Hindi and Tamil. *The Sanātana-Dharma Catechism*, a shorter work first published by the College in 1902, was translated into Gujarati, Hindi, Marathi, Bengali, Urdu, Telugu, Tamil, Kannada, Malayalam, and Sindhi.

15. These were the boys of the Central Hindu College, but it is not yet clear to me in just what form the *Textbook* actually entered classroom life. Nita Kumar is skeptical that it did, at least in any pedagogically systematic way. She concludes from her study of the institution that 'Besant's pedagogic plans restricted themselves to the publication of the Sanatan Dharma series, which the teachers were expected to familiarize themselves with and adapt in their classes with reference to the age of the children.' See Kumar, 'Religion and Ritual in Indian Schools: Benaras from the 1880s to the 1940s,' in Nigel Crook, ed., *The Transmission of Knowledge in South Asia: Essays on Education, Religion, History, and Politics* (New Delhi: Oxford University Press, 1996), p. 142.

16. In the sense that the Hinduism it represents would be intelligible as a 'religious system' parallel to other 'world religions'. Further reflections on this point will be offered at the conclusion of the essay, but for the moment it is important to note that those who spoke for the Central Hindu College itself (Mrs Besant herself?) accepted this claim as true:

> Others may follow along the same road, and copy the idea, but to the CHC. will ever belong the glory of issuing the first series of books which present Hinduism in a compact and comprehensive form.

Central Hindu College Magazine, 1 January 1904, p. 3, as quoted by Kumar, 'Religion and Ritual in Indian Schools', p. 139.

17. In the advanced version of the textbook, a sensitivity to issues involved here is displayed at the very outset:

> Dharma is not merely a set of beliefs having no necessary connection with the daily life of humanity, but it is the very principles of a healthy and beneficient life. Therefore to know those principles and act upon them is to be a true Āryan (or follower of Vaidika Dharma), and to tread the sure road to happiness, individual as well as general. The etymological meaning of 'religion' is also the same, 'that which binds together'.

Annie Besant *et al.*, *An Advanced Text Book of Hindu Religion and Ethics* (Banaras: Central Hindu College, 1905), p. 2.

18. Besant *et al.*, *Sanatana Dharma*, p. 53.

19. Ibid., pp. 57–8.

20. Nita Kumar reports that the collective morning ritual practised at the Central Hindu College included a reading out of passages from the Gītā and Mahābhārata. Kumar, 'Religion and Ritual in Indian Schools', p. 142.

21. Annie Besant and Bhagavan Das produced a full-length book on the Gītā in 1905. It was entitled *The Bhagavad Gītā, with Saṃskṛt text, free translation into English, a Word-for-Word translation, an Introduction to Saṃskṛt Grammar, and a complete Word Index.* The fifth (1926) and following reprints are copyrighted to the Theosophical Publishing House, Adyar.

22. Besant *et al.*, *Sanatana Dharma*, p. 1.

23. Ibid., pp. 2–7.

24. Ibid., pp. 1–2.

25. I am as yet unable to ascertain exactly which *pāṭhśālā* this might have been. The *Imperial Gazetteer of India* published in 1908–9 (Calcutta: Supt. of Government Printing) is apparently the first to speak in detail about educational establishments in Shahjahanpur, but it gives no guidance about particular schools that might have been called pāṭhśālā. It tells us that in 1903–4 there were 186 public schools, of which 128 were managed by various levels of government, and 60 private schools—presumably including the pāṭhśālā where Gursahāy served, if it was still in existence (vol. 22, p. 209). The gazetteer dating to Gursahāy's own period of publication (London: Trubner, 1885–7) makes no mention of such institutions, confining its attention to government, *tahsīlī*, municipal, and mission schools in the city (vol. 12, p. 357).

26. *Āryya logoṅ ko.* Gurusahāy, *Sanātanadharmamārttaṇḍa,* preface (n.p.) The reference is general, and in no apparent way determined by the presence of Ārya Samājīs in Gursahāy's immediate environment. No Ārya Samājī presence is reflected in the 1885–7 gazetteer, but its 1908–89 counterpart reports that 'A new meeting-house has recently been built by the Arya Samāj' (vol. 22, p. 210).

27. Gurusahāy states this formally on pp. 3–4. By emphasizing the manner in which Gurusahāy conceives himself to be expositing Manu, however, I do not mean to imply that he simply follows the outline that Manu provides. Far from it. Even the basic distinction between general and varṇāśram-specific dharma that structures the *Mārttaṇḍa* is not to be found in Manu, and the varṇāśramadharma frame, while not absent from the earlier document, emerges much more definitively in Gurusahāy's text. A convenient overview of the contents of the *Manusmṛti* can be found in Patrick Olivelle, *The Law Code of Manu* (Oxford: Oxford University Press, 2004), pp. 3–12.

28. Gurusahāy, *Sanātanadharmamārttaṇḍa,* pp. 1 and 67. Donald Davis emphasizes the point that *sāmānya* or *sādhāraṇdharma* is not to be regarded as being the same thing as *sanātana dharma*, at least in its classical usages. He regards the former, rather, as 'a nod to the ethicized notions of dharma held by the Buddhists and Jains' and notes that it is 'hardly elaborated upon at all in the Dharmasastra' (Davis, e-mail communcation, 7 November 2005). Given this fact, it is striking that Pandit Gurusahāy gives such priority to sāmānya dharma. On classical usages of sanātana dharma, by contrast, an aggregation of venerable, specifically enjoined

actions, see James L. Fitzgerald, '*Dharma* and its Translation in the *Mahābhārata*,' *Journal of Indian Philosophy*, vol. 32 (2004), pp. 679–80 and p. 684, note 12. On the distinction between sanātana dharma and various forms of *svadharma*, see Wendy Doniger [O'Flaherty], 'The Clash between Relative and Absolute Duty: The Dharma of Demons,' in W.D. O'Flaherty and J. Duncan M. Derrett, eds, *The Concept of Duty in South Asia* (London: School of Oriental and African Studies, 1978), pp. 96–105. Other contributors to this volume are less content than Doniger to group those forms of dharma that contrast to sanātana under the single heading of svadharma. See, for instance, Derrett, 'The Concept of Duty in Ancient Indian Jurisprudence: The Problem of Ascertainment', pp. 30–1. Also relevant is Robert P. Goldman, '*Eṣa Dharmaḥ Sanātanaḥ:* Shifting Moral Values and the Indian Epics', in P. Bilimoria and J.N. Mohanty, eds, *Relativism, Suffering, and Beyond: Essays in Memory of Bimal K. Matilal* (New Delhi: Oxford University Press, 1997), pp. 187–223.

29. Olivelle, with the editorial assistance of Suman Olivelle, *Manu's Code of Law: A Critical Edition and Translation of the Mānava-Dharmaśāstra* (New York: Oxford University Press, 2005), p. 153.

30. Gursahāy's experience with 'the English' (*agarez* [i.e., *angrez*] *log*, preface, n.p.) was probably shaped by the substantial presence of the American Methodist Mission in Shahjahanpur since 1859; it was their regional headquarters (*Imperial Gazetteer*, 1908–9, vol. 22, p. 210).

31. Gurusahāy, *Sanātanadharmamārttaṇḍa*, preface (n.p.).

32. Gurusahāy is hardly the first person to have directed attention to the lamentable effects *pākhaṇḍīs* cause in the religious life of a people. Heidi Pauwels has highlighted this element in the utterances of Harirām Vyās, who tends to use the term *vimukh* ('The Early *Bhakti* Milieu as Mirrored in the Poetry of Harirām Vyās', in Alan Entwistle and Francoise Mallison, eds, *Studies in South Asian Devotional Literature: Research Papers 1988–1991* [New Delhi: Manohar and Paris: École Française d'Extrême Orient, 1994], pp. 34–6), and the theme of degeneracy *(pākhaṇḍ)* is certainly widespread. Pauwels cites Joseph T. O'Connell's attention to the term in, 'Social Implications of the Gauḍīya Vaiṣṇava Movement' (PhD thesis, Harvard University, 1970), p. 119, and in regard to Vallabhācārya, see *Śrīkṛṣṇāśrayaḥ*, translated in James Redington, *The Grace of Lord Krishna: The Sixteen Verse-Treatises (Ṣoḍaśagranthāḥ) of Vallabhacharya* (Delhi: Sri Satguru Publications, 2000), pp. 109–111, especially verses 1 and 6. Verse 6 is particularly interesting, since it highlights the association between pākhaṇḍ and, as Redington tanslates, 'different doctrinal systems' (p. 110). There is a complementary discourse among Muslims: When Iblis sows the seeds of doubt in the primordial garden, the ultimate results are distortions and malformations that challenge the purity and integrity of Islam. They find expression in a host of schisms and sects.

33. Gurusahāy, *Sanātanadharmamārttaṇḍa*, p. 71.

34. For a review of such changes in government education policy in a neighbouring province, see Kazi Shahidullah, *Patshalas into Schools: The Development of Indigenous Elementary Education in Bengal, 1954–1905* (Calcutta: Firma KLM, 1987), pp. 37–104; a subsequent version can be found in Kazi Shahidullah, 'The Purpose and Impact of Government Policy on *Pathshala Gurumohashoys* in

Nineteenth-century Bengal', in Nigel Crook, ed., *The Transmission of Knowledge in South Asia,* pp. 119–34. For the Northwest Provinces and Oudh, somewhat more cursorily, see Sureshchandra Shukla, *Elementary Education in British India during Later Nineteenth Century* (Delhi: Central Institute of Education, 1959), pp. 2–13, 23–5. The gazetteer for 1908–9 reports that the municipality of Shahjahanpur maintained four schools directly and contributed funds to 17 others (*Imperial Gazetteer*, 1908–9, vol. 22, p. 210).

35. On the inadequacies of Farquhar's system of categorization, see Brian A. Hatcher, 'Contemporary Hindu Thought', in Robin Rinehart, ed., *Contemporary Hinduism* (Santa Barbara: ABC-CLIO, 2004), pp. 180–2; and from another angle, J.E. Llewellyn, 'Gurus and Groups', in Rinehart, *Contemporary Hinduism,* pp. 233–6.

36. The emergence of this broader landscape is described in Tomoko Masuzawa, *The Invention of World Religions* (Chicago: University of Chicago Press, 2005). See also J.S. Hawley, 'Comparative Religion for Undergraduates: What Next?', *The Chicago Forum on Pedagogy and the Study of Religion,* Martin Marty Center Occasional Papers, vol. 2 (Chicago: University of Chicago Divinity School), pp. 20–31. I must caution that much work remains to be done before I could possibly venture a conclusion about which of our two competing Sanātana Dharmas—if either—persists more successfully in Hindi-speaking environments in India itself. A tantalizing dependent clause by Nita Kumar suggests that Manu remained the standard for Sanātan Dharma in the view of Vidya Devi, who founded an Arya Mahila School in Banaras in 1926. The passage reads:

> Besant's Hinduism was challenged explicitly to the last. Vidya Devi, professing a Sanatan Dharma where Manu was the supreme authority, *herself* exemplified the opposite. (Kumar, 'Religion and Ritual in Indian Schools,' p. 150.)

37. Ed Viswanathan, *Am I a Hindu?*, p. 1. Even more striking, for those who know the Westminster Catechism, is the passage in S. Sabāratna Mudaliyār's *Essentials of Hinduism in the Light of Śaiva Siddhānta* (Madras: Meykandian Press, 1913), where the author asks, 'What is true religion?', then 'How are we to 'see' God?', and finally 'And how is He to be enjoyed?' (pp. 10–11).

38. The current publishers are Rupa Press in India and Halo Books in the United States: see http://www.amiahindu.com. The publishers' publicity (mailed from New Orleans 12 May 2005) indicates that the book is 'used by many universities in US and Canada in their religion classes.'

39. While I do believe that the adoption of a roughly catechetical format here owes a fundamental debt to manuals of Christian instruction, we should not ignore the fact that dialogue (*saṃvāda)* has ancient Hindu roots as well. And not just ancient. Exchanges that were recalled as having taken place between Pandit Śraddhā Rām and various members of his audiences appeared in Urdu newspapers of the time and were later collected and rendered into Hindi to comprise Chapter 7 of his collected writings. See Sarandās Bhanoṭ, ed., *Śraddhārām Granthāvalī* (Kurukshetra: Punjab Sahitya Academy, 1966), pp. 103–82.

40. Viswanathan, *Am I a Hindu?*, pp. 1, 3–5, 19.

41. Ibid., p. 23.

42. Ibid., p. 21.

43. Bansi Pandit, *Hindu Dharma* (Glen Ellyn, Ill.: B & V Enterprises, 1996), p. 7.

44. Ibid., p. 81.

45. Gurusahāy, *Sanātanadharmamārttaṇḍa,* pp. 2–3.

46. Ibid., p. 192.

47. Ibid., preface (n.p.)

48. Sri Jagathguru Sri Chandrasekharendra Sarasvathi Swamigal, *The Sanātana Dharma, or the Hindu View of Life,* trans. V.R. Sundararaman (Madras: Madras Law Journal Press, 1940), pp. 2–4.

49. Shankaracharya, *The Sanātana Dharma,* pp. 4–5.

50. Besant *et al.*, *Sanatana Dharma,* p. vii. The *Advanced Text Book,* published a year later, chooses an interestingly different wording for this passage (p. iii):

> The name to be given to these books was carefully discussed, and that of 'Sanātana Dharma' was finally chosen, as connoting the ancient teachings, free from modern accretions. It should cover all sects, as it did in the ancient days.

51. Besant *et al.*, *Sanatana Dharma,* p.vi.

52. Ibid., p. vii.

53. The wording of the most recently quoted passage also changes in the *Advanced Text Book,* and again the difference is worth observing. The sentence in question follows that quoted in the previous note, as a separate paragraph (p. iii):

> May this book also aid in the great work of building up the national Religion, and so pave the way to national happiness and prosperity.

That the Theosophist project was firmly embedded in the imperial frame—while at the same time seeing itself as transcending and even reversing it—is, however, beyond dispute. A sensitive exploration of certain key aspects of this subject is provided by Gauri Viswanathan in 'The Ordinary Business of Occultism', *Cultural Inquiry,* vol. 27 (2000), pp. 1–20.

12. CUSTOMS AND CANONS

BHIMA BHOI IN THE LITERARY TRADITION OF ORISSA

Ishita Banerjee-Dube

Oriya as a language, affirmed Suniti Kumar Chatterji, the renowned linguist and literary scholar of Bengal, 'has remained almost unchanged...from the middle of the twelfth right down to the twentieth'. He felt that this was 'remarkable' about Oriya 'among all the New Indo-Aryan languages'.[1] This essay will tease out the implications of this 'unchanging' nature of Oriya as reflected in distinct constructions of community. It will underscore creative deployments of the 'indigenous' and the 'western', and the 'early' and the 'modern' in twentieth-century configurations of identity centred on the vernacular. What is of particular significance is the fact that such articulations proclaim equal distance from both the classical Sanskrit tradition and the modern western tradition in order to uphold the 'native', unsoiled, oral nature of literary Oriya best expressed in religious poetry.[2]

I will focus on the tangled careers of the Oriya language and Bhima Bhoi, a late nineteenth-century poet of western Orissa, in order to track the overlapping processes through which the salient features of Oriya have been identified, its key representatives valourized, and Bhima Bhoi elevated to the position of the 'national' poet of Orissa. This would offer insights into the importance of language in discourses of identity and highlight how such discourses have 'appropriated' Bhima Bhoi—the unlettered poet-philosopher of Mahima Dharma, a heterodox religious order—as a symbol of Oriya pride, an appropriation that has been subsequently integrated by the followers of Mahima Dharma.

LITERARY ROOTS

Oriya as a distinct vernacular probably came into existence in the twelfth century. However, there are hardly any recognized literary compositions before the fifteenth, except Jayadeva's *Geeta Govinda*, which is regarded as both Bengali and Oriya. The flowering of Oriya as a language was directly related to the rule of the solar dynasty (*Suryavamsa*) (1435–1540 CE)[3] with Kapilendra (1435–69) being the first Oriya king of a roughly independent Orissa. This bonding of political independence with the independent career of a language constitutes a prominent feature of the literary history of Orissa. It is stated that the short span of the rule of the solar dynasty witnessed the most significant growth of Oriya language and literature.[4] At the same time, it bears pointing out, that the blossoming of Oriya is not linked to royal patronage but to the spread of religious devotionalism, particularly Vaishnavism, in the period. Vaishnavism again, had a long and colourful career in the region with Jagannath being transformed from his tribal beginnings into the Lord of the Universe as the ninth incarnation of Vishnu and the state deity by the southern Ganga kings in the twelfth and thirteenth centuries. The Gangas, however, had scant regard for the vernacular and patronized Sanskrit, the language of higher learning. It was under the succeeding *Suryavamsi*s that the Oriya-speaking tract came under one administration and a wave of bhakti swept the region with Chaitanya's move to Puri, the abode of Jagannath. The two together set the vernacular on a new course.

The fall of the solar dynasty and the loss of political independence in 1568 led to the fragmentation of the Oriya-speaking tract. It came under several administrative and political units which changed contours from time to time. This disunity generated an awareness of the unity of Oriya speakers.[5] It was heightened by the patronage given to Oriya by the rulers of Khurda, recognized by the Mughal general, Man Singh, as the descendants of the imperial Gangas. The Khurda rajas, in order to gain legitimacy as the first servants of Jagannath, the 'god of Orissa', encouraged greater use of the vernacular. The medieval period thus saw the coming together of Jagannath and Oriya as symbols of Oriyaness.

The 'early poets' of the language—Balaram Das, Jagannath Das, and Sarala Das—to name only the most eminent—provided vernacular renderings of the Ramayana, the Bhagavata Purana, and the Mahabharata respectively. This clearly reflected the hold of bhakti in the region. Interestingly, the vernacular renditions of Sanskrit classics signalled the independence of Oriya from the Sanskrit literary tradition. This went hand in hand with a rupture with the Brahmanic tradition as well. The early poets were all 'Sudras' and their vernacular compositions of classical texts simultaneously freed Oriya from Sanskrit and effaced the stranglehold of Brahmans over these texts and the religious ideas they advocated. These early texts were by no means translations of Sanskrit works. The stories of the Ramayana, the Bhagavata Purana, and the Mahabharata were 'retold' with significant variations. These poets used 'rustic' Oriya metre and tune to compose verses that were meant to be read out and sung. Indeed, the texts were so completely geared to collective reading that the apparent 'imperfections' in the metre were made up when they were performed with correct accent and tune. This stress on the oral and the colloquial made these early texts extremely popular and ensured their continued popularity. Sarala Das' *Mahabharata* and Jagannath Das' *Bhagavata* in particular became *the Mahabharata* and *the Bhagavata* of Orissa with regular narrations continuing up to the twentieth century. Though the butt of derogatory remarks by Brahmans in their own times, these poets were given the status of 'national poets' who raised 'the superstructure of the national literature of Orissa' in the first English compilation of *Typical Selections from Oriya Literature*.[6]

The trend of bhakti was continued by the *Panchasakhas*—Five Friends—renowned medieval mystics. The Panchasakhas were Vaishnavas but they conceived of Krishna–Vishnu as *nirguna*, beyond form and attributes. The compositions of the mystics, also pliant to performance, have acquired escalating esteem as they have become associated with the genre of popular apocryphal texts called *malikas*. Malikas, which contain vague prophecies about the destruction of the evil Kaliyuga through the appearance of a redeemer and lack an authoritative authorial voice, have arisen time and again in moments of crisis out of the constant combination of the spoken and the written. The fact that they are ascribed to the Panchasakhas lends credibility to their prophecies while it demonstrates the hold of the Five Friends on popular imagination. Equally, these works through their repeated recreations keep alive an earlier tradition as they contribute to the vitality of Oriya as a language.

In brief, the distinctiveness of Oriya as defined in the twentieth century, has been framed by compositions of popular poets in Oriya metre that make them amenable to repeated recitals. This interface of the oral and the written coupled with the dominant presence of bhakti have provided a common stock of knowledge readily drawn upon and interpreted during oral performances. This has meant that these early medieval and medieval texts have remained ever attractive as they have got transformed and recreated through frequent rehearsals. And this appealing blend of religion and literature has played a pivotal role in constructions of Oriya identities. As stated above, the early works of Oriya have been canonized as 'modern', 'national' compositions, since they caused a break with the Sanskrit tradition. The innovation and radicalism characteristic of 'early' Oriya poets constitute significant markers of Oriya pride. It is with this background in mind that we turn to the life and works of Bhima Bhoi, the poet-philosopher of Mahima Dharma, a religious order in a controversial relationship with the cult of Jagannath.

RELIGIOUS TRACKS

Mahima (Alekh) Dharma was founded by Mahima Swami, an abstemious, itinerant ascetic in the tributary states of Orissa in the 1860s when the region was rocked by a devastating famine. The new faith advocated devotion to an all-pervasive, formless Absolute who was difficult to be conceived yet accessible to all, as the only way of salvation. This seemingly simple message rendered redundant worship of idols, including that of Jagannath, the central deity of Hinduism in Orissa and the state deity for centuries, and questioned complex hierarchies of caste and kingship, and the role of the Brahmans as mediators between gods and men. The challenge implicit in the message was worked out in the practices of the founder. Mahima Swami countered authority and establishment through constant movement and acute detachment and contravened the rules of caste and commensality by asking for cooked rice as alms from all households and by eating it together with his disciples from the same pot.

Mahima Swami's radical message and his simple lifestyle appealed to large sections of subordinate peoples in Orissa. The Swami became deified in his lifetime as the incarnation of the Absolute he spoke about and his faith found a wide following, particularly among the untouchable, lower caste, and tribal peoples of the tributary states. By the time of his death in 1875/76, his disciples—ascetics and householders—numbered in thousands. At the same time, the extreme detachment of the Swami meant that he left no nominated successor and no permanent structure of the faith. Indeed, the Dharma faced a crisis after his death. It was at this time that Bhima Bhoi emerged as an important preacher in western Orissa, helping the dissemination of the message of Mahima Dharma through his bhajans and *janans* (devotional lyrics in praise of and in conversation with the Lord) which were sung in large gatherings of non-literate followers.

A dramatic incident brought the new faith to the notice of colonial administrators and Oriya literati. On 1 March 1881, a small group of anonymous men and women from western Orissa, householder devotees of Mahima Dharma, entered the main temple of Jagannath in the pilgrimage centre of Puri with the express intention of dragging out and burning the images of Jagannath, his brother Balaram, and sister Subhadra. The person who led the group had been commanded in a dream by Mahima Swami to embark on this daring mission. These ordinary men and women failed in their task. But the 'audacity' of their mission caused consternation among Oriya elites and made the colonial government order detailed enquiries into the antecedents of the faith. The extraordinary 'event' of the 'attack' on the temple, marked the entry of the new faith into colonial records as 'a sect of Hindu dissenters'.

The reports drawn up after the incident bear testimony to the importance of Bhima Bhoi. A feature titled 'Kumbhipatia Babaji' in the Oriya newspaper *Utkala Deepika* of 19 November 1881 mentioned that the Kumbhipatias as 'a community...exists in Sambalpur district', and described Bhima Khond as their leader. The report affirmed that although first propounded in Banki by Alekh Swami, the Dharma very soon 'gained special spread in the district of Sambalpur' where people of all castes except the Brahmans adopted the faith.[7] The annual report of the Orissa Baptist Mission on Sambalpur for the year 1881–2 commented: 'The Kumpatias continue to gain adherents and we are glad to welcome this as a sign of continued reactionary [*sic*] movement against the grosser forms of idolatry'.[8]

The life of Bhima Bhoi is a rich source of legends and hence of contention. What is generally agreed upon is that he hailed from western Orissa, lived in the second half of the nineteenth century, was of 'low' origin and grew up without formal education, was initiated into Mahima Dharma by Mahima Swami. The story surrounding his initiation is that the blind and poor Bhima, who fended for himself by tending cattle, fell into a well one day. He refused all offers of help to pull him out of the well stating that he would remain there until the master who had made him fall into the well came and rescued him. Mahima Swami travelled a great distance at remarkable speed, lifted Bhima out of the well and bestowed on him the eye of knowledge and the gift of poetry to spread the message of the new faith. Over the twentieth century the fact of Bhima Bhoi's blindness has been questioned and the tale of his initiation interpreted differently in diverse perceptions of the poet as well as his place within Mahima Dharma.

Mahima Swami did not only endow Bhima with the gift of poetry. He also arranged for four scribes to become Bhima Bhoi's constant companions and record his inspired utterances.[9] Bhima Bhoi is believed to have crafted four bhajans in one *raga* simultaneously. He began with the refrains for the scribes to note down, and followed them up by singing the bhajans one by one.[10] These were then sent to Joranda for the Guru's approval, and passed on to the *bhakta*s (devotees) to be sung and recited. These lyrics spoke of an all-pervasive, indescribable (*alekh*) formless Absolute as the only object of devotion. This Absolute again was the creator of the Universe and the personal Lord of Bhima Bhoi, Mahima (Alekh) Swami. The compositions of Bhima constituted the first written records as well as the early theosophy-philosophy of Mahima Dharma.

Before proceeding to analyse Bhima Bhoi's thoughts and ideas, let me pause briefly and recount two facts significant for the arguments of the essay which we will not have occasion to go into detail.[11] The first is Mahima Dharma's intricate and transforming relationship with the cult of Jagannath. This relationship was of great significance in the initial phase of the faith. *Nirveda Sadhana*, a key work of Bhima Bhoi, clearly identified Govinda Das, Mahima Swami's first disciple, with Jagannath and stated that he had left Puri in order to purge himself of the sins accumulated in his various incarnations by becoming the follower of the true Lord. According to the formal history of the faith written in the twentieth century by a leading ascetic, Mahima Swami made his first appearance on the grand road in Puri in front of the Jagannath temple and toured the neighbouring regions before moving on to Kaplias in Dhenkanal where he spent thirty-six long years in mediation. It was at the end of this that the Swami launched his career as a preacher. His message, we have noted, dismissed the efficacy of idols, priests, and rituals, and sought to give primacy to the tribal peoples of far-flung territories, who had been neglected by Jagannath's elevation in status from a tribal lord to the state deity as Buddha-Jagannath, the ninth incarnation of Vishnu. This complex relationship became more and more tendentious as Mahima Dharma evolved as a sect within the universe of Hinduism over the course of the twentieth century. The identification of Govinda with Jagannath, however, persisted and was variously understood and deployed by lay followers.

The second fact relates to the contradictory relationship of Bhima Bhoi with Mahima Dharma. An ingenious poet of ungoverned imaginings, Bhima Bhoi was not restrained by the dictates of a single faith. Indeed, songs of the genre of Dalakhai and Rasarakeli, which passionately portray the intense love of Radha and Krishna, are ascribed to him. Moreover, Bhima Bhoi transgressed the unwritten rule of celibacy adhered to by many preachers by adopting the life of a householder.[12] Apart from cohabiting with four women and producing a son and a daughter, he allowed women to join the monastic order. While this generated a host of legends and led to his near deification in western Orissa, it outraged the ascetic disciples of Mahima Swami and occasioned a parting of ways between the renouncers who constructed a memorial of the guru at Joranda in Dhenkanal, and Bhima Bhoi who set up his own ashrama at Khaliapali in Sonepur. However, in the early twentieth century, when the ascetics themselves came to clash over interpretations of Mahima Swami's teachings, one group resorted back to Bhima Bhoi's works as the only authentic record of the founder's precepts. Bhima Bhoi's colourful life and his imaginative creations have gone through the push and pull of marginalization and canonization in the twentieth century in conjunction with the turmoil within the faith and distinct discourses of Oriya identity.

POETIC PRACTICES

Let us now turn to a brief survey of the compositions of Bhima Bhoi. Believed to have been born blind to poor parents, Bhima grew up without formal education. But he had imbibed and aurally apprehended various traditions of religious and popular literature, particularly the Mahabharata and the *Bhagavata* read out regularly in the village *bhagavatghara* (room for the recitation of the *Bhagavata*) by the time he was initiated into Mahima Dharma. His imaginative and creative mind combined these received ideas with the teachings of Mahima Swami to produce original compositions. Bhima Bhoi's lyrics reflect the rich assortment of religious traditions that flourished in Orissa: there are elements of Hinduism, Buddhism, Tantra, mysticism, and bhakti. His numerous bhajans, *stutis,* and janans speak of an Absolute (Brahma), omnipresent and omniscient, who created the world out of his *mahima* (radiance, glory), but who is beyond attributes—formless and indescribable. He is the Lord of lords, the one and only Guru who had taken form and come down to earth to redeem humanity by establishing *satya dharma*. This Guru is accessible to all through devotion. His worship does not require priests, temples, or pilgrimage. The pilgrim sites are located in the body: indeed, the *pinda* (body) is a replica of the *brahmanda* (universe). Through proper concentration and control one can attain the Absolute in oneself. The worship of images, the mediation of priests and rituals thus become totally redundant in the path to salvation.

The currency of these ideas for centuries before the time of Bhima Bhoi has induced scholars to try and place him in one tradition or the other. Beginning with the characterization of Mahima Dharma as 'crypto-Buddhism' on grounds that the *sunya* (formless Absolute) of Bhima Bhoi's works corresponded to the sunya (void) of Buddhism,[13] there have been sustained attempts to trace an unbroken line of belief in an Absolute beyond attributes (nirguna) from the Naths through the Vaishnavas to the Mahima Dharmis.[14] The ingenuity of Bhima Bhoi has often been neglected in this hunt for lineage. In spite of cautionary remarks such as that 'only a stray similarity in words ought not to encourage us for an excessive comparison',[15] the effort to locate Bhima Bhoi within the history of ideas in India in general and Orissa in particular, has persisted. It is widely accepted that in thought, language, and ideas Bhima Bhoi was closest to the Panchasakhas. Anncharlott Eschmann marked out the three elements that the poet had drawn directly from the mystics: 'the worship of the sunya, the theory of Pinda Brahmanda, and the idea of a future redeemer who will come and openly establish what is for the time being a secret doctrine.'[16] For Paritosh Das, the Panchasakha Dharma and the Mahima Dharma of Orissa are both 'outcomes of a popular assimilation of the religious ideas of the later Tantrik Buddhism with those of Gaudiya Vaishnavism represented by Chaitanyadev'.[17]

This association with the Panchasakhas is significant for various reasons. After the period of the mystics, Oriya literature came to be dominated by the ornamental style of Sanskrit poetry best reflected in the works of Upendra Bhanja (about 1685–1725). Although Bhanja is hailed as *kavisamrat* (king of poets) and the ornate compositions of the *reeti-kavis* appreciated, over time this style has come to be regarded as 'artificial' and distant from the feelings of the common people. The other experiment was that of Radhanath Ray (1848–1908), acclaimed for heralding the 'modern' era in Oriya literature. Ray, however, drew heavily upon western forms and metre. Bhima Bhoi, in closely following the early poets and the Panchasakhas in thought, language, and style, represented a move back and also signified a new beginning.[18] This newness was distinct from that of Radanath Ray or Upendra Bhanja, whose styles in being derivative and imitative were not truly 'native'. Bhima Bhoi on the other hand, renovated and refurbished the native tradition, best articulated in Oriya mystic poetry, the true signifier of Oriya 'poetic consciousness'.[19]

This is evident in the way Bhima Bhoi is portrayed in *Typical Selections from Oriya Literature*. B.C. Mazumdar, the editor, commended Bhima Bhoi for his religiosity and close proximity to the earliest poets in thought and moral values. Mazumdar expressed his personal admiration for 'Sant Bhima Bhoi', whose life and teachings he considered to be 'highly interesting and educative.'[20] At the same time, he thought it fit to place Bhima Bhoi along with other 'Modern Poets of the Old School', since his style was 'altogether of the time of the earliest poets and as the civilization of the modern times did not even indirectly affect him'.[21] Indeed, this nearness to the early poets was reiterated by the reviewer of the manuscript of Nirveda Sadhana, published in the *Journal of the Kalinga Historical Research Society*. P.C. Raut, the reviewer, stated that had it not been for the facts that the authorship and the time of the manuscript were definitely known, Nirveda Sadhana could very easily be placed 'at least four centuries earlier than the time when he [Bhima Bhoi] actually lived'.[22] The text, significantly, is composed in the famous *dandi matra* (metre) of the Oriya *Bhagavata*, described as 'the Bible of the Oriya speaking masses'.[23]

Bhima Bhoi's compositions then, were in perfect tune with the dominant themes of rupture and continuity as distinctive features of the Oriya language. Moreover, the tribal poet's closeness to the 'early poets' and his distance from (Western) 'civilization' would acquire increasing import in the course of the twentieth century as significant markers of Oriya distinctiveness and pride. The following section will explore the ramifications of this on Bhima Bhoi's assessment and canonization over the twentieth century.

PLURAL PERCEPTIONS

Early assessments of Bhima Bhoi reveal an inherent ambiguity. The mix of opposites that characterized the poet—his capacity to produce works of great literary and spiritual merit despite his low birth and lack of formal education, and his success as a religious leader who transgressed celibacy but allowed women to become ascetics—confounded middle-class critics and admirers. The report of the *Utkala Deepika* of 19 November 1881 makes this evident. Speaking of Bhima Bhoi, the daily commented: 'he is born blind but very intelligent. He has had no formal education...but has composed some songs and hymns in praise of God whose beautiful style can hardly be matched by the most educated.'[24] The very next sentence stated that Bhima Bhoi had annoyed the Kumbhipatias by getting a woman pregnant through 'illicit love' (*papa pranaya*). Moreover, he had tried to deceive them by saying that the woman would give birth to Arjun, who would destroy all the non-believers. Bhima Bhoi was proved wrong when a daughter was born. Bhima now claimed that he had received an order from the Lord that the daughter was to do away with the non-believers. But the baby died within a few days. At this, the feature claimed, those 'who had even a little bit of intelligence' separated themselves from Bhima Bhoi and formed a distinct sect. Bhima Bhoi thus, was simultaneously praised for his success in propagating the faith and blamed for causing dissension among its adherents.

The same ambivalence characterized the reports of the Baptist missionaries. In 1881–2, the success of Bhima Bhoi in gaining adherents was a welcome sign that people were moving away from 'the grosser forms of idolatry'. But by 1887–8, the sign was no longer welcome. The people who had moved away from idolatry had not taken the next step of adopting the true faith, Christianity. They remained faithful to Bhima Bhoi. The missionaries now saw him as an 'impostor', a master of 'blasphemous pretensions', who gave himself out to be 'a new incarnation', an *anadi avatara* (incarnation without beginning), who had appeared on earth 'to inaugurate a new dispensation'.[25] Bhima Bhoi called his wife the *adi* avatara, the first incarnation, and named the village he established *agamya dham* (the inaccessible place). What irked the missionaries most was that this impostor could 'number his disciples by [the] hundreds, if not thousands'.[26] No doubt the messengers of Christ saw in the act of 'thousands of men giving divine honour to an ignorant man' a 'widespread disbelief in idolatry and an equally widespread restlessness of heart which was leading the people hither and thither for some way of salvation.'[27] But their sense of outrage and tone of contempt for this 'ignorant man' indicated their disappointment which lay in the fact that the poet had greater appeal than the messengers of Christ.

There was a change of tone in accounts of the twentieth century. The passage of time and Bhima Bhoi's death made the incense over incest less intense. Bhima Bhoi's poetic skills and their effects on the spread of a new faith became important. The vernacular was the first to record this. In 1908, a senior official of the court of Sonepur wrote an essay titled 'Bhima Bhoi's acquisition of knowledge'. In parenthesis he called it a legend. Published in the literary magazine *Mukur* in 1908, the essay wanted to make Bhima Bhoi and his religion known to readers.[28] In an interesting turn of events, Bhima Bhoi's fall into the well was stated to have happened after the disappearance of Mahima Swami. The fall was almost symbolic of the crisis of Mahima Dharma. A distraught Bhima called out to the formless Alekh. He heard a voice near the well asking Bhima to hold his hand and climb out of the well to avoid death. For the ardent devotee, however, death was much less painful than the pang of witnessing the erasure of the name of Alekh from the world. The number of Alekh's devotees was painfully small and was dwindling day by day. There was no written text to help people concentrate on the worship of Alekh and earn peace of mind. 'Were all the efforts of the Guru going to be in vain?' Hearing these words the voice asked Bhima Bhoi why he, a pious devotee, was blaming others instead of trying to write the text himself? But for Bhima Bhoi it was an impossible task to carry out. He was ignorant, with no knowledge of the letters, and blind. How could he write about the glories of Alekh preached by the Guru that was even difficult for learned men to understand? At that moment, the owner of the voice lifted Bhima Bhoi out of the well, set him on the right path and addressed him as the 'guru of the bhaktas'. The eye of knowledge was conferred on Bhima. The voice announced that the precepts of 'Mahima Das' and the essence of his faith would blossom in Bhima's heart in the form of Prakruta songs. He needed only to recite, scribes would write them down. Mahima Dharma would gain fame and popularity through Bhima who would spend the last part of his life serving the feet of the Lord.

This 'legend' is significant. It points to the fact that within a few years of his death, the poet had come to be recognized as a key figure of Mahima Dharma. Mahima Das had preached the faith, but it was Bhima Bhoi who saved it from extinction, and helped the dissemination of its message in a way as to become the real leader. The tale contains an important twist. The survival of a Dharma, whose founder embodied absolute detachment and disdain for institutionalization, is ensured through the composition of songs which are inscribed in writing. Written compositions alone saved the name of Alekh from being erased. In the perception of the Oriya official, oral messages and lyrics got a new lease of life only when they were committed to writing. The emphasis on the oral and the performative as critical markers of popular Oriya texts is underplayed here. At the same time, Bhima Bhoi's lack of formal education and his intricate relationship with the rich Oriya oral tradition and early texts is highlighted by the fact that he composed songs in Prakruta. Prakruta here stands both for old Oriya as well as for a language that is not Sanskrit. Here are the first indications of the onset of a process of canonization that would undergo diverse bends over the course of the century.

The cue was soon followed up in English. The year 1911 saw the appearance of two influential texts of N.N. Vasu, a scholar-administrator. In *The Archeological Survey of Mayurbhanja* and *The Modern Buddhism and its Followers in Orissa*, Vasu categorically identified Bhima Bhoi as the leader of the sect and paid him glowing tributes:

Ere long the fame of Bhima Bhoi spread far and wide. Hearing his immortal instruction helping in the attainment of real knowledge and illumining the head and the heart, the mighty pillars of the caste system stooped at his feet, though the blood of the low kanda ran in his veins. They considered him a spark from the Eternal Flame of truth and knowledge. Before several years had elapsed the Mahima Dharma could count its followers by thousands.[29]

Bijoy Chandra Mazumdar, the editor of *Typical Selections* who served as an official of the Sonepur court in the first decades of the twentieth century, credited Bhima Bhoi with the leadership of the attack on the Jagannath temple in his *Sonepur in the Sambalpur Tract*, also published in 1911.

That he [Bhima Bhoi] had a charming and commanding personality can be fully appreciated from a fact which is on Government records. Bhima Bhoi considered the celebrated idol of Jagannath at Puri in Orissa a huge nuisance, and ordered his followers to proceed to Puri and burn the idol.[30]

Government records did not in any way connect Bhima Bhoi with the attack on the temple.[31] At the same time, it is difficult to deny that the works of Bhima Bhoi had inspired the 'attackers'. Nirveda Sadhana, we may recall, had declared that Jagannath had left his abode to become the Swami's first disciple. According to government records, the attackers stated that they had come to Puri in order to burn the images of the Jagannath trinity.

The message of Mahima Dharma had spread widely through the creations of Bhima Bhoi which were sung, collectively read, and interpreted. If we are to place the message of a radical faith in the context of a crisis caused by the death of a founder believed to be a divine incarnation, it would not be difficult to understand the statement of the attackers that their leader had been commanded by Mahima Swami in a dream to march to Puri and destroy the lifeless image of Jagannath. Indeed, this act by a group of lay followers offers a rare glimpse into practices of reading and understanding as well as of the innovative reception of teachings by ordinary members. The linking of Bhima Bhoi with the incident in books that appeared in print within fifteen years of his death indicates the significance the poet and his creations had come to acquire at the turn of the century.[32]

Vasu's texts set the tone for subsequent assessments of Bhima Bhoi. For Vasu, the poet's low birth heightened his greatness and his achievements. His immortal message made 'the pillars of caste system' forget themselves and stoop at his feet even though 'the blood of a low kanda ran in his veins'.[33] The early poets, to reiterate, were all 'sudra' poets, who freed Oriya from the grip of Sanskrit and made the ideas of important Sanskrit texts accessible to the 'common masses'. Bhima Bhoi was a 'kanda' poet who had intimate links with the early poets and Panchasakhas in language and style. He also spread the message of a faith that decried Brahmanical Hindusim. Taken together, they have led to his elevation in status to the rank of 'national' poet of Orissa. In histories of Oriya literature written in the late twentieth century, Bhima Bhoi features prominently as the authentic voice of tribal Orissa.

Here are a few representative statements. In Binayak Misra's *Oriya Sahityara Itihasa* (History of Oriya Literature) Bhima Bhoi is hailed as a national poet who occasioned an awakening of the Oriya people.[34] In another history written in English, Mayadhar Mansinha calls him the greatest Adivasi poet.[35] For Chittaranjan Das, Bhima Bhoi is the 'most precious gift of Mahima Dharma to Oriya literature' and 'should also be claimed as the most precious gift of Orissa and Oriya literature to the legacy that is India'.[36]

Bhima Bhoi's low birth has increasingly become an asset in statements of Oriya pride, particularly in the second half of the twentieth century. Isn't it remarkable that Oriya society can produce such a great philosopher and scholar from among its backward 'tribals'?[37] Tied to this glorification is also a recent resurgence of nationalism in western Orissa, a story we cannot take up here.[38] The fact that Bhima Bhoi was a 'kanda' almost makes his radical thinking and creative style self-explanatory. He has come to be upheld as a *biplabi* (revolutionary), a champion of social reform, who sought to bring about a change in society by means of his protest against idol worship and caste distinctions.[39] Moreover, he experimented with language and style, making fruitful use of Sanskrit, Prakrut, and colloquial Oriya in his *boli*s. Not constrained by rules of grammar, Bhima Bhoi used 'impure' words—'words used very commonly by the illiterate'—to great effect, enriching Oriya language in the process.[40] All the 'defects' that caused consternation in the early nineteenth century have come to be forgotten in the course of the twentieth. Bhima Bhoi's stature as the national poet of Orissa is justified by his tribal origin, which brings him very close to the early sudra poets whose innovative compositions set Oriya on a career of its own. The recognition granted to Bhima Bhoi as a great poet of all Orissa is reflected in the selection of two of his couplets from *Stuti Chintamoni*, where he pleads for the redemption of the world even at the cost of his own salvation, as the *leit-motif* of the Oriya language in the Sahitya Akademi's list of languages.

CONCLUDING COMMENTS

Let us pick up the story of Oriya and Oriya nationalism again to bring these overlapping narratives to an end. We have noted that from the sixteenth century on, Lord Jagannath slowly became the pivot of language centred Oriya nationalism on account of the fact that there was a direct correspondence between the territory of Jagannath, the *rashtra devata* (state deity), and that of the Oriya speakers, although neither coincided with the shifting boundaries of the Orissan kingdoms. The British occupation of central Orissa in 1803 and the resultant influx of Bengali officials in the region boosted the sense of oneness of the Oriya speakers and heightened their aspiration of remaining united and independent under the rajas of Khurda, the first servants of Jagannath.[41] Indeed, the Paik rebellion of 1817 against the rule of the East India Company is now interpreted as a 'spontaneous though pre-mature outburst of this intensified feeling and aspiration.'[42] Whether or not we accept this interpretation, the defeat of the Paiks stalled the efforts to restore Lord Jagannath to his former glory.

It was not until the late 1860s that nationalism centred on the language grew. And this was in direct response to efforts of Bengali officials to replace Oriya with Bengali in government offices and schools in the coastal districts. The reason advanced was that Oriya was not a separate language but a corrupt version of Bengali. The *bhasha-andolan* (language agitation) that grew out of these fierce public debates, not only revived the slogan 'Orissa for the Oriyas' with great gusto, but also took up the issue of the unification of Oriya-speaking tracts under one administration. The spread of Western education and the beginnings of political nationalism aided the movement. The devastating famine of 1866, caused primarily by administrative inefficiency, bolstered Oriya nationalist sentiments while the Jagannath Temple suit of 1886–7, once again made the raja of Puri and Jagannath the rallying point of Oriya nationalists.[43] The Cuttack Printing Company was set up in 1866 and *Utkala Deepika*, the first Oriya newspaper, was published the same year. Oriya literature underwent important transformations with Radhanath Ray's experiments with English styles and metre. Significantly, history and geography of Orissa took the pride of place in Oriya literary expressions. Importantly, the coastal districts managed to stave off the substitution of Oriya by Bengali.

The move to replace Oriya with Hindi in the Sambalpur division toward the end of the nineteenth century occasioned another round of passionate propaganda for the encouragement of Oriya and the unification of Oriya-speaking tracts. Drawing encouragement from the success of the language movement in the coastal districts, people of the Sambalpur region made a very strong case for their solidarity with other speakers of Oriya and their basic identity as Oriyas.[44] This fervent activity was put on a firm institutional basis with the foundation of the *Utkal Sammilani* (Utkal Union Conference) in 1903, conceived as the 'Parliament of the people inhabiting Oriya speaking areas notwithstanding caste, creed, language and administrative division'. This sustained activity resulted in the restoration of Oriya in the courts and government offices in Sambalpur in 1903 and the transfer of the Sambalpur region from the Central Provinces to the Orissa division in October 1905. This brought to a successful end an agitation that sought to create and unify a community of Oriya speakers.

This unification and subsequent decolonization, however, have resulted in distinct perceptions and assessments of the towering figures of Oriya literature. Once Oriya gained confidence, it set its identity more and more in contrast to Bengali.[45] And in this, the 'rustic' and the religious came to be increasingly celebrated as representative of the soul of Oriya. The early poets whose 'imperfect' compositions became perfect in oral renditions gradually assumed the status of national poets. Similarly, the Panchasakhas, who have been credited with the composition of malikas, apocryphal texts that arise again and again through the interface of the written and the oral, now share the honour of being national poets. This imbrication of reading and writing, recitation and interpretation of religious poetry is the marker of 'native' Oriya. Bhima Bhoi's elevation in status fits in perfectly with these assessments. His tribal background, lack of formal education and closeness in thought and ideas to the early poets and the Panchasakhas are what render him a true native intellectual. And it is stated with pride that while Rammohan Roy founded the Brahmo Dharma with direct influence of Western ideas, Mahima Swami and Bhima Bhoi elaborated a similar faith drawing entirely upon Oriya traditions, with no borrowing. And in this, Radhanath Ray's experiments with western metre and style have also come to be dismissed as imitative. To conclude with what I began, it is in this sense that Oriya has remained virtually unchanged from the twelfth to the twentieth, retaining with zeal its native rural character which brings it very close to the heart of the common people.

NOTES AND REFERENCES

1. Suniti Kumar Chatterji, *The People, Language and Culture of Orissa* (Bhubaneswar: Orissa Sahitya Akademi, 1966), p. 43.

2. This point deserves special mention. Ranajit Guha's masterful analysis of the mindscape and world of peasant insurgency abundantly uses classical textual sources to frame arguments and facilitate understanding. Yet, here is a dominant discourse in which a regional elite posits its novelty and orginality on its distance from the Sanskrit tradition. Cf. Ranajit Guha, *Elementary Aspects of Peasant Insurgeny in Colonial India* (New Delhi: Oxford University Press, 1982).

3. Kapilendra, the founder of *Suryavamsa* (solar dynasty) is widely believed to have been a usurper. The last ruler of the preceding Ganga dynasty died without an heir. It was important for Kapilendra to re-dedicate the kingdom of Orissa to Lord Jagannath and accept the status of a *sevak* (servant) of the Lord. It is not surprising that Kapilendra linked his new dynasty to the legendary Suryavamsa of the Puranas.

4. See for instance, B.C. Mazumdar, *Typical Selections from Oriya Literature*, vol. 1 (Calcutta: University of Calcutta, 1922), p. xix.

5. G.N. Dash, 'Jagannatha and Oriya Nationalism' in A. Eschmann, H. Kulke, G.C. Tripathi (eds), *The Cult of Jagannath and the Regional Tradition of Orissa* (New Delhi: Manohar, 1978), pp. 360–1.

6. Ibid.

7. *Utkala Deepika*, part 16, no. 46, 19 November 1881.

8. *Indian Report of the Orissa Baptist Mission for 1881–82*, Baptist Missionary Society Archives, Angus Library, Regent's Park College, Oxford.

9. Biswanath Baba, *Satya Mahima Dharmara Itihasa* (Cuttack: Satya Mahima Dharmalochana Samiti, 1978), first published in 1935, p. 69. This is generally accepted by scholars who work on Bhima Bhoi.

10. S.C. Panigrahi, *Bhima Bhoi and Mahima Darshan* (Cuttack: Santosh Publications and Department of Philosophy, Utkal University, 1998), p. 13.

11. For detailed analyses of these points, see Ishita Banerjee-Dube, *Religion, Law and Power: Tales of Time in Eastern India, 1860–2000* (London: Anthem Press, 2007).

12. See Linda Hess's essay in this volume for recent contestations of Kabir's marital status by Kabirpanthis.

13. N.N. Vasu, *Modern Buddhism and its Followers in Orissa* (Calcutta: U.N. Bhattacharya, 1911), pp. 150–1.

14. N.N. Pradhan, *Prachin Oriya Sahityare Nirguna Dhara* (Cuttack: Basanta Kumari Pradhan, 1986), p. 235.

15. Chittaranjan Das, 'Studies in Medieval Religion and Literature of Orissa', *Visva Bharati Annals*, vol. 4 (1951), p. 121.

16. A. Eschmann, 'Mahima Dharma and tradition' in Ishita Banerjee-Dube and Johannes Beltz (eds), *Popular Religion and Ascetic Practises: New Studies on Mahima Dharma* (New Delhi: Manohar, 2008).

17. Paritosh Das, *Sahajiya Cult of Bengal and the Pancha Sakha Cult of Orissa* (Calcutta: Firma K.L. Mukhopadhyay, 1988), p. 175.

18. See, for instance, Sanjeeb Nayak 'A Note on the Mystic Poetry of Bhima Bhoi', in Banerjee-Dube and Beltz (eds), *Popular Religion and Ascetic Practises*, pp. 103–16.

19. Das, 1995, 163.

20. B.C. Mazumder, *Typical Selections from Oriya Literature*, vol. 2 (Calcutta: University of Calcutta, 1923), p. xxxiv.

21. Ibid.

22. P.C. Raut, 'Review of Manuscripts', *Journal of the Kalinga Historical Research Society*, vol. 1, no. 3 (1946), p. 275.

23. S.K. Chatterji, *The People, Language and Culture of Orissa*, p. 62.

24. *Utkala Deepika*, 19 November 1881.

25. *Indian Report of the Orissa Baptist Mission for 1887–88*, Angus Library, Baptist Missionary Society Archives, Regent's Park College, Oxford, p. 46.

26. Ibid.

27. Ibid.

28. Cited in Debendra Kumar Dash, 'Bhima Bhoi o Mahima Dharma', *Eshana*, vol. 34 (1997), pp. 120–52.

29. Vasu, *The Modern Buddhism*, p. 164.

30. Mazumdar, *Sonepur in the Sambalpur Tract*, Appendix iv, pp. 126–36.

31. It is surprising that the *District Gazetteer* of Bolangir published in 1968 credited Bhima Bhọi with the attack on the Jagannath temple which is stated to have taken place in 1880, N. Senapati and N.K. Sahu (eds), *Orissa District Gazetteers, Bolangir*, p. 109. A Census of Mayurbhanj also attributes the attack to Bhima Bhoi. Mohammed Laeequddin, *Census of Mayurbhanj State, vol. 1: Reports*, 1931, p. 120.

32. Scholars from western Orissa take it upon themselves to disprove Vasu and Mazumdar's assertion that Bhima Bhoi headed the attack on the Jagannath temple. The basic assumption behind their attempt is that leadership in the incident in no way enhances the prestige or popularity of the non-violent, introspective poet. B. Nepak, *Bhima Bhoi, The Adivasi Poet Philosopher*, p. 71; Kasinath Pradhan, '"Puri Jagannathanka prati akraman" ghatanare santha Bhima Bhoinka samprikta ki?' ('Is Sant Bhima Bhoi connected with the incident of the "attack on Jagannath in Puri"?'), *Saptarsi* (Sambalpur University Journal), nos 7–8, (1981), pp. 79–83. Surendra Nath Chinara, on the other hand, supports Vasu and Mazumdar in stating that if Bhima Bhoi did not actually lead the attack, he definitely inspired it. S.N. Chinara, 'The History of the Mahima Cult in Orissa' (PhD dissertation, University of Berhampur, 1982), p. 34.

33. Vasu, *The Modern Buddhism*, p. 164.

34. Binayak Misra, *Oriya Sahityara Itihasa* (Cuttack: Utkal Sahitya Press, 1928), p. 278.

35. M. Mansinha, *Oriya Sahityara Itihasa* (Cuttack: Grantha Mandir, second edition, 1976), p. 206.

36. Chittaranjan Das, *A Glimpse into Oriya Literature* (Bhubaneswar: Orissa Sahitya Akademi, 1982), p. 158.

37. As an instance of this mode of thinking, see M. Mansinha, 'The Greatest Tribals', in M.N. Dash (ed.), *Sidelights on the History and Culture of Orissa* (Cuttack: Vidyapuri, 1977), pp. 207–16.

38. For a discussion, read G.N. Dash, 'Changing one's own identity: The Role of Language in the Transformation of a Subregional Tradition' in Angelika Malinar (ed.), *Time in India: Concepts and Practices* (New Delhi: Manohar, 2007), pp. 264–8.

39. Numerous essays published in anthologies and journals bear titles like 'Bhima Bhoi the revolutionary' and 'Bhima Bhoi the radical social reformer'.

40. Bhagirathi Nayak, *Oriya Poets through the Ages* (Balasore: Grantha Bharati, 2002), p. 71.

41. The fact of late colonization of Orissa and its incorporation into the Bengal Presidency meant that from the beginning, there was a tangible sense of the Bengali as the 'other', particularly among the elites who took to English education and competed for jobs in the British administration. For a general discussion of the growth of Oriya nationalism, see, G.N. Dash, 'Jagannatha and Oriya nationalism'.

42. Ibid.

43. See Ishita Banerjee-Dube, *Divine Affairs: Religion, Pilgrimage and the State in Colonial and Postcolonial India* (Shimla: Indian Institute of Advanced Study, 2001), pp. 71–5 for a critical discussion of the case.

44. Dash, 'Changing One's Own identity'.

45. I am aware that there is no monolithic Bengali identity. As stated above, it is a trend of linguistic nationalism in Orissa which reified a single Bengali identity for self-constitutive purposes.

13. LIVING ABOVE HIPPOPOTAMUS STREET

RELIGION AND COMMUNITY IN WORKING CLASS NORTH INDIA

Daniel Gold

Hippopotamus Street[1] runs along the bottom of a hill that in the first half of the twentieth century was on the northern outskirts of Gwalior, then the capital of arguably the most important princely state in central India. With Gwalior now forming the centre of a metropolitan area of about a million inhabitants in northern Madhya Pradesh, the hill above Hippopotamus Street marks a boundary between the older princely city and extensive new development beyond it. Many of the outlying new colonies are middle class or better, their residents driving into town through a congested pass. From Hippopotamus Street itself, however, it is possible to walk to the city's main commercial district in twenty minutes or so, and many of the hill residents do so daily.

The hill above the street is framed by temples. At its top is a cluster of structures of different size and age that house several old images, the most prominent of which is Satya Narayan, who gives the hill its name: Satya Narayan ki tekri (*ṭekrī,* in the local language, means a small hill). Just below the street, opposite the steps leading up to to the Satya Narayan temple area, is another group of temples including one with an image of a Jain tirthankara of monumental (for Gwalior) proportions and another with a stone Shiva lingam about four feet in diameter, credibly said to be the thickest in the area. The hill seems blessed by impressive divine presences.

Indeed, not so long ago, when Satya Narayan hill was still on the periphery of the city, urban gentlefolk used to go there on family excursions, picnicking at the temple areas—but they don't go much any more. For over the last few decades, as the city has grown, the working poor have started making their homes higher and higher up the hillside. People from the city visiting Satya Narayan temple now walk quickly up the steps to it from the street, eyes ahead. They think of the hill as a tough, somewhat dangerous district, one that no longer invites a secluded scenic stroll. For its residents, though, the hill can be a vibrant and lively place. It forms a network of interlocking neighbourhoods, mostly mixed, with a few predominantly Muslim areas and some settlements—more and less homogenous—of specific low-caste communities. People visit within neighbourhoods and across them, mixing according to factors of caste, class, occupation, and personal affinity. With neighbours facing similar pressures of urban life, even within its diversity the hill displays multiple forms of cohesion.

This essay is based on field research done in 2005, still fairly close to the time of the paper's writing. In pursuing an extended study of urban religion in Gwalior, I had made some acquaintances on Satya Narayan hill on previous visits to the city. Having earlier focused largely on issues of middle-class religion, I was intrigued by the area's religious culture and social styles, to both of which I was unaccustomed. So on a two-month visit during the monsoon season I made an effort to expand my networks there. Although I began by asking questions of religious practice, what I found myself observing were more often patterns of social interaction among castes, classes, and communities, the ways in which individuals adhered to apparent norms and sometimes transcended them. What follows is an account of some dynamics of socioreligious and political community that I encountered. Some names have been changed, but the people described are real.

TEMPLES FOR COMMUNITIES AND INDIVIDUALS

Hippopotamus Street runs for about three kilometres from east to west, with the steps leading up to the Satya Narayan temple beginning roughly at its middle. Walking from the steps toward the West, one comes to the image-makers' district, with its shops displaying figures of Hindu deities in many shapes and sizes. At its eastern end stands a temple to Valmiki, the legendary author of the Ramayana said to be from the sweeper caste. A sizable sweeper community lives in a scattered settlement behind the temple; they call themselves Valmiks after the sage.[2] In contrast to most people living on the hill—who did not particularly favour the impressive old temples in their immediate vicinity, many preferring the well-attended places of worship in town—members of two low-caste groups, the Valmiks and the leather-working Ahirwars, did regularly pay attention to deities enshrined at local sites. These sites, however, were not old ones, but newly built structures providing each community with a religious and social centre.

For both the Valmiks and the Ahirwars, the new structures served special functions for them as historically marginalized communities with sizable settlements on the hill. But because the communities present a contrast in their economic condition and cultural priorities, the sites served them in different ways. While both the Valmiks and Ahirwars are Dalits, 'oppressed', as the former untouchable castes are now called, the Valmiks include a number of people with middle-class jobs and the higher aspirations that go with them. With a longer history of politicization in the area, further, they are more ready than the Ahirwars to express their discontent, sometimes in eloquent (and practised) ways. Their temple has thus played a role in their political as well as sectarian development—neither of which is pronounced among the Ahirwars. Although not all Ahirwars I met were happy living on the hill, many seemed happy to be living in a homogeneous settlement. On the whole less educated and leading more traditional lifestyles than the Valmiks, they valued the close-knit caste community that the settlement provided. For them, the new shrine they built on the main lane in the area had become a point of communal pride.

AHIRWAR COMMUNITY

The Ahirwars' settlement is just to the east of the steps leading up to Satya Narayan temple. It begins about half-way up the hill and stretches to the top, bordering the steps in its final expanse. About forty families live in small-roomed houses there; many have close relatives in the settlement. The majority of the Ahirwar men remain in leather-working trades, expanded these days to include sandals made from synthetic material. When asked about their work, leather workers usually specify 'manufacture' or 'repair,' with the former more prestigious. Others work in small factories or as shop assistants;

married women sometimes roll *biḍis*—coarse, country-style cigarettes. Although some Ahirwars are educated and articulate, many are not, and of these, some don't place much value on educating their children fully either.

Bhotraj Ahirwar, although not well educated, is articulate and expressed obvious satisfaction in living in the settlement. The oldest of three brothers, he lives in a joint family with them, a divorced sister, and a widowed mother. They all share a courtyard, but have separate rooms for their families. Bhotraj and his next younger brother are both in leather-working trades. Bhotraj is in repair, setting up a sidewalk shop in a bazaar in an older section of the city beyond the main commercial district, where his brother works in a small shoe factory. Bhotraj's youngest brother and almost grown son were both at the time unemployed. The youngest brother, with a twelfth-grade education, is prized in the family for his literacy and would like to find an office job where he could use it. Bhotraj's son works as a cook in a catering business, but there aren't many weddings to cook for during the monsoon. Life is hard, but together they manage, and community life has its consolations.

Bhotraj smiled warmly when asked how he liked living on the hill. 'My family is here,' he said, 'my children and grandchildren.' Moreover, the settlement itself served as an extended family in a literal as well as figurative sense: like most residents, Bhotraj had relatives living there, in his case maternal grandparents and uncles. They invited one another to eat, went to one another's weddings and celebrated the Hindu holidays together: 'the forty families keep together in everything' they do. Although this idealized picture of village-style community in an urban environment undoubtedly had unstated internal stresses, it was a vision that Bhotraj treasured, a vision that was shared to at least some extent by many of the Ahirwars on the hill.

It was not, however, shared by all. Bharati Ahirwar is the only member of the community there attending college, her absent father earning a decent government salary as a member of the Indo-Tibet Border Police. Unlike most families there, Bharati did not have an extended family in the settlement; her father's parents lived in town and he bought on the hill because it was affordable. Bharati kept aloof from the younger generation in the settlement, preferring the company of her middle-class college friends, whom she visited at their homes in town. She too would like to live like them, or better: 'in good society, where people have education and understand its meaning. Here education is given no value. They think it's bad if a girl goes out'—even to study. Still, Bharati continued to participate in the community-wide festival celebrations and weddings that Bhotraj mentioned: they were almost an obligation of local community membership.

A more typical complaint about living in the settlement came from Dal Chand, one of Bhotraj's maternal relatives, and like him a leather worker. Although Dal Chand has studied more than most in his community—through high school, working on the side—he did not express dissatisfaction at carrying on his community's traditional occupation. Having returned from a stint of shoe making in Delhi, now at twenty-eight, he lived in the family house and made fancy sandals at a small factory in town. Dal Chand's dissatisfactions were common to people at his stage of life in all castes and classes: he just wanted to be his own person. At his father's house, he said, there is 'tension,' using the English word. To get some peace, he'd like to live on his own, somewhere in the city close to where he'd be working. Not that he wanted to stay in his present job—he didn't really like working under someone else. His ambitions remained modest: 'I just want my own shop where I can work as I like.' He was happy to remain 'a small craftsman' *(chhoṭa kārigar),* but for now valued independence over family and community life.

Whatever their feelings about actually living in community, though, most Ahirwars took a collective satisfaction in a newly built shrine to Shiva often referred to as Bhole Nath. Its main donors were two of their own: Phul Chand, a driver, and Raju, who made sandals—their names duly noted on the inaugural plaque. The shrine stood on the main lane running perpendicular to the steps, a mixed area, just opposite an alley leading up to the Ahirwar settlement. It thus at once dignified the portal to the Ahirwar domain and made a respectable Ahirwar mark on the larger neighbourhood—whose members did not, however, seem to offer many prayers there. For Ahirwars, though, the shrine was the one place of worship that they all mentioned consistently visiting. In the evenings, young Ahirwar men strolling together on the street pay it reverence as they pass. On Mondays, Shiva's Day, Bhotraj claims that 'Everyone goes, I mean everyone, the whole neighbourhood, they bring garlands and incense.' The shrine is uncovered, and not particularly imposing, but it is well maintained and aesthetically pleasing, proudly claimed by the Ahirwar community as its own.

VALMIK DISCONTENT

The Valmik temple, by contrast, is a sizable building that has multiple functions—one of four Valmik temples located in disparate areas of the city.[3] Although the term 'Valmik' is normally used as a respectful caste name accepted even by professed atheists in the community, it can also refer more narrowly to adherents of a sectarian tradition (normally from the same caste) who follow the sage Valmiki. The temple serves both groups: the sect through its regularly worshipped images of Valmiki and its large hall, which may be used by visiting sectarian sadhus as a place to stay; the caste community through the same hall when used by its local members as a rest house for wedding guests and as a general meeting place. Because of the temple's role as a meeting place for Valmiks, I was cautioned about it by a high-caste acquaintance who lives within range of the hill. Yet in addition to sadhus and some good-natured youth, the people I met there were retirees from lower middle-class jobs: a policeman, an office worker, a practitioner of traditional medicine. For the latter—some of them temple officers—the temple seemed to be a bastion of intracaste respectability.

The location of the temple on Hippopotamus Street itself helps contribute to the urban ambience of the Valmiks' district. In contrast to the Ahirwars' settlement—far from the street, self-contained, and traversed by footpaths, suggesting a village in its layout as well as its community ideals—the Valmiks' is a paved street ascending the gentle eastern slope of Satya Narayan hill, where Valmiks live interspersed with other mostly low castes. This area was settled earlier than the Ahirwars' and is more integrated with the city. Its population, moreover, is also better integrated into the regular urban economy. Although the majority of Valmiks, I was told, remain sweepers by profession, many of these have secure government jobs: working at the railway station, the jail, the city offices. Some, further, have been able to avail of opportunities offered to members of historically disadvantaged castes in education and employment to secure responsible government positions. These local bourgeoisie continue to live in the area in which they were brought up, close to their relatives and having roomier accommodation than they might be able to afford in a classier part of town. Socially and politically aware, however, they often remain discontent with where they are and are quick to express outrage at the way their caste has been treated.

Nand Kishore Kadam (BA, LLB) works as a revenue inspector for the Gwalior municipal corporation. His extended family has had mixed fortunes: two of his brothers had to be satisfied working in 'maintenance' in government offices, but another has his own garage in Bombay and is doing fairly well. While Nand Kishore and his Bombay brother have started using the name Kadam, a Maratha name that suggests membership in the old Gwalior Maratha aristocracy, the rest of the family uses the more plebeian Dhaulpuria (sometimes shortened to Dhaulkar).

Entering Nand Kishore's home after becoming comfortable in the Ahirwars' neighbourhood was like entering another world. With its good-sized rooms and plentiful upholstered furniture, it had more than the basic comforts of the Indian middle class. But Nand Kishore wasn't satisfied: the house was 'sufficient', he said, using the English word, but he was *compelled* to live there—really he'd rather be living in a nice colony. (Economic circumstances contributed to this compulsion, no doubt, but family considerations also entered the picture: many of his brothers and cousins, as well as his aging parents, lived nearby.) It was true that he had made some progress personally, he said, but his caste hadn't: its members remained mostly poor, the government didn't help, and Valmiks were still subject to discrimination. 'They think we make their temples impure and go shoo! shoo! shoo!' he said with excited gestures, 'Do I have a tail or big ears? They're human beings and I'm a human being!' He was vehemently against image worship and had little use for religion in general. These views were echoed by Nand Kishore's son Anil, a stylishly dressed young man who was getting a business degree, working in a cellphone shop, and selling Amway products on the side. I had met Anil before his father and had been surprised when he told me he was an atheist—not a common confession in provincial India—but now I saw that he was just following a family tradition. Professed atheists but outspoken in voicing the grievances of their caste, Nand Kishore and Anil have ambivalent feelings about the Valmik temple standing proudly on the street below: although they disdain it religiously, they nevertheless appreciate it as a useful centre for their community.

Nand Kishore inherits his strident attitude toward caste prejudice, at least, from his uncle, an old Valmik activist, who had edited a local newspaper for the community in the middle decades of the last century. But Uncle Dhaulpuria, who lives in the neighbourhood—like the majority of Valmiks but more so—also embraces religion. He maintains a shrine to Kali in front of his house, fronting a little square on the main road, which Nand Kishore's wife regularly visits. He recognizes Kali's special powers as a supplement to Guru Valmiki's. Hindu divinities such as Kali can help with things in the world, he says, which are not Guru Valmiki's particular concern: Valmik was 'a light of God' who offered salvation but did not deign to meddle in mundane affairs. Some years ago, a guru in the Valmik tradition gave Uncle Dhaulpuria the *ram* mantra. (A popular mantra throughout north India, *ram* has a special significance for followers of Valmiki, the legendary author of the Ramayana.) 'Ram mantra is the best mantra in the world,' said Uncle Dhaulpuria, 'everyone who repeats it gets liberation.' Clearly, whatever political significance the Valmiki tradition has had for him, it also has a vital religious meaning that is comprehended within a broader Hindu world view. For him, the Valmik temple has been a centre for both political organization and salvation.

INDIVIDUAL PILGRIMAGES

Other caste temples around Hippopotamus Street play their own roles in community, often becoming focal points for both conflicts and new alliances. Over in the image-makers' district, for example, leadership at a temple to the divine builder Vishvakarma had for some time been a point of contention in the artisan community that bears his name. There was hope, however, that things would be resolved in a forthcoming intracommunal election. The Malis' temple in the temple-cluster below the street, by contrast, had recently seen separate groups come together. It had just hosted a celebration of the formal union of three small historically distinct gardening communities: one with local origins, one from Vraj to the north, and one from Rajasthan to the west. Meeting at the temple, the three groups had voted to unite their separate caste organizations, giving sanction to practices of intermarriage and intercommensality that had already begun in practice. For members of communities without local caste temples, however, temple allegiances are largely individual, determined by people's own predilections and personal histories. In these cases, a temple's proximity can be in inverse proportion to its perceived value.

When most Hindus on the hill were asked about their temple-going habits, they named one or other of the better known temples in town—most often one to Hanuman or Durga, deities generally understood to be effective in Gwalior as elsewhere for getting one's practical job done. The cluster of temples on the top of the hill also includes shrines to Hanuman and Durga, but the majority of the people who live on the hill ignore them. When I asked Narendra Mishra, a hill resident and professional religious story-teller, why this was so, he suggested that one reason people go to the temples in town is because of the effort involved in doing so: to get results from a divinity you need to make a sacrifice. At the same time, though, we can imagine that going to the big Gwalior temples reinforces the hill residents' identity as ordinary inhabitants of the city. Just because they live in a less than respectable neighbourhood that happens to have some nice old temples nearby doesn't mean that they shouldn't go to the popular temples in town like everyone else.

The Satya Narayan temple complex itself is largely visited by middle-class Hindus from outside the neighbourhood and maintained by well-to-do patrons in the city. In addition to the Satya Narayan temple and some smaller Hindu shrines, it includes an old Bhairava temple and a newer one housing the image of a Jain Tirthankara found on the hill.[4] The attendance as well as the construction and maintenance of the Jain temple, in fact, turned out to be largely a family affair. Not only was it commissioned by the mother of a Jain household in town to house a large Jain image found on the hill, but it is visited almost exclusively by members of her family. The temple is locked during the day, although an old Jain caretaker whose son keeps a small shop on the hill has a key to admit appropriate visitors. Every morning, male members of the family walk up from the city in their street clothes, change into traditional dress at the temple, and perform a service for about an hour; women from the family join in for the second part of the service. For this family, as for others from the city who visit temples at the complex, hiking up the hill is treated as an ascetic effort, reinforced by the tough reputation of the neighbourhood through which the steps pass. If the hill residents' visit to popular city temples helps normalize their identity, the city dwellers' trek up the now disreputable Satya Narayan hill can lend their temple-going practices an air of ascetic exoticism.

The relatively small number of hill residents who do regularly visit the temple complex do so for ordinary and less ordinary reasons. Upendra Joshi, the college-going son of a middle-class Brahmin family living low on the hill, is drawn to the Bhairava temple, which isn't in his immediate neighbourhood. He visits it weekly like other middle-class devotees, if with a somewhat shorter walk. For Daulat Ram Ahirwar, however, who does shoe repair off the main bazaar, a daily morning tour of all the hill temples helped mark him as socio-religiously special in his own eyes and others'. Perceived as a character by many who know him, Daulat Ram is an amiable middle-aged man who is given to high-minded talk. A visible aspect of his high-minded persona is his daily ascent to the temple complex to do ritual puja at all the Hindu shrines and temples there. (Not welcome at the Jain temple because of his caste, he avoids it.) The priests all accommodate Daulat Ram and he doesn't hurry; his daily routine takes about an hour. Although a lengthy daily morning puja at a nearby temple is a traditional Brahminic practice, if not readily kept by Brahmins these days (particularly in urban India), it was not something Ahirwars, or those from most other Hindu castes, normally do. Whatever Daulat Ram's personal reasons for his practice—and no one seemed to doubt his piety or sincerity—it also presented him as a sort of Brahmin among Ahirwars, an anomalous status that he obviously relished. As an individual, he practiced temple worship against the grain to his own idiosyncratic ends.

CASTE, CLASS, AND FRIENDSHIP

Upendra Joshi and Daulat Ram Ahirwar lived in close proximity to one another near the steps, in an area that included small, unfinished, one-room dwellings, older, multi-roomed houses with places for livestock, and a few new homes built to basic middle-class norms. Because this neighbourhood is on the path leading straight up to the

Satya Narayan temple area, it is itself sometimes referred to as Satya Narayan Hill, taken in a narrow sense. Most of its three or four thousand residents lived off small alleyways branching out from a wider lane running toward the east, perpendicular to the steps; that lane, after a few bends, turned into the wider road passing through the Valmik neighbourhood. A few houses lined the west side of the steps—older, village-style ones below, with places for animals, and newer construction above. As with most neighbourhoods on the hill, the area is mixed in both caste and class, with individuals intermingling according to caste familiarity, class style, and personal affection. In general, caste ties seemed more important for older and more traditional people and class attitudes more important for the more urbanized and young. Among the young in particular, personal friendships could transcend both caste and class—but not for everyone, and less readily for extreme divides.

JITENDRA AND JITENDRA

Upendra Joshi's younger brother, Jitendra, was best friends with a neighbour named Jitendra Gujar. The two were usually referred to by their nicknames: the first as Chikku and the second as Guddu; both were in their late teens when I met them. The two had grown up near each other in houses on the west side of the steps and remained close.

The Gujars' house is older, in a village style, and lower down on the hill. Although Guddu's grandfather had been in government service, the family had maintained the caste profession of dairying on the side and had kept milch animals there before the hill was well developed. The family had been living near Hippopotamus Street for 'a hundred years', said Guddu's grandmother, having earlier lived near the big Jain temple across Hippopotamus Street. They had moved to their present house thirty years ago. The grandparents still kept milch animals and let neighbours come for dairy products, but Guddu's father had prospered in the transport business before his premature death and had built a large house in one of the outlying middle-class colonies; Guddu had access to a family motorcycle.

Chikku's father, by contrast, was the first from his village to take a middle-class job in town: he worked in a bank. With no established city networks and limited means, he built on the hill above Guddu's family because land there was affordable. His sons were serious about their education and two had also managed to find work. Jitendra, the youngest, took both college classes and orders from shops for Cadbury's chocolate; Upendra, the middle brother, was pursuing an MA; the oldest brother had a business degree and and did specialized marketing for a big corporation. All were striving towards some recognizable goals of the educated middle class.

The Joshi family also maintained its Brahminic sensibilities about purity, which Chikku seemed to take seriously, politely restricting my access to the puja room and kitchen. He would idealize the village, which he visited, for the way in which Brahmins could maintain their separateness and regreted that it was so hard to do so on the hill. Still, Chikku tried to keep aloof. Although he would lounge on the steps like others, he often just sat alone and watched. I never saw him being chummy with any of the Ahirwars who also sometimes mingled there. He tended to speak of them and the Valmiks (both of whom he generally referred to by less dignified names—Chamars and Bhangis) in hushed tones as if even talking about them was improper. Even though he used the same tones to speak of the settlement of poor cowherding Gujars near the top of the hill, he saw his middle-class college-going friend Guddu in an entirely different light. Certainly, Gujars (despite the assumed proclivities of those in the hilltop settlement), though among the less elevated castes, are generally not seen to be unclean in the same way as Bhangis and Chamars; in Gwalior, moreover, some claimed to be Kṣatriyas. Guddu's family had some money and his grandmother was an imposing local matriarch; in the evenings, Chikku's mother could sometimes be found visiting her on her stoop. However the Joshis finally perceived Guddu's family's caste status, they included the family in their circle. Chikku treated Guddu as a middle-class friend, not as one of those other Gujars up the hill. Although his caste sensibilities were pronounced, they were not overwhelming. No doubt encompassing stereotypical ideas of low-caste behaviours, they could be transcended when he met someone who conformed to his middle-class norms.

MOHIT AND THE BRAHMINS

In some cases, though, a tension between low caste and middle class led to unwarranted social pretensions and relationships that could seem strained. Mohit Moré was one of the most prosperous residents of the neighbourhood. An electrical contractor in his mid-thirties, he was born in the neighbourhood, and—the only son of an elderly father—had inherited the house in which he grew up. He had done some recent renovations on the house, which stood on the lane running east from the steps: it now had another story on top and a living room with a shiny new floor that looked like marble. Sometimes he came in from town in a spiffy suit and chatted on his cellphone—which was not, as it was in more prosperous parts of the city, an accoutrement many people in the neighbourhood had. But Mohit could also frequently be found sitting on his stoop in an undershirt and lungi, chewing paan and shooting the breeze. He was politically active and familiar with local polling figures and became the source I trusted most for neighbourhood population estimates and, since he was in contracting business, for land values.

When I first met Mohit, he was lounging on the steps with Liaqat Khan, a young man in his early twenties who lived in an extended family occupying an old house on the west side of the steps between Guddu's and Chikku's. They introduced each other as good friends, and their relaxed demeanour suggested some genuine affection between them. But, as I was to learn, Mohit was generally garrulous and Liaqat regularly wore a broad smile and seemed friendly with everyone. Liaqat, it turned out, also worked for Mohit, learning the electrical trade, so their good friendship was not without mutual self-interest. Mohit discussed his friendships more pointedly one day at the Sharmas', a Brahmin family who lived in a new house on the west side of the hill and also rented out some nearby rooms. This house, he said was his 'own house,' as was Liaqat's. 'But over there,' he said, indicating the other side of the steps, where he lived, 'where there are a lot of chamars...the society's no good.... They play dice. They drink.' (Mohit himself had invited me to drinking parties more than once). 'I don't have anything to do with them,' he continued, and, at my expression of doubt, expanded: 'I talk with them all, but don't maintain relations with them. Here,' he added, referring to the small group of houses west of the steps, 'people are educated.'

For Mohit, then, the steps represented a dividing line between a small, demarcated middle-class area on the west and the large, predominantly lower class area to the east that included the Ahirwar settlement. And as I thought about it, this was a line that others marked, too. People living on the western rim of the steps simply walked down the hill into town; I couldn't remember seeing the young men who lived there standing about in the lane with Ahirwars and others. The steps themselves were neutral territory, where everyone could and did loiter, but there was no real neutral public space to the west of them. It was with this western area that Mohit wanted me to associate him.

Mohit had also alluded (inaccurately) to caste during his excited declaration of this to me: 'Here there are only Brahmins and Thakurs'—and it is true that the three Brahmin families in the neighbourhood lived to the west of the steps. But what the Brahmin families, the Khans, and Gujars had in common was class, not caste, in which they were more or less on par with Mohit. Still, after Mohit left, the Sharma patriarch gave me to understand that he didn't feel as close to Mohit as Mohit professed to feel for him: 'He's low caste,' said Papa Sharma, unasked. When I later inquired among my Ahirwar friends, I was told that Mohit was a Baraar—a caste from which midwives come—and, it seems, the only one in the neighborhood.

Because Mohit used the Maharashtrian surname Moré, I originally understood him—as I did the Valmik Kadams—to be part of Gwalior's formerly elite old Maharashtrian community. Mohit never dissuaded me from this view, even when I asked him if he knew Marathi—as most from that community still do. In this, he differed from Anil Kadam, who seeing my confusion, immediately responded: 'I'm not a Maharashtrian, I am a Valmik: do you have a problem with that?' Anil had an extended caste community to live in and a politicized sense of caste pride. Mohit had neither and sought an uneasy social solidarity with some of the neighbourhood economic elite through class. Anil wore both his caste and class with aplomb: even though most of his Valmik relatives were poor, he mixed with them readily and unashamedly; but because he grew up middle-class, he was also able to interact easily with his city friends. Mohit, by contrast, was a lower-class boy made good through shrewdness and energy and had never quite mastered middle-class social graces. If Mohit had actually behaved more like the Sharmas, it might have been easier for them to forget about his caste origins. But they didn't—Mohit knew it, and it made him nervous.

JAINS IN A BAD NEIGHBOURHOOD

Down the lane from the steps, just past the Ahirwar shrine to Bhole Nath, is a store run by a Jain family. Its wares are most modest—soaps and penny-candies and other small goods that might satisfy the immediate needs and desires of people with simple tastes and not much money. The family had earlier lived down in the city, and like most who migrated from there to the hill, came because they would rather own than rent and the hill was affordable. Although they participated in the urban middle-class Jain culture, they obviously weren't very prosperous.

Jitu Dholkar, Anil's cousin, often came up from the Valmik area, further east, and sat on the curb in front of the shop. Jitu's father was a sweeper in the train station, but Jitu worked for a videographer. Because the wedding season was in hiatus, he didn't have too much to do, so these days, the shop's stoop was his *adda,* his station. He seemed to enjoy the action that sometimes took place near the Ahirwars' Bholenath temple and was also friends with Amit Jain, a soft-spoken teenager who lived behind the shallow storefront and often minded it.

I first met Jitu and Amit together, high on the steps, as I was descending from the temples above. Jitu was older, with a more outgoing personality, and showed interest in my questions about the area. We arranged to meet the next day. Although he would eventually provide me an entry into the Valmik community, at the time, I couldn't place his surname. Outside any particular context, Jitu and Amit seemed like any two friends from the area enjoying the evening view. Since Jitu was with Amit Jain, I presumed he was from some caste traditionally understood as clean.

When I next saw Amit, I didn't immediately recognize him. By then Jitu had introduced me to a large circle of his Valmik relatives and friends. We were gathered in Anil Kadam's living room, the nicest place to meet that the extended family had to offer, and engaged in a rousing conversation on caste, atheism, Hindu nationalism, and patriarchy. Women from the family spoke up and diverse views were aired. It seemed very genteel, if perhaps sometimes more heated than the usual middle-class parlour discussion. In the midst of it, Amit Jain came in and sat down. I thought he was another friend from the Valmik community. When he later re-introduced himself, I did a silent double-take but then reproached myself for my jaded presumptions: what was so odd about a lower-middle-class boy imbibing some intellectual culture in a more prosperously middle-class drawing room? I soon got a good glimpse, though, of where my presumptions came from.

Finding Amit at the shop one day the next week, I asked him about the Jain temple on the hill. This led to an introduction to his grandfather, who kept a set of keys. When I expressed an interest in Jainism, grandfather called his wife and they both spoke to me at length on Jain philosophy. In a cramped little room on the hill, they took turns, lecturing me with fervour and erudition. I was impressed. When talk turned to the temple, they said it was open only for Jains. What about the *baniyas* with whom local Jains sometimes married? Well, they would open it for high-caste Hindus, as they would for an interested foreigner like me, but they didn't want the riffraff on the hill coming in. (They were likely thinking primarily of the Ahirwars who lived in the temple's immediate vicinity.) What, then, did they think of their grandson's mixing with low-caste friends? They both looked immediately stricken: they didn't like it at all. Their faces showed sincere pain. It didn't matter to them that Amit's particular low-caste friends were familiar with middle-class ways and even occasionally helped to widen his intellectual horizons. They may not even have imagined this was possible. But Amit knew who he liked and the worlds in which they lived. So what if the old folks don't like it? There wasn't much they could really do.

HINDUS AND MUSLIMS

For the most part, Hindus and Muslims lived amicably enough on the hill. Muslims, when asked, regularly reported that there was no 'tension' (sometimes using the English word), and genuine intercommunal friendships were patent. Even an ardent Hindu nationalist organizer who lived on the hill distinguished between local Muslims—who were OK—and those from outside. In part this is a factor of Gwalior's demography: because the Muslim population is so small (maybe six per cent of the total) and generally poor, the Hindu majority doesn't feel threatened and so has no real cause to be intimidating. Muslims recognize the situation and aren't especially assertive about their collective prerogatives. Particularly interesting in these circumstances are some of the variations of religious observance and identity that emerge—often within the same family—as individual Muslims live within a Hindu world.

HOLIDAYS AT THE KHANS

Liaqat Khan's was the only Muslim family that lived permanently in the neighbourhood of the steps. Some Muslim renters came and went, but Liaqat's family was a fixture. Their house was an older one, fairly low down, built before much of the recent development. Their stoop was in a prominent place—on the west side of the steps opposite the main lane to the east—and some of the household women who might be found doing chores there were strong neighbourhood personalities.

The women also seemed to have stronger Islamic identities than the men—stronger, at least, than Liaqat's. Although Liaqat's cousin, who worked as a mechanic near a large mosque, went to common prayer every Friday, Liaqat went 'very little...a couple of times a year.' When asked about his favourite holidays, he mentioned Diwali, Holi—both Hindu holidays—and Id, in that order. The daughters-in-law of the household would reverse the order, usually beginning with the 'sweet' Id, when they cook vermicelli noodles with sugar, and giving particular attention to Moharram, when they have big feasts. During that time they exchange invitations with Muslim relatives and friends in nearby areas, while distributing food to the Hindu neighbours: 'the Ahirwars come and take it as prasād,' said Liaqat's aunt Meena Begum, using the Hindi word for sanctified food.

Liaqat's aunts were ambivalent about participating in some widely celebrated festivals grounded in Hindu tradition. According to Meena Begum, they celebrate Diwali 'to make the children happy.' Anwari Begum added that they, too, like the Hindus, whitewash their houses at Diwali and give sweets to the children: 'the Hindus do these things so we have to as well.' She was clear, however, that 'we don't do *pūjā-pāṭh*' or other specifically religious ceremonies. Anwari Begum (like many respectable Hindus) didn't really appreciate Holi, a spring festival that can get a little raucous. 'We don't like it,' she said twice. Unlike some of her more rigorously observant Muslim acquaintances, however, who would pointedly not participate in Holi at all, Anwari did so as not to offend her neighbours: they 'acknowledge you and come; we don't want to refuse those people.'

Meena and Anwari were sisters who came from Sabalgarh, a town in a bordering district that had an intercommunal demographic similar to Gwalior's but was considerably smaller and more provincial. They seem to have been brought up, however, in a household that had a more definite notion of Islamic religious identity than the one into which they had married. There, as here, they lived among Hindus but had ties with Muslims in other areas not far away where it was easy to give full expression to Muslim holidays and family celebrations. Now living where they did on the hill, they celebrated in a small Muslim settlement below, just across Hippopotamus Street. This was the way Islamic life went in the neighbourhoods they've lived in—they didn't seem to mind.

MUSLIM CRAFTSMEN AND HINDU IMAGES

One of the areas on the hill with a substantial concentration of Muslims was the image-makers district. Although the owners of the five or so image-making establishments in the district—who are also the prime salesmen—are all Hindu, they employ Muslims on the manufacturing end, especially in the less-skilled, labour-intensive finishing work. These image-workers maintain their identities as Muslims and are aware of themselves primarily as craftsmen, not devotees, but they nevertheless sometimes give thought to their relationships to the Hindu images that they produce.

Ansar Khan, in his early thirties, who came from a nearby village, had been working in image manufacturing for years, mostly polishing cut images, but sometimes painting them, too. He liked the painting work: demanding higher skills, it paid more, and he hoped to get more assignments in that line. For a while, Ansar was renting a room from his (Hindu) employer on Hippopotamus Street itself, but when the employer needed the space for his own family, Ansar rented a room by the Satya Narayan steps for a few months (where I first met him) before moving in with his wife's family across Hippopotamus Street from the image-maker's district.

Ansar was fond of the figures of the Hindu divinities he polished and painted. Although he declined to name a favourite, the one he liked best was clearly Durga—whom he called (as do many in the area) simply the 'lion rider': her image 'is good to look at,' he said, 'and to make.' But Ansar's fondness for goddess figures in general went beyond the mere crafting of an image. He frequently went to a private shrine to Santoshi Ma that was run by an elderly, unmarried Maratha woman; she lived with her natal family on the hill between the Satya Narayan steps and the Valmiks' area. (Not too long ago, Santoshi Ma had been a goddess of very little renown, but her popularity was greatly heightened by a 1975 hit film about her called *Jai Santoshi Ma*.)[5] On Fridays, about 8 p.m., the Maratha woman would become possessed by the goddess, who answered questions and granted boons. The shrine drew devotees from the city, but people from the hill sometimes came, too. Not all, though, were admitted: some Valmiks reported being turned away, and foreign scholars were not welcome during the time of possession. But Ansar and his wife had no trouble going repeatedly: the couple had faith. 'I do puja,' Ansar declared with a touch of defiance, 'I am a Muslim, sure, but I accept all.' Just as many Gwalior Hindus readily visit Sufi shrines they find powerful, Ansar visits Santoshi Ma.[6]

A more complex case is presented by Irfan Khan, who himself sometimes sang at Sufi shrines. His outward identification with Hindu divinities and traditions went further than Ansar's, but it was also more ambivalent. I first met Irfan in 2003, as he was polishing an image in a shop I was visiting together with an acquaintance of the shopowner's. 'This boy not only polishes images,' the shopowner remarked, 'he also sings.' It turned out that Irfan was from a family of q*awwals* that lived on the hill above the shop. Even in Gwalior, though, they were very small-time performers and none of them seems to have made much of a living out of *qawwali*. The paterfamilias had kept a day job as a mechanic; other brothers also worked in *nauṭankī*, a popular performance tradition, and toured villages.

Irfan's main professional outlet for his music was actually not in qawwali but in Ramayana performances. Small in stature and still in his late teens, he was well suited to playing women's roles. He didn't do these performances in Gwalior, he said, where people knew him and might not accept the fact that he was a Muslim playing a Hindu divinity. As part of a professional troupe, however, he toured medium-sized towns in western UP. Because devotees gave special reverence to actors in Ram Lila performances even when they were off stage, Irfan took on an overt Brahminic identity while he was on tour: he called himself Sanjay Sharma, wore a dhoti, painted a tilak on his forehead, and kept vegetarian. Although Irfan was feeling exuberant during most of his talk, he was reticent at first about his Hindu Ram Lila persona. When asked how he felt about it, Irfan turned reflective: pretending to be a Hindu offstage during the Ram Lila was like pretending to be a woman during the performance. 'I am a Muslim,' he said, 'but my profession...my art: I transform myself—I change. It's also a big thing that even though I'm a man, I change to a woman....Then when I come down from the stage I'm a guy like you.' Irfan could play a convincing Sita on stage and a convincing Sanjay on the street. But in both cases he was demonstrating devotion to his craft, not to religious ideals.

Often performing with Irfan in both qawwali and Ram Lila is his younger brother Jamal: 'For qawwali, my name is Jamal Khan; for Ram Lila, it's Bunty Sharma.' Jamal was more energetic than Irfan and more ambitious. He had accepted a popular qawwal in town as his ustad and had learned some theatrical dance. With his drive and dancing abilities, Jamal was able to find work year round in theatrical companies that toured villages in the region, usually playing women's roles. He did not, like his brother, have to polish images on the side.

During the course of these village performances Jamal befriended Rajesh Mishra, a young brahman a few years older than him who lived on the flat top of the hill above the image-makers' district: 'Jamal plays ladies' roles,' said Rajesh, 'I play gents',' saying *ladies* and *gents* in English. (In the Ram Lila, Rajesh had usually played Lakshman—although after our conversation the sudden resignation of the actor in his troupe playing Sita had landed him *that* important role.) Rajesh's family maintained their Brahminic traditions—his father doing puja every morning in their very cramped quarters—but Jamal was obviously most welcome in their house. His mother, whom I had previously seen as stiff and dour, ashamed of their current poverty, opened up when she saw Jamal and greeted him with a warm smile. The feeling of genuine intercommunal togetherness at the Mishras' house may have inspired Jamal to comment on how he, as a Muslim, felt about his work in

Hindu religious performances. Rajesh and Jamal were discussing their craft when Jamal, talking about the Ram Lila, digressed:

I don't see things as separate. I really *enjoy* working there. Sometimes you find some of our brothers who say: Why are you working in the Ram Lila; it's not in our Sharia. But I don't accept this. Brother, it's all one.

He went on to recite a couple of verses from Hindu poets suggesting similarities of Hindu and Muslim mystical paths but concluded on a more tentative, political note, 'As far as our city goes, there's unity...there hasn't been any strife yet and there won't be. This is what I want...' Unlike his brother commenting above, Jamal here took seriously both the spiritual and communal implications of his cross-religious performance. He knew that some people, especially in his own community, could find problems with what he did, and was glad he lived in a place where those problems weren't likely to cause him trouble.

COMMUNAL CONFRONTATION FIZZLES

The religious extremists in Gwalior were sooner to be found on the Hindu side than on the Muslim,[7] but the local organizer I came across on the hill wasn't having an easy time finding causes to motivate his troops. Ashok Gupta was the chairman of one of several Gwalior divisions of the Hindu Mahasabha youth wing. The Hindu Mahasabha is one of the oldest organizations on the Hindu right and—while no longer nationally prominent—has a long history in Gwalior and remains active there. 'Youth wing' is something of a misnomer for Ashok's membership: people could remain in it well into middle age. Ashok was 32 and had been a member for twenty years. Born on the hill, he continued to live there with his family in a tall house near the Valmiks' area to the east and a Muslim settlement just up the hill. He had a shop specializing in pulses in a nearby commercial area and said he was happy with his life. I believed him.

Being a leader of the Mahasabha youth wing gave Ashok some status—he had a big sign proclaiming his position posted on his door—and an outlet for his energy. But because local issues were hard to come by, he often had to resort to some well-worn national ones. He told me about the function he was planning for later in the week in support of the Hindu nationalist leader L.K. Advani's recent statements about rebuilding the Ram Mandir at the site of the Babri Masjid in Ayodhya. (The masjid was destroyed in 1993, so by 2005 the issue had become pretty stale.) I wondered what kind of audience Ashok would get. Finding local issues took imagination: the youth wing of Mahasabha was also pressing for guards at Gwalior's major temples; because terrorists could infiltrate from Pakistan and attack them, said Gupta, there should be armed policemen there from 4 to 8 p.m., when the temples were most active. But the police demurred, finding no need.

Was it just infiltrators from Pakistan who posed this threat, I asked Ashok, or were local Muslims also involved? No, no, he wasn't worried about local Muslims. 'The Muslims that live in Gwalior say that they live in India, that they're Indian.' At first he seemed to take this attributed statement as something he believed, distinguishing local Muslims from the Islamic activists he associated with places such as Aligarh. Explaining why he would nevertheless not accept a Muslim as a friend, however, he didn't seem so sure about their Indian *bona fides:* 'How can you trust them? Tomorrow they might go to Pakistan.' Ashok lived near Muslims, didn't have much to do with them and didn't trust them, but their proximity was not a worry. I soon found out why.

We were talking on Ashok's flat roof, and he wanted to show me something. He pointed down to a small, nondescript shrine on the street that went down to the Valmik temple. 'Two or three months ago,' he told me, ' the Muslims took it over *(qabzā kar liyā).'* By this he meant that some nearby Muslims had started offering sehras there. Sehras are short strands of flowers bound together on top and customarily offered at Sufi shrines. But Ashok insisted that this was not a Sufi shrine. Instead it was a fifty-year-old Shiva temple. So they had to 'liberate' it *(mukta karna),* using the language used by those who claimed the Ayodhya site for Hindus by destroying the Babri Masjid. In this case, however, Ashok just had to threaten the perpetrating devotees with police action for them to cease and desist. It was difficult for Ashok to find opponents ready to play his game.

Frankly, the site looked to me like a Sufi shrine, of which there are surprisingly many in Gwalior (although I didn't press the issue with Ashok at the time): it was a platform that held a miniature building with a dome—no familiar Hindu image could be seen. As far as I could make out, it had long been inactive until some local people had started offering reverence to it. Perhaps because they were motivated not by communal assertion but from a surge of customary piety that had not yet led to habit, they decided it wasn't worth a confrontation that would not end nicely for them in any event. Yes, they let themselves be bullied, but this was a battle they saw no point in joining.

I passed by the site several times since my visit with Ashok and noticed neither sehras nor malas: its recent period of activity was clearly over. When I asked people about the shrine and what went on there, nobody had much to say: old inactive shrines are not particularly noteworthy. Certainly, nobody mentioned that an incident had occurred there a few months earlier. Either people wanted to keep neighbourhood secrets quiet (Ashok certainly didn't) or, more likely, whatever happened at the site never made much of a public impression. To rally his troops, Ashok would have to try harder.

OWNERSHIP AND PROTEST

There has, however, been violent protest on the Satya Narayan hill, incidents leading to front page headlines. The causes were not religious, but political and economic—issues of alleged police brutality and landownership. There weren't many renters living on the hill. Most people who moved there did so because they preferred to live in their own house—even if small and inconveniently located—rather than to pay rent in town. The land up the side of the hill was for sale, but the flat top of the hill and some land just below it on the side away from Hippopotamus Street was supposed to be held in public trust. Nevertheless, people built there anyway, sometimes buying houses and land from previous squatters. On 13 and 14 August 2002—just before India's Independence Day of 15 August—the municipal authorities decided to crack down. They ended up having to send police reinforcements to clear parts of the hilltop, an area that housed some of the hill's most unfortunate residents.

On the whole, the top of the hill was not a very desirable place to live. It was open to the hot sun and wind, not easily accessible, and had a serious problem with water. In general, the further you went up the hill, the worse conditions got. At the bottom of the hill, fronting Hippopotamus Street, a few stately homes, now subdivided, continue to house the descendants of some old, well-to-do families who first settled there when it offered room for a sizable private compound outside the central city. These families were later joined by middle-class professionals as well as artisans and storekeepers living above their shops. The first layer of houses behind the street had easy access to it, and even more important, to public taps connected to the city water supply. Some of the homes there seemed roomy and well built. Higher up the hill, however, there were no public taps. Although land was cheaper there, the daily hike down the hill for water was more onerous. Poor people built small houses. At the flat top of the hill, where water was pumped up to one spot for an hour or two in the morning, all that many people had in common were their hard-luck stories.

In particular, one hears the story of the closing of the mills. As the former capital of an important princely state, Gwalior had once been a centre for large-scale manufacturing. The maharajas were successful in attracting businesses and even starting a few themselves: mopeds were built, pottery made, and biscuits baked and packaged for national distribution. Most important for the local economy, however, was a complex of cloth mills located in a part of town called Birlanagar, named after the prominent Bombay industrial house to which the mills belonged. Founded in the 1930s during princely rule, the mills remained vital in independent India through the mid-1980s. Some of their products, moreover, lent the city some national panache: Gwalior Suiting was long advertised in national publications through ads featuring well-turned-out men with haughty gazes.

While the mills were flourishing, they offered thousands of workers steady jobs with union benefits, but when the mills became outmoded, the Birlas decided to close them and build new ones elsewhere. Although some smaller-scale manufacturing had developed during the mills' decline, it was in newer industries that demanded technical skills different from those of the mill-hands (TV monitors were a going enterprise); the jobs, moreover, were less in quantity and, largely ununionized, in quality, too. People who had spent their working lives in the mills and lived in company housing didn't know what to do or where to go. Several ended up on top of the hill. One of these was the father of Rajesh—Jamal's Brahman acting friend—Murlidhar Mishra.

Murlidhar had come from a middle-class family in the oldest part of the city—the part known locally as Gwalior proper—near the old fort gate. His extended family still had a house there, which Murlidhar's wife continued to refer to as their own. When the mills closed and Murlidhar was left without income, he moved his family to the hilltop near his wife's brother Narendra, who was also suffering from the mills' closing. The two, however, had contrasting responses to the loss of their longtime jobs: one attempting to find a new internal identity, the other pretending to have an old external one.

Narendra had worked at various manufacturing jobs at the mills—weaving cloth and printing it too. Even though he knew his way around machinery, he could not find another job in production in town. Discouraged, he underwent an apparent transformation. A Brahmin who had always had an interest in religious performance, he was now trying to make a living as a professional religious story-teller and musician. He looked the part—wearing beads and painting a tilak on his forehead—and got some work, but he wasn't very successful at supporting his family from it. Adding to his burden in advancing middle-age was a new baby boy, born from a wife they had both presumed was past child-bearing age. 'It was a mistake,' he said sadly. But it was more than that: a new baby for someone his age who dressed as he did and exhorted his listeners to traditional dharma wasn't really very seemly, either, and may have contributed to his lack of success in his new career. Narendra's transformation from a longtime factory hand to a householder sadhu seemed incomplete and not particularly fulfilling.

Murlidhar, by contrast, who had worked as an accountant in the mills, managed to keep some continuity in his profession, eventually finding book-keeping work in town. But his new job entailed keeping up pretences. 'He's let them think that he lives in the Gwalior house' said Murlidhar's wife, Lakshmi Devi. 'At the shop, they call him the Gwaliorwale Pandit, not by the name of this place...We'd be ashamed to invite the shopowner here—we live in this shack.' Lakshmi Devi's description of their house was accurate. The couple lived together with their three sons and a daughter-in-law in a single small, roughly built room with a kitchen and a little covered porch. When it rained, the roof leaked. Murlidhar had to live with pretence and poverty, too.

It was difficult for those from the fallen middle and once stable working classes to pretend they were happy on the hilltop, and most didn't even try. In addition to the two Mishra families, these included a high-school educated son of a policeman supporting his family through day labour, which sometimes made him sick, and an educated Maratha widow who moved there with her children when her husband died. Although she and her now grown son were both working at low-level jobs for the same firm and were managing, they recall better days. Lakshmi Devi seemed particularly disturbed by her family's current situation. One of the first things she said when I first met her was that they had another house in Gwalior. Even though they didn't live there, it was a mark of who they really were. She regreted that she had no nice place for visitors to sit. In addition to her current poverty, she commented on the relative isolation of the hilltop, which was not good for her grown sons—one of whom was poorly educated and chronically unemployed. 'Coming and going is a problem. When you go down, you don't feel like coming up; and when you're up, you don't feel like leaving.' She didn't like not knowing when her sons would come home, but there was no work to be had on the hill. 'At least when they're down, they do a little something.' It's finally better, for Lakshmi Devi, if her children are off the hill, even though it's home.

Still, because the hill *was* home, those with less distressing personal histories were able to look at the bright side: the air was good, some would say, and they had nice views—both of which were true. Of course there was a water problem, all admitted, but living on the hilltop was like living in a little village within the city, with a village's peacefulness and community. Some of those who spoke thus had in fact recently come from a village and were happy with a more familiar setting. Others had been there a while but seemed to be doing all right financially, with sturdy, large-roomed houses. One of these was Parsuram Gujar, who talked about the 'family relations' *(pārivarik sambandh)* among the people on the hilltop: they were all 'loving people' *(premī log)*. For Parsuram, the hilltop was indeed his community. He had actually been among the first to settle the hill twenty-two years before and was treated by many as a local elder.

Parsuram in fact has had an interest in politics and was sometimes referred to as *netājī*, 'respected leader,' an epithet for politicians that is sometimes used ironically but not, apparently, here. He thus assumed an important role in the events of 13 and 14 August 2002 when the people on the hilltop did rally as a community against a common foe.

On 13 August following the city magistrate's orders, a joint force from the city and district administrations came to clear the hilltop's illegal settlements. The only way to go was by a narrow access road up the back side of the hill. Once the news of their impending arrival reached those on the hill that morning, they organized quickly. Largely women—who were most likely to be home during the day—they offered unexpectedly effective resistance, slowing the advance of the force with their bodies and then protecting the houses. Not until police reinforcements arrived were eleven homes razed. According to news reports these were new, well-made houses, and it wasn't easy to level them.[8] This destruction, however was not enough: the full job that the force had come to accomplish was left undone, and the officers in charge said they'd be back. That first day, at least, there were no reports of injuries.

The next day, both sides were better prepared. The civil authorities brought in more police, while the people armed themselves with rocks and a plan of attack, surrounding the intruding party on all sides as they started up the hill. Rocks hit many in that party—including some of its leaders—but no one was hurt too badly. The most seriously injured was a driver named Munnalal Valmik who was bleeding from the head and would require eight stitches.

It was difficult for the police to make the people stop stoning them. The tear gas they first used was ineffective, so they fired in the air (one report says the ranking policeman wanted to fire into the crowd at this point, but the civil magistrate said no). In the melee that followed the shooting, the police started grabbing people to arrest—women, men, young persons—not all, apparently, people who had actually thrown stones. Once those arrested were hauled away, the bulldozers came in. The police, understandably angry and jumpy by now, are said to have forcibly removed people from their homes, sometimes injuring them and damaging their property; there were specific allegations of wanton brutality.[9] Twenty-four houses were razed that day, and forty-two people arrested—more women than men[10]—charged with disturbing the peace. Netaji was among them, and, known as a leader, was a prime defendant in the court case that arose from the day's events. He was held for ten days, he said, although the case against him continued for two years more. But it was finally dropped for political reasons.

The city government at the time was dominated by the Congress party, most often championing the cause of the poor but in this case deciding to enforce the law. The member of the national parliament from the area, however, was from the BJP, a party more oriented toward middle-class Hindu interests and a sometimes aggressive nationalism. The city government's unfortunate timing of the raid ('it had to take place sometime')[11] together with the overzealous reaction of the police made it easy for the local Member of Parliament to make political hay of the situation. 'It's a pretty sorry state of affairs', said Jaybhan Singh Pavaiyya, the member of parliament, 'when one day before the anniversary of our independence the police do a demonic dance of destruction. The city and police officials on the spot at the time must be held completely responsible...' He himself was on the spot right away, listening to victims' stories of horror and offering them sympathy and promising support. Members of his party, he said, were on their way to the state capital to intercede there.[12]

In fact the organized response of the hilltop residents and the consequent reaction of the public took the city government by surprise. Sympathy for the residents was not so difficult to muster even among middle-classes prone to favour property law. Not only were the allegations of wanton police brutality too numerous to ignore, but the hilltop settlement didn't really conflict with any practical middle-class interests: it bordered no nice new colony and did not block any imminent development. It was just a case of poor people staking claims on isolated land nobody else really wanted. Some had even paid previous squatters for their places and had notarized documents to show for it: there were rumours of a land mafia with government officials involved.[13] The city magistrate's claim that he wanted to stop further encroachment on government lands[14] did not seem enough of a reason. In any event, the outcome of the pre-Independence day raid was messy enough to stall both further threats to the settlement and the case against the residents. Then, in the 2004 elections—

despite the Congress victory at Delhi—the Gwalior city government swung toward the BJP, which fulfilling some electoral promises, managed to get the case closed. The result of the local Congress government's attempt at enforcing the law was to solidify both the de facto ownership rights of the remaining hilltop residents and to make them give their political support to the BJP, whose major interests are not typically their own.

The dramatic events on the top of the hill can help give some perspective to life on the slope leading up to it. Although the mix of the people on the hilltop is similar to that at other places on the hill, people there seem less rooted: more are newly arrived, many in the last eight or ten years. Many, further, have come compelled by very difficult circumstances and with the knowledge that their rights to their homes, while apparently secure for now, are in fact tenuous. On the hilltop, one doesn't get the feeling of urban density that one finds on the hillside: the houses are often flimsier—why invest in construction when your title isn't clear?—and dispersed on larger plots, sometimes appearing as solitary shacks. The (un)built environment conveys a greater sense of individual isolation.

Much of the community that exists there was stimulated by the ill-fated pre-Independence day police incursion, which did bring the residents together into intense, active cooperation, and three years later a sense of mutual solidarity remained: many could remember in detail their part in the collective experience, while injured victims recounting their stories of injustice found empathetic listeners. But the community thus born was primarily one of resistance, deriving from the unfortunate circumstances of many of its members and a traumatic, galvanizing event. In this it differed from most of the communities on the hillside: which were older, denser, and generally happier—if not integrated by caste, than by ripened personal relationships. On the hilltop, community seemed more circumstantial: people found themselves in the same place through different forces of economic adjustment, were brought together by a magistrate's ill-conceived and poorly timed order, and kept together in part by shifting political tides. In the communities closer to Hippopotamus Street, by contrast, coherence came through no accidental political sparks, but through cultural and personal affinities that seemed more rooted and enduring.

NOTES

1. 'Hippopatumus Street' translates the Hindi *gendevālī saḍak*. Although there are no hippopotamus in India (they are found in Africa), rhinoceros are native to the subcontinent, and the same word, *gendā*, is used for both. Perhaps in the old days, when the street was on the outskirts of the city, rhinoceros sometimes came to the area. When I asked local people what the name meant, however, they all told me 'hippo', a trendier expression than rhinoceros (or even rhino) in common north Indian usage, so I adapted the popular term.

2. On Valmik history and community organization, see Vijay Prashad, *Untouchable Freedom: A Social History of Dalit Community* (New Delhi and New York: Oxford University Press, 2000).

3. I was told that the temple—which also serves as a community centre—was built in 1953 with the help of some government aid to low-caste groups.

4. All three of these temples find regular support from sources in town. The Jain temple, as described in the text, is maintained by a single mercantile family, and the temple to Bhairava by a foundation of the royal Scindias; the latter temple also, for many years drew support from admirers of a well-respected sadhu who lived there until his death at the beginning of the 2000s. The Satya Narayan temple is actually new, constructed by a prosperous builder to house an old image of the deity whose previous abode not far away was in a state of disrepair. The builder continues to sponsor religious events such as Ramayana readings there.

5. For an insightful discussion of the film and the scholarly literature about it, see Philip Lutgendorf, 'A Superhit Goddess: Santoshi Maa and Caste Hierarchy in Indian Films', *Manushi*, vol. 131 (July–August 2002) and 'Made to Satisfaction Goddess': Jai Santoshi Maa Revisited', *Manushi*, vol. 131 (July–August).

6. On Hindus visiting Sufis in Gwalior, see Daniel Gold, 'The Sufi Shrines of Gwalior City: Communal Sensibilities and the Accessible Exotic under Hindu Rule', *Journal of Asian Studies*, vol. 64, no. 1 (2005).

7. The city has given more than its share of Hindu rightist politicians to the national scene, including two of the founders of the BJP, the main rightist political party: A.B. Vajpayee and Rajmata Vijayaraje Scindia.

8. 'Illegal Structures Levelled', *Dainik Bhaskar*, Gwalior, 14 August 2002, p. 7.

9. 'They Kicked and Punched then Dragged us Out', *Dainik Bhaskar*, Gwalior, 17 August 2002, p. 8.

10. The newspaper accounts agree on the substance of what happened, although details differ. *Nav Bharat* gives 42 arrests and mentions the rumour that the police in-charge wanted to fire into the crowd: 'Battle between the Police and the People—Satya Narayan Tekri, 16 Wounded', *Nav Bharat*, Gwalior, 15 August 2002, p. 1. The *Dainik Bhaskar* noted 40 arrested, 24 women and 16 men: 'Stoning of a Force Come to Level Illegal Structures', *Dainik Bhaskar*, Gwalior, 15 August 2002, p. 1.

11. Attributed to Wasim Akhtar, district magistrate in 'Who Saw What', *Dainik Bhaskar*, Gwalior, 15 August 2002, p. 2.

12. 'They Kicked and Punched'.

13. 'Everyone's Eager to Get Hold of Land', *Dainik Bhaskar*, Gwalior, 15 August, 2002, p. 2.

14. 'Who Said What'.

REFERENCES

'Battle between the Police and the People on Satya Narayan Tekri, 16 Wounded', *Nav Bharat*, Gwalior, 15 August 2002, p. 1, continued on p. 9.

'Everyone's Eager to Get Hold of Land', *Dainik Bhaskar*, Gwalior, 15 August 2002, p. 2.

Gold, Daniel, 'The Sufi Shrines of Gwalior City: Communal Sensibilities and the Accessible Exotic under Hindu Rule', *Journal of Asian Studies* vol. 64, no. 1 (2005), pp. 127–50.

'Illegal Structures Levelled', *Dainik Bhaskar*, Gwalior, 14 August 2002, p. 7.

Lutgendorf, Philip, 'A Superhit Goddess: Jai Santoshi Maa and Caste Hierarchy in Indian Films', *Manushi*, vol. 131 (July–August 2002), pp. 10–16.

____, 'Made to Satisfaction Goddess': Jai Santoshi Maa Revisited', *Manushi*, vol. 131 (July–August 2002), pp. 24–37.

Prashad, Vijay, *Untouchable Freedom: A Social History of Dalit Community* (New Delhi and New York: Oxford University Press, 2000).

'Stoning of a Force Come to Level Illegal Structures', *Dainik Bhaskar*, Gwalior, 15 August 2002, p. 1, continued on p. 10.

'They Kicked and Punched, Then Dragged Us Out', *Dainik Bhaskar*, Gwalior, 17 August 2002, p. 8.

'Who Said What', *Dainik Bhaskar*, Gwalior, 15 August 2002, p. 2.

CONTRIBUTORS

PURUSHOTTAM AGRAWAL is currently a Member of the Union Public Service Commission of India. A scholar of bhakti traditions and a public intellectual, he has published extensively in Hindi and was formerly Professor at the Centre of Indian Languages, Jawaharlal Nehru University, New Delhi.

ISHITA BANERJEE-DUBE is a Professor at the Centre for Asian and African Studies, El Colegio de México. Her authored books include *Divine Affairs* (2001) and *Religion, Law, and Power* (2007). Among her several edited volumes are *Unbecoming Modern* (2006) and *Caste in History* (2007).

R. CHAMPAKALAKSHMI was formerly Professor of History at the Jawaharlal Nehru University, New Delhi. Her numerous publications on art, religion, society, state, and urbanization in south India include *Vaisnava Iconography in the Tamil Country* (1981), *Trade, Ideology and Urbanization* (1996), *The Hindu Temple* (2001), and (co-edited with S. Gopal) *Tradition, Dissent and Ideology* (1996).

FRANK F. CONLON is Professor Emeritus of History and International Studies at the University of Washington, Seattle. He has written on the social and cultural history of South Asia, particularly with reference to western India and Mumbai, and is presently preparing a revised and expanded edition of his seminal work, *A Caste in the Changing World* (1977). He is co-founder and co-editor of H-ASIA.

SAURABH DUBE is a Professor at the Centre for Asian and African Studies, El Colegio de México. Among his authored books are *Untouchable Pasts* (1998), *Stitches on Time* (2004), and *After Conversion* (forthcoming). His several edited volumes include *Postcolonial Passages*

(2004) and *Historical Anthropology* (2007).

DANIEL GOLD is Professor of South Asian Religions in the Department of Asian Studies at Cornell University, Ithaca. His publications include *The Lord as Guru* (1987) and *Aesthetics and Analysis in Writing on Religion* (2003).

JOHN STRATTON HAWLEY is Professor of Religion at Barnard College, Columbia University. His many single authored books include *Three Bhakti Voices* (2005) and *The Memory of Love* (forthcoming). Among his several edited volumes are (with Vasudha Narayanan) *The Life of Hinduism* (2006) and (with Kimberley Patton) *Holy Tears* (2005).

LINDA HESS teaches in the Department of Religious Studies at Stanford University, California. Her publications include (co-translated with Shukdev Singh) *The Bijak of Kabir* (1977) and *Singing Emptiness* (2008).

BENJAMÍN PRECIADO-SOLÍS is Director of the Centre for Asian and African Studies, El Colegio de México. His books include *The Krsna Cycle in the Puranas* (1984) and *India: La democracia más grande del mundo* (1986).

ROMILA THAPAR is Professor Emeritus of History at the Jawaharlal Nehru University, New Delhi. Her several path-breaking books include *Aśoka and the Decline of the Mauryas* (1961), *Cultural Pasts* (2001), and *Early India* (2003).

THOMAS R. TRAUTMANN is Marshall D. Sahlins Collegiate Professor of History and Anthropology at the University of Michigan, Ann Arbor. Among his many authored books are *Aryans and British India* (1997), *Languages and Nations* (2006), and *The Clash of Chronologies* (forthcoming). His edited volumes include *The Aryan Debate* (2005).

DAVID GORDON WHITE is Professor of Religious Studies at the University of California, Santa Barbara. He is the author of *Myths of the Dog-Man* (1991), *The Alchemical Body* (1996), *Kiss of the Yogini* (2003), and *Sinister Yogis* (forthcoming).

INES G. ŽUPANOV is a Senior Research Fellow in History at the Centre National de la Recherche Scientifique (CNRS) in Paris and a member of Centre d'Etudés de l'Inde et de l'Asie du Sud (CEIAS). Among her many publications are *Disputed Mission* (2000), *Missionary Tropics* (2005), and (co-edited with C. Guenzi) *Divins Remèdes* (2008).